BEYOND THE FRONTIER

American Museum Sourcebooks in Anthropology, under the general editorship of Paul Bohannan, are published for The American Museum of Natural History by the Natural History Press. Directed by a joint editorial board made up of Dr. Bohannan and members of the staff of the Museum and the Natural History Press, this series is an extension of the Museum's scientific and educational activities, making available to the student and general reader inexpensive, up-to-date, and authoritative books in the field of anthropology. The Natural History Press is a division of Doubleday & Company, Inc., and has its editorial offices at The American Museum of Natural History, Central Park West at 79th Street, New York, New York 10024, and its business offices at 501 Franklin Avenue, Garden City, New York.

PAUL BOHANNAN is Professor of Anthropology at Northwestern University, where until 1963 he was also chairman of The Center for Social Science Research in African Affairs.

Born in Lincoln, Nebraska, he graduated from the University of Arizona and, a Rhodes Scholar, attended Oxford University where he received his B.Sc. and D.Phil. With his wife, Laura Bohannan, also an anthropologist, he spent a total of twenty-six months from 1949 to 1953 among the Tiv of central Nigeria and in 1955 he spent nine months with the Wanga of Kenya.

Before going to Northwestern in 1959, he taught at Oxford University and Princeton University. He is the author of numerous monographs and articles and two books, *Social Anthropology*, a textbook, and *Africa and Africans*. He has edited *Homicide and Suicide in Africa, Law and Warfare,* the first volume of the American Museum Sourcebooks in Anthropology, and, with George Dalton, a symposium, *Markets in Africa*. He wrote the Encyclopedia Americana's article, "Africa: Peoples and Cultures."

FRED PLOG is a graduate assistant in the Department of Anthropology at the University of Chicago. A native of El Paso, Texas, he was graduated with distinction from Northwestern University in 1966. He is an honorary Woodrow Wilson Fellow and holds a National Science Foundation Traineeship.

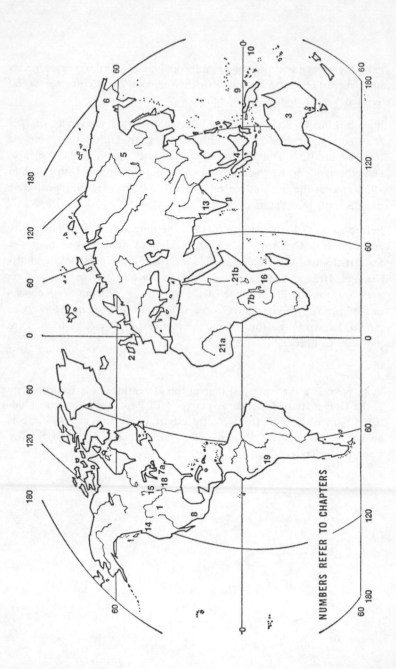

NUMBERS REFER TO CHAPTERS

BEYOND THE FRONTIER

SOCIAL PROCESS AND CULTURAL CHANGE

EDITED BY PAUL BOHANNAN
AND FRED PLOG

NHP

AMERICAN MUSEUM SOURCEBOOKS IN ANTHROPOLOGY

PUBLISHED FOR

THE AMERICAN MUSEUM OF NATURAL HISTORY

THE NATURAL HISTORY PRESS

1967 · GARDEN CITY, NEW YORK

The illustrations for this book were prepared by the Graphic Arts
Division of The American Museum of Natural History.

Library of Congress Catalog Card Number 67–12891
Printed in the United States of America
First Edition

CONTENTS

INTRODUCTION

Paul Bohannan

IN THE CENTURIES since the Renaissance, Western culture has spread throughout the world. Somewhere or another, there has been a frontier. Usually several. And, armed by the most effective technology ever invented, Westerners pushed on, beyond the frontiers, creating new frontiers but, at the same time, leaving less space for the other peoples of the world to stand. Today, the frontiers have reversed themselves. Westerners are becoming doubly aware of boundaries and frontiers. They themselves are the people who are in the way, who are beyond the frontiers of non-Western peoples experimenting with new and effective technologies. Things look different from this side—and the world looks different to everyone from its look in 1945.

Anthropology, as a discipline, was formed by and battened on the frontier—but, from a relatively early stage, anthropologists were interested in the "great beyond." What was the effect of the frontier on the peoples who felt the impact of Western culture? Were there regularities or "laws" of impact and changing culture that resulted? In this process, anthropology has itself had a considerable impact on the world. The major influence of anthropology on Westerners has been to allow them to see themselves and their own institutions more clearly by daring to tear away the veils of ethnocentrism that kept them from seeing that other peoples had institutions as complex and histories as full as their own. The job is far from completed—but the headway is also far from inconsiderable.

One of the largest literatures in all of anthropology is that devoted to acculturation and culture change. It also contains the most disparate of materials. In order to bring a semblance of order into it within a small compass, an editor must divide it and classify it. He must also take a theme or a thread that gives him a criterion of relevance beyond the primary one of "culture change."

THE FRONTIER AS A THEME

The frontier as a theme allows us to throw our work directly into touch with some of the most important work of historians. Frederick Jackson Turner is usually recognized as the founder of the "frontier hypothesis" of American history. But I suspect that Turner little realized the stir he would create when he read his paper at a professional meeting at the turn of the century. He was interested in the influence of the frontier in producing Americans and America. He probably overstated his point. He was taken up—indeed, blown up. His hypothesis was tested by all and sundry and it was either rejected with vehemence or embraced with passion. Today, the frontier as a recurring historical feature has been studied extensively and comparatively.

Yet, interestingly enough, historians have shown little interest in the "other side of the frontier." With a few major exceptions, that has been the preserve—indeed, until recently, the reservation—of anthropologists. Anthropologists have had two main tasks out beyond the frontier: one of them is examination of the facts of cultural traditions and change of the peoples who were feeling the impact of Western growth and expansion. The other task was voicing moral outrage when they found that the very standards and values of Westerners themselves were not applied to other peoples, or when they found Westerners claiming in their ethnocentricity that other people were "stupid" or "unfit for civilized life." For all this Cassandra'ing, anthropologists got little thanks either from the Westerners or from the people whose cudgels they thought they had taken up. Too often, perhaps, the moral outrage set in before the facts were anything like complete. Yet, anthropology has been the main—indeed, until recently, almost the sole—source of sober facts about the area beyond the frontier. They share their distinction with a few—but very few—missionaries and traders.

The frontier has changed in our own day. Seeing its reversal allows us more easily to appreciate the problems of the new nations. As Euro-America itself moves "beyond the frontier" of other peoples and cultures, a wealth of studies are being done by behavioral scientists of many persuasions who have "found" the field and the riches that comparison can yield.

Seen thus, the frontier becomes a device, so to speak, for viewing cultural and social change.

The first section (Part I) of this book contains accounts of some frontiers, and of the effect of such frontiers on the peoples of one side or both. Billington's article contains a thorough and exciting summary of the research in American history that was undertaken in response to Turner's thesis. MacLeod's is a statement of the English frontier in Scotland and Ireland, which was established and run by the same people, who at the same time, were manning another frontier in North America. There is also material on frontiers in Australia, Southeast Asia, and Soviet Asia. Anthropologists must not forget the people who created the frontiers any more than historians can afford to forget those who were beyond them.

THE "PERIODS" OF STUDIES IN CULTURE CHANGE

For purposes of this book, we have divided the studies of culture change into three general time periods. The first of these (Part II) can be called the discovery of ethnocentrism, the second (Part III) can be called the "high period" of acculturation studies, and the third (Part IV) can be called the "modern" or "post-colonial" period.

THE DISCOVERY OF ETHNOCENTRISM In the middle of the last century, before anthropology developed as any more than an esoteric branch of philosophy and the practical arm of museology, most reports about people beyond the frontier were studded with statements of values and emotional reactions. They are difficult to read without annoyance today, and what little information is in them seems the less because it has to be disentangled from emotional reactions we no longer share. Reports of early American Indian agents, and of early missionaries are rife with these judgments—the Indian agents and missionaries who looked at and learned to talk with these people were few. Westerners had absolutely no talent for cross-cultural communication and understanding. For "practical" purposes, indeed, such a talent becomes supererogatory with their acquisition of their formidable technology. Only an occasional artist like Catlin, or writer like Schoolcraft, or missionary like Conrad Weisser gives us much information today. This period was marked by the fact that, with the development of anthropology and the changes in values that made that development possible, there was an increasing capacity to be concerned with those "other" people and to try to understand the situation in which they found themselves. Anthropologists such as Hocart translated the *cri de coeur* of the "natives" (colonialism created "natives" according to Fanon 1966). Others such as Rivers were concerned with their reaction to illness and overwhelming power and authority. Still others such as McGee did quite early and serviceable analyses of types of acculturation. And yet others such as Radin (1917) and Wissler (1914) made studies of particular situations. In those years, anthropologists in America were concerned primarily with learning to deal intellectually with the kind of data they were acquiring from reservation Indians; most specifically they wanted to "recover" the "primitive" or "pre-contact" culture. Those were the days before we realized that anthropology is characterized by a set of methods rather than bound by a subject matter; hence there was some attempt to exhaust as fully as possible the information about the Red Indians.

THE "HIGH PERIOD"   Although concern with culture change per se as a scientific concern as well as an historical and practical one can be traced back into the nineteenth century, and although the specialist studies of culture change became fairly common about 1910 (Keesing 1953), it was not until these studies became a flood tide in the early thirties that any real organization of the subject set in. The Social Science Research Council appointed a committee to handle the subject. The report of that committee (Redfield, Linton and Herskovits, reprinted below) acted as a point of collection, rally and departure in 1936 in America. At about the same time, Malinowski's seminar—for many years the primary growing point of British anthropology—turned to the same subject (Malinowski 1937).

Anthropologists handled the investigation of acculturation and social change in a very distinctive way, which grew out of their method of study and of the personal impact of such a study. Redfield (1955: 20) has stated the basic position: "The primitive culture or society is a complete world, a mental universe with its own special cast or character, and to begin to make the science [of anthropology] you must come to live, in some measure, within such a world and see it from the inside out. To understand it so is an intensely human experience." The anthropologist, quite naturally, took this "complete world" as his unit, and examined the way in which it was hit from the outside, and the influence of the West on that unit. Often, the unit persisted more by anthropological definition than in any other way. It is just this point of view— the alien, contained culture which one has one's self experienced from the inside, as it was hit from the outside—that dominated most of these studies. The lurking assumption was that the society with which that humanly experienced culture is associated is, in some sense, a permanent entity. Actually, of course, it was this very society that had to disintegrate or develop—or both—if the culture were to change.

By 1953, quite literally mountains of very fine studies had been published. And there was again need to assess progress. The Second Memorandum, if we may call it that (Broom *et al*, see below) gave the subject a very firm outline—and it became even more apparent than ever that the "theory" of culture change could never escape either remaining programmatic or else breaking up into many theories—indeed, that "change" would necessarily once again become a dimension of all social and cultural theory. It became clear by the end of this period that the investigations had been about the wrong thing, for all that they had been highly rewarding. By the late 1950s the *Zeitgeist* had changed to the point that it was apparent to all. The classical acculturation study had, like the classical distribution study before it, reached its climax and must from this point on be interpreted as a part of the history of anthropology.

THE "MODERN" "POST-COLONIAL" PERIOD Such did not mean, of

course, that studies of "change" ceased to be made. It meant only
that a sea change occurred in the way they were to be done.
They have, in fact, vastly increased in number. But they are now
made on a different set of assumptions. Whereas the earlier assumption was that the small society, totally and vitally experienced by the anthropologist, was the unit of study, it now
became evident that the creation of new national, social and cultural units was of even greater moment. The Spindlers (1959:
60–61) have noted in their survey of the studies for 1957–58
that there were no "schools" of social change theory, and that the
techniques, assumptions and data ranged widely—"approaches to
the analysis of culture change have always changed as the intellectual milieu and the conditions of reality undergo change." Put
into terms of the political "conditions of reality," the concern
is no longer with colonialism, but rather with nationalism and, in
Africa, with the search for "modernized" societies throughout
the "uncommitted, third world," the search for cultural "opportunity" and "modernization" in a revolution of "rising expectations," and with what Americans call "civil rights movements."

The "plight" of a people, whether they be American Indians,
American Negroes, Asians or Oceanians looks very different in
the 1960s from what it did in the middle 1950s. This fact, con-
joined with the advent of economists, political scientists, psychologists and many others onto the scene, at the very time that the
reservations of the anthropologists disappeared, has led scholars
(including anthropologists) to deal with more restricted and
specialized topics. Moreover, Euro-American Westerners have become more specifically concerned with their own actions in bringing about change, and have in some cases actually begun to
engineer change (Tax 1958; Holmberg, see below). We have become increasingly interested in the sources of our culture—especially those that do not spring from the civilization of Europe
(Hallowell, see below). But the wave of the future would seem
to be the growing awareness of Europeans that they are themselves on the other side of the frontier of developing and expanding people. We are being told (and a few are listening) that
Europe is brutal and brilliant, successful—and dead (Fanon, see
below).

A "THEORY" OF "CHANGE"

Perhaps most important of all, however, is that "change" is no longer a substantive, but rather has become an adjective. We are now studying changing economies, changing polities, changing art forms and all the rest. "Change" has in fact become the dynamic of history. Historians themselves, although they often do not like to be charged with so doing, are using the behavioral sciences lavishly in explaining historical change and development. This move has not yet hit the schools—it has hardly hit the historians—but the day is not far off when history and behavioral science will again be keeping open company, even in America.

Indeed, as we compiled this book, I came to look upon change as the "blue flower" of the romantic movement in anthropology. In the romantic movement of the German littérateurs at the end of the 18th and beginning of the 19th centuries, the search for a "blue flower" became the mark of a man who was looking for something so fine and so rare that it could never be found—but only in the search itself were rewards to be found. The very unattainability made the search the more nearly exhaustive, and hence more valuable. "Change" did not exist in the form in which it was sought during the "high period." Today, the romantic movement in anthropology is dated. We have replaced the blue flower with correlations, and romantic serendipity with "research design." We have moved into a period when we see change as a dimension and quality of all social, psychic and cultural life. The task is not to explain "culture change" but to explain "culture" and why it changes as it does.

In less colorful terms, to seek a theory of "change" is like seeking a theory of "velocity." "Velocity" itself is a theory—which can be stated precisely, given certain conditions held constant. Velocity must be computed by measuring the distance between points in different spatial locations at different times. Change can be computed only when traits or institutions are in different conditions at different times. The constant is the trait, the institution, the "culture," or whatever. The "change" becomes a mode both of explaining and experiencing the working of the institution and its people and its milieu, including, of course, its social and cultural milieu.

"Change" as a topic rather than as a mode of many topics does still have a lot of practical value, however. It is basic to the vocabulary in which behavioral scientists of different disciplines talk to one another. We live in an age when the topic "change" is being totally reconsidered—just as we live in an age of computers that make us reconsider all our thought processes and scientific methods, and just as we live in an age when the frontier has been turned into cultural Babel. The new frontier is no longer distinguished by space alone. The people on it no longer merely face one another in a struggle for a common culture for their interactions. Rather, the frontier is marked by the cultural selectivity of peoples and interest groups in a world in which variety is rapidly swelling, not ebbing. The frontier is all around us.

The vast literature on cultural and social change has left us with a great legacy and a lot of current problems. No Introduction to it can do it credit. We have tried to make this one do three jobs: show the development of the topic, provide some case histories, and to show the unity of the historical, anthropological and other behavioral scientific approaches.

PAUL BOHANNAN

Evanston
October 4, 1966

Part I | FRONTIERS AND THE FRONTIER HYPOTHESIS

1 THE AMERICAN FRONTIER

Ray Allen Billington

FOR MORE THAN half a century the most useful—and contro-versial—concept employed in interpreting American history has been the "frontier hypothesis."[1] Advanced in 1893 by Frederick Jackson Turner *as one means* of explaining the distinctive features of the nation's civilization, it was generally accepted and enthusiastically applied until the 1930's, when it was subjected to a barrage of criticism by a group of younger scholars. More recently historians have rallied to the support of the thesis, stated now in somewhat modified form, and are again finding it an essential device for an understanding of the past. A knowledge of the hypothesis as applied by today's historians is necessary for a proper interpretation of United States history.

The thesis as stated by Turner is too well known to require extended comment. The differences between the civilizations of Europe and America, he believed, were in part the product of the unique environment of the New World. The most distinctive feature of this environment was "the existence of an area of free land, its continuous recession, and the advance of American settlement westward." During each advance men not only shed

Originally published by the American Historical Association. Reprinted with permission of the author and the publisher.

[1] A second major concept, that of the economic interpretation of politics, has been judged by some historians to be even more influential. Yet its originator, Charles A. Beard, declared that the essay in which Turner advanced the frontier hypothesis had "a more profound influence on thought about American history than any other essay or volume ever written on the subject." [—Author.]

"cultural baggage" and adjusted themselves to an unfamiliar physiographic environment; they also sloughed away many of the complexities of civilization. The primitive outposts that they planted along the frontier required fewer social, political or economic controls than the compact settlements of the East, just as the people within them found little time for cultural pursuits as they devoted their energies to subduing the forest. Eventually, as newcomers drifted in, these communities struggled back along the road to maturity, but the resulting civilization differed from that of the East, its institutions modified by the strange environment, the accident of separate evolution, and the contributions of the divergent groups constituting the social order. An "Americanization" of men and their society had occurred.

CRITICISMS OF THE FRONTIER HYPOTHESIS

This thesis was subjected to a vigorous criticism during the years immediately following Turner's death in 1932. The time was ripe for such an attack. During the decade of the Great Depression many of the basic values of American civilization were searchingly re-examined, and the frontier hypothesis embodied too many of those concepts to escape censure. If the United States was not the land that it seemed, some scholars asked, had it ever been such a land? The popularity of Marxist doctrine among depression-oriented intellectuals also made suspect a theory that emphasized geographic rather than class forces. Liberals similarly found little to their liking in a concept that stressed frontier individualism at a time when governmental controls seemed essential to social salvation. Trends in historical thinking also activated the anti-Turner movement; historians suddenly awakened to the importance of intellectual history looked askance at a theory which stressed the western rather than the eastern origins of civilization, while others rebelled against Turner's emphasis on a single force to explain the nation's development. This seemed singularly unrealistic when the depression daily demonstrated the complexities of the social order.

Responding to these forces, historians by the score unleashed their attacks on the hypothesis. Some took exception to Turner's loose terminology and inexact definitions; others singled out passages from his essays that could be condemned for contradictory theories, unsupported generalizations, and inadequately based assumptions (Pierson 1940; 1942; Hofstadter 1949; Riegel 1952, 1956; Lokken 1941; Burkhart 1947; Almack 1925; Beck 1955; Gressley 1958; Rundell 1959). More launched their barbs against specific statements, quarreling especially with Turner's belief that the frontier had served as a safety-valve for the East's discontented, or that it had fathered democracy. More serious were two charges that struck at the basic assumptions of the hypothesis. On the one hand Turner was charged with denying a basic principle in modern historiography—that of multiple causation—in ascribing America's development to the frontier and ignoring such vital forces as the class struggle (Hacker 1933, 1935), industrialization, urbanization, and the rise of transportation systems (Beard 1921, 1928). On the other he was blamed for encouraging provincialism and isolationism through his failure to recognize the continuing influence of the East (Pomeroy 1955; Wright 1955) and Europe on the American West. Far from discarding the "bedraggled garments" of their heritage, critics insisted, pioneers clung to those garments even when they proved unsuited to the environment. Turner's indifference to the continuing impact of the Old World on the New, operating through the flow of ideas as well as people, not only distorted history but helped warp the American mind, it was charged. Over-impressed with the uniqueness of their past, Americans had developed an intellectual isolationism that ill-equipped them for their twentieth-century role in the world (Hayes 1946; Fox 1935).

The validity of many of those criticisms cannot be disputed. Turner did pen unsubstantiated generalizations; Turner did allow his poetic instincts to lead him along metaphorical by-paths that obscured rather than defined his exact meanings. He did overemphasize geographic forces, although he was not, as often charged, a geographic determinist. He did generalize too widely on the basis of limited observation. He did minimize the continuing influence of Europe's civilization on that of the United States, just as he did the impact of industrialization, urbanization, and immigration. But the question remains: did these attacks on Turner's *presentation* of the frontier hypothesis prove the hypothesis itself to be wrong?

Certainly many of the most outspoken critics were guilty of the very faults ascribed to Turner. Some of the criticisms resulted from a too-limited reading of his works; his earlier and later writings reveal a historical philosophy with which few modern historians could quarrel. Others were based on theories voiced by some of Turner's overenthusiastic disciples rather than by Turner himself, but the principal error of his critics was their refusal to recognize that Turner was advancing a hypothesis rather than attempting to prove a theory.

During the past dozen years defenders of the frontier hypothesis have done much to restore both Turner and his thesis to their rightful place in historiography. This has been accomplished by a detailed examination of Turner's background and concepts, by a re-examination of his frontier hypothesis in an attempt to determine its validity in the light of criticisms levelled against it, and by an extension of the frontier concept to include areas of the world not embraced within the United States as well as aspects of history not treated in the original statement by Turner.

THE FRONTIER HYPOTHESIS RE-EXAMINED

Yet Turner did devote his own scholarly efforts to frontier history, and it is as a frontier historian that he will be known. Hence it is proper to ask: what validity do historians today attach to the hypothesis that he stated in 1893 and partially developed in his later writings? What aspects of his thesis were demolished by his critics, and what portions are recognized as useable at the present time? And, most important, can the hypothesis be restated in the light of the criticisms directed against it as a theory necessary to the interpretation of American history?

A preliminary step in such an inquiry is to arrive at a satisfactory definition of the term "frontier." This Turner himself never attempted. To the despair of his critics, he repeatedly interchanged "West" and "frontier" in his writings; to their even greater despair he defined either term as the whim of the moment directed. At one time the frontier to Turner was "the meeting ground between savagery and civilization"; at another it might become "the temporary boundary of an expanding society at the edge of substantially free lands," or a "migrating region," a "form

of society," a "state of mind," a "stage of society rather than a
place," a "process," or "the region whose social conditions result
from the application of older institutions and ideas to the trans-
forming influences of free land." On still other occasions he accepted the census bureau's definition and considered the frontier
to be that area where the population ranged from two to six
persons to the square mile (Mood 1945, 1948, 1952; Forbes
1962; Pearce 1962; Strickland 1960; Lottick 1959, 1961).

This varied usage suggests that two definitions are necessary,
one of the frontier as a geographic area, the other of the frontier
as a process. The "frontier" can be defined as "the geographic
area adjacent to the unsettled portions of the continent in which
a low man-land ratio and abundant natural resources provide an
unusual opportunity for the individual to better himself economically and socially without external aid." The "frontier process"
may be described as "that process by which individuals and their
institutions were altered through contact with an environment
which provided unique opportunity to the individual by making
available to him previously untapped natural resources." The first
definition suggests that the "frontier" was not a narrow line but
a migrating zone of varying width, peopled by a variety of frontier
types ranging from fur-trappers on the west to town-builders on
the east. The second implies that the social devolution and evolution occurring within this zone varied with time and place depending on the nature of both the individuals and institutions
entering the region and the environment awaiting them there
(Billington 1963).

Did the "frontier," defined in this manner, attract settlers exactly in the manner suggested by Turner? That it did not is
scarcely to his discredit, for he shared the misconceptions common to his day. Like most literate Americans since the days of
Benjamin Franklin and Thomas Jefferson, Turner believed that
the frontier served as a "safety valve" to drain off the dispossessed eastern workers in periods of depression, thus raising wage
scales in the East and hindering the emergence of radical philoso-
phies such as those common in other industrializing nations. "The
wilderness," he wrote in one of his books, "ever opened the gate
of escape to the poor, the discontented and oppressed. If social
conditions tended to crystalize in the east, beyond the Alleghen-

ies there was freedom" (Turner 1935; Holt 1948; Robbins 1933). Few aspects of the frontier thesis have been so vigorously attacked by Turner's critics, or so staunchly defended by his champions.

To comprehend the "safety-valve" controversy we must recognize that both nineteenth-century theorists who accepted the doctrine and their twentieth-century critics were speaking of at least four different safety valves. One was a "direct" valve through which displaced eastern workers could escape to the West's cheap lands in times of depression. A second was "indirect"; eastern farmers dislodged by competition with western agriculture went west themselves rather than competing for factory jobs. A third was a "resources" safety valve through which the sequential exploitation of natural resources kept wages high and slowed the growth of radical unrest. Finally, a "socio-psychological" safety valve has been identified, on the ground that workers who *believed* they could escape to the West were less discontented than those in non-frontier nations who could harbor no such hope.

Recent studies have not only re-defined the nature of the frontier safety valve, but have revealed the migration process to be far more complex than pictured by Turner. His "orderly procession of civilization, marching single file" westward—fur trapper, hunter, cattle-raiser, pioneer farmer—omitted countless types essential to pioneering: miners, soldiers, explorers, missionaries, lumbermen, land speculators, road and railroad builders, merchants, flour millers, distillers, blacksmiths, printers, lawyers, and a host more. Nor did these frontiersmen obey the laws of social evolution to which Turner subscribed; instead of advancing in an orderly procession as they subdued the wilderness they moved in a helter-skelter fashion that was as unreasonable as it was confusing.

Rather than picturing the frontier advance as an orderly succession of types representing progressive stages in the emergence of civilization, today's historians despair of any division beyond two broad categories. One comprised pioneers bent on *using* nature: fur trappers, missionaries, soldiers, prospectors, herdsmen, and others whose livelihood depended on preserving the wilderness intact. They played their role in the drama of expansion, for they unwittingly prepared the way for later comers by exploring the countryside, discovering transportation routes, advertising favored spots, and lessening the self-sufficiency of the Indian occupants. Behind them, but sometimes at their sides, came the second group bent on *subduing* nature: farmers, land speculators, town planters, merchants, millers, tradesmen, artisans, and dozens more, all dedicated to building a civilization on the ashes of the wilderness. They too refused to follow any neat pattern; at times the first-comers on a new frontier might be backwoods farmers or land speculators, at others town planters or grist millers who hoped that a village would grow up around the favorable spot they selected. The frontier was actually a broad, westward-moving zone, in which a variety of individuals were applying a number of skills to the conquest of nature, unmindful of any orderly pattern that later theorists might expect to find in the evolution of society (Steckler 1961).

Two frontier types neglected by Turner have been subjected to particular scrutiny in recent scholarship. One comprised the town planters or promoters who flung their dream villages into the very depths of the wilderness. The towns that they planted exhibited characteristics markedly different from their eastern counterparts, both in economic functioning and in political philosophy. Not only was the economy of every frontier village shaped to supply the needs of the rural area surrounding it, but in each the welfare of the community was protected by tight controls over such public businesses as grist-milling or retail selling. The governments of these communities were somewhat more democratic than those along the seaboard, with the mayor reduced to a mere figurehead and the popularly elected council, which was in actual control, kept under the public thumb with annual elections (Still 1941; Harper 1963; Wade 1959).

The land speculator played an even more important role than the town planter in the life of the frontiersman. He was omnipresent, either in the form of the eastern or southern or European capitalist who engrossed vast estates against future sale, or in the garb of the pioneer farmer who acquired more land than he could till in the hope of selling off at a profit to a later comer. Between 1785 and 1841 speculators served as middle men between the government land offices and farmers by dividing large parcels into useable units and disposing of them on the credit system. After 1841 when the Pre-emption Act legalized squatting—thus allowing pioneers to let the lands pay for themselves—speculators concentrated on securing town sites and other favored locations, forcing farmers either to pay their price or accept inferior sites (Billington 1945; Gates 1942; Bogue and Bogue 1957; Morton 1951). Nor did the Homestead Act of 1862 lessen their activities. Taking advantage of the generous government grants to railroads and state educational institutions, or buying bonus script from soldiers, or appropriating Indian reservation lands, or capitalizing on faulty features of congressional acts for the disposal of swamp and timber lands, speculators managed to engross much of the land in the Far West that was useable by farmers. Pioneers had either to pay their price or take out homesteads distant from transportation and on poor soil. As a result six or seven newcomers purchased their farms from jobbers for every one who obtained a free grant from the government (Gates 1936, 1963; LeDuc 1950; Shannon 1936).

In the light of this record, Turner's oft-repeated emphasis on "free land" as the principal inducement for migration obviously needs modification.

While modern scholarship has modified aspects of the frontier hypothesis as it relates to the nature of expansion, it has also critically examined Turner's conclusions concerning the influence of the frontier on the institutions and character traits of the American people. The result has been to alter some of the more extravagant claims made by Turner and his disciples, but to recognize that their basic thesis remains valid. The pioneering experience did contribute to a uniquely American type of democracy, nationalism, and individualism, but not exactly in the manner that Turner postulated. It also accentuated the rate of social mobility, the wandering instinct, the materialistic attitudes, and the inventive urge of the frontiersmen and their descendents.

More recent examinations of American democracy suggest that Turner was groping in the right direction, and that the three centuries of frontiering did alter imported theories and practices to a recognizable degree. Scholars point out that the frontier provided an ideal breeding ground for the growth of democratic governments. This was the case for two reasons. On the one hand, the low man-land ratio allowed a wider distribution of property rights than in older communities, with a corresponding insistence on political participation natural among those with a stake in society. On the other, the relatively common level of economic and social status stimulated belief in egalitarianism, just at a time when lack of national or external controls made self-rule a "brutal necessity." In this situation governmental structures had to be created, and with no prior leadership structure existing, every man had an opportunity to win office if his abilities warranted such an award. Moreover the necessity for co-operative social efforts—in cabin-raisings, logrollings, road and school building, law enforcement, and the like—created a sense of municipal responsibility that was easily translated into political activity, assuring a wide choice of candidates for each post. A careful study of three frontiers, that of New England in the seventeenth century and of the Old Northwest and Old Southwest in the pre-Civil War years, has demonstrated that democratic institutions developed with surprising rapidity in all communities, but that their growth was least rapid where a prior leadership structure existed, as it did in the plantation South (Elkins and McKitrick 1954; Curti 1959).

That the democratic spirit evolving in these frontier outposts was embodied in more permanent form was due to the constant opportunity for political experimentation created by the westward expansion of the American people. New territories had to be erected with each advance of the frontier—thirty-one in all—and each required a frame of government. The territories in turn eventually became states, again providing a chance for constitution-making. These constitutions were framed by a majority of relatively poor recent arrivals whose democratic ideals were unassailable, and a minority of upper-class leaders who were publicly committed to democracy in their capacity of leadership, for they realized that any taint of aristocracy would discredit them with the people. The result was a constant democratic trend as constitution-makers adopted the most liberal features of existing frames of government. "American democracy," one student of the subject has written, "derives its strength from the fact that it is the product of the people practicing over and over again the art of creating their own government" (Nichols 1954; Abernathy 1938).

But if democratic practices were strengthened, even though

not originated, along the frontiers, why have other frontier nations failed to devise political institutions comparable to those of
the United States? Recent studies indicate that on every frontier
imported practices were modified in the direction of recognizing
greater equality and allowing a wider participation in governmental affairs. The result was a democratization of inherited institutions, although the degree of democracy resulting naturally
varied with the base on which it rested. The frontier experience
in Russia and New France illustrates this point particularly well.

Russia's eastward-moving Siberian frontier attracted some
7,000,000 people, most of them peasants in search of cheap land,
during the nineteenth and early twentieth centuries. The communities that they reared were noticeably lacking in the aristocratic
institutions common to Russia itself; guilds, the established
church, and village communities were absent while even the provincial and district assemblies of the nobility exerted little influence. When the Russian prime minister P. A. Stolypin visited the
frontier in 1910 he expressed fear that the "enormous, rudely
democratic country" taking shape through the influence of the
small homesteads that were the typical living units would soon
"throttle European Russia" unless it was brought under control.
Tsarism, he believed, was doomed if the egalitarian forces gen-
erating there were allowed to spread (Treadgold 1956; Beazley
1942).

New France underwent a similar transformation long before
1763 when French control ended. There the seigniorial system
with its lordly seigniors, its serf-like *habitants,* its absolute royal
controls, and its authoritarian church still existed in name, but
in practice the opportunity created for the individual by the presence of cheap land had wrought a social and political revolution.
Habitants not only dressed well and affected good manners but
bore themselves with a lordly air that reflected their independence; seigniors on the other hand labored in the fields and were
often to be distinguished from their *habitants* only by their pov-
erty. The common people demonstrated their love of freedom by
refusing to pay tithes to the church and taxes to the crown even
though this meant defying two respected authorities. When the
French monarch in 1704 proposed a *taille* or direct levy his officials ignored the order, knowing that a rebellion or a dispersion

of peoples into the forest would surely follow. Political power in New France was vested not in the monarch but in a local militia captain in each parish. In theory this official represented the aristocracy and was appointed by the seignior; in practice he was elected by the people and his appointment only confirmed by the seignior and governor. Yet his popularly-vested authority was unquestioned from above as he met with the people after mass each Sunday to post the orders of the day and see to it that they were obeyed. Frontier conditions in New France had introduced democratic practices which, although different from those in England's colonies, thoroughly demonstrated the liberalizing influences of cheap land (Burt 1940).

Despite this impressive evidence, most historians today would agree that political institutions have been altered but not completely transformed by the frontier process. The later history of both Siberian Russia and New France illustrates this point well. In each the people showed little tendency to follow the road toward complete democracy as far as their English-speaking counterparts; the *habitants* of New France during the nineteenth century accepted a re-asserted church authority just as docilely as the peasants of eastern Russia bowed to the new statism of the communist leaders in the twentieth. In neither case did the people enjoy a theoretical basis for freedom such as that shared by the colonists under Britain's flag (Lower 1930). The history of the frontiers of Russia and New France demonstrated that both environmental and hereditary forces were needed to perpetuate democratic practices, just as that history proved that equalitarian land ownership patterns on all frontiers liberalized imported institutions.

The spirit of nationalism, no less than the trend toward greater democracy, was strengthened by the frontiering experience, just as Turner theorized. On this point most scholars agree, although they differ with Turner as to the nature of the frontier as a nationalizing force. He reasoned that the constant pressure of Indian and alien enemies on the borderlands quickened western patriotism, that commonly-shared problems created a bond among frontiersmen which served as a national unifying force, that the mingling of peoples in the West diminished sectional loyalties, and that the demand of pioneers for roads, military protection, cheap land, and other necessities that only the federal government could provide led to a constant expansion of federal power. "Loose construction," he wrote, "advanced as the nation marched westward." Most important of all, Turner saw the successive Wests as melting pots where peoples from differing backgrounds were merged into one—as regions of rapid Americanization.

Individualism, labeled by Turner another by-product of frontiering, is also recognized by modern scholarship as a distinctive trait of Americans, but once more in a somewhat different form than originally supposed. During the 1930's, when the spirit of collectivism was high, this concept was a favorite target of critics. The West, they insisted, was an area where co-operation was more essential than in the East; pioneers depended on their neighbors for help in cabin-raisings, logrollings, Indian defense, law enforcement, and dozens of other necessary activities. Too, frontiersmen demanded aid from their government—to build roads, construct forts, finance schools, and the like—more than did inhabitants of older communities (Pierson 1940, 1942; Boatright 1941). How, asked the anti-Turnerians, could such an atmosphere stimulate individualism?

Actually, today's historians are aware that frontier co-operation was entirely reconcilable with individualism. The pioneer was dependent on the social group and was not in the least reluctant to solicit aid from his government when his own betterment was involved. With a larger property stake in society than the Easterner, and with the promise of even greater holdings as he utilized the unusual opportunities available in an expanding economy, he was willing to adopt any expediency to improve his lot in life. So he welcomed government aid when this was to his advantage, and protested government regulation when he thought this to his disadvantage. This is the brand of individualism still current in the United States; the American follows the decrees of fashion designers and the examples of social leaders unquestioningly, but outdoes the European in vigorous protest against governmental regulatory measures that threaten his economic freedom. He behaves exactly like his frontier ancestor, and with as little regard for consistency (Ward 1960; Bogue 1960).

While the pioneering experience contributed to the emergence of a distinctly American brand of democracy, nationalism, and individualism, it also, Turner and his disciples taught, helped alter certain traits exhibited by the people. Americans, partly as a result of their frontier heritage, were unusually inventive, uniquely mobile in both the geographic and social sense, thoroughly materialistic, and so prejudiced against the creative arts and abstract thought that their culture lagged behind that of Europe. All of these concepts have been subjected to rigid scrutiny by later generations, and all have been modified. Yet scholars agree that basically the frontier played a role—often a minor one—in endowing the people of the United States with these distinguishing character traits.

Certainly an inventive spirit would be expected on the frontier, for the unique problems demanding solution, the premium placed on labor-saving machinery by the scarcity of manpower, and the absence of a tradition that would require the use of time-tested practices, all favored innovation. Yet critics of Turner have pointed out that the pioneers showed a surprising reluctance to experiment and that they lagged behind Easterners in inventiveness. Eastern draftsmen and eastern engineers produced the tools that won the West: the Kentucky rifle, farm machinery, well-digging equipment, fencing, windmills, improved agricultural techniques, and dozens more. When inventors failed to meet this challenge (as in the 1840's when new tools were needed to conquer the unfamiliar grasslands of the Great Plains), they endured the hardships of the long journey to the more familiar environment of Oregon and California rather than attempt to meet the situation by themselves. Not until the 1870's and 1880's, when inventors from the East and the Mississippi Valley produced the machines and techniques needed to subdue the Great Plains province, was that region occupied (Webb 1931; Shannon 1940). Yet the existence of a frontier did stimulate innovation, partly by creating a demand for new products, partly by fostering an attitude receptive to change. Certainly new products were always in demand as settlers moved westward over differing environments; the tools suitable for one were outmoded by the next. This, combined with the relative lack of manpower, created a demand for a variety of machines that was supplied by eastern inventors. At the same time the advance of population helped create a social atmosphere receptive to innovation.

Pioneer communities, with their plastic social order, their lack of tradition, their absence of established producers who would resist changes threatening their products, their freedom from political pressures produced by vested interests, and their need for labor-saving devices to offset a lack of manpower, proved ideal testing grounds for anything that was new (Bogue 1958; Miyakawa 1964). That the United States of today is relatively less hidebound and more prone to experiment than older European nations seems traceable in part to the social atmosphere derived from the frontiering past.

The absence of traditionalism in pioneer communities also helps explain the social and physical mobility that existed there and that has become part of the frontier heritage. Within them the low man-land ratio, the abundance of unexploited natural resources, the exploding economy, and the relatively fluid state of the social order allowed every man of ability to rise to his own level, whatever his lineage or breeding. Class lines did exist, for stratification began almost with the first settlers, but they were less rigidly drawn than in older societies, and more easily breached. Vertical mobility was a built-in feature of life along the frontiers. Today the rate of vertical mobility is approximately the same in the countries of western Europe as in the United States, for full-employment and an expanding economy have created job opportunities comparable to those of frontier America (Lipset & Bendix 1959; Reavis 1957; Roberson 1960). Yet there remains one all-important difference; in America the majority *believe* that vertical mobility is inevitable. They have been weaned on the rags-to-riches saga that originated in the frontier opportunity until this has become the great dream, the drive that motivates a considerable portion of the population. Belief in the inevitability of progress sets the goals for Americans as it does not for Europeans.

Still another trait isolated by Turner as a product of the pioneering past was the tendency to emphasize materialistic attitudes at the expense of intellectual or aesthetic values. Students today recognize that the pioneer did not willingly abandon his cultural heritage; his purpose was not to flee civilization, but to plant in the West a patent-office model of the society that he had known in the East. To this end he carried with him school systems, literary and debating clubs, libraries, museums, theatrical societies, and all of the other symbols of culture that he had maintained in his old home (Wright 1955; Moore 1957). Yet conditions doomed his efforts. The mere fact of migration retarded cultural growth, for the adventure of westering failed to attract the speculative, the cultured, or the intellectually sensitive. In the pioneer settlements the thinly scattered population, the necessary preoccupation with practical tasks, and the driving ambition for status betterment inevitable in a land of unusual opportunity, all meant that cultural pursuits must be shelved while material affairs absorbed the energy of the people. Brains and brawn were necessary assets along the frontiers, but they must be applied to the endless practical tasks demanding attention. Book learning and abstract thought were of less value to society, and were down graded in popular estimation. Americans today still reflect that background by placing the "intellectual" well below the "practical business man" in their ranking of folk heroes (Curti 1955). They are still suspicious of leisure, still chained to a belief in hard work as a solution to all ills. These were frontier attitudes, and they persist as part of the frontier heritage.

Most modern scholars, then, would agree with Turner that the frontiersmen did develop certain unique traits, and that these have been perpetuated to form the principal distinguishing characteristics of the American people today. Americans do display a restless energy, a versatility, a practical ingenuity, an earthy practicality to a degree unknown among Englishmen or other Europeans. They do squander their natural resources with an abandon unknown elsewhere; they have developed a mobility both socially and physically that marks them as a people apart. In few other lands is democracy worshipped so intensely, or nationalism carried to such extremes of isolationism or international arrogance. Rarely do other peoples display such indifference toward intellectualism or aesthetic values; seldom in comparable cultural areas do they cling so tenaciously to the shibboleth of rugged individualism. Nor do residents of non-frontier lands experience to the same degree the heady optimism, the blind faith in the future, the belief in the inevitability of progress, that is part of the American creed. These were pioneer traits, and they have become a part of the national heritage.

EXPANSION OF THE FRONTIER HYPOTHESIS

While the frontier hypothesis has been both challenged and defended by some scholars, others have applied the thesis to areas unrecognized by Turner. Their findings have led to further modifications, but in general have tended to substantiate the basic concepts. Among historians in this group are those who have demonstrated that a frontier of "myth" existed side by side with a frontier of fact throughout the nineteenth century, as well as those who have expanded the hypothesis to apply to other areas and other time periods than those described in the original essays.

Certainly modern scholarship has proved that two frontiers have traditionally influenced American thought, and that they bore little relationship to each other. One was the actual frontier, where sweating pioneer farmers braved the greed of their fellowmen and the savagery of nature to eke out an existence. The other was an imaginary frontier which persisted only in the minds of Americans and some Europeans. From the eighteenth century on this image of the West influenced statesmen, fired the imagination of authors, and helped shape the attitude of the people toward their own land as well as toward other nations of the world.

In this imaginary borderland beyond the Appalachians the safety-valve operated freely to drain the discontented westward. "The new settlements," wrote Benjamin Franklin, "will . . . continually draw off the spare hands from the old," while Thomas Jefferson added that "whenever it is attempted by the upper classes to reduce them to the minimum of subsistence they will quit their trades and go to labouring the earth." In the West, according to the frontier myth, a veritable Garden of the World awaited to transform newcomers into superior beings. There, where nature's abundance stifled the competitive instinct, men lived together in peace and contentment, freed of the jealousies and meanness inevitable in the crowded East. There happy yeoman farmers, their muscles rippling beneath shirts of blue, sang merrily as they tossed sweet-scented hay or milked placid cows beneath sparkling skies; there clean log cabins provided a haven rivaled only by Eden itself. With care and want alike unknown, all men not only lived but thought as kings, for perfect equality was inevitable in a land where riches were so abundant. "We have no princes, for whom we toil, starve, and bleed," wrote St. John de Crèvecoeur. "We are the most perfect society now existing in the world." Complete democracy, complete security, complete comfort—these were the rewards that awaited all comers to the Garden of the World that was the West (Smith 1950, 1951).

That this frontier of myth did persist in the imagination of Americans has been amply demonstrated, just as it has been shown that this false image of the West was perpetuated by novelists, poets, and government politicians throughout the nineteenth century. There is also little doubt that Turner was influenced by the misconceptions of his day, and that many of the more romantic effusions in his essays were inspired by the distorted picture of the West with which he was familiar. Yet these distortions cannot diminish the importance of the actual frontier which, if it created no yeoman farmers such as those that cluttered nineteenth-century novels, did alter the characteristics and institutions of the pioneers to a degree at least.

This is substantiated by recent studies of comparative frontiers which have done much to answer Turnerian critics. If the pioneering experience was responsible for democracy and nationalism and individualism, these critics asked, why did not New France and Russia and Australia and Canada develop similar characteristics? Some modern scholars answer that traits ascribable to a frontier background have manifested themselves in every country in which a frontier existed in the sense that Turner employed the term. For the frontier to Turner was not merely a borderland between unsettled and settled lands; it was an accessible area in which a low man-land ratio and abundant natural resources provided an unusual opportunity for the individual to better himself. No such frontiers existed in countries that controlled the free movement of peoples, or in which resources were either lacking or required extensive capital outlay for exploitation (Sharp 1955).

If this definition is applied, the world areas providing a frontierlike opportunity are rigidly limited. The forests of medieval Germany did offer an outlet for a small portion of the population, with noticeable changes effected among those under their influence, but feudal controls were too rigidly applied to allow complete freedom of land usage (Thompson 1913). In Africa the few Europeans were so outnumbered by native occupants that the need for protection transcended any impulses toward democracy or individualism (Neumark 1957). Latin America offered surprisingly few regions suitable to use by individual pioneers; in that land of rugged mountains and steaming jungles only the Argentine Pampas and the Brazilian plains provided the equitable climate, good lands, navigable rivers, and other ingredients needed for pioneer agriculture. These did attract some frontiersmen, although in Argentina the prior occupation of most good lands by government-supported cattle-growers kept small farmers out until railroads penetrated the region. By this time governmental controls were too firmly established to be altered (Belaunde 1923; Aiton 1940).

Australia similarly provided few opportunities for individual pioneers. When settlement of the continent began after the gold rush of 1851 frontiersmen pushing through gaps in the coastal mountains found their way blocked by giant sheep-ranches whose control of all arable land was supported by the government; beyond the ranches lay arid deserts where not even sheep could exist. One Australian writer has pictured the result in language reminiscent of Turner:

> There is a famous gap in the range of Blue Mountains, that wall of rock and scrub which for a quarter of a century hemmed in this colony of New South Wales within the coastal plains. Stand at this gap and watch the frontiers following each other westward—the squatters' frontier which filled the western plains with sheep and laid the foundations of Australia's economy, the miners' frontier which brought Australia population and made her a radical democracy, the farmers' frontier which gradually and painfully tested and proved the controls of Australia's soil and climate. Stand a few hundred miles further west on the Darling River, and see what these controls have done to the frontier. The farmers have dropped out of the westward-moving procession, beaten by aridity. Only the pastoralists and prospectors pass by. In the west centre of the continent, aridity has beaten even the pastoralists. On the fringe of a dynamic society there are left only a few straggling prospectors and curious anthropologists, infrequent invaders of the aboriginal reserves (Hancock 1940).

With the pioneer farmer driven back by aridity, Australia's hinterland became a "Big Man's Frontier," occupied only by giant
sheep-ranchers and wealthy irrigationists. The little man was confined to the coastal plain where competition for the few dwin-
dling resources hurried the growth of an industrialized society
(Alexander 1947; Fitzpatrick 1947; Kershner 1953).

Canada also provided a setting radically different from that of
the United States. In the St. Lawrence Valley and southern
Ontario good lands and a favorable climate did encourage pioneer
agriculture, with results comparable to those south of the border,
but beyond this point expansion to the west and north was
blocked by the Laurentian Shield. This tangled mass of hills and
brush-covered sterile lands occupied the northern and eastern
two-thirds of the country, deflecting settlers southward into the
United States in their search for farms. Not until the latter
nineteenth century when railroads finally penetrated the shield
could the mass occupation of western Canada's lush prairies
begin. Then pioneers arrived by rail directly from the East, bringing with them attitudes and techniques that had not been modified by a prior frontier experience. The result was to perpetuate in
the Prairie Provinces practices that reflected eastern rather than
western attitudes: a humane Indian policy, orderly law-enforce-
ment methods imposed by the central government, and a well-
functioning land system unmarred by squatting or claim's
associations. Some techniques employed in making a living were
altered by the environment, but governmental, religious, and
social institutions underwent almost no adjustments (Zaslow
1945; McDougall 1929; Landon 1941; Sage 1928; Careless 1954;
Stanley 1940).

Only Russia among the frontier nations of the world provided
a physical environment comparable to that of the United States,
and there the pioneers were too accustomed to rigid monarchical
and feudal controls to respond to frontier forces exactly as did
Americans. They began moving eastward into the relatively unexploited wastes of Siberia in the seventeenth century, but not
until serfdom was abolished in 1861 did the flow reach flood
tide. Between that time and 1914 some 5,000,000 newcomers
invaded Siberia, most of them seeking homes in a four-hundred-
mile-wide strip paralleling the Trans-Siberian Railroad. There

they acquired land in quantities undreamed of in European Russia; their holdings after seven years averaged eleven dessiatines (of 2.7 acres each) rather than two and one-half as at home. Cultivation of such extended tracts required new tools and techniques which were mastered as readily as in the United States. More significant was a newly awakened attitude toward government; the Siberian peasants exhibited some of the same individualistic, self-reliant traits that characterized the American frontiersman. Those Russian pioneers, wrote an observer in 1914, "indeed differ from the remaining mass of the Russian peasantry . . . in their greater steadfastness, . . . their greater mobility and readiness to accept every kind of innovation" (Treadgold 1952). They, like their American counterparts, were responding to a frontier environment in their own way.

Proponents of the frontier hypothesis can easily exaggerate the similarities between the experience of the United States and that of other countries. Certainly the differences between Russian, Australian, Canadian, and Latin American pioneers on the one hand, and American frontiersmen on the other, remained greater than the likenesses. Yet comparative studies do justify the generalization that imported institutions and traits were modified by the environment everywhere, and usually along roughly parallel lines. Thus on all frontiers pressure from settlers forced a liberalization of land laws, just as their squandering of natural resources created an eventual demand for conservation measures. On all there was a tendency to employ labor-saving devices and to stimulate the inventive processes that produced them. All endowed their pioneers with a new energy and with a faith in progress; nearly all modified political institutions along democratic lines. In most lands the pioneering experience fostered a sense of racial superiority that found expression in subduing or eliminating the native populations, as well as a lusty nationalism which culminated in a sense of "manifest destiny."

These conclusions are endowed with an even greater validity by the findings of one eminent historian, Walter Prescott Webb, whose important book, *The Great Frontier* (1952), seeks to add a new dimension to the frontier hypothesis. Not only American history but the history of the modern world, Professor Webb argues, can best be explained by the application of the hypothesis. He writes that until 1492 the social pattern of Europe had remained static for centuries, with a fixed population, absolutist controls over the secular and spiritual life of man, and a rigidly stratified society that precluded either the fact or the idea of progress. Then came the voyage of Columbus and the dawning of the Age of Discovery. Overnight mankind gained access to a Great Frontier which dropped the man-land ratio from 26.7 to 4.8 to the square mile. As the resources of this windfall poured into Europe, or Metropolis as Webb calls it, population increased by 625%, the supply of precious metals 18,308%, and goods by an even greater degree. Amidst this atmosphere of plenty, man adjusted himself and his institutions to an environment of ever-broadening opportunity; capitalistic free enterprise replaced serfdom, democratic governments challenged autocratic rulers, religious freedom ousted religious authoritarianism, and legal practices were adjusted to provide justice for the individual. Above all else the spread of the idea of progress endowed mankind with a new hope as well as committing him to a gospel of work that would hurry the coming of better times.

As exploitation of the resources of the Great Frontier went on, the settlement of the new worlds slowly closed the door of opportunity to the individual. By 1930 the man-land ratio again stood at 29.5 to the square mile for the first time since 1500. As man approached the end of the era of cheap land, the controls necessary in compact social units began to reappear. Giant corporations and increasingly powerful institutions gradually encroached on the freedom of the individual; free enterprise was threatened by the rise of totalitarian governments and the extension of the welfare-state principle. Nor does Professor Webb foresee a reversal of this trend in the future; technological advances may allow mankind to exist and even prosper, but frontier democracy and individualism appear to him to be doomed in a world where opportunity for the individual is continually contracting.

The bold hypothesis advanced by Professor Webb still awaits testing by historians. Some have already questioned his data, calling attention to the fact that his exclusion of Russia from Metropolis would invalidate a portion of the statistical evidence used to substantiate his thesis (Barraclough 1954). Yet his challenging generalizations are evidence that the frontier concept is still stimulating controversy and influencing an ever-widening field of historical thought.

2 CELT AND INDIAN:
BRITAIN'S OLD WORLD FRONTIER
IN RELATION TO THE NEW

William Christie MacLeod

DURING THE sixteenth and seventeenth centuries England and Scotland, united dynastically in 1603, were developing frontier policies on the Celtic frontier as well as in the Far East and in America. The experience gained by James VI of Scotland in his attempt to subjugate the "wild" Celtic-speaking inhabitants of the Hebridean Islands off the western coast of Scotland was useful to him when in 1603 he succeeded Queen Elizabeth as King James I of England. The first colonizing business corporation actually to get under way was one chartered by James as King of Scotland in 1599, and was designed to do for a large section of Celtic Scotland what the Virginia Company was to do in Virginia. The first English colonizing business corporations designed to effect settlement in Ireland and in America were chartered by this same King several years after he ascended the English throne, in 1606 and 1609.

In these and many other incidents appear the historical relationship of developments on the Celtic frontier of Britain and Britain's frontier in America. There is, for further example, the fact that many of the most important personalities concerned in frontier development were operative on both frontiers. Sir Walter Raleigh held feudal tenure of lands in both Celtic Ireland and Indian America, and failed lamentably in the exploitation of both. John Mason, responsible for the brutal burning and massacre of the Pequot village in Connecticut in 1637, learned his

Chapter XIII, pp. 152–71, of *The American Indian Frontier* by William Christie MacLeod, New York, Alfred A. Knopf, 1928. Reprinted with permission of the original publisher, Routledge & Kegan Paul, Ltd., London.

butcher's trade in warring on Scotch clansmen (Mason 1637). Edward Wingfield, first president of the first council of the first colony in America (Virginia), had seen service in Ireland. So had many other of the colonists. "We observed a pathway like to an Irish pass . . .", notes Percy, fighting Indians in Virginia with John Smith. Again, Roger Williams in New England saw that the thick woods and swamps afforded refuge to the Indians in wartime, "like the bogs to the wild Irish". Another observer notes even that the Indian houses were "like the houses of the wild Irish" (Smith 1910; Williams 1634).

The colonizing activity on both Celtic and American frontiers called for colonists, and the two frontiers competed for them with each other (Cheyney 1907; Smith 1910; Morton 1637). The first "reservations" were designed for the "wild" Irish of Ulster in 1609. And the first Indian reservation agent in America, Gookin of Massachusetts, like many other American immigrants had seen service in Ireland under Cromwell (Gookin 1674). At the same time that the rich and undeveloped fisheries of the Celtic Scotch Hebrides were adding incentive to British expansion there, the rich fisheries off Newfoundland and New England also were an incentive for development on the American frontier (Scott 1912). Finally, let us note that one of the largest sections of early emigration to the American frontier was from Celtic Scotland and Celtic Ireland (De Villiers 1924; Strieby 1895; MacLean 1900).

All the relationships I have mentioned and many more are important and should be developed in a full comparison of both frontiers. But here we shall go into detail only in several matters which we consider of especially deep underlying significance, especially in making adequate note of the development of frontier-developmental policies by King James VI of Scotland, James I of England.

THE CELTIC LANDS

In and about the year 1600, Celtic-speaking tribes, quite free of all subjection to the Crowns of Scotland and England, held virtually all of Ireland and all of the Scotch Highlands and Islands (the Hebrides). The Scotch clan and the Irish *tuath* or petty kingdom were merely tribes such as typical Indian tribes were. The clan chief was a petty king, lord of all he surveyed. In Scotland and Ireland all told there were perhaps seventy-five of these sovereign states, each at war with its neighbours. The population gathered under one head-chief was often as little as about three thousand and its territory only about ten or twenty square miles. Politically the Celts were about on a level with the Indians of North America, and were, of course, inferior to those of Peru and Mexico.

Although they had a knowledge of agriculture and cattle raising, these arts were very crudely developed. They required five men, for example, to handle a horse and plough. Nearly the entire Celtic territory was wild woodland. The population was only about twice as dense as that of the Indian population in non-desert United States, and was only about one-seventh or one-eighth that of civilized Scotland and England. Relatively, therefore, despite their use of cattle, these Celts were about as primitive economically as the American Indian in agricultural North America.

Let us note, moreover, that they were as much Nordic in blood as the English were, despite their Celtic speech. The Scotch Hebrideans (islanders) were almost purely Scandinavian in type. And the red-hairedness so prominent in Scotland and Ireland is the result of a large admixture of Danish blood. The Viking raids of the ninth and tenth centuries had given much of the best blood of Scandinavia to these Celtic-speaking peoples.

THE ECONOMIC ASPECT

In the decades during which civilized Britain was turning to exploitation of North America, these primitive Celts held just about *fifty per cent. of the area of the British Isles,* and they bitterly resisted every attempt of the British sovereigns to extend the frontier of sovereignty, political administration, and economic development.

This frontier problem at home was more serious in some ways than frontier problems abroad. The subdued Celtic lands offered a foothold or base for foreign invasion. And in their uncivilized

condition they represented a waste which might be filled with a
loyal British civilized population which would add to the wealth,
man-power, and defence of Britain, instead of remaining a weak
spot in the insular defence.

Note, for illustration, the fact that in 1570 England had a
population of only 4,000,000, with a density of seventy-six to the
square mile. France (without Alsace-Lorraine) had a population
of 20,000,000, a density of ninety-six to the square mile, and a
corresponding superiority in national wealth, for these were the
days before the development of coal and iron in the machine
industry. London, the metropolis of England, had a population
of 120,000! The possibilities of the Celtic lands, notably of
Ireland, may be seen in the fact that merely through the improvement of agriculture, Ireland, having in 1600 a population of perhaps only 500,000, in 1800 had a population of 4,000,000, while
the population of England had increased only to 8,000,000. By
1845, again with practically no development of industrial centres,
the Irish population had increased to 8,500,000.

COLONIZING COMPANIES IN THE HIGHLANDS

James VI of Scotland in 1597 determined on a plan for the subjugation of the Scotch Highland clans. On paper the Highlands
and Islands were divided into three royal burghs. The clan chiefs
were ordered to report to Edinburgh within a few months on
pain of dispossession, and preparations were begun in anticipation of their refusal. Some of the mountain chiefs submitted.
The chiefs of the Islands were the most obdurate. They had the
advantage of insular position.

Two years later (in June, 1599) the colonizing company
method of extending the frontier was devised by James for the
Highlands. The Crown's resources were inadequate to the task of
conquering the Highlands, nor did there appear to be any feudal
noble otherwise qualified who was financially able to undertake
the task.

THE FIRST ACTUAL COLONIZING COMPANIES
IN NORTH EUROPEAN HISTORY

Two joint-stock companies were organized. One was given title
to the lands of the Camerons of Lochiel, the MacDonalds of
Glenelg, and the MacLeods of Harris. Another was given title
to the largest of the Hebridean islands, the Lewes, the territory
of a second MacLeod tribe, the *Siol Torquil* or MacLeods of
Lewes. It was planned to dispose of the rest of the Highlands
later when the results of this first experiment appeared.

The natives of the territories turned over to the colonizing
companies, were declared outlaws, and the companies had the
right to make war upon them and destroy them. The companies
planned to make their profits, as did also the Virginia Company
later in Virginia, in considerable part from real estate development, that is, by disposing of land to stockholders as dividends.
The fisheries were also of economic importance. Money profits
would, of course, be distributed as cash dividends to the share-
holders of the companies.

The Lewes Company began operations first. The Harris Company delayed operations to await perhaps the results of the Lewes
Company's enterprise. Six hundred hired soldiers, a number of
"gentlemen volunteers", and artificers of all sorts for the building of a town, were landed on the Lewes in the autumn of 1599.

At that time there was civil war in the tribe occupying the
Lewes. The side led by one Niell made terms with the colonists in
order to get their help against the other party, which was led by
the MacGilmore family. Niell, after winning a victory over his
enemies, and making terms with the colonists, left for Edinburgh
to talk things over with the King, "taking along with him also the
heads of ten or twelve of the MacGilmores whom he had lately
put to death!" (Pitcairn 1830).

Niell, or course, had played a game like that of many Indian
chiefs. For a year he watched colonization of his island, lulled
by the colonists into such a sense of security that they felt obliged
to go to very little further expense for defence. The company was
making so much money that it promised to begin payments of
rents to the King within a year, instead of at the end of seven

years as had been expected. The directors of the company began to sink their whole personal fortunes into the enterprise.

THE MASSACRE OF 1600

Then, in 1600, the storm broke. Niell and his tribesmen massacred the colonists. In the first attack sixty of the colonists were slain. Within a few weeks their town was wiped out and the island cleared. Two noblemen, members of the directorate of the Lewes Company, were captives.

The stockholders then began to throw good money after bad. In 1602 they again tried to conquer the tribesmen; and in 1605, once more, failing again despite the fact that this time the King's fleet was sent to help them. Other tribes of the islands sent galleys to the assistance of the Lewes tribe. By 1607 some of the members of the company were dead; *others had sunk and lost their fortunes.* They surrendered their charter. In 1609 a new company was chartered to try the job; it too failed.

EXTERMINATION OF THE LEWES TRIBE

James then adopted a new scheme. The MacKenzie tribe of the mainland had submitted and their chief was made a noble. They had long coveted the island of the Lewes. The King decided to use barbarian against barbarian, armed the MacKenzie chief with a commission of fire and sword, and turned his tribe with its seven hundred swordsmen loose on the Lewes islanders. The Lewes tribe, weakened by years of civil war and strife with colonists, was soon crushed. Some of the lower orders submitted; but the entire ruling clan and the upper classes were by 1626 completely exterminated. A contemporary account by a MacLeod chronicler writes: "And so ends the lamentable historie and decay of mcleod of Lewes together with his trybe the Shiell Thorquill." But a contemporary MacKenzie account speaks of their chief as, "This noble conqueror."

The land of the Lewes was then colonized by MacKenzies and their septs. But the fisheries were held by the Crown. In 1629 a Dutch company was licensed to exploit the fisheries. John Mason, in 1636, organized a joint-stock company to take over these rights to the fisheries (Mason 1637; Scott 1912) and made much money from the enterprise.

The colonizing company which was to have conquered the Camerons and others never began operations, after witnessing the early massacre of the settlement of the other company.

A GENERAL EXTERMINATION PLANNED

In 1607 James was sovereign of both England and Scotland, and we shall speak of him now as James I of England, or, of Great Britain. He had just the year before chartered joint-stock companies to colonize Virginia and New England, and was busy organizing the Ulster Plantation, making use there to some extent of the joint-stock company. But he had become disgusted with the colonizing company as an agent of frontier extension in the Highlands of Scotland. He turned then to his more powerful Scotch nobles.

The failure of the Lewes Company lay in the fact that it had come to terms with the barbarous natives and attempted to absorb them into the colony. To James it now appeared that colonization must be preceded by a vigorous military campaign which would exterminate the natives. The Scotch Crown did not have at its command adequate financial or other resources to prosecute such a campaign. The Marquis of Huntley did.[1] James opened negotiations with Huntley with a view to contracting with him for the work.

Meantime the Earl of Argyll was commissioned to[2] subjugate the MacDonalds, MacNielles, MacIans, and others of the southern Hebrides. But as soon as these clansmen heard of this they took the offensive, raided the coasts of the Lowlands, and struck so much terror everywhere that they remained for the time unmolested. All the northern Hebrides except Lewes and Skye, which were still held on paper by joint-stock companies,

---

[1] The Gordon chief had always acknowledged the sovereignty of the Scotch Crown. The chief was made Earl of Huntley first by James II of Scotland in 1449.

[2] The Campbells and their Earl of Argyll occupy the lands first taken from the Pictish Kingdom by the Irish invaders (Scots) from Dalriada in Ulster.

were to be given in fee to the Marquis of Huntley. The Marquis was to conquer the islands at his own expense. After one year from the signing of the contract he was to begin payment of rents to the Crown.

Huntley replied to these tentative terms that it would take at least nine years to conquer the islands. The Marquis, moreover, was evidently planning to attempt to come to an agreement with the natives as the Lewes Company had done. But James, by insisting on completion of operations within one year, was planning to oblige the Marquis to put all his available forces into immediate and concerted action in the islands. If this were done he thought that he could have the natives exterminated. Moreover, by insisting at the same time on the extermination of the natives, and on payments of rent by the Marquis within a year, it would force the Marquis to bring Lowland immigrants immediately into the islands.

James, speaking from his London throne, through his privy council in Scotland, was very clear on these points. He insisted that it be agreed in writing that if the Marquis left any natives alive on the islands after a year had passed the lands should revert to the Crown and the Marquis get nothing for his expense. To his privy council James wrote that "you are to enjoin the said Marquis that, anent the extirpating of the barbarous people in those bounds he specially undertake and bind himself to extirpate and rout out the chief of Clan Ranald with his whole clan [Mainland MacDonalds] and their followers within the Isles . . . and also the MacNiel of Barra with his clan, and the whole Clan Donald in the north [northern MacDonalds]. . . ." And further, "that he end not his service by agreement with the country people [natives] but by extirpation of them". And finally, "that the said Marquis before the expiring of the year, shall plant those isles with civil people, and under no circumstances with", and here he explains that the immigrants must not be from the subjugated Highland regions of the mainland, but civilized Lowlanders. (This provision he also laid down in the plantation of Ulster.)

Huntley accepted these conditions. His acceptance indicates that the extermination preliminaries were practical. There is no doubt that they could have been carried out by the Lewes Company in 1599. *But in the Scotch colonization projects as in those in America we find always a reluctance on the part of the colonizing agencies to take the chance of laying out the large initial expenses involved in carrying on a campaign of subjugation or extermination of the natives. In this financially motivated caution in North European colonial enterprise in America, first evidenced here on the Celtic frontier, we have a glaring contrast with Spanish methods, which called first for subjugation or extermination and then for agreements.* Had the Crown of England or of other North European nations like the Crown of Castile managed, directed, and financed its own colonial enterprise instead of delegating it to private interests, it were inevitable that the policy pursued on the North American frontier had been similar to that of Spain.

The Marquis of Huntley was a Catholic, and for this reason, while he was negotiating with the King over the matter of the amount of rents to be paid, the Presbyterians, then all-powerful in Scotland, stepped in, jealous of the possible extension of power of a Catholic, and prevented the signing of the contract and the carrying out of the work. The King then developed a new idea.

THE PLANTATION OF ULSTER

James, often so short of money and credit that he could not regularly pay his own palace servants (Scott 1912; Hannay 1926), unwilling himself to spend one cent in the extension of his own sovereignty or in the extension of Christianity to the heathen over the frontier, was fertile with ideas as to how to get his subjects to invest in his work. In the same year that he was negotiating with Huntley concerning the Highlands of Scotland, and witnessing the plantation of Jamestown by the London Company, he was talking over plans for the plantation of northern Ireland.

The Scotch Celts never became so thoroughly subjugated that a reservation system could be introduced to take care of them. For this we must look to Ireland. Queen Elizabeth's nobles who received lands and governing powers in Ireland provided they could conquer the natives in the territories assigned, generally decided that it would be necessary to exterminate the Irish. In 1594, when Raleigh had been given lands in the New World, the poet Spenser, and other nobles had been assigned lands in Ireland.

Spenser, whose family was burned to death in a castle destroyed by the natives, was one of the most enthusiastic advocates of extermination. But neither the Crown nor any feudal lord was wealthy enough to finance the work of extermination.

Instead, to protect the English settlement in and around Dublin (the Pale) annual tribute was paid to the neighbouring Irish chiefs or kings in order to keep them at peace. This tribute was a regular charge on the state. It is decidedly comparable to the annuities paid many Indian tribes (King William in 1688 likewise bought peace from the Scotch Highlanders.) (Johnstone 1815). Sometimes, late in the sixteenth century, the Irish chiefs were also induced to submit to the Crown's sovereignty by offers of British titles of nobility; but this method was usually a failure because of many broken promises (Gwynn 1923). In 1556 and in 1571 "plantation" schemes of some interest were devised for parts of southern Ireland which involved placing the natives in reservations; these were not pushed, however, with sufficient energy to be successful (Gwynn 1923; Ford 1915; MacManus 1921).

In 1603, about the time of Elizabeth's death and James' succession to the throne of England, matters came to a head in Ulster. The native nobility there thought it well to flee the country and go to the Continent. This was the beginning of a never-ending emigration of the Irish nobles,—the Wild Geese,—for, "ransacking all nature for its most desolate image, . . . and its most lamentable cry" (MacManus 1921), the tribesmen called their fleeing chiefs after the wild geese. In 1605 James declared the lands of Irish Ulster to be Crown domain. In 1607 (the year of the settlement of Jamestown, Virginia), Chichester suggested a reservation system for the leaderless natives; or, as an alternative, a campaign of extermination. In 1609 James used this plan in his final scheme for the colonization of Ulster.

IRISH RESERVATIONS

The natives of the region, divided into six British counties, were ordered to leave the country immediately or to gather together on reservations. Of course they had nowhere to go, and the order called for death for any found outside reservations after a certain date. The lands assigned to these reservations occupied one-fifth of the whole territory, but they were scattered evenly here and there over the whole of Ulster. The title to the land of each reservation was granted to one or another of the rich English nobles, to be called "servitors"; they were required to contract to erect a fortified castle on their land, to maintain a military force, and to protect the colonists outside the reservations; and to pay a rental to the King. The reservation natives, in order to subsist, had to meet the terms of their "servitors"; they were required to lease the reservation lands from him and cultivate them to pay the rentals demanded. Under the then civilized methods of grazing and agriculture, one-fifth of Ulster would in fact be plenty for furnishing subsistence for the native population.

THE RESERVATIONS OPENED

The entire county of Derry, with its town, was, for the sum of £20,000 and a yearly rental, turned over by the Crown to the Corporation of the City of London. From the corporation the twelve corporate guilds of the city each took title to a subdivision of the county. The other five counties were divided among wealthy private persons, many of whom organized joint-stock companies for the exploitation of their areas.

The London Corporation in Derry, and the private grantees and stock companies in the other counties contracted to introduce English, Scotch, or Continental immigrants along with cattle, ploughs, and other necessary capital. These immigrants were to lease the land of the grantees. They were forbidden to permit any native Irish on their lands.

Many immigrants were brought in. But pirates infested the channels; shipping of immigrants and capital was costly; and even the scum of the British cities who furnished many of the tenant immigrants, were, curiously enough, reluctant to leave their dirty but to them comfortable hovels for what they considered the wilderness. Those who were willing were often called by the lure of Virginia, where they could meet the expenses of passage by becoming indentured servants, and hope ultimately not to be tenants but owners of land. The bars to the immigration of the now half-civilized Celtic Scotch had to be somewhat lifted. Many French Huguenots came and developed profitable flax growing. But by 1660 or thereabouts the natives began to trickle off the reservation in large numbers and were accepted as tenants outside the reservations. Without chiefs to lead them they were in time economically assimilated, though they never ceased dreaming of revolt. Leasing to natives remained illegal, however, and the natives held leases only year by year, which gave them little incentive to improve their lands.

A TREATY WITH THE WILD TRIBES IN SCOTLAND

While the frontier was making headway in Ireland, James was trying out a new plan in the Hebrides. Away back in the eleventh century, William the Conqueror had established a frontier county of England as a county palatine or palatinate, establishing a bishop as its feudal head in possession of almost sovereign powers (Surtees). James in 1606 had reëstablished the episcopate in Scotland. Apparently inspired by the Durham example, in 1608 he created of the isles west of the Scotch mainland a domain under the feudal lordship of Andrew Knox, a clergyman who was first made Bishop of the Isles, and was then given power to conquer and subdue and govern the natives given in his charge.

But like all the King's agents, the Bishop too looked for compromise. He sailed into the isles with a well-armed vessel; he persuaded an assembly of the clan chiefs on board ship for a conference, and by trickery locked them down under the hatches, took them to Edinburgh dungeons, and there came to terms with them!

The King had ordered that the tribal system of government be utterly and completely abolished. But the Bishop wanted compromise to avoid bloodshed and got it. In 1609 on the Island of Iona (Icolumbkille) he got the signatures of the chiefs to an agreement which later received the approval of the King. The treaty was signed by the chiefs of the MacLeans, MacDonalds, MacKinnons, MacLeods of Harris, MacQuarries, MacFies, Mac-Allens, and others.

In Virginia the London Company and the Indian tribes were making treaties which did not demand submission to the English Crown. These Celtic tribes were required to submit to the Crown's sovereignty, and stop internecine warfare, but they were

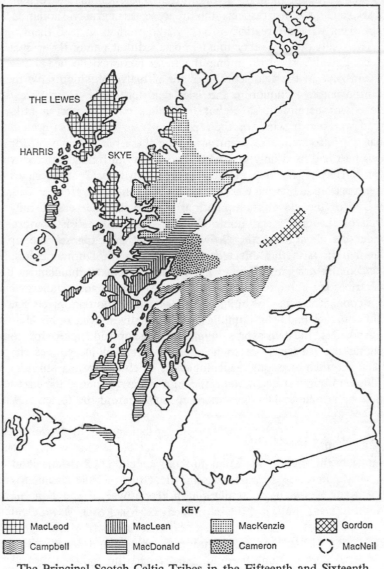

KEY

⊞ MacLeod	⦀ MacLean	⦙ MacKenzie	⊠ Gordon				
≈ Campbell	☰ MacDonald	⠿ Cameron	◯ MacNeil				

The Principal Scotch Celtic Tribes in the Fifteenth and Sixteenth
Centuries

allowed to retain their tribal organization for administrative purposes, and in other respects the treaty is remarkably similar to
typical early Indian treaties.

The treaty, among other things, observed that one of the causes
of continued barbarism among the tribesmen was the heavy use
of whiskey. So the treaty provides for virtual prohibition. Sale or
transportation of liquor in the isles was forbidden. Home brew
alone was permitted, save that the chiefs might import a little
good whiskey or wine for their personal use. It was also argued
that the introduction of firearms among these barbarians who for
ages past had used only the sword and dagger and bow and arrow
was terribly destructive in their internecine wars. So the use of
firearms even in hunting was forbidden!

One of the cleverest stipulations agreed that the eldest children of the chiefs and nobles be educated in English schools,
under the direction of the Crown though at the expense of their
parents. In time this effected some Anglicization of the chiefs.
Incidentally, trial marriage, a native custom, was forbidden; and
the tribes were required to submit in religion to the established
Episcopal Church, to build churches, and support a clergy.
Hitherto, they had been Catholics, first Celtic, then Roman.

And, last, the bards or *seannachies* were forbidden to sing to
remind the tribesmen of their ancient, primitive glory, and the
chiefs of their age-long genealogies. The chiefs were even forbidden to support them, and the bards were to be doomed to
starvation or manual labour—and silence (MacLeod 1927).

JOHN MASON IN SCOTLAND AND IN AMERICA

Naturally this treaty was often broken, and in 1625 the trouble-
some MacIans had to be exterminated (Gregory 1881), while as
late as 1633 the new population of the Lewes was still giving
trouble (Scott 1912). In fact immediately in 1610, serious re-
volts had broken out and these brought John Mason on the
scene. The Bishop required help and the King could not afford it.
Mason, a wealthy English commoner, seeking the royal favour, at
a cost of £2,000, equipped ships of war and commanded them in
the service of the Bishop for fourteen months, until 1612. His
£2,000 expenditure was considered a loan to the King's treas-

ury; the King promised to give Mason lands in Ireland in payment, but Mason never got either these lands or his money. But
in 1615 Mason became governor of Newfoundland for the joint-
stock company which had acquired title to it. Then he and Gorges
acquired title to lands in New England and he himself became
the founder of what is now the state of New Hampshire. In
1647 he was the leader of the massacre of the Pequots in Connecticut.

THE END OF SCOTCH TRIBAL ORGANIZATION

The tribal organization remained in existence all through the
Scotch Highlands until their revolt in the interest of the Pre-
tender in 1745, when the government suppressed the tribal
system, forbade the use of the native costume, worked for the
suppression of the Gaelic language, and so on. The disheartened
tribesmen, sometimes headed by their chiefs and retaining their
clan organization even in foreign parts for a time, then began a
large-scale emigration to the Carolinas, Canada, and other parts.

Those who remained at home showed themselves incapable
of rapidly assimilating the agricultural methods of civilized
peoples. The Highlands were civilized economically only as a
result of the importation of tenants from the Lowlands.

THE PURITANS ON THE CELTIC FRONTIER: EXTERMINATION;
AND RESERVATIONS

Once in the course of the development of the frontier *did the
sovereign directly prosecute its extension, and we see immediately
the absence of the timid policy of hedging and compromise exhibited by private agents on the Celtic and Indian frontiers.*

The plantation of Ulster effected the end of any serious native
problem there. But the other three regions of Ireland remained
tribal and barbarian (although Catholic in religion). These three
provinces were subjugated by the Puritan dictator, Oliver Cromwell, who had no doubt read the book on Spanish Indian mas-
sacres which so affectionately had been dedicated to him by the
nephew of John Milton, the poet who made Satan a hero.

From 1642 to 1651 Charles I and the Protestant Parliamentarians fought each other in a civil war. From 1651 to 1660 Cromwell, exactly in the fashion of Lenin, Mussolini, *et al.*, to-day, was a zealous, haughty dictator, whose strength was in the army. In 1660, the masses of the English people, sick to the death of evangelical fanaticism, restored the Stuarts in the person of Charles II and took bloody revenge on the fanatical regicides.

During his dictatorship Cromwell suppressed religious freedom as rigorously as did his fellow Puritans in America. Anglicans, Jews, and Catholics were forbidden to worship unless they wished to worship in Presbyterian or Congregationalist churches. He went with his army into Ireland determined not only to wipe out the tribal system but the native religion, and to force the natives to submit to the English Parliament and his dictatorship and to the Congregationalist religious belief and organization.

The butchery he proceeded with there, even in the light of the ethics then generally prevalent in Europe, was more than in any way could be condoned. But it was successful. "The Curse of Cromwell" brought civil government to Ireland. At a terrible cost in human suffering, however. Over eighty thousand natives were shipped to the West Indies as chattel slaves, there to toil alongside the negroes, and alongside the Indians enslaved and shipped abroad by the Puritans of New England in the same period. And of the native population of at most one million, about one-fourth died by the sword and by starvation.

Even at this Cromwell did not attain all his ends. For although in 1654 the hand-picked Parliament denied it officially, it was evident that the object of Cromwell and the hope of Parliament was the extermination of the million natives of wild Ireland!

Resistance ending on the part of the natives, open extermination was no longer planned or hoped for. A unique reservation scheme was devised, which was planned to result in the death of hundreds of thousands. In September, 1653, order was given that all natives still living in the two provinces of the east and south should get out and emigrate to the western province, Connaught. Any native found outside Connaught by May 1, 1654, was to be put to death. The Puritans apparently anticipated a substitute on May Day for the May Pole which they so detested. Those who were not executed on May 1, if they reached Connaught would probably starve, for barren, stony Connaught had

all the population it could support. The natives started to trek
to their great reservation in the West, but before the coming May
so many exceptions to the rule had been made that most of them
never had to leave. It had been soon realized that native labour
was necessary for the east and south, immigrants enough not being
available (Gwynn 1923; MacManus 1921).

So much for a frontier intimately linked with that which we
shall now consider at much greater length.

3 REACTION AND INTERACTION: A FOOD GATHERING PEOPLE AND EUROPEAN SETTLEMENT IN AUSTRALIA

A. P. Elkin

THE AUSTRALIAN ABORIGINES

Reaction and Cultural Conditioning

THE REACTION of an aboriginal people to the presence and culture of an intrusive and settling people is not based necessarily on curiosity, acquisition and imitation. Such drives are familiar to us of the western world, even in cross-cultural situations; we might infer, therefore, that because our culture is comparatively rich, the less well-endowed peoples, when confronted with it, would desire to examine, acquire and imitate it.

In Australian Aboriginal culture, however, the individual is trained not to show curiosity, indeed, not to be curious. Thus, during initiation he only looks at rites and objects when told to do so, and he does not ask the "why"; he waits until he is told— and that in instalments. Moreover, both men and women grow up accepting the fact that sections of knowledge are restricted to one or more groups, and are not free to all.

With this background, the Aborigines consider quite naturally that the ways, possessions and beliefs of the white man are his secret, his own possession, and are not to be "taken by storm" or imitated. They are just factually "another kind" and neither envy nor acquisitiveness is aroused. They do not expect the white man to pry upon their life—and this seldom occurs (anthropologists apart, who must make out a case for doing so), though the or-

Originally published in *American Anthropologist*, Volume 53 (1951), 164–86. Reprinted with permission of the author and of the editor of *American Anthropologist*.

dinary white man's motive for this lack of interest is not based
on the idea of mutual respect for cultural tradition; it is very often
just a matter of superiority and prestige. The native way of life
is "queer," especially in the degree in which the Aborigines do
not seem to act from the same motives or for the same inducements as the European.

Further, imitation for the native is not imitation of the fortui-
tous, of the strange, but of the traditional, of the cultural, of the
ways of the cult-heroes—or "Dreamings" as the Australian Aborigines call these. Life consists in maintaining continuity with the
past—the culture-stream—not in imitating the culturally unrelated
exotic. In spite of this, many benefactors have been disappointed
that Aborigines have shown no desire to join a mission or settlement and partake of the benefits—material and spiritual—which
were openly displayed to them. But, of course, houses, and farming, church-going, and school were not only exotic; they also
interfered with the established routine of nomadism and ritual.

Likewise, acquisition is not a universal trait; it is itself an ac-
quirement in certain cultures, but not in others. To the Aborigines
goods are made to use or to give away or to exchange (mostly
ceremonially); food is obtained to eat and to share according to
rules; and the semi-nomadic necessities of the economic life of a
food-gathering people, without pack-animals or vehicles, places
a heavy discount on possessions as such; they are needless
impedimenta. Even the land is apportioned among the food-
gathering groups on kinship and spiritual as well as on economic
bases; indeed the real tie to the land is spiritual. The title deeds
are spiritual. A man's country is the home of his pre-existent
spirit, and no other "country" is the same to him. To acquire
land is meaningless to him, and he finds it hard to understand
the European's motive in wanting another's land. "White man
'nother kind."

Thus, the Aborigines' reaction to white intrusion is not a matter of curiosity, imitation and acquisition. Indeed, it is only indirectly an individual matter. Rather is it a matter of cultural
determination. This surely is true in all cases of cultural intrusion.
The attitude shown by the natives is conditioned by their cultural background, by their social, economic and political organi-

zation, by the degree of their cultural self-sufficiency and integration, and to some extent by their numbers.

In the case of an integrated village and tribal organization centering on the headman or chief, the latter can either oppose the newcomer and his ways and demands, or decide to co-operate with him in some degree or other, and to accept new culture traits. Sometimes, indeed, his acceptance may be too avid for the stability of his community.

Even if central tribal and political organization be weak (as in much of Melanesia), the local village economy with its headman and defined gardens provides a base, a means and symbol of continuity and of independence, which can slow up the process of acculturation in spite of the persistence of the bearers of the new ways and strange demands; it can also provide a retreat and a rallying point if disintegration has gone far and is to be stayed.

On the other hand, a semi-nomadic, food-gathering, and therefore scattered people, with neither settled villages, anchored gardens, nor centralized organization, has no such points of resistance to the newcomer and his ways, nor means of recovery. Moreover, the obvious absence of these features gives the invader (settler, administrative officer or missionary) the impression that the natives are almost cultureless and that whatever he does can interfere but little with them. Therefore, he is very unlikely to respect native ways, customs, beliefs and values, or to adjust to these his method of economic, administrative or spiritual invasion. He sees no objective symbols of their existence. In his opinion, adaptation must be all on one side, that of the indigenous people. And he thinks it is.

In all cases of contact of western and aboriginal peoples, some degree of western culture and some of the bearers sooner or later break through. On the one hand, this depends on the economic attraction (to the settler) of the natives' country, on the strength of the civilizing urge of the administration implicated in the doings of frontier-minded men, and on the zeal of religious missionaries.

On the other hand, such break-through also depends on some degree of acceptance of the new by the native population. That is, some point of weakness must appear in the local social structure. This may come through the cupidity or ambitions of the chief of a centralized tribal society. He, in return for certain goods or equipment, for assistance in warfare and raiding, or for fancied increase of prestige, mortgages himself or his people or land to the newcomer. The latter's desire for land, for labor, or for converts, is thus met. In this type of society, the effective point of weakness is not likely to be an ordinary individual, such as a commoner or a youth, but rather a person of authority.

Economic Re-adaptation Inevitable for a Food-gathering People

The situation, however, is different in the case of a food-gathering people like the Australian Aborigines. White settlement, with its usurpation of hunting and food-gathering grounds quickly undermines its economic life, that is, the tribesmen's means of livelihood, and interferes drastically with the give and take of social life. The activities of an invading gardening or agricultural people can dovetail in with the indigenous activity of a settled, gardening people, provided, as is likely to be the case, there is spare land, and that the newcomers are not as "the sands of the sea-shore." But if, as in Australia, the Aborigines depend on food-gathering over the whole tribal region, according to rules governing groups, areas and times, and if the settlers are farmers, at once certain areas are put out of bounds for tribal food-gathering activity. This in itself would not prevent all such activity, at least not unless most of the tribal land were arable and had been put under cultivation. But when cultivation is associated with grazing cattle and sheep, or when the latter is the primary occupation of the settlers, competition with the native's means of livelihood is unavoidable. The settler's cattle and sheep, ever increasing in numbers, require all the grass and must not be disturbed by the huntsmen's activities. So the native fauna must go, including the Aborigines, unless they change their way of living and adapt themselves to the white man by working for him and existing on the new foods thus earned.

PHASES IN THE PROCESS OF REACTION

Tentative Approach

The general picture all over Australia from 1788 onward is that on first contact with definite settlement the Aborigines are usually shy and harmless. They gradually make a nervous and tentative approach to the trespassers, and if not rebuffed, readiness is shown by some to help the latter in small ways when asked. This is no doubt based on the assumption that the newcomers are temporary sojourners only. It is a transition phase marked by observation and careful contact. Incidentally, this applies also to the settler or settlers.

Clash

But the months pass by and the Aborigines realize that the settler or missionary intends to remain, or that the number of settlers is increasing. They see their land usurped as though they had no ties to it, their manpower used for labor, and their women for work and to some extent also for concubinage. This interference with their social, ceremonial and economic activities creates a condition of incipient clash, which becomes patent in various circumstances. The settler may try to stop the natives hunting in their country, now his. If native foods become scarce, as a result of white settlement, sheep and cattle may be killed and eaten, or the lonely settler's hut raided for the food stored in it, and he himself possibly killed. Or the raiding and killing may be a matter of restoring self-confidence and prestige by successfully damaging the intruder. Perplexity or resentment aroused by the white man's attitude to his native workers because of their lack of interest in, or ignorance of the tasks he sets them, may lead to their absenteeism. Likewise their absences for ritual and social purposes irritate him. And finally the settler's attitude to the husband of the native woman with whom he desires to associate, may lead to resentment and to the use of force.

The Aborigines feel justified in resisting the white man both by non-cooperation and by physical means, until they learn through punitive expeditions and police action that the intruder's power is paramount, that clash means defeat and death. They have nowhere else to go, for they are tied by spiritual bonds to their tribal and horde country, now possessed by another. They must therefore accept the changed position—the diminishing hunting grounds and the demands and economic activities of the European, and adapt themselves to it according to the circumstances

in each locality and according to the personality of each white
person with whom they have to deal.

Adaptation

So the young men work with the settler's stock or in his gardens,
and the older men do less arduous tasks, while some of the women
work around the house and carry water—no one, as a rule, doing
more than will ensure rations and some extras. It is bare subsistence labor—not paid labor, and as such is naturally for the
most part uninterested and inefficient. The "employer" realizes
this, and whether or not he could or would pay reasonable wages
for efficient work, he recognizes that he too is adapting himself to
a situation, of which he is the cause—the economic disturbance
of the tribe or local horde. He knows, too, that this situation includes the old men who remain in the background, and are the
real masters of his workers. He is concerned not only with those
who work for rations but with what are called their dependents—
that is, the rest of the tribe. He must put up with his "payments"
being shared around the camp; and he accepts the fact that more
men and women than necessary infiltrate into his bevy of "employees," even though they "go slow" and he knows that they
are "tucker (food) lines" to those who do not work for him at
all, but are "sitting down on him." However, he feels unable to
do anything about it for he is dependent on the natives for assistance; if they deserted him, he would be almost helpless, and
if he antagonized them to the extent of their retaliating by killing
his stock or himself, he would not be compensated by the police
or punitive action that would follow. Thus both parties work out
a *modus vivendi*.

This includes the rôle of the native women. Concubinage (usually temporary) and prostitution have been and are methods
of maintaining peaceful relations with, and of obtaining food and
newly desired objects from the white man, who in the marginal
regions of settlement, is seldom accompanied by any of his own
females. And so, the European, in spite of loudly protesting his
superiority to the "blacks," often accepts the fact that he is sharing his native woman with her own "black" husband—a loose
polyandry.

This attitude of superiority adopted by the European—and possibly believed by him to be well-grounded—plays into the hands of the natives. Being credited with only low intelligence, they are expected to be stupid and uninterested in their work. They play down to this expectation and so flatter the "boss," and incidentally "justify" their lack of efficiency and the "employment" of an unnecessarily large number.

The native "doctor," too, plays the part attributed to him; he "makes" rain for a consideration, or makes up legends for tobacco. Parents leave their children at the mission school to be fed while they themselves move about on tribal affairs—only to take them away, if they can, when it suits them, especially when initiation or marriage requires them in tribal life. And the natives on the Trans-Continental Railway line ply a well-developed art of "preying" on the passengers, most of whom have not seen bush Aborigines before. Donning tattered garments, and borrowing babies if they have none of their own, groups of men and women visit the train stopping places to sell their own few artifacts, to amuse and to beg. The provision of clothing and ration depôts and the work of missions have failed to prevent this active, successful, interesting, and new form of "hunting."

Thus, in these various ways a stage of *intelligent parasitism* and of equilibrium is built up in the marginal regions. Adaptation, which was formerly to nature, its seasons and bounty, is now to the settler and other persons and institutions.

Adaptation—Inevitable, General and Particular

It must be emphasized that this is based on the necessity for adaptation, not on a desire for civilization, nor on a respect for the white man because of his possessions. The latter interest him in an impersonal and objective way, but only some of them are of use to him. These are basic foods to replace the indigenous sources, no longer available, or extras (like tea and sugar) to add to them. The useful articles also include axes, knives, iron, and razor blades, string, tobacco, pipes, matches, combs, and some articles of clothing. But no credit is given to the white man (settler, missionary, or official) for having these things at his disposal. They simply come from his country—are its products, just as kangaroo, grass-seed, spears and stone axes come from the Aborigines' country. And they do so because their "shades," spirit-parts, "Dreamings," belong there, just as the "shades" of the native goods and artifacts belong to *their* own country. The credit in both cases goes to the ancestors and cult-heroes, widely known as the "Dreamings."

Moreover, it is obvious to the Aborigine that white men are not his superior—at least not in his "bush" environment, the only one he knows. Indeed, most Europeans are helpless in it. Setting out with no possessions whatever, they would probably die, whereas the Aborigine by hitting one stone with another would have a knife, chisel and axe, with which he could make other implements and weapons, and by rubbing two sticks together, would have fire, cooking, warmth and some protection from mosquitoes. In other words, his prestige does not suffer in his own eyes when he compares his achievements with those of the Europeans in his midst.

This is true also in the moral field. Trained to fulfil the reciprocal duties and taboos of kinship, age, sex, clan and other groupings, and to guard faithfully the secrets ceremonially imparted to him, he judges others by the standards implied in these duties and responsibilities. As I found in part of Central Australia in 1930, all the white men over a large area were classified by the natives according to whether they kept their word or not, fulfilled or did not fulfil their spoken or implied social and economic obligations (to the Aborigines); in the first case they were good, in the second, bad. The second were in danger of being speared. Likewise, an early observer in South Australia said: "The natives discover the differences of intelligence and conduct between the different classes of settlers, and in their remarks upon it, recognize the superior excellence of truth and honesty." They certainly prefer the truthful and honest man, and the one who is just and consistent. For the very adaptation they are compelled by circumstances to make is both general and particular. It is not only to a changed economic environment and organization in general, but also to a particular expression of the change, as mediated through the settler, station manager or employee, prospector, missionary or official who has become the focus and point of contact with the change. His character, attitudes and idiosyncrasies, strength and weakness, must be noted, and allowed for in the behavior to be adopted by the tribe or its remnant. The natives must make the best of being disinherited or disturbed. And so the generalized adaptation is particularized according to the type of white person or persons who control the local situation.

The Double Rôle and the Breakdown of Equilibrium

Thus in the phase of intelligent parasitism, the Aborigines act a part, but it is not one which is easily integrated with native life. It is external to it, though in many marginal regions economically essential. In spite of the necessity of adjusting themselves to and working for the white man, the increase of his sheep and cattle and crops has not been provided for in their ritual. Not only are these things recent and not mythological, they are the white man's "business." Fun may be made of the latter's work and possessions in ordinary corroborees, but they are not elevated to the realm of the sacred. Moreover, the language used by the white man (except by a very few missionaries) with reference to his demands and possessions is not the tongue of the native; it is usually pidgin, or at best broken English. Among themselves too, the native men and women usually employ pidgin when talking about their work. If, however, the subject be tribal, the native language is used.

But when they finish their "outside" work, with its aspects of inefficiency (both attributed and actual), superficiality and parasitism, they return to their own world of traditional security, mythological depth, social warmth, and technical efficiency (e.g. in the making and use of implements and weapons, ritual and food-gathering). Here they find life. In the other—the periods of work, they obtain a meagre existence; but this latter alone will not maintain the equilibrium sought. The former, which is social, psychological, and spiritual in context, is essential. But it may fail through depopulation, resulting from disease, unbalanced diet, high infant mortality, fall in the birth rate or other cause. If so, the phase of intelligent parasitism breaks down, and that of pauperism ensues. This phase is seen at numbers of pastoral stations and even at some missions, which have been established for two or three generations and which are usually no longer on the real frontier of settlement, but are within the sparsely settled zones of the continent. It is also the usual condition found around townships in these zones.

Conflict of Interests and the Breakdown

One important indirect factor contributes to this breakdown of equilibrium. It is the growing desire of at least some of the younger natives, in particular those born and brought up in station, township, and mission camps, for some of the white man's goods, in addition to basic food. This desire makes them more amenable to, and dependent on, the white man. "The latter has plenty, let us get some of it," is their attitude and plan, even at the cost of their tribal birthright. Attention must now be given to him, not to intra- and intertribal duties, activities and exchanges, linking individuals and groups in bonds of reciprocity.

In addition, sensing his point of view that much Aboriginal custom and belief is baseless or else stupid, they tend to ignore and even despise the old men's knowledge and authority; and yet they are not sure of themselves, for the white man does not really share with them his view and way of life. This causes conflict in their own minds as well as conflict and strain in the camp. One effect, apart from possible spearings, is that these young people are not entrusted with sacred knowledge, and when later on in middle age, they find themselves disillusioned through their lack of admission into the white man's social and economic life, they have no spiritual retreat. As the natives say, they have lost their Dreaming (their mythological and ritual anchor and compass); and "he who loses his Dreaming is lost." Thus, psychological disturbance is added to the reduction in numbers and strength—and the remnant is "lost."

This breakdown leaves the Aborigines in small remnants scattered about the sparsely settled regions—mostly within their tribal countries—working for the white man, unable to return to the old ways, perhaps ignorant of the Dreamings—and waiting!

The "mat" to which they will return is death alone—for the pattern of life's weaving has been lost.

The Sequence of Phases Not Constant

In the earliest periods of settlement in the main coastal centers, when the "invaders" were endeavoring to establish themselves firmly and quickly, the local tribes became landless in a very short time, and were reduced to penury. Physical clash, when it did occur, was harshly dealt with, locally and privately rather than officially, and the Aborigines found themselves separated tribal remnants, decreasing in numbers and dragging out their last days on the crumbs which fell from the invaders' table.

A change came when the invaders' rate and intensity of settlement slowed down; while consolidation within the first settled coastal regions was being effected, individual settlers ("squatters") pushed beyond the frontiers, each an outpost with flocks and herds, not a colonizing unit hundreds or thousands strong. This spread which was at first frowned on by authority, was later controlled by regulations, partly aimed at preventing, or lessening the severity of the clash between white and black. In these frontier conditions, the Aborigines had time to realize the position and adjust themselves to it, though slowly, because as has been implied, the settlers also had to learn to accept the natives as part of the situation—often a very necessary part to them. Some refused to learn and remained high-handed and callous. Generally, however, fear and clash gradually gave place on the part of the whites to a recognition of dependence on the natives, and of intelligent parasitism on the part of the latter.

Pauperism and Protection Policies

The lag in the development of intelligent parasitism is no doubt one reason why the difference between it and the phase of pauperism has been seldom appreciated. Another is that neither the natives, nor the white man concerned, publicized their *modus vivendi*. Moreover, the impression was gained very soon after Europeans settled in Australia that the process was one of disinheritance, followed by clash and pauperism, or else by the latter without incidents of clash, and sooner or later, but inevitably, by the disappearance of the Aborigines. This became the accepted and publicized dogma. Intelligent adaptation was not suspected, for the failure of the attempts made to civilize, educate and Christianize the Aborigines (which was the early official policy, particularly from 1820 to 1840) was accepted as a sign that they were poorly endowed with intelligence. The dogma appeared, and was rationalized and justified, that a primitive, food-gathering people was doomed to extinction when overtaken by civilization. Nothing could be done except to avoid unnecessary harshness and to "smooth the dying pillow"—a concept over one hundred years old.

This was the inspiration and theme of the protection policies adopted by the governments within Australia at various dates during the last three decades of the nineteenth century. The Aborigines would not, or more likely, could not be civilized. Diseases and clashes in the marginal region meant their reduction to pathetic remnants. Positive measures for their progress such as education, wages, housing and health services were not thought of, or else were deemed futile. All that was required was protection from harshness and injustice and the provision of rations for the aged and sick. In the long run and in essence this meant pauperism, though in the marginal zones intelligent parasitism was being evolved.

Advance from Intelligent Parasitism

The significance of this protection-pauperizing policy was realized in the 1930's, and positive policies designed to ensure the welfare and progress of the Aborigines have been progressively put into operation, though in different degrees in different parts of Australia. Citizenship is the aim; the means are education, effective dietary and health measures, child endowment, satisfactory conditions of employment, Government Aboriginal Stations and usually co-operation with missions.

Where pauperism has been reached, however, it is doubtful whether progress can be expected, especially as the Aborigines usually prefer to remain and die out in their own "countries" rather than that the remnants should be gathered together to form communities of reasonable size. But where intelligent parasitism persists, a further phase is possible, provided that certain general conditions are present. At least the will and the ability to live and persist are still operating.

The conditions are first, the maintenance of the tribe as a community, provided it is not reduced below twenty or thirty families, even though nomadism be only an occasional diversion, and all live on one or two permanent sites on the same or neighboring stations or missions. Second, there must be the functioning of community life through the native language, with its aspect of continuity and of common heritage, and through a respected, not a flouted, social organization, including the headmen with their knowledge and custodianship of the moral and social sanctions—the mythology and "Dreamings."

The possibility of such a further phase is suggested by several examples in northern Australia. One illustration comes from the Roper River, Northern Territory. The larger part of the Mungarai tribe is on one station, on which most of them work, have worked or will work. The smaller group is on the neighboring station. There is still opportunity for occasional "walk-about" and living off the country. A threatened serious decline in numbers was arrested on the first station by providing food for the mothers and children. The conditions for survival are present: the Mungarai language is retained; the number of families makes communal life possible; after forty years of contact there is seldom a "wrong" marriage. Respect is paid by the owner as well as by the tribesmen to the headman. There are few white persons and little missionary activity, so the natives have had to adjust themselves to only one external factor, and that unaggressive—the small station staff and, occasionally, the owner. In this case, education, health measures, and improvement of employment conditions should ensure the increase and future of the tribe, provided that the authorities do not shift families elsewhere on the ground of shortage of employment—at least, not until the numbers are greater and tribes in the area have coalesced more. Education and self-dependence will gradually make such coalescence possible.

A similar condition obtains at Bathurst Island Mission. The economic life has been changed very little, though small groups of men go to Darwin for short periods to arranged employment. Work is also done at and for the mission. The language is maintained and respected. The community life, with its rules of marriage and behavior, somewhat modified, is strong. Health and diet are carefully watched, especially of mothers and children. Literacy in English is aimed at. The religious position has not been determined yet, but a blend of Roman Catholicism and native belief is indicated, though most of the adults are still pagan. The population is about 800 and increasing.

A Lutheran mission in North Queensland presents a more advanced stage. The tribe, the Kokoyimidir, has preserved its community life and numbers; as a result of education through two generations, these people are literate in both English and their own language; they are good Lutherans, and also reliable farmers. In spite of the change to Lutheranism and to Christian moral principles and of the adoption of a settled life in houses and in farming, the Kokoyimidir are still Kokoyimidir, largely the result of the preservation of their language and of its use as a written medium. This preserves continuity, and also some degree of pride in their past, while the acceptance of Lutheranism provides a sanction for social cohesion, education enables them to understand western modes of life, and the training in making their own living ensures self-respect.

The Phase of Intelligent Appreciation

The suggestion is that Aborigines can pass from intelligent parasitism to *intelligent appreciation* of the culture and way of life which has spread across their tribal lands. That is, they pass from an external adaptation, making the best of the inevitable, to an inner understanding of the new way and of the part they might play in it. Associated with this change is the attitude of the white man. The preceding phase implies an adjustment, even though little recognized, on the part of the settler or pastoralist to the tribe or natives on whom and on whose country he depends for his living, and whom he professes it is better not to understand. Indeed, the maintenance of this ignorance, and also the use of pidgin or broken English rather than English or a native language, and the withholding of education from the Aborigines, are part of this external adjustment. White and native are foreigners to each other, getting what they can from each other, but sharing little. There is also the type of missionary, who, like so many in the past, refuses to learn to use the tribal language, or to try to infuse his Christian doctrine and precepts into the tribal social organization and view of life, of both of which, in disdain, he remains ignorant, and who considers it impossible to educate the Aborigines beyond third grade in school—he belongs to the same stage of external adaptation. His efforts are usually met by intelligent parasitism, though in time this may break down through a conflict of interests and a disturbance of equilibrium, as explained.

Intelligent appreciation, however, can only be attained by the Aborigines if the white man intends that they should, and helps them to do so. This means, on his part, intelligent appreciation in thought and action of the Aborigines' condition, social, cultural and economic, and of their right to shed their parasitic position and to become self-dependent members within the wider community of reciprocal rights and responsibilities, both native and white. But this is not an individual or casual matter. Enlightenment has come slowly, and to it anthropological field research has contributed much; indeed, this has provided the substance without which good-will and humanitarianism would have remained ineffectual forms. On the basis of organized knowledge and sound interpretation, both governments and missionary authorities can and have been brought to the phase of intelligent appreciation. As a result new policies are framed and new methods of working are tried. This means and requires administrative officers and missionaries trained and specializing in this intelligent appreciation of native affairs in general, of native culture, the contact problem, and of native advance. Employers and other white persons in the marginal and sparsely settled zones must abide by the regulations drawn up to make this new phase possible; failure means the complete disappearance of the "fullblood" Aborigines.

Rapid Change Inevitable

The position is now markedly different from what it was in 1930. Then one could speak of almost "untouched" regions and Aborigines, and advocate inviolable reserves for them as a means of preservation. But contact has been rapid and relentless—settlers and missionaries moving beyond the frontiers, and natives moving in to see the white man, and sometimes to take the place of extinct local Aboriginal groups. Then came the war with the army, air force and navy in their respective spheres, by choice or by accident, penetrating almost everywhere; and natives, many of them previously having no associations with white men, working for the forces, being treated well, and learning much. Scientific

parties, photographic expeditions and tourists have added to the intensity of the contact.

The effect is that there is an unsettlement, a ferment almost everywhere among the younger virile Aborigines who have any contact whatever with non-natives—townships, settlers, stations, mines or missions. Cultural diffusion and mixing are going on apace. Many want the best of both worlds, the old and new. Others, who have had very close association with whites in towns or at larger stations and missions, want a fair deal and good education. Some of the inducements, of course, are not laudable, being but the froth and jetsam of western culture; but that, too, is part of the change, the rate of, and desire for which was very much increased during the 1940's.

Intelligent appreciation is thus called for, and quickly. Efficient health and dietary measures; education based on bilingual literacy wherever native community life remains, and designed to impart an understanding of the drives and values in the culture which has come upon them, of the purpose of its economic activities, and of its moral and social codes, as well as to preserve a respect for their own native heritage; training and the opportunity to earn a living and to appreciate the responsibility of the individual to work and be self-dependent; and the provision of attractive recreation—such measures implemented vigorously, generously and without niggardliness in spirit or in financial outlay, are suggested as the means for making the stage of intelligent appreciation and mutual participation a reality.

The Alternative: "The Return to the Mat"
—A Transition Phase

Unless this phase is successfully reached, disillusionment will ensue. The Aborigines quickly detect the failure of the prospect and promise of economic, social and cultural opportunity to become more than a form without content. They become resentful, even though this may not be noticeable except in lack of cooperation and in absence of dependability in work. In addition, they seek to "return to the mat," to retreat within themselves and their own past, and at the same time to refurbish the "implements" of intelligent parasitism, or if their group life and pride be broken, to be clamant paupers, shirking and denying social responsibility.

The condition of pauperism and disintegration is inevitable if in the process of adaptation to western modes of life the native language has been ignored and its use discouraged, and if no appreciation has been shown of the aboriginal community system with its reciprocal rights and duties—that is, if the rising generation has been divorced, or encouraged to divorce itself, from the tribal community, its sanctions and its past. For in such a case the passing generation does not hand on, and feels unable to hand on, the mythical, spiritual and moral heritage of the community, except in a very extenuated and exoteric form. Consequently, an attempt to "return to the mat" cannot be successful. It is made, however—even by groups of mixed castes; indeed, it is more likely to be made by them than by small tribal remnants hanging around small settlers and outback townships, fatalistically waiting for the end, meditating in their own language and quietly conning the chants of old.

Amongst larger and persistent groups, including half and even lighter castes, which have been subjected to the forms of European culture without receiving its content, the attempted return is sometimes very definite—even if not obvious to the casual observer. This is not merely a matter of the continuing influence of native culture, but a conscious retaking, re-establishing and re-using of those elements in the tribal past which are not lost and which can serve to build up cohesion, to provide comfort, to express difference and even defiance, and restore prestige in what is obviously an outcast, depressed and underprivileged condition.

At the back of this is a resentment deeper than any which appears in the disillusionment or disappointment which is the lot of the middle-aged who in their youth were attracted to the white man's way of life, believing they would really share in it, and who later realized they had followed a mirage. For the most part, this was self-induced. But the case is different when official policy and promise are felt to have no content or to be inordinately slow, or to be the focus of strong and noisy prejudice on the part of the non-natives.

I first detected this in embryo among the Aborigines of the north coast of New South Wales in 1936, where resentment was strong because of a feeling and conviction of injustice, that the government's promises had not been kept, and that they had been evicted from areas where they were making a living. Native religions, sanctions, and doctrines were then being acclaimed as the equal of the Christian, and initiation ceremonies were being practised, with some modifications in form and content. What has been most striking, however, has been the revival of the native language, particularly in the northern Clarence River and neighboring districts. Persons have been seen and heard who speak good English, window-shopping in Bandjelong language. In government settlements, where the group life is maintained, the latter is the normal means of communication. One motive here as in the south-west of the state, is that in their own language, they have something which the white man does not possess; in it they can converse secretly and in defiance of him.

Another indication of their condition is the popularity of evangelical religious missions, conducted mainly by visiting native preachers. Friends and relatives congregate, packing into the available houses and tents, attending the meetings en masse, singing loudly and vehemently pronouncing the hallelujah interjections. Of course, they are re-experiencing and reaffirming their own solidarity, and through the voice of the same preacher express their sense, often extravagantly, of the injustices they suffer. For a fortnight after, when the visitors have gone and the excitement abated, the local people still "hallelujah" their way about, and find it hard to settle to work.

The real content and some of the form of the tribal ceremonies of an earlier day have been recaptured. There is one interesting difference. Then, the ritually uninitiated could not approach. Now, the white man is for the most part on the outside, and wants to be; while to the acculturated Aborigines, these meetings are an expression of his solidarity over against white society into which he is not admitted.

The "return to the mat," with its blend of native and European custom, is itself a transition phase in Australia. Wisely acknowledged and accepted as a basis for policy, it can lead to assimilation into the general cultural and economic life, the Aborigines contributing something worth while out of their "treasures new and old." If, however, this "return" be ignored, it will in time lead to further resentment, and to opportunities for demagogues. Finally, unless the numbers of Aborigines of the darker castes

TABLE 1.   ABORIGINAL REACTION

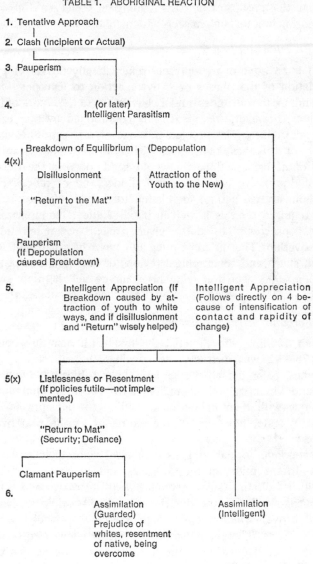

1. Tentative Approach

2. Clash (Incipient or Actual)

3. Pauperism

4.   (or later)
                Intelligent Parasitism

4(x)   Breakdown of Equilibrium   (Depopulation

          Disillusionment   Attraction of the
                                       Youth to the New)

          "Return to the Mat"

Pauperism
(If Depopulation
caused Breakdown)

5.   Intelligent Appreciation (If   Intelligent Appreciation
            Breakdown caused by at-   (Follows directly on 4 be-
            traction of youth to white   cause of intensification of
            ways, and if disillusionment   contact and rapidity of
            and "Return" wisely helped)   change)

5(x)   Listlessness or Resentment
            (If policies futile—not imple-
            mented)

            "Return to Mat"
            (Security; Defiance)

Clamant Pauperism

6.
                Assimilation   Assimilation
                (Guarded)   (Intelligent)
                Prejudice of
                whites, resentment
                of native, being
                overcome

increase very greatly, it will lose its impetus and leave dissatisfied and protesting groups of outcasts, loafing on society and gradually disappearing in it through miscegenation.

White Reaction and Policy

Table I is an attempt to represent schematically the development and relation of the phases of native reaction to European settlement and to the attitudes and behavior of settlers and officials. This latter, however, was also partly conditioned by the reaction of the Aborigines. The process was one of interaction. Some indication of this has been given. Therefore, to understand the phases of native reaction, we would need to trace the development of non-native behavior and attitudes and of official policy and administrative action, in relation to the Aborigines. The research required for this is well in hand. Table II summarizes the historical process. The dates given are approximate and the phases overlap. The different rates and types of settlement in the different states and geographical regions of Australia must always be remembered. The following brief survey will help to explain this table.

The Aborigines—British Subjects

Governor Phillip, who directed the first settlement in Australia from 1788–92 was instructed to conciliate the affections of the Aborigines, to enjoin all the settlers ("our subjects") "to live in amity and kindness with them," and to report in what manner intercourse with them might be turned to the advantage of the colony. In spite, however, of the efforts of Phillip and his immediate successors, the usurpation of native land, with its inevitable economic, social and psychological consequences, led to clashes. In the midst of these clashes, indeed because of them, the British Colonial Office crystallized its instructions of "amity and conciliation" into the doctrine that the Aborigines, living in a country over which the monarch exercised sovereignty, were British subjects. Therefore, war could not be deemed to exist between them and the white settlers, and acts of violence on either side should be dealt with according to the practice of British justice.

Further, associated with this doctrine was the development of opinion in England that the principles of humanity and justice demanded active measures to civilize and Christianize the Aborigines. This demand was met, especially during the 1830's and 1840's, missions and "civilizing institutions" being established from Moreton Bay to Perth.

From 1820 to the early 1840's, the decades in which free settlement, as distinct from penal colonization, became significant, was the period during which the authorities enunciated the policy of the Aborigines as British subjects to be civilized and Christianized, as well as to be treated justly. It was the period in which the influence of Buxton and Wilberforce was felt in native affairs, frequently to the annoyance of settlers in the colonies.

This policy failed. It did so, because it was very costly; because it required sound knowledge of native society and culture, of the process of culture-contact, and of native administration, and such knowledge was not available; and because the spread of settlement caused the Aborigines to become parasitical on the "invader," or else to become hostile. This was inevitable, however carefully officials and individuals made their first approaches to the natives, and even though they did not regard themselves as competing with, or conquering, them. In fact, the settlers were competing for the same living areas, and were destined to conquer.

"Pacification"

Consequently, this British subject and civilizing phase passed into one of recognized *clash* and of *pacification by force*. In early days of settlement, attempts were made to adjust the clashes by just means. By the 1840's, however, the method of suppressing the natives by force was demanded by the settlers and by much opinion. Moreover, it operated unofficially, at least in the marginal regions, though it was not unknown officially. Of course, justification was found: for example, it was held that the Aborigines were low in the scale of humanity, the very failure of the attempts to civilize and Christianize them being a "proof" of this. As local legislatures gained more power, with their representatives from the marginal regions, little more than formal recognition was given to the position of the Aborigines as British subjects; it was just hoped that the settlers in "protecting" their ventures, would be as restrained as possible. The Aborigines for their part had to adjust themselves to the unavoidable fact of white settlement, with all its implications, or else take the physical consequences of being overcome by force. Here lay the origin of the punitive expedition. Thus, they were reduced to a servile condition.

Such was the development in the decades 1840 to 1880. It continued, at least in the background, in the more distant frontier regions up to the early 1930's.

The Phase of Protection

In the meantime, a third phase appeared. From 1870 onward the comparatively new study of anthropology had turned its attention to the Australian Aborigines. L. H. Morgan, E. Tylor and James Frazer abroad, and L. Fison, A. W. Howitt and B. Spencer in Australia, showed that the Aborigines with their complex social and religious systems were not so "low" as had been asserted. They were human and of great interest—indeed, they were worthy of benevolent treatment.

Further, by this time, a considerable population was growing up in the main centers of each state, which had little, if any experience of the natives, and no recollection of the clash with them in the early days of settlement around such localities as Port Jackson, Port Phillip, Adelaide or the Swan River. But now stories and reports drifted in of "atrocities" in the frontier pastoral regions, in which the Aborigines seemed to suffer through little fault of their own. Urban opinion was disturbed. Moreover, anyone who travelled past the country towns saw too often the sorry plight of full-blood remnants and of mixed bloods.

But what could be done? Attempts to "civilize" them had failed. Dispossessed of their lands, bereft of their social and economic structure, and reduced by unaccustomed diseases, they presented a hopeless picture. All that seemed possible was to protect them against abuses and provide the little groups about the country with some rations, blankets and medicine.

Such was the Policy of Protection which was drawn up and put into practice in the various states—Victoria in 1860, when the Aboriginal remnant was under 2,000; South Australia, 1880—which instituted food depots; Western Australia in 1886; Queensland in 1897; New South Wales, 1909; and the Northern Territory in 1911. This policy was in part continuous with the earlier attempt to bring Christianity to the natives but now the outlook had become pessimistic and negative. The only sign of hope expressed throughout this long Protection period, from 1860 in Victoria to 1934 in the Northern Territory, was that if the Aborigines were allowed to roam on inviolable reserves, their extinction might be averted. But how keep them on these reserves and how keep the latter inviolate, if these proved to be of reasonable economic value?

So negative protection prevailed. Its theme was well expressed as long ago as 1843 by a writer in the *New South Wales Magazine:*

"I wish to see our means applied to rendering the current of events by which the grave is closing on our sable brethren, smooth and regular." "Smooth the Dying Pillow" became the comfortable rationalization, repeated *ad nauseam.* "A stone age people must go under when confronted by civilization." Let us do the right thing and make their passing smooth. Give them some food; cover their nakedness; write about their strange customs; administer some medicine; hold their hand (perhaps only in thought) and say a prayer as they pass on. "The Passing of the Aborigines" was a phrase which did much to fix in men's minds and in policies the idea that the Aborigines are doomed; and therefore to ensure that doom.

The Phase of Mutual Adaptation

During this long period of official protection, clashes and punitive expeditions were reported from time to time in the marginal or frontier regions. Such a condition of affairs, however, was not continuous, and as was pointed out, a phase of external adaptation of the natives and settlers to one another was quietly worked out. The former realized they would have to adjust themselves to the white man's presence and use of their country. The latter realized he was dependent for labor on the natives, and so had to give them enough to keep them around him. From this the custom grew up for the pastoralist to "keep," that is, to give some rations to, his native workers' dependents, or "tribe"—but no wages were paid. Unfortunately, this *modus vivendi* did not prevent the Aborigines from dying out; not enough future stock-boys

TABLE II WHITE REACTION AND POLICY

Phases of Native Reaction		Reaction of Settlers and Public	Period	Policy
1 Tentative Approach	i	Careful approach, not meant to be competitive nor conquering.	1788–1820	a i. "Amity and conciliation"
			1820–1840	a ii. Aborigines, British subjects; to be civilized and Christianized.
2 Clash Incipient, Actual	ii	Competition and clash unavoidable. Attitude of superiority. "Aborigines cannot be civilized." "Too primitive." Objection to influence of humanitarian societies. Punitive expeditions.	1840–1880 But continued later in central, northern and northwestern Australia.	b Legislation to control clash. But "pacification" by force is semiofficial method in marginal regions. Adjustment worked out locally; servile position of natives.
3 Pauperism	iii	In cities and main centers of population: Recognition of remnants. Some pity. "Dying Pillow" slogan. Some scientific interest.	1880–1936	c Protection policies (negative). But clash and pacification still possible and occur in marginal regions.
				d Protective policies

4(x) If 4 breaks down and passes to 5x or 5.	iv(x) Search for native workers still tribalized. Competition between "employers."	"1920's" up to 1936	d(x) Uncertainty. Some improvement in acts based on belated recognition of native rights. Policy of reserves and segregation —as protection and buffer.
5 Intelligent Appreciation (from 4 or 4x)	v Growing understanding and appreciation of Aborigines by public and governments. The rôle of anthropology.	1934–1939	e Positive policies studied and acts and. administration modified.
5(x) Listlessness and Disillusionment (plus resentment if mixed bloods)	v(x) Opposition of employers and most local groups to positive policy; to rights of natives. Prejudice against mixed bloods.	1940–	e(x) Positive policies slowly, hesitantly but surely imposed. (Citizenship, social services, franchise, education, employment conditions)
6 Assimilation Guarded and Intelligent	vi Condemnation of prejudice. Gradual appreciation of assimilation.	1946–	f Assimilation, citizenship.

Phases 3 to 5, iii to v and c to e are still present, but emphasis on v, vi, e(x) and e is very noticeable and increasing, as a foundation for 6 and f.

were born on the various pastoral stations, with the result that stations sometimes competed with each other for native employees, and accused each other of enticing their "blacks" away.

It was not until after World War I, when ideas inherent in the League of Nations Mandate principle began to influence thought, that any signs of dissatisfaction with the protection policies appeared in Australia. Some modifications were made in Aboriginal Acts, and the plan of providing reserves on which the natives would be segregated, and which would act as buffers in the contact process, was implemented. The land, it was held, was the Aborigines'; it was their life and only hope.

Further, at the very end of the 1920's, missionary and humanitarian bodies felt that the Commonwealth government should make an endeavor not only to prevent abuses in the north, but also to save the Aborigines. The attention, however, of these groups was still concentrated very largely on reports of injustice and ill-treatment, and too much energy was expended in protests. It was pointed out to them that this negative attitude would not prevent untoward incidents, and that the only hope lay in drawing up and working for a positive policy to be implemented by all governments. Such a policy would take for granted that the Aborigines had a future, but to be successful must be based on a knowledge of Aboriginal life and of the contact process, and must include education in the wide sense of the term. This positive policy was elaborated in addresses, articles and conferences and widely disseminated, and by the end of 1933 was widely accepted as a goal.

In this context, anthropology played an important part. The Department of Anthropology had been established mainly by the Commonwealth Government in the University of Sydney in 1926 for several reasons; among them was the view that anthropological research in New Guinea and anthropological training of administrative officers and missionaries were a necessary basis for sound administration. If this discipline was of practical value in New Guinea, why not in Australia also?

Anthropological field-workers returning from the northern and central parts of Australia, bore public witness to the qualities—often estimable—of the Aborigines. In some cases they drew attention to the unsatisfactory contact conditions which prevailed.

But what was more important, they provided first the humanitarian societies, and then the governments, with systematized knowledge of the essentials of native social and cultural life, and of the principles operating in the contact situation, of which both missions and administrations should be aware. Public interest, particularly in eastern Australia, was aroused in the Aborigines as a people and in their sad plight. The quickly increasing fund of knowledge, based on sound field-research, was used to inform this opinion, especially from 1934 to the outbreak of the war—a series of events—"incidents"—in 1934 in the Northern Territory and their repercussions making that year a turning point. From then onward the Commonwealth Government sought ways to improve Aboriginal affairs, and readily accepted the help of the Professor of Anthropology and has done so ever since.

Not only the Commonwealth government, but also state governments felt the impact of the rising and informed opinion that protection policies were not enough, and in any case were not always successful in protecting. Positive policies were needed; the progress of the Aborigines towards citizenship had to be the goal. So acts and administrative machinery and methods were modified in the 1934–39 period, and from 1940, especially in the post-war period, positive policies have been slowly, hesitantly, but surely developed and implemented. The same stage has not been reached everywhere in the continent; history and conditions vary; but appreciation of the Aborigines is increasing; prejudice is being tackled; and the opposition to the education of the Aborigines as citizens of Australia is being firmly faced and overcome.

The following, then, summarizes the approximate sequence of phases of "white" attitude and policy:

(1) From the beginning of settlement to the 1840's, but especially from 1820 to 1840—an abortive "civilizing," Christianizing, British-subject phase.

(2) "Pacification," determined locally, often by force—unofficial and semi-official; developed during 1840–80.

(3) Protection—negative in content—and ineffectual to stop clashes; from the 1880's to 1930, with Victoria (and its few remnants) twenty years earlier.

(4) Within this Protection period, a phase of "intelligent" mutual adaptation in the marginal regions, where protection had little mean-

ing, and where a local *modus vivendi* usually took the place of clash and "pacification."

(5) A period of uncertainty, which marked the change from protection as a goal to (6) the phase of positive policy, which is now being recognized as directed towards assimilation and full citizenship. The years 1934 to 1939 were preparatory; small steps were taken during the war; but from 1945 on, the policy has been slowly but definitely implemented over an ever wider field, both geographical and also social and economic, that is, in the spheres of employment, living conditions, social services (benefits), and franchise (Elkin 1944).

If the whole picture of this interaction be considered, and if the succession of phases be considered in relation to the general background, two problems emerge: first, the possible logical sequence and the aspect of determinism manifested in them; and second, the possibility that the sequence might be the same in the contact situation between European (and American) settlers and native people in other regions during the past one hundred and fifty years (Elkin 1949).

4 HISTORICAL PATTERNS OF
CULTURE CONTACT IN SOUTHERN ASIA

Konrad Bekker

SOUTHERN ASIA has a long history of contact with countries that were relatively advanced in one or the other aspect of their civilization. Certain elements of these other civilizations were assimilated, others were not, and today the cultural diversity of the area is as great as it has ever been. The processes of intercultural communication are traced here in their broadest outlines to bring out the main patterns of transmittal and of resistance which we can discern.

EASTERN AND WESTERN PATTERNS OF EXPANSION

Sir George Sansom calls attention to the contrast between the cultural influences exerted by the two great self-centered Oriental land powers China and India on the one hand, and the small expansive European sea powers such as the Greek city states on the other (Sansom 1950). It will help place our problem in perspective if we point out a few of the characteristic features of Greek colonization.

Within the city states themselves there was a close identification of political, economic, military and cultural leadership. When Greek civilization was carried east by Alexander and his successors, enough of this integration persisted to make Greek influence felt in government, military organization, arts and trade alike. Greek society was so organized that its various elements

Originally published in *Far Eastern Quarterly*, Volume XI, No. 1 (November 1951), 3–15. Reprinted with permission of the editor of the *Far Eastern Quarterly*.

cooperated and complemented one another abroad as at home. They were effective exponents of their own civilization but were not limited to functioning in exclusive relation to one another. The impact of this both integrated and open civilization was aided by a second significant aspect of Greek colonization: the area of contact between Greek and Near Eastern civilization was very broad. Geographically, Greek influence operated at many points throughout Alexander's empire. Socially, contact was immediately established at all levels of society from craftsman, common soldier and merchant to royalty. A third determinant of Greek cultural influence was the structure of the society on which it was exerted. In this respect, the response varied. But in general, assimilation of elements occurred at many points where they fitted into the indigenous pattern. Indian Buddhists began to make statues of the Buddha, and other artistic influences were transmitted to China. Arab-Indian trade was enlivened by Greek competition.

In contrast to the Greeks, most of the carriers of foreign civilizations who reached Southern Asia did not represent the whole of their society but only a fraction of it. In many instances they were marginal elements on the fringe of their own society. Their points of contact with the local population were limited. The diffusion of cultural influences occurred through tortuous channels and remained incomplete. The elements that were selectively absorbed were few compared with the vast range of cultural influences to which Southern Asia was exposed. In following some of these processes, I shall take my examples principally from Southeast Asia because this area was the meeting ground of all the major cultural currents in the Far East and on the whole received them all with relaxed hospitality.

TRADE AS A CARRIER OF CULTURAL INFLUENCE

In historical times, the most obvious channel of culture contact throughout Southeast Asia was trade, and we are inclined to think of the trader as a pioneer of an expanding civilization, followed in short order by the missionary and the colonial administrator. But this is only one possible pattern, suggested to us by the colonial expansion of Catholic countries since 1500. The Catholic traders and missionaries were sponsored by their home government, and the only instance of colonization somewhat along this line in Southeast Asia was in the Philippines. Chinese traders were not followed by missionaries and have never acted as pioneers of Chinese civilization. Arab merchants traded in the Far East for 1,000 years as a culturally inert element until they became carriers of Islam. Indian traders opened the path to Hindu kingdoms and to Buddhist missions, but the Hindus did not missionize and the Buddhists did not colonize. The political dependence of distant European colonies on the metropolis with all the economic and cultural effects of this dependence has no parallel among the outposts of Far Eastern civilizations.

If we look at the accounts of early trade relations in Southeast Asia, we find in fact that limitations of contact are usually worked out as carefully as the facilities for contact themselves.

In the Philippines, for instance, Chinese traders turned their merchandise over to native traders at established trading beaches. After disposing of the goods, the native traders returned and settled accounts with the Chinese. The area of social contact was extremely limited. Presumably it was further restricted by language difficulties, custom, mutual security precautions, and other measures designed to make possible a specific contact for a mutually recognized purpose. Centuries later, Nagasaki served as such a 'trading beach,' and similar restrictions were traditionally imposed on foreign merchants in China.

Even if geographical and physical limitations were less severe, social barriers were built around trade both by the local people and by the foreign merchants. In Malaya's heyday as a trading center, the royal courts shared in the profits of foreign trade through port duties, customs, piracy, and through participation in foreign commercial ventures. But they guarded the monopoly of this participation jealously against their subjects. Stringent sumptuary laws kept the Malay population in its place. The formation of commercial capital in private hands was effectively prevented, and when the Portuguese and Dutch took over control of the foreign trade, the one avenue was closed through which all contacts between Malay society and the outside world had been channeled (Winstedt 1950).

As for the foreign traders themselves, one of their principal concerns was the limitation of all foreign contacts that might interfere with their own purposes. During the period of Western colonization, the theory and practice of indirect government was worked out so as to establish a social barrier around a circumscribed area of foreign contact through trade. Even in Catholic countries traders and missionaries overseas were in constant conflict, with the missionaries favoring, and the traders opposed to cultural assimilation. For earlier periods and for traders of Far Eastern nationalities we have no explicit theory of this sort, but we have other evidence of the limitations of trade and traders as a channel for cultural influence. We shall return to this point shortly.

But what of the stimulus to cultural exchange through new commodities and techniques? The spread of copper, tin, iron and silk working techniques, to name only a few, must have been linked closely to trade. But even here, social as well as technical assimilation of new skills was necessary. Both usually required the migration of a group of craftsmen and their integration in an alien society. Tin and gold mining in Malaya, which are very ancient arts, were apparently carried on during the bronze age by a group of Mon-speaking specialists from north of the peninsula (Winstedt 1950). We don't know what sort of relationship existed between them and the native Sakais. It was almost certainly not that of teacher and pupil. We ourselves have only recently come to think of the bearers of technological progress as benefactors of humanity. To the Sakai, the Mon tin miners may have been the possessors of a devilish and well guarded magic. To other Indonesians a few centuries later, foreign craftsmen must have appeared as servants following in the train of conquering princes, or as luxury slaves that changed hands as part of the spoils of battle. In each case, the social context as much as the technological environment of both carrier and recipient determined the nature of stimulus and response. If there was a particulary close link between trade and the transmission of cultural influences, it was perhaps due to the fact that early trade was in luxuries, and luxuries were the part of the material culture of Southeast Asia which was most flexible and responsive to outside influences.

If we turn now to a brief characteristic of the patterns of influence developed by the principal civilizations that affected

Southeast Asia, we take it for granted that opportunities for contact, and particularly trade relations, were always present.

THE HINDU KINGDOMS

We have only a few clues to the factors that made for the beginnings of Indian colonization during the first and second centuries A.D. Many of the earlier traders had been Buddhists, while the new kingdoms professed Hinduism and were under the control of Brahmans and Kshatriyas (Coedes 1944; Sastri 1949). The role of the high caste Hindus in Southeast Asia can be seen from the spectacular development of the new states. For one thing, administrative and military operations assumed vastly larger proportions. And second, the new states developed a source of wealth and power that had been untouched by the Indian traders: indigenous agriculture. There was an integration of tribal into state functions under a despotism tempered by the power of the priesthood. To this, the Indian visitors contributed experience in the administration of centralized tax systems and large-scale irrigation works, the breaking down of local autonomy above the village level, and the religious glorification of absolute government. The cross-cultural link in this process was from the ruling caste of India to the tribal leadership of Southeast Asia, and the principal transfer was not in foreign relations, but in internal organization. Trade continued of course as a source of wealth, but the support of vast courts, armies and capital cities, and the resources for the building of the Borobudur and Angkor Vat had to be drawn from the surrounding countryside.

The ruling castes of the Hindu kingdoms in Southeast Asia may have thought of themselves as Brahmans and Kshatriyas, but the local population never identified itself with the Vaisyas and Sudras of the Hindu system. Nevertheless, many elements of Hindu civilization penetrated to the population at large. Most of these were channeled through the principal instruments of social control by which the local aristocracy exercised its leadership. The punitive and deterrent sanctions of Hindu law were substituted for the generally milder provisions of the traditional law. Written records were substituted for oral traditions. Even where Hindu institutions were imposed from above upon a subject population, they required active participation from below through ceremonial and compliance.

In addition to compulsive participation there must have been a large field of contact with Indian civilization in which the local population could respond spontaneously and selectively, and where this occurred, Hindu civilization underwent a change in function. Hindu mythology and cosmology as expressed in royal temples and sculpture may not have had a truly religious significance for the Indonesian and Cambodian craftsmen who built the Borobudur and Angkor Vat, but they had a tremendous impact on their skill, their art and their literature. In this esthetic reinterpretation, Hindu tradition was compatible with Islam and Western control. Thus it was capable of surviving political changes that swept away Brahmans and Kshatriyas.

Perhaps the most significant of these changes in function is that which occurred in Indian script. The knowledge of Indian writing was first acquired as a means of access to Sanscrit texts and as the script of official documents. But it soon became adapted to the languages of Southeast Asia and was used to develop Southeast Asian versions of Hindu literature and to transmit Southeast Asian traditions. A modern parallel to this development can be found in the Philippines where the spread of literacy in English has led to the spread of literacy in the local languages and has reinforced their hold.

BUDDHIST MISSIONS

Buddhism was the first of the great Indian religions to reach Southeast Asia and may have been a decisive factor in breaking down self-imposed restrictions on Hindu contact with the outside world. But the many accounts of Buddhist penetration of foreign countries do not deal with the introduction of new systems of government. They deal with the history of Buddhist dogma and with the wide travels of Buddhist students. The systems of local government remain a foil for the study of the Buddhist classics. As soon as we have documented accounts of Buddhist monks as distinct from traders, they were teachers and scholars absorbed in nonpolitical pursuits.

The absence of explicit political ambition in Buddhist literature does not mean that Buddhist missions did not represent a social ethos that had a strong and differential impact on the social strata of Hinduized Southeast Asia. It rather expresses the Buddhist protest against the aristocratic organization of Hindu society. In implicit opposition to Hinduism, Buddhism made a broad appeal to the population at large. It rested on community participation. Its monks, drawn from the laity and often returning to it, subsisted on the charity of the poor. Even the Buddhist monarch, far from being singled out for veneration, shed his royal robes to enter the priesthood for part of his life. Where Hinduism was identified with privilege, Buddhism stressed equality and set up standards of individual merit and attainment. Under Buddhist influence, literacy in Southeast Asia reached standards rarely attained elsewhere before the development of modern democratic government in the West. It is tempting to compare the relationship between Buddhism and Hinduism with that of the monastic orders in Europe and the feudal hierarchy. If the comparison is valid, it may illustrate how as a social force, and as an instrument for the transmission of Indian civilization, Buddhism in Southeast Asia was complementary to Hinduism rather than opposed to it.

The substratum of Indian culture created at the popular level by Buddhist teaching was less affected in periods of war, governmental decay, and economic distress, than the Hindu court civilization. It may also have merged more thoroughly with indigenous traditions than did the court Hinduism. Buddhism with its recluse and unpolitical bias proved in the end the most penetrating and most lasting instrument of Indian cultural expansion.

CHINESE PATTERNS OF CULTURAL EXPANSION

Chinese and Indian cultural influences in Southeast Asia were exerted initially under strikingly similar conditions. Nevertheless, the permanent impact of Chinese civilization was comparatively negligible.

Chinese, like Indian, merchants had traded in Southeast Asia since long before the Christian era. Diplomatic missions by both metropolitan countries were established no later than the middle of the third century A.D. when the first Chinese ambassador in

Fou-nan met there the first Indian ambassador. By that time, Chinese as well as Indian traders were living in the major port cities. The Chinese immigrants who have made their homes in Southeast Asia since then greatly outnumber the Indians. In many respects the Chinese shared the advantages of the early Buddhist traders. They were free of race and caste prejudice and dealt and intermarried freely with the local people. They represented a civilization far advanced in comparison with the local civilizations. Their trade goods, silk, porcelain, and glazed pottery, were widely sought. Many features of their clothing and ornaments were imitated. In at least one respect, Chinese civilization had better apparent opportunities for penetration than Indian civilization: all of Southeast Asia was at one time or another under Chinese suzerainty, and most of the area acknowledged some sort of political bond with China for many centuries. If Chinese civilization failed to take hold in Southeast Asia, the reasons must be found beyond the points of contact in structural characteristics of Chinese society.

In feudal China, combinations of aristocratic, military and official elements such as the Hindu colonizers of Southeast Asia had not been uncommon, but by the end of the Han dynasty, which coincided with the beginnings of Hindu expansion in Southeast Asia, China's feudal structure had been thoroughly obliterated for 400 years. The bureaucracy was drawn from classes that had no military background. The eyes of Chinese officialdom were fixed on the center of a vast bureaucratic machine. To go abroad as a knight errant, marry into the family of a barbaric chieftain, conquer territory and set up a new dynasty must have seemed an adolescent dream to the civil servant of the later Han just as it would to most of us. (It nevertheless happened at least in one instance in Champa, and almost once more in the Philippines.)

The reverse side of the medal was that Chinese traders abroad could not carry Chinese political institutions with them regardless of how deeply they themselves were imbued with Chinese tradition. Their own position in China was an inferior one, even more so than that of the Vaisyas in India, and was deliberately kept so as a matter of high social policy. Many of them, moreover, came from a small coastal area around Amoy and Swatow that was geographically and linguistically isolated from the main centers of Chinese government. But in any case, the Chinese system of government could not be introduced piecemeal in a foreign environment. Because its controls were systematically centralized, its elements were not workable in isolation. The civil service system, the study of the Confucian classics, the systematic use in local functions of officials drawn from distant provinces, the careful checks on the power of the military bureaucracy, the concept of education as preparation for government service, all these characteristic elements in the Chinese system of government were of one piece. Even the Chinese character script fits into this closely integrated pattern.

Dr. Beyer has pointed out how there has developed "a more self-sufficient and independent type of existence among Chinese merchants and settlers in foreign lands . . . than was established by almost any other type of trader or immigrant" (Beyer 1948). This condition reflects both the intensive cultural integration of Chinese communities abroad with the homeland, and their inability to integrate their cultural heritage with their local environment. The characteristic pattern for these Chinese communities has been that they preserved their cultural identity only where they were compact and isolated and where contact with the home country was continuous and close. These conditions were not met for any length of time except in a few trading centers. In the vast majority of cases, the Chinese abroad lost their identity very rapidly. Where they were able to gain prestige and political influence in the local community, they did so in terms of local political institutions and as local citizens.

Since Chinese civilization could be transferred only as a whole, none of the channels of culture contact which we have so far described could carry it abroad. The instances where it spread successfully all involve central government coordination of a systematic effort at all social levels. This was true even in Japan where the Japanese Emperor rather than the numerous local Chinese used Chinese methods to weaken his feudal vassals. We might distinguish three forms of Chinese expansion: the assimilation of contiguous peasant societies, the imposition of Chinese civilization through conquest, and the systematic adoption of the Chinese technique of government in other countries. The first

form of expansion is illustrated by the spread of Chinese civilization throughout present-day China and continues to the present
day in Manchuria, Cochinchina and elsewhere. An outstanding
example is the gradual penetration of Indochina by the Vietna-
mese. This was accomplished by the establishment of new settlements through spontaneous migration, as penal colonies, or as
military colonies. In every case, a complete self-contained and
self-sufficient Chinese community was established. There was no
question of converting the local population. The Chinese (or Viet-
namese) who were the pioneers of this type of expansion were
peasants, and what they carried with them by way of cultural
tradition was implicit in their way of life and community organization. The local people were pushed back, but over a period of
time they became assimilated. This type of community depended
for the administrative, literary, and otherwise explicit aspects of
Chinese civilization on a parallel expansion of the governmental
machinery. That is probably the reason why it occurred only along
the borders of Chinese cultural territory. Isolated Chinese peasant
communities, say in Malaya, were unable to generate out of their
own resources a political organization reflecting their cultural
heritage. Even though they preserved for some time their personal discipline, family cohesion, and economic efficiency, politically they remained fragments out of context.

The other two forms of Chinese expansion, imposition through
conquest, and deliberate imitation by the indigenous government,
were not characteristic of South and Southeast Asia except as
secondary elements in the Chinese penetration of Vietnam. The
one brief period of Chinese naval and military ventures in the
Southern Seas under the Ming dynasty began and ended during
the first half of the 15th century and left no permanent mark. And
none of the many embassies from Southeast Asia to the Chinese
court led to deliberate experiments in Chinese practices of government such as were made in Japan and in Korea.

ISLAMIC PATTERNS OF CULTURAL EXPANSION

In India, Islam imposed itself on new territory first by plundering
raids, then by conquest. Its active protagonists in the initial stages
of advance were military leaders who were often illiterate in

Islamic traditions. These leaders had to be in control of a feudal military machine that collected booty from conquered territory and tribute from subject peoples. Its economic support rested on the grant of land holdings to the soldiers and threatened to weaken whenever these holdings became the outright inheritable property of the holder. In the top echelons, the fight for control of the military machine was bitter and ruthless and had little to do with religious sanctions. After the 9th century, the link with the Caliphate was purely nominal and the Moslem conquests in the East remained outside the struggle for hegemony among the Moslem countries in the Mediterranean basin.

The Moslem conquerors set up a civil administration that required little change in the practices of the Hindu rulers, but differed radically in the ease with which members of the conquered people could join the new ruling group. At a time when the Hindu rulers of India made deliberate efforts to mend and strengthen the caste system, the Moslem rulers in India were not only themselves of foreign and often humble descent, but they drew into their service foreigners from all over the Arab world as well as converted Indians without regard to caste. There was a gradual progression from the superficial indoctrination of new converts under political, military and economic pressure to the establishment of orthodox Islam. This transition was accompanied by increasing opportunities for participation in the responsibilities and rewards of government. Thus all Moslem regimes soon were in large measure indigenous in the conquered territory. They continued to discriminate against non-believers, but they fully identified themselves with the local Moslem population. Moslem missionaries came to soften the impact of foreign domination, to demand spiritual allegiance to a distant center of learning rather than to a foreign power, and to open paths by which the humble citizen could gain access to the written sources and to the holy places of Islam. Like the Buddhist missions, the Moslem teachers provided not a one-way channel for cultural influence, but opportunities for contact that were responsive to social conditions in the recipient country as well. It was this grass-roots educational movement that secured the lasting impact of Islam.

In Southeast Asia there was a striking parallel between the advance of Islam and that of the early Hindu kingdoms. Again we had a penetration on two distinct social levels, that of royalty and that of the popular religious-educational center. Again it was the latter that maintained its hold when political control of the area was lost. Again this expansion was even less a matter of war, conquest, and forcible conversion in Southeast Asia than it had been in India. And since it drew, somewhat like the Buddhist missions, on the support of the broadest indigenous group that could respond to the appeals of literacy and participation in government, it outweighed the efforts of the few European missionaries a hundredfold.

WESTERN PATTERNS OF CULTURAL EXPANSION

Portuguese, and later Spanish, Dutch and English penetration of Southeast Asia, excluding the Philippines, stimulated the voluntary adoption of Islam by native rulers as a counterweight against Christianity. This not only facilitated the spread of Islam among the local population, but it softened Islamic standards of orthodoxy which were already affected by the influence of Indian mysticism on the early Moslem missionaries in the Far East. Both the political and the dogmatic connotations of Islam thus had an immediate indigenous appeal in Southeast Asia. Christian missionaries, in contrast, were conspicuously allied with alien powers that constituted a political threat and that would not compromise with local traditions. In both its temporal and its spiritual aspects, European colonization remained under the control of the metropolitan countries. Where Jesuit missionaries attempted to recast Christianity in local molds, as they did in both India and China, they were soon taken to task by the Church. The elements of Western civilization that were carried to the East remained defined in terms of their European cultural context.

It was one expression of this rule that Europeans, contrary to Hindus, Chinese, and Moslems, did not settle in the Far East. They did not take their families, much less did they attempt to introduce the political institutions of their home countries. The Protestant nations that replaced the Portuguese and Spaniards in most of Southeast Asia restricted even the field of the missions that might have acted as carriers of Western civilization. As a general description of Western cultural influence in Southeast

Asia it can be said that it was almost entirely negative during the first three hundred years of contact. It did not carry European culture or institutions to Southeast Asia, and it froze Southeast Asia's acquaintance with foreign civilizations at the level of the 16th century. Furnivall has given a classic analysis of the various internal changes that accompanied the adaptation of Indonesia and Burma to the changing policies of the colonial powers (Furnivall 1948). The process was not limited to colonial areas. It affected Thailand, Burma and Indochina even before the latter two came under the control of European powers.

More than Hindus, Buddhists and Moslems, the European representatives were unrepresentative of their own society as a whole. That does not mean that they were not typical or important in their particular function. In its domestic environment, a Dutch or British joint stock company could be considered an expression of cooperative individual initiative under an impersonal system of law. It represented the equalitarianism of the rising middle class and the competitive and progressive aspects of an expanding Europe. But this is describing the highly specialized service the company performed in Dutch or British society. Removed from the control of courts of law, political interests, civic responsibilities, and family ties, and placed in positions of absolute power, European traders in the Far East represented not the spectrum of modern Western civilization, but only one of its colors. They were adventurers of a rough and ready kind, and represented the England of Shakespeare as John Jacob Astor's men represented the United States of Emerson. The very degree of individual specialization encouraged in the West meant that the element gravitating toward sea trade knew and cared little about European cultural traditions if it was not deliberately turning its back on them. Even in their own field, competition and risk bearing did not appeal to these men for their own sake, but were a function of their domestic environment. In the Far East, the European traders were largely successful in holding both to a minimum. As an incidental result, the establishment of the European trade monopolies brought about the permanent elimination of the indigenous high seas trade of Southeast Asia and temporarily eliminated Arab, Indian, Chinese and competing European shipping from certain areas. This was the beginning of a continuing process of cultural isolation of the European colonies from one another. Until the turn of the 20th century, when Dutch ethical policy brought a new emphasis on social welfare, it is difficult to find a positive Western cultural impact in Southeast Asia. Certainly, what there was did not compare in magnitude or indigenous sponsorship with the impact of Indian and Moslem culture.

The Philippines presents a sharp contrast to the pattern just described, but it illustrates further how elements of European civilization were transmitted selectively to the East through channels capable of carrying only part of a European civilization. In the Philippines the conflict between traders and missionaries was resolved in favor of the missionaries in a more extreme application of Spanish colonial policies evolved in Latin America. From 1571 until 1811 only one ship a year, the Manila Galleon, was permitted to make one round trip from Mexico to Manila and back. All other trade with Europe or America was prohibited, and although trade with China continued, the Chinese community in the Philippines was decimated by periodic persecutions. Spanish grantees and their retinue obtained large landholdings as they did in other Spanish colonies. But by 1600, Manila was an archdiocese, the number of priests was more than 400, and in 1601 the church established the first college in Manila. Filipinos had opportunities to visit Spain, and many of them entered the Catholic hierarchy. From 1810 to 1835 the Philippines was represented in the Spanish Cortes. Carried by religious and educational channels, Spanish civilization took a hold comparable to Indian and Moslem civilization elsewhere in Southern Asia. The Filipinos adopted not only Catholicism, but European dress, music, dance and script. Again, these influences persisted when the political bonds with the metropolitan country were broken.

CONCLUSION

Our discussion stops at the point where Western powers began to show concern about cultural contact with their colonies, and where Western civilization began to be mediated through indigenous elements: civil servants, seamen, students, military, and many others at different social levels. If there had been time for these new trends to bear fruit, many of the earlier omissions might have been made up for, just as the contact of indigenous Buddhists, Hindus and Moslems with the foreign centers of their civilization served to correct the distortions of earlier contacts. In India and Pakistan much progress along that line was made, but in Southeast Asia the time was very short.

On the whole, the difficulties in the way of effective culture contact may have increased with the increasing differentiation and stratification of the former colonial societies. Certainly, the general characteristics of a Western society are no more likely to describe its cultural impact abroad today than they were in the past. Beyond that, few of the tentative generalizations that might occur to us stand up when confronted with historical facts. No two patterns of culture contact we have mentioned were alike. Some of the most effective transmission of Far Eastern civilizations occurred not through the elite, at least not through the existing political elite, but at the popular level. In most instances there was not one channel of culture contact, but there were several complementary ones, and their impact was extremely complex. Foreign contacts remained inert unless they were made at focal points of social development. Apparently there is no instance of lasting cultural influence in Southeast Asia that was not associated with an intensive and broad educational program, but on the other hand, cultural diffusion was not always from a higher to a lower level of civilization. Government was an effective agent of cultural influence in some instances, but played no role in others. The initiative for culture transmission lay as often with the receiving as with the giving country.

Perhaps we should not expect uniform patterns in the transmission of cultural influences. As we look back on the history of South Asian countries, the foreign elements which they absorbed stand out conspicuously while the detail of their everyday lives is lost. But this is a distorted perspective. At any given time, foreign contacts occupied little more than a marginal place in a vast field of continuing local activities with dynamics of their own. In this field, culture contact did not introduce new social forces as much as it released and shaped existing ones. These pathways of cultural interaction lead deeper into the indigenous social matrix than we can follow them here.

The diversity we found in the patterns of culture contact in Southern Asia can be restated in terms of the criteria set forth at the beginning of this paper. There were vast differences in the structure of the foreign cultures to which the area was exposed, ranging from the closely integrated Western cultures represented fractionally by trading companies and missionaries. There were equally large differences in the area of social contact, ranging from the aristocratic level of Hindu colonization to the broad scope of Muslim cultural penetration. Finally, there was a great deal of variation in the critical areas of response although Southern Asia was generally open to foreign influences. Given the various factors that controlled the transmission of cultural influences first in the country of origin, then on the way, and again in the receiving countries of Southern Asia, the cultural diversity of the area becomes less astonishing than the common elements that have been preserved.

5 RUSSIAN EXPANSION
IN THE FAR EAST

A. Lobanov-Rostovsky

SCRATCH A Russian and you will find a Tartar" was the saying coined by Polish *émigrés* in Paris after the Polish Revolution in 1831 to win sympathy for their cause against the Russians. Earlier, in 1799, Nougaret, the French historian, wrote of "a catastrophe which seems to be preparing before our eyes and which may make the second Rome fall into the power of the Tartars who are now called Russians" (Vasiliev 1952). In both cases, the propaganda implication of horror and danger by associating the Russians with the ruthless Asiatic conquerors was obvious and could be explained in the first case by the failure of the Polish insurrection, in the second by the Russian army's conquering Italy under Suvorov and menacing France. But the question of whether Russia belongs to East or West, whether she may be regarded as the vanguard of Asia menacing European civilization or as the bulwark of Europe against Asia, was hotly debated in Russia itself at the time.

To answer this question, one must turn to the impartial verdict of geography and the role of the frontier in Russian history. The pertinent fact is that the history of Russia is a history of the colonization of the vast expanse stretching from the Baltic to the Pacific by a Caucasian people, the Slavs, whose original home was in east-central Europe, approximately eastern Germany, Poland, and western Russia. Hence this colonization moved west-east, towards Asia, and not from Asia. Furthermore, by obtain-

Originally published in *The Frontier in Perspective*, edited by Walker D. Wyman and Clifton B. Kroeber, Madison, University of Wisconsin Press, 1957, pp. 79–94. Reprinted with permission of the University of Wisconsin Press.

ing their religion, their written script, and the basis of their culture from Byzantium, these Slavs had definitely associated themselves with the cultural stream of Christian Greco-Roman civilization and not with the great competing Asiatic civilizations such as the Persian, Arabic, or even Chinese.

But nature abhors a vacuum and the Great Russian or Eurasian plain was just such a vacuum. Hemmed in to the south and to the east by great Asiatic empires, this vast expanse sucked into it the restless barbarian tribes from the fringe areas, and they spread as a thin layer over it and became dissolved in it. Thus came the Sarmatians, Scythians, and other Indo-European or Iranian tribes and the subsequent waves of Turco-Mongol peoples ranging from the Huns, the Avars, the Khazars, the Bulgars, and the Magyars to the Pechenegs and Cumans—roughly fifteen hundred years of continuous invasions from Asia, limited, however, to the broad belt of the steppes north of the Black Sea. Further to the north stretched the limitless forest, across which veins were cut by slow, meandering rivers. There the Slavs settled amidst peaceful Finnish folk; here along its western fringe passed the Goths on their trek south from Sweden, down the rivers. Had there not been the lure of trade down these same rivers to the great markets of Byzantium and of the Arabic East as far as Bagdad, it is possible that the Asiatic invaders, nomads preferring the wide expanse of the steppe, would never have clashed with the Russians.

But the Russians trespassed upon the nomad by coming out into the steppe. Kiev, the capital of the first Russian state, was boldly set in the plain outside of the forest zone, and the war was on—a war of attrition which lasted four centuries, roughly from the ninth to the thirteenth century, a war between Europe and Asia fought not west-east, but north-south. In this war, the Russian state, with a more intricate political organization and a highly promising and rapidly rising Christian civilization, had the advantage over the nomadic tribes, but it was drained of its strength by this everlasting task of keeping the nomad at bay. Then in the thirteenth century, the pattern reversed itself. Kiev and the whole of the forest zone of Russia fell prey to the Chinese-trained Mongol armies led by a conqueror of genius, who had overnight created the greatest empire the world was to see.

For the next two and a half centuries, the Russian principalities were to be integrated into the vast Mongol dominion stretching from Korea to Bagdad, and Western Europe forgot Russia since Russia had become a part of Great Tartary. But the Mongols themselves looked upon Russia as a European colony that could be ruled by remote control from their capital, Sarai, on the lower reaches of the Volga. Hence Russia's national consciousness was not lost, and it rallied around a new center—Moscow. Moscow reunited Russia under the Tartars and then threw off the Mongol yoke in 1480.

The weakened Mongol state could not oppose this resurgence of Russia. The Mongols had ruled a Russia divided into many principalities, but now the roles were reversed. Moscow had reunited these states into one powerful state, while the Mongol Khanate was breaking up into three weak states. These could not any longer oppose the Russian drive into Asia.

It is well to stop here and draw a parallel between the westward movement in America and the eastward movement of the Russians, both aimed at the same goal, i.e., the Pacific, but in reverse directions, the great difference being the time lag, the Russian movement being infinitely slower. It took the Russians some six centuries to reach the Ural mountains and then a century more to reach the Pacific. The reason for this was the onrush of counterinvasions from Asia, which like breakers submerged the Russians or blocked their advance, while in the westward drive in America the greatest resistance came from local Indian tribes.

Thus the pivotal point in Russian history was attained when the course of the Volga was reached and incorporated into Russia by the middle of the sixteenth century. Indeed, in 1552 and 1556, Ivan the Terrible conquered the two fragments of the Mongol Empire which had survived to the east of Moscow, the Khanates of Kazan and Astrakhan, both situated on the Volga. This ended the centuries-old duel for the possession of the Eurasian plain between Russia and Asia, and fate decreed that henceforth the Russians were to be its masters. The logic of history and geography seemed also to prove that states of various races could not cohabit peacefully on this plain and that the domination of the whole plain from one center, i.e., Moscow, was to become unavoidable through the very nature of the plain.

The Volga thus enters Russian history much as the Mississippi with the Louisiana Purchase enters United States history. It becomes the economic backbone of Russia, the river of legend, song, and tradition, and more important, the jumping-off-place for the great drive to the Pacific Ocean, much like the Mississippi three centuries later, for the westward drive. Thus, the axis of Russian colonization and advance, after having been northeast in the preceding centuries, changes to due east. The drive east beyond the Volga opened immediately, and thirty years after the fall of Kazan, in 1581, a band of Cossacks under Yermak crosses the Ural mountains and conquers Western Siberia up to the Irtish River. Once the drive had started, it could not be stopped, and by the 1640's both the Pacific Ocean and the Amur River, the boundary with China, had been reached. In 1697, Kamchatka was annexed, and throughout the second half of the eighteenth century Russian pioneers crossed the Bering Straits and settled in Alaska.

The technique of this expansion originally resembled the conquest of the overseas empire by Spain but later came to resemble more and more the American westward drive. At first, bands of adventurers led by conquistadors were driven into the wilderness by the urge for finding wealth in the nature of silver and furs. That these adventurers were Cossacks and that their leaders were known as *Atamans,* be they a Yermak, a Vlassiev, or an Atlassov, did not change the picture. They fought their way with firearms against bows and arrows. Yermak with eight hundred men broke the resistance of some thirty thousand men defending the capital of Khan Kuchum, Sibir. Vlassiev with one hundred and thirty men conducted a fierce war against many thousand Buriats in the region of Lake Baikal, while Atlassov all but exterminated the peaceful Kamchadals. On occasion, these bands were accompanied by priests who baptized the natives but were unable or unwilling to restrain the Cossacks from committing terrible atrocities. The territory once conquered, the Cossacks would erect a fort (an *Ostrog*), and its garrison, perhaps fifty men, would patrol hundreds of miles of adjacent territory. Behind these screens the peasant-colonist would settle, government administration would be established, a *Voevoda* or governor responsible to the Siberian Department in Moscow would be appointed. Little by little, cities grew out of the forts and Siberia became more and more the extension of Russia proper, with the natives either dying out or assuming the position of the American Indians.

Two striking idiosyncrasies of Russian colonization, however, must be mentioned. The first was the systematic use made by the government of the Cossacks from about the middle of the eighteenth century for the purpose of colonization. Prior to that, the Cossacks were bands of adventurers acting pretty much on their own. Now they were formed into "hosts" or irregular cavalry and were used for the purpose of advance colonization and as a protective screen. Thus a chain of Cossack hosts came into existence and were planted as "hedges" along the advancing frontier: first came the Ural (or Yaik) Cossack host, then the Seven River host, then the Transbaikal host, then finally the Amur and Maritime hosts at the turn of the twentieth century along the borders of Manchuria and Korea. The second feature to be noticed is that the Russian is not racially minded and shows no discrimination toward the natives. Though the Siberian colonist would often cruelly exploit them and take advantage of their ignorance and credulity, he treated them as equals and made no attempts to change their way of life or religion. If the natives became Christian and orthodox, the Russian would consider them members of his own family and would intermarry freely with them. If there was any distinction, it would be more along religious than racial lines.

The question arises at this point whether it is possible to apply the Turner theory to the Siberian frontier and what similarities or dissimilarities can be found in comparing the westward movement in America and the eastward movement in Russia. If we compare the Cossacks with the pioneers—which can be done without straining the point if we limit ourselves to the earlier days before the Cossacks were organized into a semiregular military force, we will find that the starting point and the goal of both movements are the same. Furthermore, the Cossack turns from warrior and conqueror to trader, or, as the expansion proceeds, the trader joins him. The demand for the furs, silver, and other wealth of Siberia led to the supplying of the native with arms, liquor, and primitive manufactures, thus creating what Turner calls the "trading frontier." In both western America and in Siberia the resistance was sporadic. After the opposition of Mah- metkul's forces was broken by Yermak, the Khirgiz tried to block the southern expansion and the Buriats fought desperately to pre- serve their independence in the region of Lake Baikal. After their resistance was broken, it was not till the Russians reached the Amur River that they again met determined warlike foes. These were the Daurians, bolstered up by Chinese regulars. Thus the fighting did not have the unifying and consolidating effect of bring- ing the whites together which the Indian wars did in the United States. Moreover, by the turn of the eighteenth century all fight- ing had ceased in Siberia, which was henceforth strongly governed by a centralized administration directed from the capital. Peaceful colonization replaced what might be termed the "heroic age" of conquest. The nineteenth century did see an organized military drive, but only in Central Asia.

Turner describes the colonization of the frontier as proceeding in three waves. Quoting Peck's *Guide to the West,* published in 1837, he mentions first the pioneers who occupy and start ex- ploiting the land; then the emigrants who purchase the land and open it up by building roads, bridges, etc.; and finally, capital enterprise which builds the cities and industries. The first and third waves are found in Siberia in a fairly clear-cut fashion; the second wave differs considerably owing to special conditions in Russia.

> Cossacks went in their boats along northern rivers, sent bands out in every direction, brought the natives under subjection, built ostrogs. After them came the fur traders. Hunters scattered in the forests far across the subjugated territory and built themselves huts and small blockhouses. They formed *artels*—co-operatives—for hunting and fish- ing, they prospected ores . . . (Semyonov 1944).

and again

> the Cossacks saw that men can live in this country. There was plenty of freedom there, an abundant nature, and a scarcity of authorities. They determined to settle there (Semyonov 1944).

So much for the first phase. The second wave was composed of prisoners and peasant colonists evading the hardships of serfdom in Russia proper. Both have to be examined in more detail, since Siberia owes its development to these two elements.

The idea of using Siberia as a penal settlement seems to have appeared in Moscow shortly after the conquest. The great jail in Nerchinsk in eastern Siberia was erected in the 1730's, while in the same period many leading statesmen of the day who had fallen out of favor were sent in exile to Beriozov, a city far north in western Siberia. These included such men as Princes Menshi-kov and Dolgoruky, General Münnich, and others. Thus from the outset, a distinction was made between *katorga* (hard labor) and *ssylka* (exile). When in the 1750's Empress Elizabeth abolished the death penalty for ordinary nonpolitical crimes, Siberia received a further influx of life termers. This forced colonization brought into Siberia two elements—on one side the hardened criminal, on the other the most enlightened, cultured, and advanced strata of society. To the latter belonged the so-called Decembrists (the later Nihilists), the cream of Russian aristocracy, involved in the revolutionary outbreak of 1825. A great many of these, after having served their terms, remained permanently in Siberia and contributed powerfully to the development of the country. In the main, however, the criminal element far outnumbered the political exiles. It has been calculated that during the nineteenth century somewhere between eight hundred thousand and a million prisoners were sent to Siberia, of which the political cases represented some 10 to 15 per cent. As the revolutionary movement grew in virulence after 1860, the number of political cases increased. But on the other hand, toward the end of the century most of the *katorga* cases were transferred from eastern Siberia to the island of Sakhalin.

The free peasant colonization of Siberia, which by the very nature of the case caused that land to become a haven for runaway serfs, was strenuously fought by the government. After the liberation of the serfs in 1861, this colonization was still frowned upon by the government and remained limited, though schemes of organized settlement were very occasionally put into effect without too much success. A natural hindrance was the problem of transportation. In the 1880's, for instance, an attempt was made to bring settlers to coastal regions near Vladivostok by the sea route around Asia.

The situation changed completely after the building of the Trans-Siberian Railway and the Russo-Japanese war. Under the energetic sponsorship of Stolypin, the last great statesman of the Tsarist regime, a special department of internal immigration was created which earmarked the land available for colonization in Siberia, provided free transportation, monetary aid, and agricultural implements for volunteer settlers. This policy resulted in the settling of some four million peasants in western Siberia in the great agricultural belt along the Trans-Siberian Railway. Under the Soviet regime, as already noticed, the colonization of Siberia has become one of the main concerns of the government and all methods have been used from "slave labor" camps to rendering free settlement more enticing by grant of special privileges, coupled with widespread industrial development of the area.

The coming to life of Siberia in the nineteenth century produced the appearance of the third type mentioned by Turner, namely, the capitalist and industrial promoter. A special type of the Siberian millionaire came into existence. Like his American counterpart of the sixties and seventies, he was a rugged individualist, adventurous, energetic, often ruthless. He loved ostentation and was proud to show off his acquired wealth. There is a story about such a millionaire hiring all the droshkies (horse-drawn taxis) in one of the larger cities of Siberia and forming a procession of empty droshkies through the city streets, led by himself in the first droshky, to impress the citizens with his power and wealth. However, again like his American counterpart, he generously donated his money for philanthropic or civic purposes, and many Siberian cities boasted fine school and hospital buildings bearing the name of the donor. It is curious to note that this type is to be found as far back as the seventeenth century. Indeed, Khabarov, the great explorer of the Amur region in the 1650's, was a peasant from Veliki-Ustug in Russia, who had made a fortune in Siberia in salt and real estate and who equipped his expedition down the Amur at his own cost.

The importance of Siberia as a colony to Russia may be seen by the growth of the population. By 1662, the population of

Siberia was around seventy thousand. Fifty years later it was two hundred and fifty thousand, and a post road with regular mail service had reached Yakutsk on the Lena. In 1822, the growth of Siberia necessitated an administrative split into two governor-generalships, one for western Siberia and one for eastern Siberia. By 1914, the population had risen to nine million, and at present it is around forty million.

This drift of the population, though far from filling the empty spaces of eastern Siberia, produced the inevitable result of over-flowing into neighboring areas beyond its borders. It must be remembered that Siberia is encompassed on the north by the Arctic Ocean and on the east by the Pacific. The only overflow possible was east into Alaska and only a handful of the hardened pioneers went across the Bering Straits. The greater mass drifted across the land frontier to the south and thus the first contact with China was established. It started as early as the beginning of the sixteenth century, when the early conquerors of western Siberia made their way up the Irtish and penetrated into Dzungaria (west of Mongolia), the home of nomads owing a loose allegiance to the emperors of China. It was through this contact that tea was received in Russia and became the national drink. Also, since this territory was inhabited by the Kara Kitans, Kitai remained the name given to China in the Russian language. Half a century later, the Russians sailed down the Amur River and began to infiltrate into Manchuria, along its tributaries. This led to a thirty-year undeclared war with emperors of the newly established Manchu dynasty, who were particularly sensitive to this Russian colonization of their homeland. The war was concluded by the treaty of Nerchinsk in 1689, which forced the Russians to evacuate not only Manchuria but the valley of the Amur River as well. But the Russians gained the inestimable advantage of the right to trade freely in China a century and a half before the other powers of Europe. It is interesting to note that this is the first of the three times in history when the Russians made an attempt to settle in Manchuria; the second time was in the 1890's and the third during the final months of World War II. They were never able to stay. The logic of history and geography seems to have drawn a line to their colonization, saying thus far and no farther—and this line is the Amur River.

The Treaty of Nerchinsk supplemented by a treaty in 1727 established peaceful and friendly relations between Russia and China for well-nigh two centuries. Russian diplomacy was occupied elsewhere, and the Far East faded out of the picture. Perhaps we may call this period, which lasts up to the middle of the nineteenth century, a time of sporadic accidental exploration and expansion. Certainly the movement of Cossacks into Manchuria, and of pioneers into Alaska was spontaneous, while the Russian Academy of Sciences in coöperation with the navy had initiated in the eighteenth century a vast scheme of exploration and geodetic survey of the coasts of Siberia, and owing to this Russian vessels found themselves in Japanese waters. The second and much more important phase opens in the 1850's.

This chapter starts as a result of the double impact of England and the United States on the Far East. The treaty of Nanking signed by the Chinese after the loss of the Opium War in 1842 had opened the China Coast to British trade and had resulted in the cession of Hongkong to Britain. Eleven years later, Perry carried out his successful venture to open Japan. These two events changed the balance of power in the Far East and deeply affected Russia's interests, particularly since the Anglo-Russian rivalry in western and central Asia was reaching a culminating point. Worried that the coast of Siberia on the Pacific was completely undefended and that the British, having established themselves in the treaty ports along the coast of China, had merely to push a little northwards to reach the mouth of the Amur, Czar Nicholas I appointed an energetic young governor-general, Muraviev, to eastern Siberia with the task of making Russia's coastline secure.

Muraviev lost no time. He founded a naval base at Petropavlovsk, Kamchatka, and ordered a naval explorer, Captain Nevelskoy, to sail around the Sea of Okhotsk to find a better base. The latter, sailing up the River Amur in a sloop, annexed the territory north of the river (which nominally belonged to China) and on August 6, 1850, established a base a few miles upstream. The resulting diplomatic conflict with China ended with the signing of treaties in 1858 and 1860 in which China ceded not only the territory north of the Amur but also the coast of the Pacific from the mouth of the Amur to the Korean border. Here in a fine bay was founded the city of Vladivostok, which became the definitive Russian naval base on the Pacific and later the terminal of the Trans-Siberian Railway. The border between China and Russia drawn in 1860 has remained the same to the present day. This completed the expansion of Russia on the mainland of Asia. But opposite the newly acquired coast stretched the island of Sakhalin, populated by Ainus. Japan claimed the island as an extension of the Japanese Archipelago, north of Hokkaido. The energetic Nevelskoy sent his lieutenant Boshniak on dog sleigh across the frozen straits of Tartary and the Russians took possession of Sakhalin as well in 1852.

The very next year and exactly at the same time that Perry was in Japanese waters, a Russian squadron composed of three vessels under Admiral Putiatin sailed into Nagasaki Bay with the mission of obtaining for Russia what Admiral Perry was demanding for the United States, namely, the opening of Japan to Russian trade and navigation. Putiatin was instructed not to use force but to achieve his ends through patience and diplomacy. Though Putiatin lost his flagship, which was sunk in a tidal wave following an earthquake, he was able to achieve his goal by the signing of the treaty of Shimoda in February, 1855. There remained, however, friction with Japan over the seizure of Sakhalin. Still too weak to face Russia, Japan came to terms with Russia by accepting an exchange of Sakhalin for the Kurile Islands in 1873. Thus came to an end the second wave of Russian expansion, which, in contrast to the earlier unorganized, glacierlike advance, was carried out by diplomatic and naval means.

The third phase, which opens in the 1890's, introduces a new factor into the picture. As a result of the industrial revolution gaining momentum in Russia, we now enter the period of economic imperialism and the scramble for foreign markets. Not being able as yet to compete successfully with the more highly developed industrial nations, Russian industry profited by the geographical advantage of having an undeveloped area along the Siberian border, which was relatively remote from the ports of entry for western manufactured goods. Thus a belt of territory running from northern Persia through Sinkiang to Manchuria came within the economic orbit of Russia, and here all the earmarks of economic imperialism were displayed, from obtaining concessions

for the development of these areas to the establishment of banks
to carry out the required transactions. Thus Russian financiers
founded the Discount Bank of Persia to be followed with the
aid of French capital by the Russo-Chinese Bank and the Bank
of Mongolia. Railway building kept pace, so far on Russian
territory. In the 1880's, the Russians built the Transcaspian Railway from Krasnovodsk on the Caspian to the gates of Sinkiang.
This railway skirted the northern border of Persia, and a branch
line led to the border of Afghanistan. After the revolution, the
Transcaspian was extended through the Turk-Sib to link up with
the Trans-Siberian, encompassing western and northern Sinkiang.
The Trans-Siberian, built a decade later, reached the Pacific at
Vladivostok and encircled China from the north. Next came
the phase of building on foreign soil.

The spectacular defeat of China at the hands of Japan in 1895,
revealing the weakness of the decadent Manchu Empire, initiated
this phase. The Li-Lobanov treaty of 1896 gave Russia the right
to build across northern Manchuria a railway which was named
the Chinese Eastern Railway. A branch line cut southward from
Harbin to the Yellow Sea at Port Arthur. In the twentieth century, the Russians built a railway to Tabriz in Persia, and in our
own days a branch line of the Trans-Siberian was extended to
Ulan Bator, the capital of Mongolia, and now has been extended
across the Gobi to Peiping.

The next phase following the signing of the Li-Lobanov treaty
of 1896 resulted in the nearly complete absorption of Manchuria
by the seizure of the Liaotung Peninsula with two ice-free ports,
Port Arthur and Talienwan, the first of these converted by Russia
into a naval base and the second, renamed Dalny, into a commercial port. Strengthened by the Anglo-Japanese alliance of 1902,
Japan struck back and the Russo-Japanese war put an end to
what may be termed the period of runaway Russian imperialism.

Considering the gravity of the defeat inflicted upon Russia by
Japan, the destruction of Russian naval power at Tsushima, and
the revolution breaking out in Russia, the treaty of Portsmouth,
which ended the war, was most favorable to Russia. She retained
northern Manchuria and the Chinese Eastern Railway, ceding to
Japan half of Sakhalin, Port Arthur, and Dalny and approximately
half of the branch line leading from the main trunk of the Chinese

Eastern Railway to these ports. She also acknowledged Japan's right to a free hand in Korea. Russian diplomacy took a realistic view after this disastrous war and let bygones be bygones. By the agreement with Japan in 1907, a division of spheres of influence in the Far East eliminated all points of conflict between the two countries. Manchuria was divided by a line passing through Changchun (Hsinking), and Russian influence was consolidated over northern Manchuria, through which passed the Chinese Eastern Railway. Japan similarly was given control over southern Korea, which she annexed in 1910, while in compensation Japan acknowledged Russia's interests in Mongolia. Thus Mongolia, which after the Chinese Revolution had proclaimed its independence from China, became the next field for Russian economic and political penetration.

The subsequent World War, the Russian Revolution, and the collapse of Russia invalidated the whole picture and it looked for a moment as if the Russian factor had been eliminated from eastern Asia. Between 1919 and 1922, all frontiers disappeared in anarchy, and the contending White and Red Russian armies swept freely over the Manchurian and Mongolian borders, Japan occupied eastern Siberia up to Lake Baikal, and the Chinese Eastern Railway passed under Allied control. But when the new order, i.e., the Soviet regime, finally emerged out of the chaos and brought Russian Asia under its control again, a remarkable and significant thing happened. The border was once more restored as of 1914, or more exactly as of 1860, proving that the logic of geography and history demanded the restoration of this line. The next milestone in this long procession of history was the Sino-Soviet agreement of 1924 which brought Russian influence back into Manchuria, and the administration of the Chinese Eastern Railway was placed on a joint fifty-fifty basis between Russia and China. Concomitantly, the same year saw the proclamation of a Soviet republic in Mongolia, thereby eliminating the weak theocratic regime of the Khutukhtu which had precariously ruled independent Mongolia. The Chinese were perturbed, and in 1929 Chang Hsueh Liang, the Manchurian war lord, attempted to drive the Russians out of Manchuria. This brought swift Soviet retaliation, and in an undeclared war the Soviets reasserted their hold over northern Manchuria and the railway by a lightning

invasion by the Red Army. Thus the pendulum swung in favor of
the Soviets, who were rapidly regaining their strength in Asia.
But just as dramatically the pendulum swung to the other extreme, when Japan in 1931 embarked on her great conquest of
Asia, partly because of the great fear of Russian resurgence.

Once more the stage seemed to be set in the Far East for a
headlong clash between Russian and Japanese imperialism, with
a weak and divided China paying the costs; only the roles were
now reversed, with Japan aggressively pushing forward in Manchuria and the Soviets on the defensive, particularly in view of
the Hitler menace on their European border. Notwithstanding
hundreds of armed clashes along the Amur and Ussuri borders,
war was avoided. But the inner workings of obscure historical
forces were actually favoring China. Millions of Chinese were
settling in Manchuria under Japanese occupation, making it more
Chinese than it ever was. The evanescent hold of Japan on the
conquered territories in Asia was revealed by World War II,
and on the surface Russia seemed to have garnered the fruits of
Allied victory in Asia. Indeed, the all-time high watermark of
Russian expansion was achieved by Russia in 1945 with the return of Sakhalin and the Kurile Islands.

But the postwar years revealed a different outline, gradually
shaping itself, of the real balance of forces in Asia. For one thing,
the collapse of Japan, coupled with the expansion of Russian influence, produced the appearance of the United States as a bal-
ancing factor in Asia as revealed by the Korean War. For another,
whatever be the temporary ideological alignment between Russia
and China, the factor determining the future is the rapid transformation of China into a first-class military and, possibly later,
industrial power. China is usurping the position previously held
by Japan. In the past, when China was strong, she tended to
overflow into the neighboring belt of states, be it Mongolia,
Sinkiang, Tibet, or Annam. A similar trend is visible at present
under Communist rule and may form an automatic barrier to
further Russian expansion. Thus the belt of territories lying between the Siberian border and the Great Wall of China, nominally
Chinese but in reality the field for Russian economic and political penetration, will inevitably become more and more the bone
of contention between the two great Communist powers of Asia,

and the Chinese are showing an active interest in countering Russian economic development by their own. For example, the Russian railway network reaches the gates of Sinkiang, while the Chinese are constructing a line from Lanchow to Urumchi (Tihwa) and thus linking up with the Russian railheads. It must be remembered that if Siberia is the land of the future for Russia and is being colonized and industrialized by Russia, the territories stretching from Sinkiang to Manchuria play the same role for China. Thus demographically and economically, both countries are coming nearer to each other, and their borders, previously separated by vast desert regions, are now becoming contiguous in reality, not only on maps. Though it must be granted that China has a long way to go to become economically developed, it must not be forgotten that Russia changed herself in two generations from a weak economy to a leading industrial nation. This seems to be the main problem and the main trend in the balance of power of Asia. Whatever the present alignment or ideological conformities, the day may not be so far off when Russia will be on the defensive on her Siberian border, as this border once more proves to be the real frontier between Slav and Chinese.

Thus if the Turner hypothesis is in the main applicable to the Siberian frontier, as we have seen, it is equally applicable to China's far western and northern frontiers, and to understand the real balance of forces in Asia we have to consider a situation which Turner did not have to face, namely, the existence of two parallel, expanding, and competing frontiers. It is this aspect of the frontier problem that makes the greatest difference in the development of the American and Russian frontiers.

6 THE CHUKCHI OF
THE SOVIET FAR EAST

Walter Kolarz

COMMUNISM AS a materialistic teaching cannot aim at the preservation of national groups and minorities. Their right to an existence as separate political and cultural individualities depends on their contribution to the communist cause. If they fulfil a useful and 'progressive' task, from a communist point of view, they are able to enjoy the very considerable material blessings which communism has in store for backward areas. On the other hand, if they are an obstacle to communism they may be exterminated.

The extermination of ethnic groups can take many forms both in communist and non-communist societies. Open violent genocide has been practised only in a few exceptional cases, for instance, by Imperial Germany which wiped out entire tribes in South-West Africa, by Hitlerite Germany which destroyed the bulk of the Jewish population of Eastern and Central Europe or by Soviet Russia which suppressed such nationalities as the Chechens, Ingushi, Crimean Tartars, Balkars and others. But genocide does not always culminate in one single dramatic event, it may be spread out over many years. A large number of political, economic and cultural measures may be put into effect to bring about the ultimate extermination or at least disintegration of an ethnic group. Let us recapitulate shortly the principal measures leading to national oppression which we have seen at work in various parts of the Soviet Far East and Eastern Siberia:

Originally published as pp. 179–80 and pp. 89–99 of *The Peoples of the Soviet Far East*, by Walter Kolarz, New York, Frederick A. Praeger, 1954. Reprinted with permission of the publisher.

1 Industrialization and de-tribalization which is linked with migration of natives to big urban centres.

2 Destruction of the native economy through state interference such as the fostering of class struggle and the confiscation of cattle.

3 Mass colonization of 'national territories' by Europeans.

4 'Liquidation' of the native upper class and of the intellectual *élite*.

5 Persecution of religious beliefs peculiar to minority nationalities.

6 Prohibition of cultural and political integration of kindred tribes and nationalities.

7 Imposition of an alien ideology, of a foreign language and culture.

8 Suppression of historical and cultural traditions which are essential to the survival of the national consciousness of a given ethnic group.

It may be argued that none of these eight measures is the exclusive weapon of communist nationalities policy. Their application may be traced not only in Russia but also in areas which are notorious as 'dark spots' of Western colonial policy. Ruthless industrialization and de-tribalization, for instance, may be seen in operation in a city like Johannesburg or in the mining areas of the Belgian Congo. The liquidation of the intellectual *élite* does seem to be the result of the policy pursued in Madagascar. Mass colonization by Europeans has jeopardized the interests of the native peoples of Kenya and the Rhodesias. Attempts at establishing unity have been frustrated in the case of the Ewe people in West Africa and in the case of the Somali in East Africa. But in comparing conditions in Siberia to those in the more problematic parts of the African continent one important reservation must be made. The numerical strength of the African people is such that ultimately they will triumph over the limitations which result from European colonial rule. Ultimately Africa will belong to the Africans. In Siberia things are different. There the peoples can have no hope of an end of European rule. They are too small in numbers to withstand the communist offensive which combines the implementation of economic development schemes with social experiments and attacks on tribal institutions and customs.

CHUKOTKA—THE RUSSIAN COLONY FACING ALASKA

The National Area of the Chukchi occupies the north-eastern tip of Asia facing Alaska, and is bordered by the Arctic Sea on the north, and the Bering Sea on the east and south. Several islands are part of the Chukcha National Area, including the Soviet island of Big Diomede, which is separated by only four miles from the Little Diomede, which belongs to the United States.[1]

The Soviet nationalities policy has done its best to take advantage of the indisputable geo-political importance of the Chukcha National Area—in short, Chukotka. This policy had to allow, in the first place, for the fact that the natives of Chukotka, both the Chukchi themselves and the Eskimos, who are related to them, had a long tradition of close economic co-operation with their American neighbours, whereas links between Russians and Chukchi had been tenuous.

The danger of an Americanization of 'Chukotka' was not caused by a deliberate offensive of 'dollar imperialism' against that territory, but was due to the natural inter-dependence of the more highly developed American Alaska and the underdeveloped Russian territories on the western shore of the Bering Strait. *De jure*, Chukotka has been a Russian possession ever since the middle of the seventeenth century, when Cossacks had first penetrated into the land of the Chukchi. *De facto*, however, the Russians did not exert any sovereign rights over either the territory or the territorial waters around the north-eastern tip of Asia. A few Russians who had settled down in Chukotka in the seventeenth century, became completely intermixed with the native population, and quite indistinguishable from them as far as their exterior appearance was concerned. In 1897 there were 300 Russians in Chukotka, and 500 persons officially described as 'Russianized natives', who might easily have been Russians turned native. The

---

[1] The Diomede Islands are also known as Ratmanov Island and Kruzenshtern Island respectively. Admiral Kruzenshtern commanded the first Russian round-the-world voyage and Ratmanov participated in this expedition.

bulk of the population—the 11,771 Chukchi—lived in complete
segregation from the Russians, and had they not been so primitive, it might have been said that they formed a State of their
own. Up to the end of the nineteenth century the Chukchi were
completely ignorant of Russia. They were even unaware of the
existence of a Russian Czar. Nor did the Chukchi ever pay the
Russians any 'yasak', the famous fur tribute by which the Siberian peoples implicitly recognized the overlordship of Russia
(Silnitsky 1897).

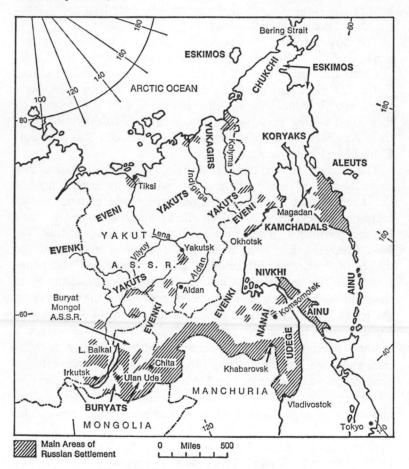

The Aborigines of the Soviet Far East

In the middle of the nineteenth century the Americans started the exploitation of Russian coastal waters in the Bering Strait, and in the Okhotsk Sea, with its vast abundance of whales. Since the Russians displayed no interest in whaling, the Americans soon became the unchallenged masters of those Russian waters. 'Predatory American whaling' had nearly exhausted the whale stock of the north-western Pacific before the Russians even thought of organizing whaling expeditions of their own.

After the purchase of Alaska by the United States in 1867, American whalers were almost the only civilized people with whom the inhabitants of the Chukot peninsula came into contact. The Americans sold them all the goods they needed, including rifles and ammunition, and later even little boats in which they went to Alaska, trading and intermarrying with Alaskan natives. Both the Chukchi and the Asiatic Eskimos learned English, and some of them travelled with the assistance of American whalers and traders as far as Seattle and San Francisco. Eskimo children from Chukotka went to Alaska to attend mission schools.

A learned Russian traveller to Chukotka, said, as early as 1888, that nearly all Chukchi of the Chukot peninsula, women and children included, understood some English, and that many Chukchi spoke it as well as a 'genuine American'. Gradually the Americans became so familiar to the Chukchi that they used to call all foreigners appearing on their shores 'Americans' (*Izvestiya* 1888).

It was only in 1889 that the Russian Government transformed the land of the Chukchi into a separate administrative unit—the Anadyr District—and it was not before the 'nineties', when the district was under the command of a young, broad-minded District Commissioner, N. L. Gondatti, that Russian rule over the Chukchi became more effective, and attempts were made to counteract American commercial competition. Gondatti ordered regular fairs to be organized for the benefit of the Chukchi, and every native coming to his headquarters was offered a meal and a small present.

The attempts to consolidate Russian rule in Chukotka were, however, checked by the development of Alaska at the beginning of the twentieth century. To the American public the advance of economic and cultural life in Alaska seemed to proceed at too slow a pace. But what the Americans criticized as 'neglect' the Russians praised as the most astonishing progress. In 1909 the Russian scholar Kokhanovsky described the Alaskan town of Nome as 'an outstanding cultural centre' (*Izvestiya* 1909). Obviously nothing in Chukotka, Kamchatka or around the Okhotsk Sea could bear comparison with Nome during its short-lived boom at the beginning of the century. At that time the danger of the United States expanding economically from Alaska into Chukotka was particularly real. Between 1902 and 1912 there existed an American 'North-Eastern Siberian Company', which eagerly propagated the idea of American investments for the exploitation of Chukotka's national riches—gold, iron-ore and graphite. The company was entitled to exploit 60,000 square miles of Russian land. During the ten years of its existence, it established an American trading monopoly on the Russian side of the Bering Strait. About 200 Americans settled more or less permanently in Chukotka. Their solid, well-furnished houses aroused the envy of the few local Russians, and the admiration of the natives. After the Second World War Soviet propaganda gave a very coloured version of the 'American period' in Chukotka's history. To show the far-flung ambitions of American imperialism, the Soviet Press made great play of a very unrealistic private American project to link Alaska with Chukotka by a submarine tunnel, and to build a railway across Northern Siberia (Ogonyok 1952; Melchin 1909). The scheme had caused a minor sensation at the beginning of the century, but it was never taken very seriously.

THE SOVIETIZATION OF CHUKOTKA

Only the Soviet régime transformed Chukotka into a safe Russian possession and held foreign influence at bay. It could not raise Chukotka to a higher cultural and economic level than that of Alaska, but it could at least destroy the old interdependence of the two territories. Even this could be achieved only gradually and incompletely. Friendly direct contact between Alaska's and Chukotka's natives went on for several years after the establishment of Soviet power in the areas east of the Bering Strait. A fairly large number of Chukchi continued to speak some sort of broken English and there are indications that trips between Chukotka and Alaska went on until as late as 1944. Until that year parties of as many as forty people were observed to arrive from Siberia on the Alaskan coast on hunting, fishing and trading expeditions whilst American Eskimos visited Siberia for similar purposes (*Military Review* 1952).

The transformation of Chukotka into an integral part of the Soviet Empire has been described in detail in Syomushkin's novel *Alitet goes to the Hills*. The book was published in 1947. It was awarded a Stalin Prize for prose, for, from the point of view of the régime, it had the great merit of drawing the attention of a large Russian public to the strategic and political importance of the Chukotka outpost in the 'cold war' against America. Later, a film was produced on the basis of Syomushkin's book, but this was not such a great success.

Syomushkin, who had lived eight years in Chukotka, depicted in detail the methods which the Soviet governor employed to achieve the Sovietization of the land of the Chukchi. This man, whom Syomushkin called 'Los', was posted to Chukotka as he might have been to Kursk, Tula, or any other place in Central Russia. He had not the slightest knowledge of the country which he was to administer. He did not know anything about its customs. On the very first day of his arrival in Chukotka, without having gained even a superficial knowledge of local conditions, he stated flatly to his Russian companion: 'We'll make communists and komsomols out of them, mark my words.' And the Soviet administrator did make 'communists' out of the Chukchi, but these 'communists' were unable to understand such words as 'communism', 'Soviet' and 'revolutionary'. His assistant, a young intellectual called Andrey Zhukov, who had studied the customs and languages of the Chukchi, was more sceptical of the transplantation to the Arctic of the Communist Party jargon. When Los asked him to translate the word 'revolutionary' to a Chukcha, Zhukov said: 'I should like to see you translate the word "revolutionary". It is not so easy.' Los was not impressed by this refusal, but assured his subordinate that he would get the word translated, and that the Chukchi would learn the word. After gathering some experience in propaganda work among the

local people, Los and his assistant drew up a political vocabulary.
Here are some of its principal terms:

Communism	The new law
Lenin	The Russian who invented the new law of life
Communist	A man who wishes to remake life
October Revolution Anniversary Celebration	Feast of the big speech-making. (The Chukchi themselves call it 'The Russian Feast'.)
Communist Party Card	Bearer of the good spirit
Petrol	Good Spirit Benzine

The most difficult thing was to translate the word 'State'. How
could one explain to the Chukchi that a thing called 'State' had
confiscated the reindeer, and that it had become the most important property owner in Chukotka? A Chukcha woman, Rultina,
found an adequate and truthful translation of 'State' by suggesting that the State was just a white man. A young Chukcha communist answered to this that the State was not only the Russian
administrator, but 'many, many people'.[2]

Syomushkin's novel showed that the Soviet régime had to make
a particularly great display of its efficiency in Chukotka because
the Chukchi had an opportunity to compare the respective merits
of Russian and American technical skill, even if only in the form
of Russian and American matches. At one point of his book

---

[2] The Soviet régime is not the only one trying to teach the peoples of the
North the political A.B.C. in a simplified and even over-simplified language.
This is how *The Eskimo Book of Knowledge* of the Hudson Bay Company
explained to the Eskimos of Labrador the transformation of Canada into a
dominion—'In his wisdom, the King of Britain said to the people of these
new countries beyond the seas, his sons: "You have always loved me and
the things which I love. You are now grown to full manhood, you have
learned the things which I can teach you, you have your families and your
children. It is right that you should direct your ways for the benefit of your
children. I will appoint a Governor for your lands, but he shall be guided
by your wishes. For are not your wishes my wishes?"' (Binney 1931:
38–40).

Syomushkin said that a pro-American Chukcha settlement had to be bribed by a motor whale boat before it would agree to join the Soviet hunting and fishing co-operative. Russia's position *vis-à-vis* the United States was also strengthened on a larger scale by the building of new settlements opposite Alaska—the Eskimo village Naukan and the administrative base Uelen, which was mainly populated by Chukchi.

The fight against native kulaks and traders was one of the most important activities of the Soviet authorities in Chukotka. The Russian communist officials tried to take control of fur hunting, fur trading and reindeer breeding. This was a difficult task, since the measures for collectivization were less understood in Chukotka than in most other 'backward' territories of the U.S.S.R. Syomushkin himself had to admit these difficulties when he described the effect of the imprisonment of the 'wicked kulak Alitet' (a Chukcha trader of this name really existed) on the local atmosphere in Chukotka. The local people saw in Alitet's arrest not a measure taken by the champions of the proletariat against the kulaks, but the persecution of a Chukcha by Russians. This is how Syomushkin described the despondency which the 'Alitet case' had created in Chukotka:

'Something amazing had happened on the coast. The Russians had locked Alitet up in a wooden yarang, and he sat there like a seal in a net. The news spread like wildfire, magnified by monstrous rumours. Alitet was in everyone's mouth, in the yarangs of the seal hunters, among the trappers, at meetings on the trail, in the depths of the tundra and wherever men came together in twos or threes.'

'The Shamans said that the Russians were building strong wooden yarangs in order to catch and lock up the Chukchi in them'.

'People dare not live now on the big rivers. The Russians would come down in the summer on their self-going whaleboats, and seize all the reindeer herds in order to do away with them. The reindeer men must not live in big encampments. They must break up into small camps of one or two yarangs, not more. The Russians want to destroy the herds' (Syomushkin 1948).

CHUKOTKA DURING THE WAR: ECONOMIC EXPLOITATION
AND 'IDEOLOGICAL' CONCESSIONS

The story of Syomushkin's book is carried further in the novel
Swiftmoving Reindeer by Nikolay Shundik. It describes life in
Chukotka in the years of the war. The situation is then fundamentally different from that presented in *Alitet goes to the Hills*.
The Soviet régime has already won the first round in the fight
for Chukotka, the Soviet administration is firmly established, the
collective farm system dominates and the young Chukchi are organized in the Komsomol. Many of them, it is true, do not know
what the 'Communist Youth League' really stands for[3] but this
does not matter as long as the Chukcha Komsomol members
support the régime wholeheartedly and make their contribution
to the development of local economy. The emphasis of Shundik's
book is on this economic aspect. The Russian officials who figure
in his novel are of a quite different type from the Los and Zhukov
of Syomushkin. They are no longer interested in indoctrinating
the Chukchi and explaining to them the essence of communism
and the working of Soviet power, they do not even talk about
Lenin and Stalin. Their primary objective is to make the Chukchi work harder and to extract from them greater material contributions, particularly in the form of fur supplies.

The Russian officials and their Chukcha collaborators need all
their ingenuity to increase the trapping of fur animals. Although
the hunters are working under great strain, day and night, they
must raise their targets further—under the pretext that the front
expects more. To achieve this every collective farmer must look
after a larger number of fox-traps. Women, too, are enrolled into
the 'fox-hunting brigades'. One Russian administrator even has
the idea of forcing reindeer-breeders to give up their herds and
devote themselves entirely to hunting. This scheme is tried out

---

[3] Shundik's definition of the Komsomol as put into the mouth of a Chukcha
girl is very similar to the definitions of political terms in *Alitet goes to the
Hills;* 'The Komsomol is a very big family of young lads and girls. These
lads and girls are honest and strong. They do one big job that is necessary
to all, namely, to build life anew. The Komsomoltsy do not fear anything,
neither an enemy, nor heavy work, nor snowstorm, not even death'.

but it does not work. It puts an unfair burden on the remaining shepherds and provokes profound dissatisfaction among the Chukchi who for generations have been used to combining fox trapping with reindeer-breeding. As a result less furs are provided than before. The man responsible for this failure, Karaulin, the head of the economic department of a Communist Party District Committee in Chukotka, is dismissed. He had been highly unpopular with the local population and it is interesting that this final removal occurs over an economic problem and not because of the high-handed way in which he had for several years been treating the Chukchi. One of his 'exploits' was the confiscation of a number of charms and idols belonging to an old Chukcha. Such arbitrary actions against helpless natives must have frequently happened in the past, both in Chukotka and in other native territories of the Far North and Far East. Nobody took exception to them in 1935 or 1938 but in the new situation that existed during the Second World War confiscation of idols became a 'left-wing distortion'.

Far away, in Moscow, Stalin gives the example. He has revised the official policy towards religion and concluded an armistice with the Orthodox Church. The Party secretary in Chukotka thinks that somehow he must adapt this new line to the conditions peculiar to North-Eastern Siberia. So he disowns his too zealous subordinate, Karaulin. The confiscated idols and charms are neatly wrapped up and bundled and restored to the owner who, incidentally, is a first-class and generally respected reindeer-breeder the régime can ill afford to antagonize.

CHUKOTKA AND THE 'COLD WAR'

The situation of Chukotka in 1945, as depicted in Shundik's novel is still not quite satisfactory from the Soviet point of view. The author introduces us to such 'hostile elements' as a reindeer-breeder who still refuses to join the kolkhoz, a kulak who, though formally a kolkhoz member, continues to be harmful and treacherous, and even an alleged American spy who for a certain period successfully poses as an official of a Soviet trading post. What is even more remarkable is the survival in Chukotka of 'devilish superstitions' but about this point at least a more official testimony is available than Shundik's book. 'In the minds of the Chukotka peoples', says *Pravda* of July 2nd, 1947, 'the old times are still surviving.' 'The Party organization', the newspaper adds, 'must carry out a tremendous cultural and educational work among the local population. Books are needed in the languages of the Chukchi and the Eskimos[4] to expose the prejudices of the past.'

The main handicap to communist activity in Chukotka has always been the fact that the country is ruled from Khabarovsk, which is as far away from Uelen, the settlement of the Chukchi on the Bering Strait, as Murmansk is from Tiflis. The communist leadership of Khabarovsk has found it extremely difficult, for obvious geographical reasons, to become interested in the special economic problems of the Chukchi, and in their cultural and economic needs. When the Party secretary of the distant National Area went to Khabarovsk in 1947, he had more than one reason for complaint. His most urgent grievances were the following: none of the Khabarovsk communist leaders ever visited Chukotka; the Khabarovsk paper *The Pacific Star* (Tikhookeanskaya Zvezda) rarely reported on events in the territory; no literature on Chukotka was published by the Regional Publishing House, Dalgiz; and the Khabarovsk trade organization, Severotorg, did not supply the goods badly needed by the population, such as tea,

---

[4] The 'Russian or Asiatic Eskimos' live in the coastal areas of the Chukot peninsula. The part of the Chukcha National Area which they inhabit, and which also comprises Wrangel Island and the island Big Diomede, forms a special Chukcha-Eskimo National District of 150,000 square miles. It includes about one-sixth of the National Area. The Soviet régime has attached considerable importance to 'its' Eskimos in view of the large number of their kinsmen living in North America. The first expression of a Soviet 'Eskimo policy' was the organization in 1929 of an 'Eskimo Congress of Soviets'. The Soviet Government has also published pamphlets in Eskimo on basic political topics, as well as on reindeer-breeding, and an experiment was made with an Eskimo wall newspaper.

In 1947 the Soviet authorities decided that the Eskimo language hitherto in use in the U.S.S.R. was based on a 'wrong alphabet', and a 'wrong spelling'. The Minister of Education of the R.S.F.S.R., Alexey Kalashnikov, issued a decree by which the existing Eskimo alphabet was changed, and a more phonetic system of spelling adopted. The changes made it necessary to rewrite the existing Soviet literature in the Eskimo language in accordance with the new spelling rules. The new Eskimo alphabet was the third one to be introduced by the Soviet régime within less than twenty years.

tobacco and petrol stoves. The publication of the article in *Pravda* coincided, quite accidentally, with the beginning of the 'cold war', and it constituted a turning point in the official Soviet attitude towards the Chukotka problem. Once again events in Alaska had a bearing on the situation in Chukotka. In view of the importance which Alaska acquired in the defence system of the Western hemisphere, the Soviet authorities paid increased attention to Alaska's neighbour, the National Area of the Chukchi. Educational activities, for instance, were greatly extended. At the beginning of 1950 there were as many as 76 schools in the National Area, with more than 3,000 pupils (*Soviet Monitor* 1950).[5]

Hand in hand with the development of schools for the children of Chukotka has gone the increase of propaganda activities among the adults. The Party secretary of the National Area stated, in May 1952, that Chukotka had as many as 350 'agitators', who had been recruited from among the Chukchi, Eskimos, and other 'natives'. Some of these locally recruited agitators were trained in the Territorial Party School in Khabarovsk. Others were indoctrinated in Party schools working in the National Area itself. In 1951–52 alone, 900 Party and Komsomol members of Chukotka, including both natives and Russians, studied the 'classics of Marxism-Leninism', and the 'Short History of the All-Union Communist Party' (*Pravda* 1952).

All this indoctrination work among the Chukchi is concentrated in the hands of a Russian Party secretary, who shares his political power with the native Chairman of the Executive Committee of the Chukcha National Area. The division is very unequal, for the Party secretary has the powers of the governor of a colony, and the Chairman of the Executive Committee is only a figurehead and a spokesman of native interests. A man called Kukai was chairman just before the war. During the war the job was filled by a graduate of the Leningrad Institute of the Peoples

---

[5] The record of the Canadian Government in providing education for the Canadian Indians is at least as good as that of the Soviet government in Chukotka. In 1949, out of the 135,000 Canadian Indians, 23,285 were attending school, that is to say more than one out of six. By comparison the school population in Chukotka is roughly the same, granted that the National Area has about 18,000 inhabitants, which is a very low estimate. The figure includes not only Chukchi and other natives, but also the Russian colonists.

of the North, Otke. He has frequently been mentioned and quoted in the Soviet Press, and there is no other native of the Soviet Far East and Far North who has come into such prominence. Not only does he serve as an example of how the Chukcha people have advanced under the Soviet régime, but he is also used for anti-American propaganda purposes. As a small boy, so his official biography says, Otke was offended by an American merchant, who poured the contents of a whole bag of duck feathers over him. Otke never forgot this episode. Apart from telling the story of the duck feathers, he is credited with making more profound political statements, such as the following: 'From Chukotka to Moscow there are 15,000 kilometres, and to Washington the distance is naturally considerably less. But there are different kinds of distance. There is a very great distance between the thoughts and feelings of people working in Chukotka and the intentions of the people in Washington. In this respect there is no distance whatever between Chukotka and Moscow.'

IMMIGRATION OF RUSSIANS AND RESETTLEMENT OF CHUKCHI

It is impossible to say what is the numerical proportion of Russians to natives in Chukotka. It is a fair assumption, however, that the Russian element has greatly consolidated its position after the end of the Second World War, when something approaching a mass immigration seems to have taken place for the first time. Before the war the Soviet Government had mapped out a big colonization plan for Chukotka, the population of which was supposed to increase to 30,000 by 1938, the end of the Second Five-Year Plan. Luckily for the Chukchi, but very much to the detriment of Russia's strategic interests, this plan failed to materialize. Chukotka's population remained stationary, at about 15,000. A substantial increase of the Russian immigrants after the war may be assumed from the fact that, in 1951, as many as 31 per cent of all deputies of local District and Area Soviets of Chukotka were officially classified as not belonging to the northern peoples (Sibirskie Ogni 1952). In other words, they were Russian and European colonists and officials. If the council seats were distributed in accordance with the proportionate strength of the nationalities inhabiting Chukotka, an inference which cannot be made with absolute certainty, then almost one third of its population must have been European immigrants. This must be compared to the situation around 1930, when only 3·8 per cent of the population of the National Area consisted of non-natives. 76·3 per cent were Chukchi, and almost 20 per cent were Eskimos and other aborigines (Sergeev 1934).

Apart from Russian immigration, the National Area was the scene of yet another important development after the Second World War—the liquidation of nomadism. The complete triumph of the Soviet system in the Far North will be possible only when the entire population becomes sedentary, and within easy reach of the Communist Party and State organs. This is why active measures have been taken to settle the nomads in the various National Areas of the Soviet Arctic. The task has been a difficult one. It has required considerable financial investments, and a great deal of work on the part of the Soviet authorities (*Uchitelskaya Gazeta* 1951). In 1947 Chukotka's first nomadic collective farm engaged in reindeer breeding decided (according to an official statement) 'to settle down completely, and for good' (*Soviet News* 1947). In the middle of 1952 it was stated that a 'mass resettlement' took place, whereby the Chukchi were moved from their yarangs into 'comfortable houses'. This meant a greater concentration of the Chukchi in a number of larger collective farm settlements, probably for many of those concerned a rather painful operation (*Pravda* 1952).

Both the immigration of Russians and the resettlement of the Chukchi have set civilization in Chukotka on a higher level. On the other hand, these two measures are bound to pave the way to the extinction of the Chukchi as a separate national group. Accordingly, the forecast of the great Russian anthropologist Professor Bogoraz-Tan with regard to the Chukchi seems to be coming true: 'If civilization comes too near, the Chukchi will probably follow the way of other primitive peoples, and will die out and disappear' (Bogoraz-Tan 1934).

Part II | EARLY ANTHROPOLOGY
AND FRONTIERS

7 "CIVILIZED MEN" AND "NATIVES"

A Series of Excerpts from a Debate held before
The Anthropological Society of London in
1865, and from the Report of the U. S. Bureau of
Indian Affairs for 1867.

Fred Plog and Paul Bohannan

WHEN PEOPLES OF two cultures meet, they have no way of
interacting with one another except each according to his
past training. They must work out a way in which they can communicate adequately with one another and judge the meaning
and the temper of each other's actions. Ethnocentrism means
acting in accordance with one's own values in a situation to which
they are not relevant: sometimes there is an additional feeling
of willfulness in the word, as if someone were positively refusing
to look beyond his own values and impressions.

Ethnocentrism among Westerners began to show up immediately the reports of travelers and colonizers began to appear.
Initial ethnocentrism is probably unavoidable, although if one is
aware of it, one can be very sensitive to situations in which it is
operative—one can sense one's own ethnocentrism in one's impatience, anger, fear and homesickness while dealing with foreign peoples. We have taken the following illustrations of ethnocentric attitudes and the painful processes of self-examination
that are necessary to recognize them from the Report of the U. S.
Bureau of Indian Affairs for 1867 and from the report of a debate about missionaries in Africa which occupied the meetings
of the Anthropological Society of London between March 14 and
May 16, 1865.

The selection obviously represents a comparatively late period

Excerpts reprinted from the *Journal of the Anthropological Society of London*, Volume III (1865), clxiii–ccxciv. London: Trubner and Co.   *Report
of the U. S. Bureau of Indian Affairs for 1867*, Department of the Interior,
1867. Washington: Government Printing Office.

in the history of Western frontiers and contact. However, that is
useful because the effect of the people beyond the frontier and
of ethnocentric attitudes is felt more strongly than it was earlier.
Try as they will to examine merely the Indians or the Africans,
the people who created these reports found it necessary to examine themselves as well.

Anthropology is one of the weapons for overcoming ethnocentrism. When these reports were written, anthropology was in its
infancy. The excerpts are frankly selected with a bias that stresses
certain points: that Europeans applied their own, necessarily ethnocentric, criteria in judging other peoples, and that they (and
many others) have had to learn to recognize and combat their
own ethnocentrism. We are not branding Europeans or Americans, missionaries or Indian agents; neither are we trying to take
a sentimental attitude toward "natives." Our point is that seeing
beyond one's own cultural dimension is a considerable achievement that has been developed to at least some degree in the last
hundred years.

The excerpts are set out under headings which form a set of
postulates that are the "lurking hypotheses" behind both sources.

POSTULATE I   The difference of the native "atmosphere" from
the "civilized" atmosphere is a difference that can be associated
with geography and with "moral" (today we would say "cultural")
limitations of "primitive" peoples.

COROLLARY 1   The "native" "atmosphere" is not conducive to
civilization.

We know that man is modified to a certain extent by the atmosphere in which he breathes. In the same manner men live in a moral
atmosphere, which varies immensely in different parts of the globe,
and of which religion may be said to be the oxygen, or universal gas.

Now there can be no doubt that we live in an air which is purer
than that which permeates a savage people. This incontestable fact
has induced some thousands of our enthusiastic, but ignorant, fellow-
countrymen to adopt a wild scheme for the remedy of this evil. They
endeavour to change the religious climate of whole continents by

bottling up our moral atmosphere in missionaries, and in exporting it at a very great expense.

(Africans, p. 164)

Now what can Europe do to assist West Africa? I reply that it can do nothing. The only manner in which we could elevate the negro would be by establishing a commercial mission, of which the churches should be workshops, and master artizans the priests. But, owing to the pestilential nature of the climate, all efforts of this kind would result rather in degrading the white man to a level with the negro than to elevate the negro to anything like our own standard. Thanks to the exertions of Mr. Adderley, we may soon hope to see the emancipation of the white men from this accursed coast.

(Africans, p. 167)

COROLLARY 2   "Immoral" family and property institutions or settlement patterns are specific blocks to civilization.

"As long as Indians live in villages they will retain many of their old and injurious habits."

(Indians, p. 75)

I have been convinced by personal observation for some time that the system of holding land in common is very unfavorable for educating an Indian to personal independence. Though he may build and improve for a time, he must to some extent be subordinate to his tribal government, and this will operate against continued personal efforts in building, enlarging fields, planting orchards, or acquiring other property of an immovable nature, the permanent possession of which is uncertain, and may be disposed of contrary to the wishes of the owner without personal remuneration for the value thereof. The very fact of his enjoying some home comforts will render him suspicious of the uncertain tenure by which they are held, and make him irresolute in regard to prosecuting further improvements. As timber becomes scarce, and pastures contiguous to their improvements become worthless, contentions will originate that will mar the pleasant relations that existed between them when a wigwam and a patch sufficed for their wants. I believe that to obviate these difficulties, to break down the traditional rule of Indian government, and to aid the Indian in achieving mental independence, each Indian should receive an allotment of a subdivision of land, and should hold the same by certificate-title. They can then feel secure in the possession of their homes, can protect the timber belonging to their claims from either white or Indian depredators, and will be invested with a feeling of pride and contentment that will incite them to greater energy in cultivating the soil and raising cattle. I respectfully invite an earnest consideration of this subject by the Department.

(Indians, p. 121)

As to polygamy, he believed it was one of the greatest obstacles to the spread of Christianity. It was a practice which he thought ought to be tolerated in the first instance, and that it would die out in the second generation. It was a great crime for a man to put away his wives, who then became prostitutes; and for that reason he considered it desirable that polygamy should be allowed amongst the first converts.

(Africans, p. 181)

COROLLARY 3   If "natives" become "civilized" the fact may be attributable to "civilized" (perhaps illegitimate) ancestors.

"Bishop" Crowther is frequently cited as an example of the civilised negro, improved by the missionaries out of the hold of the slaver. Now, unless Mr. McArthur has had some positive physical evidence of "Bishop" Crowther's truly negro parentage (I mean such physiological evidence as would satisfy a jury in the Divorce Court), I must throw all the weight of proving his improbable thesis on himself. The predominance of Haoussa blood in the neighbourhood where "Bishop" Crowther states that he was born is significantly omitted from the discussion, and those who have ever seen this highly educated African will, while admitting the darkness of his complexion and the woolliness of his hair, prefer, as in many other cases where the parentage of the negro is discussed, to avoid this delicate question.

(Africans, p. 239)

COROLLARY 4   If "natives" become "civilized" the change may be "nominal" or purely superficial.

But it was soon discovered that, however readily they consented to be baptised (the more so as eating salt, which they are very fond of, was part of the ceremony) and to call themselves Christians, they utterly refused to give up their plurality of wives, and were very indignant, as well they might be, at the impertinence of these foreigners in making such a request. They could not see the connection between marriage and religion; and the wives, especially, were furious. Women are always the pillars of the church; and when these were withdrawn, the missionaries were ridiculed as madmen, and Congo relapsed into paganism.

(Africans, p. 166)

COROLLARY 5 Education works, if it works at all, only with a complete change of "atmosphere."

Touching the matter of the education of the Utes, I regret to have to report that no progress has been made in this direction during the year. While I have grave doubts as to the practicability of establishing and maintaining a school which would be *really* beneficial to the Indians, still I should certainly have tried the experiment had there been any building suitable for school purposes. A mere *day-school* would, I am convinced, be of but little benefit to them, if, indeed, it would not be worse than useless, when the labor and expense entailed are taken into consideration. In order to advance the education of the children they should be entirely removed from the influences with which they are surrounded in the wigwam, and be gradually weaned to the manners and customs of civilization by being brought in constant association with white people. With the establishment of a boarding-school something in this way might possibly be accomplished, for there are many bright children among the Utes who would seemingly make apt scholars. Some few of the better-informed chiefs and headmen are in favor of education, but the great majority are either indifferent or else strenuously opposed to what they consider a harmful innovation.

The prejudice against the performance of manual labor which exists among Indians as a class is, perhaps, in no instance so strongly marked as in the Ute. He considers it a disgrace to labor, and ridicules the very idea of his ever being required to do anything of the kind. The child who has been trained under the influences of civilization and taught to regard labor as an honorable pursuit is seldom or never proof against the sneers and taunts of his Indian associates, and is pretty sure to yield to the common prejudice, and before arriv-

ing at manhood exhibit as strong an aversion to toil as the most
ignorant of them.

(Indians, p. 43)

Our native youths leave school at a critical time, and return, as
they will and must, to the native kraal. It would be folly to attempt
to keep them at such an age: their passions, pent up, would only
break out in some more gross and abnormal form. The parents will
expect them to return: the boys will reckon upon it as their right,
and will probably, if refused, take the law into their own hands, and
enforce their claim by running away. Nor can we dispense with or
ignore the natural affection between parents and children, if we wish
to elevate, to educate, the latter in a truly human manner. If we
could eradicate it—which, indeed, some missionaries seem almost to
wish they could—we could not get on without it. No new ties to their
teachers can or ought to take the place of their love to fathers and
mothers, sisters and brothers. How can they learn the Christian faith
—trust in, and obedience to, a Heavenly Father—if they have begun
by learning to despise their earthly parents?

We must, therefore, face this difficulty also, of our educated youths
returning home from school, as one of the primary inevitable draw-
backs upon our missionary efforts. For I need not say that, returning
thus to their kraals, removed from the influence of their teachers,
and coming again under that of their native friends, they are very
likely to return also—for a time, at all events—to the native mode of
life, to lay aside their books, to forget their lessons, to throw off their
clothing, and fall back into the idle habits and the vicious practices
of heathenism.

(Africans, p. 262)

COROLLARY 6   Failure to change the atmosphere results from the
natives' unwillingness or inability to make one or a few "simple"
changes which the writer deems crucial.

Ponies and rifles should be taken away from them, must be taken
in order to settle them down. There is nothing to hunt in Dakota that
requires rifles and horses; water-fowl and birds abound in their season. Permission for the most orderly to have shot-guns would afford
means of adding to the food supply. The ownership of a rifle and
pony is an invitation to wander off, which is seldom resisted. Many
good friends of Indians regard taking away arms and ponies as a

hardship where friendly Indians are exposed to hostiles; this is correct. In this superintendency there is no such danger, and as a friend of the Indians I assure other true friends that arms and horses are to them "unqualified mischief." Many of them understand this, and if the taking away is conducted justly and prudently, will occasion but little trouble. Last year those taken by way of precaution were seized at a time that rendered their loss inevitable. It is a painful story. A large part died of starvation and cold. Those remaining brought little. What Government received I trust will be no measure of what we give them in return. They were taken from Indians not hostile at the time. The full value should be paid in domestic cattle. It is not their fault that we lost most of the property. We cannot afford to be unjust. Ponies should be taken in June, not later, when grass is good, and they can be sent to market without loss. The proceeds, and more, should be invested in cattle and chickens, the possession of which makes moving about difficult, and encourages remaining in settled habitations. To reap the full benefit of taking away horses and arms, the Indians should be located as near the agencies as possible, close enough to render horses unnecessary.

Tepee-cloth should be discontinued, and as soon as proper locations can be had, log or frame houses should be substituted. Blankets and paint interfere with work and white men's ways. They should be discouraged, with as little violence as possible, but persistently. The use of paint, beads, and blankets should be stopped, and strong, coarse clothing provided. Such blankets and cloth as are furnished should be of quiet colors.

(Indians, p. 50)

Once more, I believe that the course which the great body of missionaries have taken on the question of polygamy is a very serious impediment to the progress of our work. Here again, without any authority from the Church of which they are ministers, there are many of the missionary clergy, and even Bishops, of the Church of England, who have laid down the law, that every convert admitted into the Christian Church shall put away all his wives but one, if he had more than one, before baptism.

(Africans, p. 274)

The men have adopted citizens' dress in full, the women partially. They still cling to their shawls, which they use for bonnet and shawl. I think there is great need for work among the women, for the men of this agency are making more progress than the women, and the men need to be supported by the women more than they are at this time in the proper performance of their household duties.

(Indians, p. 147)

They still maintain their tribal organizations, though not with the strength and influence of former years. These tribal ties are loosening, which augurs well for the future. Individualism is becoming more marked and should be encouraged. Aside from this I note but little change or progress toward civilization, except in the matter that some two or three hundred families are disposed to agriculture; but even here most of the work devolves on the squaws. Their civilization is still remote.

(Indians, p. 67)

POSTULATE II   Agents of contact are dangerous or inadequate.

COROLLARY 1   Contact agents are not qualified.

But on the subject of "ignorance," I fear, and want of due fitness and preparation for the work, a great deal might be said. The work of a missionary, when regarded in a true light as that of endeavouring not to save a few individual souls from everlasting burnings, but to raise a whole race to the true dignity of man, as a child of God, a being endowed with intellectual, moral, and spiritual faculties, is one of the highest, most interesting, most ennobling, that can engage our powers. Yet this great work is left for the most part in the hands of men comparatively ignorant and illiterate, with narrow views and limited education,—earnest in spirit it may be, simple and pure in life, unwearied in industry,—yet greatly deficient in some of the primary qualities, which go to make up the true ideal of a missionary.

(Africans, p. 267)

COROLLARY 2   Contact agents cannot communicate.

Good interpreters are essential to successful dealing with Indians. I have only seen one in this superintendency fit for the place. Important statements become absurd when made through an ignorant man, who only understands the simplest and coarsest forms of expression. Many charges of bad faith on the part of Government, and broken promises, arise, no doubt, from faulty interpretation. The pay should be increased so that a better class of men can be employed—as a business proposition. The Government can afford to pay liberally for teaching the English language. Difficulty in communicating with them adds very much to the vexatious problems embraced in our Indian policy.

(Indians, p. 51)

COROLLARY 3   Contact agents practice racial discrimination.

There was one of the missionaries married a coloured woman. This so annoyed the white saints that he was compelled to leave and go to Monrovia; and this feeling with regard to black people is more or less shown amongst all missionaries. You never see them received into the house, and associated with as an equal one of the black pastors, although these men do the greater part of the work, and live in the villages amongst the people, where, of course, their black coat has to be found, and white necktie kept as well starched as their more fortunate brethren in Freetown.

(Africans, p. 203)

COROLLARY 4   Contact agents engage in competition, which reduces their effectiveness.

One very great cause of the want of success amongst the natives is the continual opposition of one denomination to the other; this causes the natives to argue with themselves in this manner: these white men say they all worship one God, and are all followers of one Saviour. How is it they are always quarrelling, and no two of them go the same road to heaven; which one is right? This creates so much doubt in the small mind of the savage, that it ends in his professing whichever pays best. A few months back the whole body of missionaries in Freetown combined to preach against the Roman Catholic mission just establishing in Freetown, and advertised sermons to be preached by the different ministers on the subject. This caused a great sensation, and was the best advertisement that the Roman Catholics could have had, and I have no doubt was the means of getting a great many converts to the Roman Catholic faith.

(Africans, p. 203)

The general condition of the Papagos, considering the little that has been done for them, is on the whole satisfactory. Though there are exceptions, as in any community, they are generally industrious, honest, and well behaved. Mingling more with other people than do the Pimas, they are gradually acquiring the ways of the white man, and may be said to be a numerous people, standing on the threshold of civilization. The Mexican population of this Territory stands in the way of the Indians learning our language and manners, as they assimilate more readily and naturally with them, which is probably no advantage to the Indian. Intemperance and prostitution are to be found among them, but they are as good and virtuous as their surroundings and advantages would be likely to permit.

(Indians, p. 33)

The Mohammedan teachers have been described as "the agents of perpetual mischief to the best interests of the people," whilst for proofs of their ignorance and imposture, I would refer those who feel an interest in the subject, or may be inclined to doubt the justice of, to *Sketches of a Missionary's Travels,* by the Rev. M. Macbriar, a Wesleyan missionary, or to the *African Memoranda* of Captain Beaver.

(Africans, p. 191)

COROLLARY 5   Contact agents (other than one's self) bring "bad" aspects of Western civilization.

It was in this most unpromising sphere that the missionary commenced his labours; and, as if circumstances were not already sufficiently discouraging, he met on every hand jealousy and opposition, the last culminating, "at the instigation of the slave-dealer, in the destruction by fire of the churches, schools, and stores" erected with such toil, and cemented with the life-blood of their builders. Nor was this all. When the missionary, despite oppositions, dangers, and persecutions, had gathered around him those whom he fondly hoped would be the nucleus and seeds of that Church which should evangelize and civilize the great region of Tropical Africa, he found his efforts foiled by European example and European means. What availed it that he should preach chastity and purity, when his fellow-countrymen scoffed at both, and practised neither; when the Bible that he presented was met by the rum-bottle of the trader, whose whole life was a violation of those laws which the missionary inculcated, and whose example was such, that well might the heathen exclaim, "Why preach to us, or expect us to believe, when your own countrymen refuse to receive the message you bear, or to live by the rules you lay down!"

(Africans, pp. 186–87)

In regard to the evil of intemperance, no material change can be noted. It is now too deep-rooted to be easily eradicated. It would give me pleasure to say decidedly it was not on the increase. It is a more terrible foe than the dread Apache was. It brings lasting misery and degradation to this people. No village or settlement is free from its curse. It robs women and children of the necessities of life, and murder follows in its train. Human beings are transformed into demons. It brings about in part the prostitution of the women of the tribes, an evil scarcely less terrible in its moral and physical effects. In view of these facts is it too much to ask that a strong effort be made to punish those guilty of the great crime of selling whisky to the Indians? That the hands of the agent may not be tied while there is a chance of making an example of some of the mercenary outlaws who traffic for gain in the misery of their fellow-beings? The extent of the reservation, its proximity to many small towns, a great thoroughfare running through its entire length, the nearness of the Mexican boundary line, the numerous unprincipled Mexicans surrounding the reserve, the absence of the example of the better home-life of our own people, together with the determination of the Indians not to give information against the offenders, the difficulty of indicting any person for crime against an Indian, and the insignificant penalty for the offense under territorial law, make it a most difficult task, even with well-appointed means, to suppress this enormous crime.

(Indians, p. 32)

COROLLARY 6   Contact agents are unjust and rigid.

Orders have also been received to stop cutting wood by Indians, to pay them for what they have already cut, to take possession of and sell it. This, I am advised, is under a decision which deprives

Indians of any ownership in the wood until the land is taken by them in severalty. If agents do not enforce these orders they lay themselves liable. If they do enforce them the Indians are deprived of what little motive they have for labor. In the mean time, aliens of all nations cut wood on Indian land, sell to steamboats, fill contracts for the Army and for Indian agencies at high prices. Agents should, at their respective agencies, cut all the wood required for their own use and for adjacent military posts, and that may be required by steamboats in Government service. Cutting wood is one of the very few things an Indian can do in Dakota at this time. Of course such a policy will breed a storm among contractors and traders, but the work, discipline, and money are sadly needed by the Indians. The present system is absurd and expensive.

(Indians, p. 50)

COROLLARY 7   Contact agents do not fulfill promises.

This reservation was established in 1856, and by an act of Congress, March 3, 1873, was established in its present form. The Indians were encouraged to believe that they would soon have this as their permanent home, and have land given them for their *individual* homes. Four years have passed away. Messrs. Thomson, Bourne, and Eberly hold their former homes under a claim of swamp and overflowed land, and the stockmen hold the range as they did in 1872. With this range for sheep, together with our hops, mills, &c., this reservation would be self-sustaining; but the Indians failing to get the land and range promised them, and Congress cutting down the appropriations annually, they are fast losing confidence in promises, and, as a fearful result, a reaction has taken place. Scores are lost to the church—lost all their interest therein—and I fear will be forever lost.

A failure on the part of the Government to keep faith with the Indians is the cause of most of our troubles with them. The wisest man that ever lived has said, "Hope deferred maketh the heart sick." It is as true to-day as when first spoken.

(Indians, p. 41)

The greatest drawback to our Indians farming to any extent is the fact that they are entirely without oxen, wagons, harness, plows, and other farm-implements, and they complain bitterly of their "Great Father" for not giving them these articles, especially as they hear of Indians at other agencies receiving them, and they are constantly asking me, "Why cannot we have them?" and when I urge them on to work, their reply is, "How can we work without anything to work with? Give us what we need, and you will see what we can do." I feel this is true to a great degree, as it is utterly impossible for them to do much work so long as they are without proper means to do it with. I would recommend that such necessaries as cattle, wagons, harness, and the various farm implements be given to them, and I do not hesitate to say that the result will be very gratifying, and during the coming year more work will be done here than ever has been accomplished before. I believe the Brulés are now inclined to the ways of civilization, and that by kind and considerate treatment much can be achieved in another year. On the other hand, if they do not receive some encouragement from the Government they will become entirely discouraged, and will not try to aid themselves.

(Indians, p. 61)

POSTULATE III   Partial acculturation is the "cause" of *anomie*.

Dr. Seemann said he did not object to a religious discussion in that Society, for the form of religion might partake of a race character; but he objected to the introduction of sectarian views. With regard to cannibalism, he believed the real history of cannibalism had not yet been told. The fact was, that many of the nations had abandoned cannibalism from their own conviction of its atrocity; for instance, he believed that, if the missionaries had not gone to Fiji, cannibalism would soon have disappeared. His own impression was not favourable to missionary efforts. One of the supposed most successful missions was that to the Sandwich islands. After the murder of Captain Cook they were abandoned for a long time, but about twenty years afterwards a great change came over the natives. They had found that their own system had completely given way, and tried to live without any religion whatever. The Americans then sent a mission to the islands and converted them. But what was the condition of the people now? Every woman among them was a prostitute, and in about thirty years time there would not be one of the natives left. Morality was there at the lowest ebb; and he mentioned as an instance that a man connected with the missions offered his wife for two dollars.

(Africans, pp. 180–81)

In many cases that have come to my knowledge, the boys who have been brought up in the mission-schools, when they return to their homes become the worst characters in the country. This is to be accounted for in this way: they lose faith in their greegrees and other native customs, but do not gain a sound knowledge of Christianity, for it to have any effect upon them; and you will always find that the boys return to the native custom of wearing greegrees, trying people for witchcraft by the sarcy-wood test, etc.

(Africans, p. 202)

POSTULATE IV   If you've seen one, you've seen 'em all.

The condition of these Indians differs but little from all the wild tribes of the mountains, who know nothing of the restraints of civilization, except that they have for many years been friendly to the whites. They boast in all their talks and speeches that they have never "shed a drop of white men's blood," and those who know them best believe them entitled to the honor they claim, except, perhaps, some renegade Indian who may have attached himself to their enemies. Of course they are savages untamed, and wild as their mountains, ravines, and streams. They seem to copy and keep all the vices of the white men and but few of their virtues.

(Indians, p. 133)

I found that my Christian servants, although they believed in Jesus, and refused to work on the Sabbath, and sang hymns in a very high falsetto voice, made mental reservations about the eighth commandment; and their wives, according to all that I heard and saw, were equally ready to infringe the seventh. In plain words, I found that every Christian negress was a prostitute, and that every Christian negro was a thief.

(Africans, p. 165)

Some of these ideas are still expressed a century later—but they are becoming rare. It was against just such a background that anthropologists began their analyses of acculturation and culture contact.

8 PIRATICAL ACCULTURATION

W. J. McGee

HUMAN DEVELOPMENT is essentially social, and may be measured by the degree in which devices and ideas are interchanged and fertilized in the process of transfer—*i. e.*, by the
degree of acculturation. In the higher culture-grades (civilization
and enlightenment) the interchange is friendly and purposive;
this is amicable acculturation. In the lower culture-grades (savagery and barbarism), on the other hand, the interchange is
largely inimical and adventitious; this may be called piratical acculturation.

The law of piratical acculturation is strongly suggested by one
of the two phases of stone-work among the Seri Indians. The
first phase is indigenous and represents the commonplace industries of the tribe; it involves merely the selection and use of cobbles suitable for crushing shells and seeds, breaking bones, and
severing tough tissues with the aid of a larger stone as an anvil,
together with the subsequent retention and incidental wear of
especially convenient specimens; this phase of stone-work being
that already designated *protolithic* (McGee 1896). The second
phase involves chipping and purposive shaping of quartz or other
tough rock into arrowpoints and spearheads used for war purposes; it is little known and seldom practiced, the very name for
stone arrowpoint being known to but few of the tribe; since the
process involves preconception—including a definite model and a
distinctive design—it may be called *technolithic*. Manifestly the

---

Originally published in *American Anthropologist*, old series, Volume XI
(August 1898), 243–49.

two phases are widely distinct, not only in type of object but even more in the mental operations illustrated by the objects; for the protolithic implements represent undesigned adaptation and modification of cobbles picked up at random, while the technolithic weapons represent designed shaping of obdurate materials in accordance with preconceived ideas. The coexistence of the two incongruous types seemed puzzling at the outset, and was provisionally ascribed to the diverse occupations of the sexes, the women using the protolithic implements and certain of the warriors making and using the technolithic weapons. Further study showed that the arrowpoints imitate in every essential respect the aboriginal weapons of the hereditary enemies of the Seri, including the Papago and Yaki Indians; and this fact, coupled with the mysticism thrown around the chipped stone objects by the Seri shamans—a mysticism expressed by the ignorance of the name for stone arrowpoint among the common people—suggested that the idea of the technolithic weapons was acquired through warfare. Examination of other characteristics of the Seri Indians in the light of this interpretation served to explain various puzzling features displayed by them, and, at the same time, tended to establish the validity of the interpretation.

The Seri appear to be practically autochthonous; they have been at war with alien tribes almost constantly since the time of Columbus, and indeed long before, as indicated by archeologic evidence; and most of their arts and industries are exceedingly primitive. Yet here and there features imitating those characteristic of neighboring tribes or even of white men are found: They carry water in ollas which are fairly distinctive in type, though apparently based on alien models, yet make no other use of baked clay; they substitute cast-off rags and fabrics obtained by plunder for their own fabrics wrought with great labor from inferior fibers; since the adjacent waters have been navigated they have learned to collect flotsam, and to use tattered sailcloth in lieu of pelican-skin blankets, cask staves in lieu of shells as paddles for their balsas, hoop-iron in lieu of charred wood as arrowpoints for hunting, and iron spikes in lieu of bone harpoons for taking turtles; and, during recent years, each marauding group carries one or two guns taken from previous victims, though they seldom possess ammunition and make little good use of it when they do. Almost without exception, these modifications in custom have arisen without amicable relation and despite—indeed largely by reason of—deep-seated enmity against alien peoples.

Too little is known of the inner life of the Seri Indians to warrant statement of their own ideas concerning the acculturation whereby their customs are slowly changing; but something of the way in which piratical acculturation progresses may be learned from the history of the Papago and Apache Indians. These tribes have been bitterly inimical from time immemorial, the oldest cosmogonic legends of the Papago describing the separation of the peoples at the creation; yet there is hardly a custom, at least among the Papago, which has not been shaped partially or completely by the inimical tribe: The habitat of the Papago in the hard desert is that to which they have been forced by the predatory enemy; their industries are shaped by the conditions of the habitat and by the perpetual anticipation of attack; the traditions nightly recounted by the old men are chiefly of battle against the Apache; even the beliefs and ceremonies of the Papago are connected with that eternal vigilance which they have found the price of safety, or with the wiles and devices of the ever-present enemy. The early observations on the exoteric life of the Papago revealed plain evidences of an inimical acculturation, conspicuous as that of the Seri; while later studies of their esoteric life brought to light the concepts and motives by which the acculturation was guided. As the studies advanced it became manifest that the most important element in the acculturation is connected with belief. To the primitive mind the efficiency of a weapon is not mechanical but mystical, an expression of superphysical potency connected with the primitive pantheon of zoic deities; and each enemy strives constantly to coax or suborn the beast gods or other mystical potencies of the antagonist. So the Papago shaman seeks to identify the Apache deities from their symbols used in warfare, and then to invoke their aid; and the Papago warrior goes confidently to battle against the Apache when protected by a fetish including an Apache arrowpoint taken in conflict, and feels sure of victory if his warclub is made in imitation of that of the enemy and potentialized by a plume or inscription appealing to the Apache deity. This indicates the real essence of piratical acculturation; it represents the aim of shamans and warriors to obtain favor from the mystical powers of the enemy, and thus to win easy victory; and it results, incidentally, in painstaking imitation of articles seen and captured in battle. The commonplace explanation offered by the Seri warrior for carrying an ammunitionless gun is that "it frightens the enemy" (though both they and the enemy realize that even a Winchester with full magazine is less effective in the unskilled hands of one of their warriors than a bow and quiver of arrows, in the use of which they are marvelously expert), and in the light of Papago ideation it becomes clear that to the Seri the rifle is a symbol of mystical potency; and, in the same light, the Seri passion for rather clumsy stone arrowpoints in lieu of teeth or fish-spines or charred hard-wood becomes fairly clear.

Among many primitive peoples marriage is one of the most efficient means of acculturation. Numerous observers have noted that actual or ceremonial capture of the bride is a feature of marriage among certain tribes, and have assumed that this was the initial form of mating. Researches among the American Indians have shown that in the lowest of the four great culturestages paternity is ill-recognized or not recognized at all, and that mating is regulated chiefly by the female relatives of the bride with the sanction of their male kindred; so that, in this stage of development, marriage-by-capture of brides is hardly conceivable. It is probable that in this stage the blood-mingling of tribes arises chiefly in capture and enslavement or adoption of wounded or defeated warriors; yet there is a step early in the stage of paternal organization (perhaps arising late in the antecedent stage of maternal organization) in which a certain form of marriage-by-capture has arisen in America, as shown by Powell, and may easily have become prominent on other continents. When peoples are in that unstable condition of amity characterized by peaceful interludes between periods of strife—a condition found in higher savagery and much of barbarism—the intertribal association occasionally results in irregular matches between members of the alien tribes; such mating may be punished by one or both tribes, though sometimes there are special regulations under which the offense may be condoned—*e. g.*, the groom or the couple may be subjected to fine, to ostracism until children are born, etc. While both bride and groom may incur displeasure and even risk of life through such matches, there is a chance of attendent advantage which measurably counterbalances the risk, for the groom, especially if of the weaker tribe, may eventually gain the amity and support of his wife's kinsmen, while the eldermen and elderwomen of one or both tribes may recognize the desirability of a coalition tending to unite the tribes and thus to strengthen both. There is reason to suppose that in earlier savagery the irregular mating was frequently but a source of intertribal strife, and that the custom of condonation arose slowly and gradually transformed such unions into intertribal bands. Certainly the recognition and regulation of intertribal marriage are common among primitive peoples and are expressed in the customs of exogamy and endogamy; and the researches among the native Americans have shown that the customs expressed by these terms are correlative, the former referring to the clan and the latter to the tribe or other group; they have also shown that the limitation of exogamy and the extension of endogamy are effective devices for uniting tribal interests and promoting peace.

The definiteness and complexity of marriage regulations among all primitive peoples thus far studied imply clear recognition of the importance of what may be called marital acculturation; yet they do not necessarily indicate the motives in the minds of the tribesmen. Fortunately the motives are known in some cases, and are found to have a strong fiducial factor: Among the clans of the Kwakiutl, as shown by Boas, the aim of marriage settlement is the acquisition, not of property or kindred *per se,* but of family traditions—*i. e.,* of the gods to which the traditions relate; among many tribes the marriage of a Wolf-man and an Eagle-woman results in an exoteric bond between the clans which, viewed from the esoteric side seen by the Indians themselves, is a union between the Ancient of Wolves and the Ancient of Eagles, and thus a coalition of mystical potencies able to shape the careers of both clans, and, by combination, to give them enlarged domain; the same sentiment survived in ancient Greece and Rome, in which a feature of marriage was the disposition of the lares and penates.

Now, the marital acculturation characteristic of barbarism is not strictly inimical, since the antagonistic element (which survives in curious fashion even in civilization and enlightenment) is gradually subordinated; neither can it be regarded as strictly amicable by reason of this antagonism. On the whole, it seems fairly clear that intertribal marriage, whether by the espousal of captured warriors by women of victorious groups, by common agreement, by mutually arranged elopement, or by actual or symbolic capture of the bride, is simply a means of uniting aliens largely through their deities, and thereby of raising acculturation from the martial plane to that of amicable interchange.

There is a third phase of acculturation which is commonly recognized, and indeed implicitly assumed to represent the sum of social interaction; it arises in barter and matures in commerce. In this phase the idea of property grows dominant; the interchange begins with personal property and passes to lands and waters; and its effect is to unify ideas and motives and to bring peoples and nations into harmony.

There remains a phase of acculturation which is unimportant among primitive peoples, increasingly important in civilization, and paramount in enlightenment; it is the free or regulated interchange of ideas by processes which in the last analysis are essentially educative.

Briefly, there are four phases of acculturation which practically represent stages in human development. The first phase is characteristic of savagery; it is expressed in the imitation of weapons and symbols, with the esoteric purpose of invoking new deities;

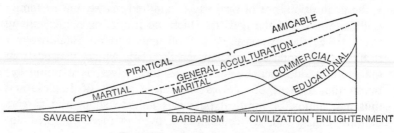

Four Phases of Acculturation

it may be styled martial acculturation. The second phase is characteristic of barbarism, though arising earlier and persisting later; it is expressed in semi-antagonistic mating between tribes, with the initial esoteric purpose of strengthening tribal pantheons; it may be called marital acculturation. These two phases are essentially piratical, though the antagonistic element is gradually weakened as amity arises with increasing intelligence. The third phase is characteristic of civilization, though it begins in barbarism and plays a role in enlightenment; it is expressed in interchange of goods with the purpose (at first esoteric and afterward exoteric) of personal profit or gain; it may be designated commercial acculturation. The fourth phase is characteristic of enlightenment, though its beginnings may be found much lower; it is expressed in the spontaneous interchange of ideas for the purpose of increasing human power over nature; it may provisionally be styled educational acculturation. The last two phases are essentially amicable.

The four stages combine to express the law of acculturation, the applications of which are innumerable: In the light of the law it becomes easy to understand how inimical tribes are gradually brought to use similar weapons and implements, to adopt similar modes of thinking and working, to worship similar deities, and thus to pass from complete dissonance to potential harmony, which becomes actual concord whensoever the exigencies of primitive life demand; thus the course of that convergent development, which is the most important lesson the American aborigines have given to the world, is made clear. Based as it is on scattered facts in the history of mankind, the law seems to illumine the history of acculturation; it indicates that the human prototype was too provincial to profit by acculturation, and lived unto himself like the beasts of the field; also that piratical acculturation of the martial type began early in savagery, as exemplified by the Seri Indians, gradually declining as a higher type arose; that marital acculturation became dominant, as exemplified by most of our Indian tribes and by the barbaric peoples of other continents; and that amicable acculturation of two types succeeded to give character to civilization, and prepare the way for the enlightenment already illumining the world.

The relations between the stages of acculturation are set forth graphically in the accompanying diagram, which is designed to show the cumulative progress of general acculturation, together with the rise and decadence of the special forms of acculturation characteristic of the four principal stages in human development. The successive curves in the diagram indicate the rhythmic character of progress and the cumulative value of its interrelated factors. Representing as it does the law of normal growth, and indeed of cosmic progress, the diagram is widely applicable; in the special case under consideration it exhibits relations more clearly and in a more natural manner than any arbitrary scheme of typographic arrangement, and at least suggests the complex history of the long course of human acculturation beginning with savagery and coming up to enlightenment.

9 THE PSYCHOLOGICAL FACTOR
IN THE DEPOPULATION OF MELANESIA

W. H. R. Rivers

THE PAPERS BY members of the Melanesian Mission and other workers in Melanesia published in this book show conclusively that this great archipelago is undergoing a process of depopulation. In some parts the decline is taking place so rapidly that at no distant date the islands will wholly lose their native inhabitants unless something is done to stay its progress.

In the New Hebrides the loss of native population is especially great and is progressing rapidly. Not long ago Fate, or Sandwich Island, had a considerable population in which, as usual in Melanesia, it was possible to distinguish between the bush-people and those living near the coast. Now the bush-people have wholly disappeared and the few survivors of the coastal districts have left the main island and live on one or other of the small islands, such as Eretap and Erekor, which fringe its coasts. In the island of Epi further north, the numbers of the people are said to be rapidly declining.

In Espiritu Santo, usually known as Santo, the largest island of the New Hebrides, the inhabitants of several villages on the west coast have entirely disappeared and their places have been taken by a few wretched people who have moved down from the interior. The little island of Tangoa was formerly the site of three villages, each of which must have been a community of considerable size, for the people are said to have had different

Originally published as Chapter VIII of *Essays on the Depopulation of Melanesia*, edited by W. H. R. Rivers, Cambridge University Press, 1922, pp. 84–113. Reprinted with permission of the publisher.

dialects. Now all the people of the island live in one small village. At the southern end of Santo the people of Vulua twenty years ago numbered at least 200 according to the estimate of the Rev. F. G. Bowie, the missionary of the district. Now there is only a miserable handful of people, herded together in one village with hardly any children, and they will soon be altogether extinct.

In the Santa Cruz group, large islands which are said to have been well peopled are now uninhabited, the decline here having been especially great during the last few years. In the Solomon Islands, the tale is less pitiful, but here also the population of many islands is diminishing so rapidly that unless something is done to stay the decline, it will soon share the fate which has already overtaken so many parts of the New Hebrides.

The Rev. C. E. Fox of the Melanesian Mission has given a striking picture of the decrease of population in San Cristoval in the Solomons. The Spaniards in 1546 spoke of the large population of the island (Mendaña 1901). At Wango in 1887 H. B. Guppy (1887), estimated the population at about 500; now there are less than 100. From one hill-top Mr Fox was shown the sites of forty-six once flourishing villages of which only three are now inhabited.

Since my visit to Melanesia in 1914 the archipelago has been visited by the severe epidemic of influenza which, here as elsewhere in the Pacific, has done much to hasten the process by which the people of Oceania are disappearing.

Various causes have been given to account for the dying out of the people, different factors having been stressed by different authors. I propose to attempt a more complete survey of the causes which lead to decrease of population.

Before beginning this survey it will be well to deal briefly with a supposed fact which has frequently been brought forward as a means of accounting for the decrease of the population of Melanesia. It has been supposed that the Melanesians were already a dying people before the European invasion, and that their decline was due to faults inherent in their own culture. In the first place there is no evidence of any value that the people were decreasing in number before the advent of Europeans.

It may be true that here and there the people already showed signs of diminution on the arrival of the missionaries.[1] It must be remembered, however, that the people had already been subject for many years to certain European influences, such as that of the sandal-wood hunters, which were far from being of a harmless kind.

When apologists for the effects of their own civilisation give reasons for the supposed original decadence, these often bear their own refutation on the face. Thus, one writer blames the heathen custom of polygamy, but in the same paragraph states that the practice is confined to the few.

Another cause which has been put forward is the special kind of consanguineous union known as the cross-cousin marriage.

This marriage is orthodox in several parts of Melanesia and is especially frequent and important in Fiji. This subject was fully investigated by the Commission which more than twenty years ago inquired into the decrease of the native population of Fiji. In their *Report* (1896), which forms a storehouse of most valuable facts concerning the topics of this book, it is shown conclusively that this factor had not contributed towards Fijian decadence, but rather that these consanguineous marriages were more fruitful than marriage between wholly unrelated persons.

I shall deal presently with native customs in relation to our subject and hope to show that it is rather the indiscriminate and undiscriminating interference with them which stands forth prominently among the causes of decay.

I can now consider the conditions to which real efficacy in the process of destruction can be assigned. In studying this subject the first point to bear in mind is the double character of the factors upon which fluctuation of population depends, a double character which holds good of Melanesia as of more civilised parts of the world. Diminution of population may be due to increase of the death-rate or to decrease of the birth-rate, or to both combined. I can bring forward evidence to show that both

---

[1] In some cases this decrease in early times is almost certain. Thus, there is little doubt that the northern end of Ysabel in the Solomons was decimated by the activity of the head-hunters of Ruviana and Eddystone, but this decrease was purely local and had no appreciable influence on the general population of Melanesia.

factors have been active in Melanesia. I will begin with the conditions which have affected the death-rate.

In a subject in which we can find little on which to pride ourselves, it is satisfactory to be able to exclude one cause of depopulation which has contributed in no small measure to the disappearance of native races in other parts of the world. There has been no deliberate attempt to exterminate the people such as has disgraced the history of our relations with regions more suited to European habitation than the sweltering and unhealthy islands of Melanesia. The injurious influences due to European rulers and settlers have been unwitting. Owing to the need for the labour of those accustomed to the tropics, it has always been in the interests of the settlers that the native population shall be alive and healthy. In so far as native decay is due to European influence we have to lay the blame on ignorance and lack of foresight, not on any deliberate wish to destroy.

In considering the death of a people as of an individual, it is natural to think first of disease. Disease is the name we give to a group of processes by which the size of a population is adjusted so as to enable it best to utilise the available means of subsistence. Before the arrival of Europeans, Melanesia had its own diseases, by means of which Nature helped to keep the population within bounds. Everything goes to show that the population of Melanesia was well within the limits which the country was capable of supporting, but it is not so certain that it was far within this capacity in relation to the very simple means the people possessed for exploiting its resources. So far as we can tell, there had been set up a state of equilibrium between the size of the population and the available resources of the country. Recent knowledge goes to show that the diseases due to infective parasites tend to set up a state of tolerance and habituation which renders a people less prone to succumb to their ravages, and there is no reason to suppose that Melanesia was any exception in this respect. Thus the people are largely habituated to the malaria which certainly existed among them before the coming of European influence.

Into this community thus adapted to the infective agents of their own country, the invaders brought a number of new diseases: measles, dysentery, probably tubercle and influenza, and last but unfortunately far from least potent, venereal disease. These maladies had effects far more severe than those they bring upon ourselves, partly because they found a virgin soil, partly because the native therapeutic ideas were not adapted to the new diseases, so that remedies were often used which actually increased their harmfulness. Many of these introduced diseases are still drawing a large toll on the numbers and energies of the people, the two which seem to be exerting the most steady influence, so far as my observations show, being dysentery and tubercle.

A second group of introduced causes of destruction is composed of what may be called the social poisons, such as alcohol and opium. Though it is possible that the people use tobacco somewhat to excess, the only poison which needs to be considered in Melanesia is alcohol. In certain parts of Melanesia there is no question that it has exerted in the past and is still exerting a most deleterious influence, but it is satisfactory to be able to say that its noxious influence has been reduced to negligible importance in those parts of the archipelago wholly subject to British rule, where it is penal to sell or give alcohol to a native. Alcohol is still, however, potent as a cause of disease and death in the New Hebrides. In those islands there are regulations against the sale of alcohol to natives, but under the present Condominium Government they are not obeyed.

A third direct cause of increase of death-rate is the introduction of fire-arms, by means of which the comparatively harmless warfare of the natives is given a far more deadly turn. This cause is still active to some extent in the New Hebrides owing to breaking of the regulations of the Condominium Government, but fire-arms have never had great importance as an instrument of destruction in Melanesia.

I come to a more serious cause when I consider European influence upon native customs. I begin with one which excites perennial interest whenever native welfare is discussed. Before the advent of Europeans the people of some islands went wholly nude or wore only garments, if they can be so called, which fulfilled neither of the two chief purposes for which the clothing of civilised people is designed. In other parts the native clothing consisted of petticoats, loin-cloths, or other simple garments thoroughly adapted to the necessities of the climate. One of the first results of European influence was the adoption of the clothing of the visitors, and clothes were adopted in such a manner as to accentuate the evils which they necessarily brought with them. The Melanesian is not uncleanly. He bathes frequently, and where he preserves his native mode of clothing, his ablutions are amply sufficient for cleanliness. When he wears European garments, he fails to adopt measures, such as the frequent change of clothing, which then become necessary. He continues to bathe in his clothes, and instead of changing his garments frequently, wears them continuously till they are ragged, and even when new clothing is obtained, it is put over the old.

It is a great mistake, often made, to blame the missionaries for this use of foreign clothing. It is true that its use was directly encouraged by the early missionaries, but this encouragement was unnecessary. To the native, trousers and coats are the distinctive mark of the white man, and nothing short of prohibition could have prevented their use. Where we can now see the missionaries to have been at fault is that they did not recognise the evil of the innovation and set themselves steadily to minimise it. They should have insisted upon attention to the elementary principles of the hygiene which the use of clothes involves.

At the present time the influence of missionaries is steadily directed to this end. Having been privileged to live among missionaries of different schools of thought in Melanesia, I can testify that no subject is more frequently discussed and more thoroughly and anxiously considered than how to lessen the use and injurious influence of European clothing.

Another modification of native custom, which is less widely recognised, but in my experience quite as much in need of consideration at the present time, is housing. The native Melanesian house is usually rain-proof and of good proportions, while owing to its mode of construction it is well ventilated and thoroughly adapted to the climate. Instead of being content with houses of similar construction or with houses of the kind used by Europeans living in other tropical countries, settlers have built houses with thick walls and very imperfect means of ventilation. These have in some cases been copied by the natives, or even built by the missionaries for the use of their followers. Such buildings might have been specially devised for the propagation of tubercle, and if they are allowed to be built will certainly increase the already far too heavy ravages of this disease.

The modifications of housing and clothing which I have just considered touch especially the material side of life. I have now to consider a number of modifications and interferences with native custom which I believe to have been quite as important, if not more important, in the production of native decadence. When Melanesia became subject to Europeans, magistrates and missionaries were sent to rule and direct the lives of the people. They found in existence a number of institutions and customs which were, or seemed to them to be, contrary to the principles of morality. Such customs were usually forbidden without any inquiry into their real nature, without knowledge of the part they took in native life, and without any attempt to discriminate between their good and bad elements. Thus, in the Solomon Islands the rulers stopped the special kind of warfare known as head-hunting, without at all appreciating the vast place it took in the religious and ceremonial lives of the people, without realising the gap it would leave in their daily interests, a blank far more extensive than that due to the mere cessation of a mode of warfare. Again, in Fiji, the custom according to which the men of the community slept apart from the women in a special house, a widespread custom in Melanesia, seemed to the missionaries contrary to the ideals of the Christian family, and the custom was stopped or discouraged without it being realised that the segregation of the sexes formed an effectual check on too free intercourse between them.

In the New Hebrides again, the missionaries put an end to, or where they did not destroy, treated with a barely veiled contempt, a highly complicated organisation arising out of beliefs connected with the cult of dead ancestors. In some cases it was apparent enough that the institution with all its elaborate ceremonial was heathen and prejudiced church attendance, while elsewhere stress was laid on occasional revels and dances which gave opportunity for licence. It was not recognised that in forbidding or discouraging without inquiry, they were destroying institutions which had the most far-reaching ramifications through the social and economical life of the people.

If these and similar institutions had been studied before they were destroyed or discouraged, it would have been found possible to discriminate between those features which were noxious and needed repression or amendment, and those which were beneficial to the welfare of the community. Even when their destruction was deemed necessary, something could have been done to replace the social sanctions of which the people were thus deprived. The point I wish to emphasise is that through this unintelligent and undiscriminating action towards native institutions, the people were deprived of nearly all that gave interest to their lives. I have now to suggest that this loss of interest forms one of the reasons, if indeed it be not the most potent of all the reasons, to which the native decadence is due.

It may at first sight seem far-fetched to suppose that such a factor as loss of interest in life could ever produce the dying out of a people, but my own observations have led me to the conclusion that its influence is so great that it can hardly be overrated. I venture therefore to consider it at some length.

When you inquire of those who have lived long in Melanesia concerning the illness and mortality of the natives, you are struck by the frequency of reference to the ease with which the native dies. Over and over again one is told of a native who seemed hale and well until, after a day or two of some apparently trivial illness, he gives up the ghost without any of the signs which among ourselves usually give ample warning of the impending fate. A native who is ill loses heart at once. He has no desire to live, and perhaps announces that he is going to die when the onlooker can see no ground for his belief.

The matter becomes more easy to understand if we consider the ease with which the people are killed by magic or as the result of the infraction of a taboo. The evidence is overwhelming that such people as the Melanesians will sicken and die in a few hours or days as the result of the belief that an enemy has chosen them as the victim of his spells, or that they have, wittingly or unwittingly, offended against some religious taboo. If people who are interested in life and do not wish to die can be killed in a few days or even hours by a mere belief, how much more easy it is to understand that a people who have lost all interest in life should become the prey of any morbid agency acting through the body as well as through the mind. It is this evidence of the enormous influence of the mind upon the body among the Melanesians and other lowly peoples that first led me to attach so much importance to loss of interest as the primary cause of their dying out. Once this belief has been formulated, there is seen to be much definite evidence in Melanesia to support it.

Certain islands and districts of Melanesia show a degree of vitality in striking contrast with the rest. These exceptional cases fall into two classes: one includes those islands or parts of islands where the people have so far been fierce and strong enough to withstand European influence. There are still certain parts in Melanesia which as yet the footprint of the white man has not reached, and others where, after successful encounters with punitive expeditions, the people still believe themselves to be a match for the invader. Here the old zest and interest in life persist and the people are still vigorous and abundant.

The other group of peoples who show signs of vitality are those who have adopted Christianity, not merely because it is the religion of the powerful white man, but with a whole-hearted enthusiasm which has given them a renewed interest in life. Here the numbers are increasing after an initial drop. Christianity and the occupations connected with it have given the people a new interest to replace that of their indigenous culture, and with this interest has come the desire to live.

The special point I wish to make in my contribution to this book is that interest in life is the primary factor in the welfare of a people. The new diseases and poisons, the innovations in clothing, housing and feeding, are only the immediate causes of mortality. It is the loss of interest in life underlying these more obvious causes which gives them their potency for evil and allows them to work such ravages upon life and health.

I can pass to the second of the two groups of influences by which a people decline in number, having so far dealt only with those which increase the death-rate. I have now to consider those which produce decline by diminishing the birth-rate and will begin by stating briefly the evidence that this factor has played and is playing a part in the dying out of the Melanesians. This evidence has been gained by a mode of inquiry adopted originally for purely scientific purposes. When in Torres Straits with Dr Haddon twenty-four years ago, I discovered that the people preserved in their memories with great fidelity a full and accurate record of their descent and relationships (Rivers 1910). It was possible to collect pedigrees so ample in all collateral lines that they could serve as a source of statistical inquiry into such features as the average size of a family, infant mortality, and other subjects which furnish the basis for conclusions concerning fluctuations of population. I have found this interest in genealogy wherever I have worked, and the collection of pedigrees has always formed the basis of my ethnographic inquiries. In Melanesia this instrument shows conclusively that the fall in numbers is due quite as much to decrease of the birth-rate as to increase of the death-rate.

I will begin with the evidence from the Solomon Islands. I have a large collection of pedigrees from two islands of the group, Eddystone Island and Vella Lavella. The result of the analysis of these pedigrees is given in the two following tables, which make it possible to compare, if only in a rough manner, the fertility of the present with that of preceding generations. The tables record in percentages the size of the family, the proportion of childless marriages, and other data for three successive generations. The chief difficulty arose in dealing with the third or present generation, for its marriages evidently include a number which, though childless or with only a small family at present, may be expected to result in offspring, or more offspring, in time. A certain number of marriages, viz. 9·1 per cent. of this generation were therefore set aside as doubtful, as shown in the eighth column of the table. It is possible that a certain number of the marriages included in the childless category of the fourth column may also become fruitful, and there may also be a slight increase in the figures recording the number of children per marriage. Thus, though the record of childless marriages only includes cases where it seemed safe to assume that the marriage would be permanently sterile, the figure is probably somewhat larger than it would be if the record could be taken ten years hence. Similarly, the figures giving the size of the family in this generation would also show some increase.

The division into generations was necessarily rough, but was effected before any attempt was made to estimate fertility. The objections which I have considered do not apply to the comparison of the two earlier generations, though there is the possibility that persons of the earlier generation may have been altogether omitted from the pedigrees because, owing to the absence of children, they were not of social importance, so that their existence had been forgotten. It is possible that this factor may have come into action to some extent in the pedigrees from Vella Lavella, but it is improbable that it has had any influence on the Eddystone figures, for these were collected from several sources and verified in many ways. It is possible that persons who failed

Table I. Eddystone Island

Generation	Total number of marriages	Total number of children	Childless marriages, in per cent	Marriages with			Number of children doubtful	Children who died young, in per cent	
				1 or 2 children	3 to 5 children	6 or more children		M	F
I	207	447	19.4	43.5	32.8	4.3	–	6.4	4.5
II	295	379	46.1	29.0	18.9	3.3	2.7	18.5	8.1
III	110	72	52.7	32.7	5.5	0	9.1	31.1	14.8

Table II. Vella Lavella

Generation	Total number of marriages	Total number of children	Childless marriages, in per cent	Marriages with			Number of children doubtful	Children who died young, in per cent	
				1 or 2 children	3 to 5 children	6 or more children		M	F
I	116	279	12.1	4.2	41.4	4.3	–	1.7	2.7
II	209	297	35.4	37.8	21.1	1.4	4.3	6.3	3.7
III	57	15	71.9	22.8	0	0	5.3	25.0	28.6

to marry may have been omitted, but improbable that persons who married would have escaped record.

The Eddystone figures are more satisfactory than those of Vella Lavella in many respects, for they are based on a fairly complete genealogical record of the whole population of the island, whereas the pedigrees of Vella Lavella are only samples collected here and there from a population very much larger than that of Eddystone.

The Eddystone figures show decisively how great has been the influence of some factor or factors leading to decrease in the size of the family. Childless marriages increased in frequency from 19·4 to 46·1 per cent. in passing from the first to the second generation. As I have already mentioned the increase to 52·7 per cent. in the present generation may possibly be illusory owing to certain families being still incomplete, but this factor cannot possibly explain the great increase in the number of childless marriages in the earlier generation. Equally striking are the figures showing the total number of children recorded for each generation in the pedigrees. Whereas two generations ago, 207 marriages produced 447 children, or well over two children per marriage, the figures for the following generation were 379 children from 295 marriages or an average of less than a child and a half per marriage. In the present generation the record is even worse, only 72 children having been born from 110 marriages, or less than one child per marriage. This figure may be expected, however, to become somewhat larger when recent marriages have produced their full effect upon the population.

The figures recording the size of the family are equally depressing. They show a striking decrease in the number of families of more than five. The last two columns give the infant mortality of the two sexes. It is a question whether children who died young may not have been in many cases forgotten in the case of the earliest generation and therefore omitted when the pedigrees were collected, and in this case the increase in infant mortality would not be as great as represented in the table. It will be noted that the mortality is definitely greater in the case of male children, but here again there is the possibility that male children who died young would be remembered better and that some female children who died in infancy may have been forgotten and therefore omitted.

The record of the island of Vella Lavella in the Solomons is similar in its nature but shows an even more serious decrease of fertility. As I have already mentioned, however, the record is less trustworthy. The island is much larger than Eddystone and the figures given in the table are derived from random samples taken from various villages of the coast. The record differs from that of Eddystone in that the number of childless marriages has shown a progressive increase to the present day, but as I did not know the people and their circumstances as I knew them in Eddystone no great significance should be attached to the figure for the present generation. It is significant, however, that the proportion of childless marriages two generations ago, viz. 12·1 per cent., does not differ greatly from the Eddystone figure.

Especially noteworthy is the total disappearance of families of more than two children in the present generation of Vella Lavella. Equally striking is the great diminution in the total number of children in this generation, the names of only fifteen children from marriages of this generation being recorded.

The two islands which show this striking fall in birth-rate are of especial interest in that in them, and especially in Eddystone, the chief factors to which the dying out of peoples is usually ascribed are absent. In Eddystone, about which a residence of several months enables me to speak with confidence, there is no record of any very severe epidemics. Tubercle and dysentery, the two most deadly diseases in Melanesia, do not appear to be, or to have been, especially active; and though both the chief forms of venereal disease exist in the island, they do not seem to have done any great amount of mischief. The island has never had a white missionary; the people still wear their native dress and live in houses of native build. Alcohol is little known and other poisons not at all, while any effect of fire-arms on mortality is negligible. Few of the people have left the island as labour or for any other reason. All the factors to which other writers in this book ascribe the decrease of the population of Melanesia are practically absent, and yet we have a striking diminution of population, due in the main to decrease of the birth-rate.

If now we pass from material to mental factors, the decrease in the birth-rate becomes easier to understand. No one could be long in Eddystone without recognising how great is the people's lack of interest in life and to what an extent the zest has gone out of their lives. This lack of interest is largely due to the abolition of head-hunting by the British Government. This practice formed the centre of a social and religious institution which took an all-pervading part in the lives of the people. The heads sought in the head-hunting expeditions were needed in order to propitiate the ancestral ghosts on such occasions as building a new house for a chief or making a new canoe, while they were also offered in sacrifice at the funeral of a chief. Moreover, head-hunting was not only necessary for the due performance of the religious rites of the people, but it stood in the closest relation to pursuits of an economic kind. The actual head-hunting expedition only lasted a few weeks, and the actual fighting often only a few hours, but this was only the culminating point of a process lasting over years. It was the rule that new canoes should be made for an expedition to obtain heads, and the manufacture of these meant work of an interesting kind lasting certainly for many months, probably for years. The process of canoe-building was accompanied throughout by rites and feasts which not only excited the liveliest interest but also acted as stimuli to various activities of horticulture and pig-breeding. As the date fixed for the expedition approached other rites and feasts were held, and these were still more frequent and on a larger scale after the return of a successful expedition. In stopping the practice of head-hunting the rulers from an alien culture were abolishing an institution which had its roots in the religion of the people and spread its branches throughout nearly every aspect of their culture, and by this action they deprived the people of the greater part of their interest in life, while at the same time they undermined the religion of the people without any attempt to put another in its place.

I need only consider here very briefly the agencies to which this fall in birth-rate is due. It is well known that certain forms of venereal disease will produce sterility, and it is noteworthy that the dying out of the people of Vulua is ascribed by their neighbours to the ravages of this disease brought by returning labourers from Queensland. There is little doubt, however, that if we take Melanesia as a whole, causes of this kind are trivial or of slight importance as compared with voluntary restriction. Throughout Melanesia the people are acquainted with various means of producing abortion and also practise measures which they believe to prevent conception, and processes of this kind almost certainly form the main agencies in lowering the birth-rate. We have here only another effect of the loss of interest in life which I have held to be so potent in enhancing mortality. The people say themselves: "Why should we bring children into the world only to work for the white man?" Measures which, before the coming of the European, were used chiefly to prevent illegitimacy have become the instrument of racial suicide.

It is satisfactory that before I leave this subject I am able to point to a brighter side. I have already said that in certain parts of Melanesia the downward movement has been arrested and that the people now show signs of growth. I mentioned also that this was occurring especially in islands where the people have really taken to their hearts the lessons of their Christian teachers.

The teachings of the missionaries concerning the evils of racial suicide may possibly have contributed in some degree to this recovery, though I doubt whether in general they have been aware of the part which voluntary restriction has taken. I believe that their influence has lain much more in the fact that the religion they have taught has given the people a renewed interest in life which has again made it worth while to bring children into the world.

Until now I have said nothing of a cause of depopulation which has been especially active in Melanesia. The causes I have so far considered have been treated under two headings, according as they have enhanced the death-rate or lowered the birth-rate. The labour-traffic which I have now to consider is more complex and involves both of these factors.

In dealing with this cause of depopulation it is well that it is possible to begin by distinguishing between the traffic as it was and as it is. It would be difficult to exaggerate the evil influence of the process by which the natives of Melanesia were taken to Australia and elsewhere to labour for the white man. It forms one of the blackest of civilisation's crimes. Not least among its evils was the manner of its ending, when large numbers of people who had learnt by many years' experience to adapt themselves to civilised ways were, in the process of so-called repatriation, thrust back into savagery without help of any kind. The misery thus caused and the resulting disaffection not only underlie most of the open troubles in the recent history of Melanesia, but by the production of a state of helplessness and hopelessness have contributed as much as any other factors to the decline of the population.

I must not, however, dwell on the crimes and mistakes of the past. Our object in this book is to call attention to existing evils in the hope that they may be remedied before it is too late. At the present time Melanesians are only recruited as labourers to work within the confines of Melanesia, and both the recruitment and the conditions of labour are subject to Government control. Its grosser evils have been removed, at any rate in those parts of Melanesia which are wholly governed by Great Britain, though it would appear that there are still very grave defects in those parts of Melanesia under the control of the Condominium Government. But however closely and wisely the traffic is controlled, the removal from their own homes of the younger men, and still more of the younger women, of a declining population is not a factor which can tend to arrest the decline or convert it into a movement in the opposite direction. Even in its improved form, and limited to Melanesia though it be, the labour traffic continues to act as a cause of depopulation. It acts directly by taking men and women away from their homes when they should be marrying and producing children, while other evils are that, as at present conducted, the traffic tends to spread disease and to undermine an influence which I believe to be at the present time the most potent for good in Melanesia, the work of the missionaries. Moreover, the use of natives as labourers on plantations fails to give that interest in life which, as I have tried to show, forms the most essential factor in maintaining the health of a people.

Thus far in this contribution I have been dealing with the causes to which the dying out of the Melanesian people must be ascribed. To use medical language suitable to such a state of affairs as that recorded in this volume, I have been attempting to make a diagnosis. It is now time to turn to treatment and inquire what can be done to arrest the decline and make the Melanesians again a thriving and vigorous people. If I am right in my diagnosis that the chief cause of decline is lack of interest, it is not difficult to see the general lines upon which successful treatment must be based.

I shall pass, therefore, with a mere mention those lines of treatment, dictated by the ordinary principles of hygiene, by means of which faults of clothing, housing and feeding may be remedied, and shall confine my attention to the factor which I believe to stand first and foremost among the causes of the dying out of the Melanesian—the loss of interest in life from which at present he is suffering.

The main problem of treatment is how far it is possible to restore the old interests, or maintain them where they have not yet been destroyed, and how far they must be replaced by others. As I have already mentioned, there are still certain parts of Melanesia where the old life still persists with but little change. It would be an interesting experiment to see how far it is possible in these cases to maintain the old interests and make them the foundation on which to build a culture which would not conflict with the ethical and social ideals of the people who have come to be their rulers.

To most of the writers in this volume, and probably to most of its readers, such an experiment would not appeal, for it is naturally to the total replacement of the old religious interests by new that they will look for the remedy. It may be instructive, however, to consider for a moment how far it would be possible to modify the old customs and institutions of the people; to preserve enough to maintain interest while removing all those features which conflict with the ideals of modern civilisation. For this purpose I will take an extreme case and consider whether it would have been possible to have modified such a practice as the head-hunting of the Solomons. At first sight it might seem a hopeless task, and so it would be if one attended only to the outward practice obvious to the European observer and ignored the meaning which the institution of head-hunting bears to those who practice it. If we turn to this inner meaning, the case becomes less difficult. The essential motive for the head-hunting of Melanesia is the belief that on various important occasions, and especially on occasions connected with the chiefs, a human head is necessary as an offering to the ancestral ghosts. There is little doubt that the custom is a relic of an earlier practice of human sacrifice, and the head-hunting of the Solomons was but little removed from this, for till recently it was the custom to bring home from expeditions captives who were killed when some important ceremony created the need for a head. In other parts of the world there is reason to believe that, where human beings were formerly sacrificed, the place of the human victim has been taken by an animal, and even that the place of a human head has been taken by that of an animal. I have no doubt that it would have been possible to effect such a substitution in the Solomons, that officials with the necessary knowledge of native custom and belief, and with some degree of sympathy with them, could have brought about such a substitution and thus avoided the loss of life and money which has accompanied the suppression of head-hunting in the Solomons. At the same time they would have kept up the interest of the people in their native institutions until such time as the march of events produced new interests, including new religious interests, connected with the culture which was being brought to bear upon their lives.

The substitution of the head of a pig for that of a human being would not, however, wholly solve the problem. I have already mentioned that the chief stimulus to the making of canoes in Eddystone Island came out of the practice of head-hunting. The substitution of a porcine for a human head, while satisfying many of the ceremonial needs, would leave no motive for the manufacture of new canoes and the maintenance of this industry. Here it would be necessary to provide some new motive for the making of canoes. This might be found in the introduction of canoe races as elements in the ceremonial connected with the ancestral offerings, while to this might be added economic motives connected with fishing or trade. It is probable that in such a process of substitution the native canoe would be displaced by the boat of European build, but much as this would be regretted by the anthropologist or the artist, this form of craft would be probably fully as efficacious in maintaining interest and zest in life and would thus contribute to the purpose which the writers of this volume have before them. Only, it is essential that the change should grow naturally out of native institutions and should not be forced upon the people without their consent and without any attempt to rouse their interest.

In this brief sketch of the lines upon which native customs might be modified so as to bring them into harmony with European culture I have already mentioned incidentally the introduction of new economic interests. I must now consider this subject more explicitly. In former days the chief need of the people outside their own island or district was for certain weapons and for kinds of food which did not flourish at home. Here it is noteworthy that the need for food from without was often connected with religion. Thus, one of the chief reasons why the people of Eddystone went elsewhere for the taro which did not flourish in their own island was its inclusion among the foods which should be used in certain ceremonial feasts, an example which shows how motives due to trade and the interest arising therefrom are often closely connected with religion. If religious interest flags, other interests, which might at first sight seem wholly devoid of any connection with it, will flag also.

At the present time the natives of Melanesia have acquired certain new needs through their contact with European influence, especially the need for tobacco and calico, while in many parts external influence has produced a liking for rice and other introduced foods which have had a most destructive influence on native horticulture. In order to obtain the articles thus needed the Melanesian has to do a certain amount of work, chiefly that involved in the collection and drying of coconuts to make copra. This takes little of his time and has in it little or nothing to arouse interest.

One of the chief needs of Melanesia is that the native shall be given a real interest in the economic development of his country. The Melanesian is a keen trader and there are cases in the New Hebrides in which he has shown much ability when he has entered as an ordinary trader into competition with the European. There is no question that if he were given a fair chance, he could take an important part in any organisation which had as its object the encouragement of native industry. Until recently the missionary societies of Melanesia have made no attempt at industrial development, either to encourage the old industries or to introduce new, and the Government has done even less in this direction. The only neighbouring region of Oceania where any progress in this direction has been made is in Torres Straits, where "The Papuan Industries Company" has endeavoured to give to the natives that share in the management of the industries of their country which is the best means of bringing back the old interest and zest in life. In other parts of the world, and pre-eminently in West Africa, such movements have had the most striking success and there is no reason why the success should not be as great in Melanesia.

It is doubtful, however, whether the modification of native custom and the replacement of old economic interests by new will be sufficient to allow the Melanesian to enter once more upon an upward course of progress. The old life of the people was permeated through and through by interests of a religious kind, based on a profound belief in continued existence after death and in the influence of the dead upon the welfare of the living. Experience has amply shown that Christianity is capable of giving the people an interest in life which can take the place of that due to their indigenous religion. Even if it were thought desirable to maintain the native religion in a modified form, it is highly improbable that there will be found people of our own culture sufficiently self-sacrificing to guide the progress of the people in the way which comes so naturally to the missionaries of the Christian religion. But if this religion is to help in the restoration of the material welfare of the people it is essential that its leaders shall recognise the difficulties which beset their path and should have a definite policy in connection with these difficulties.

Few things have done more harm in the past than the absence of such a policy and the consequent doubt and uncertainty concerning the attitude towards native institutions. Where one missionary has seen nothing but the work of the devil in some native institution and has willed its complete destruction, another, perhaps even of the same Mission, has seen in it a means of preparing the ground for the truth and has, to some extent at least, encouraged its activities. Faced with this difference of attitude the native has in his doubt been led into dissimulation. He has tried to combine the old and the new without discrimination and without the guidance which should have come from those whose business it should be to understand the religious practices they were displacing. If a new gospel is to be taken with success to such a people as the Melanesian, it is essential that the indigenous

point of view shall be understood and that the misunderstanding
to which the new views are inevitably subject shall be appreciated.
Even if it were decided utterly to destroy the old religion there is
no way in which these difficulties can be met so successfully as by
a study of the old religion and of the mental attitude upon which
the old religious practices rested, for this attitude must inevitably
influence the reception of the new religion. If, on the other hand, it
be decided to preserve such elements of the old religion as are
not in conflict with the new, this study is even more essential.
How can it be possible to decide whether a native practice shall
be preserved unless the nature of the practice is thoroughly
understood and its relations with other aspects of the native
culture realised? Whatever the policy adopted towards the indigenous religion, it is of the utmost importance that this religion
shall be understood and that, even if no concerted effort to study
native religions is made, attempts in this direction made by individual missionaries shall be encouraged.

Another question of policy which must be faced concerns the
attitude which the missionary is to take towards economic development. I have already pointed out the close relation between
religion and economics in the indigenous society of Melanesia.
Such institutions as the *Sukwe* of the Banks Islands (Rivers
1914) or the ancestor-cult of the Solomons stand in the closest
relation to economic needs and cannot be modified or abolished
without producing far-reaching changes in the social and economic life of the people. These are only individual instances of
a feature of early forms of human culture according to which they
show a far greater interdependence of different aspects of social
life than exists among ourselves. Even in our own society a new
law intended by legislators to act upon some one branch of
social life often produces changes of a far-reaching kind on other
aspects which were wholly unforeseen when the law was passed.
Such interdependence is even greater in such simple societies as
those of Melanesia, and it is very unlikely that this interdependence will cease with the introduction of new customs from without. The economic life of the people of Melanesia is being profoundly modified by external influence, but it is doubtful whether
the close relation between economic and religious interests will
disappear. It is essential that the missionary shall face this prob-

lem and make up his mind concerning the attitude he is going to adopt towards the economic life of the people. In the past many of the best missionaries of all denominations have set their faces against mixing economic problems with their religion. It has seemed to them that in so doing the spiritual side of religion must inevitably suffer, and no one who has had the opportunity of observing sporadic examples of the mixture can fail to sympathise with them. It must be recognised, however, that there is a problem and that it is in urgent need of settlement. If, as seems natural, economic development is made the business of the civil power, while the missionary occupies himself wholly with religion, there will be endless opportunities for conflict. The best course is one in which Government and missionary societies join in common council to decide how they can avert the disappearance of the Melanesian. The lesson of this article is that something must be done, and done quickly, to give him that renewed interest in life to which the health of peoples is mainly due.

10 A NATIVE FIJIAN ON THE DECLINE OF HIS RACE

Translated, with an Introduction and Notes, by

A. M. Hocart[1]

THE FOLLOWING essay came to my notice accidentally. I took a copy, which I translate as closely as possible, attempting to render every word, even the so-called expletives, which are really most important, as qualifying and colouring the whole sentence. English, of course, is compelled to be more precise and must use different words to render the same in different contexts. I have kept the original brackets, but otherwise modified the stops.

The essay seems worth publishing both for theoretic and practical reasons.

For theoretic, because it shows the interaction of two given cultures: the European which we know well, and the Fijian which we may still hope to know. Because it shows religion moulded by social organisation; for as the rise of chiefs promoted ghosts to be gods, so now British rule is shaping the spiritual world into a colonial government. The reader should bear in mind that the writer is well acquainted with colonial administration.

For practical, because it shows exactly how an intelligent Fijian may conceive Christianity. That is a point we need to know badly, for most missionaries see the bare surface. It also contains hints how the best intentions of a government may be miscon-

Originally published in *The Hibbert Journal*, Volume 11 (1912), 85–98. Reprinted with permission of the publisher.

[1] Mr A. M. Hocart was a member of the Percy Sladen Trust expedition which went to the Solomon Islands in 1908. Since then he has been in charge of the Government school at Lakemba in eastern Fiji, where he has gained an intimate acquaintance with the Fijian language and with Fijian modes of thought.

strued, and suspicion engendered on one side, impatience and reproaches of ingratitude on the other, which a more intimate knowledge of native thought might remove.

ARGUMENT

The decline of native population is due to our abandoning the native deities who are God's deputies in earthly matters. God is concerned only with matters spiritual and will not hearken to our prayers for earthly benefits. A return to our native deities is our only salvation.

THE ESSAY

Concerning this great matter, to wit the continual decline of us natives at this time, it is a great and weighty matter. For my part I am ill at ease on that account; I eat ill and sleep ill through my continual pondering of this matter day after day. Three full months has my soul been tossed about[2] as I pondered this great matter, and in those three months there were three nights when my pondering of this matter in my bed lasted even till day, and something then emerged in my mind, and these my reflections touch[3] upon religion[4] and touch upon the law, and the things that my mind saw stand here written below.

When this emerged from my mind, it was perfectly plain to me that the people of quality[5] and the common folk will judge me at large: they will say that I am one of the foolishest men.[6] But I deem it inexpedient that we should continue to take no thought of it, or continue to follow one single path year after year; but the right course is that we adopt some other methods and try them, in case we might thereby leastwise be able to multiply. Well, the point at which I shall begin is the Beginning when the World was first made, and thus it stands:

---

[2] *Vei tu yaki:* "standing all about."
[3] *Lakova:* lit. go to.
[4] *Lotu,* which means Christianity, church, chapel, service, prayers, etc.
[5] *Turanga:* usually translated "chiefs."
[6] *Lialia* means mad, stupid, ignorant, foolish, silly, etc.

The first thing to be kept foremost in mind is this: "What kind of God is Jehovah? A God of the spirit[7] or a god of the flesh?" (Let each of you think over the proper term.)[8]

Turn to the Creation of the World:—When God created the World, whether there was anything created along with it or not? Was the very first thing to be created Adam and Eve? Yes; we are told so in the Bible (Genesis).

Well, if the very first thing that lived in the world is Adam, whence did he come, he who came to tell Eve to eat the fruit? From this fact it is plain that there is a Prince whom God created first to be Prince of the World, perchance it is he who called the Vu God (Noble Vu).[9] With him abides the power given to him by Jehovah, the Great God of *Spirit* who dwells in Heaven, that is, the second heaven, the dwelling-place of Spirits. I think, sir, this may be he whom the God of Spirit appointed to be leader of the World, that we might be subject to him, we men who live in the bodily life. The power which originated from the Great House,[10] from the Vu God, the channels of transmission[11] thereof to the life in the body are the nobly born (Lords of the body).[12] That is why the anger of chiefs has virtue (*mana*), etc., etc.

It may be that some of us will say: "If what you here say is true, Mr What's-your-name, why is it not written in the Bible?" Consider this: It is written in the Bible that there were only two children of Adam, to wit Cain and Abel. But whence did the woman come who was Cain's wife? (Some wise men say that the couple were brother and sister; Adam had a child, a daughter, who is not set down in the Bible.) Now if it is not set down in the Bible that Adam had a daughter, it is possible that some Prince of the World, Vu Spirit, is not set down. With him is authority[13]

---

[7] *Kalou yalo:* properly this means ghost, lit. soul, spirit; but the author uses the words in a new sense, as opposed to *Kalou yango,* or god of the flesh.

[8] My copy has *kena idha,* which I amend to *kena idhavu.*

[9] *Kalou Vu* is really "ancestor ghost"; but the author uses *kalou* in the new sense of God, and *Vu* for Fijian deities. Noble Vu = *Vu Turanga.*

[10] *I.e.* the Chief's House.

[11] *Indewandewa.*

[12] *I.e.* the native chiefs are the vicars on earth of the Vu Spirit.

[13] *Sau:* that is the title of the highest chief and of his office.

and might, because Jehovah has given him to be the ruler of men, to be the Vu of men. Here are the words from a passage in the Bible: "God is glorified when he hideth things; kings and men are glorified because they inquire diligently into things or devise things." For this reason it is right that you censure me not for these my reflections.

I believe, sir, that there is in truth a Prince whom God created with the world before the creation of man (the name we give him, I suppose, is Vu God, or God whose words came true[14] in matters pertaining to the body only); his authority does not extend in the least to the soul; impossible.

Why? Because they are different in kind; the body is one and the soul another; as for him, he is not a devil or enemy of religion, he is merely God Vu; the power of the Spirit God with which he was anointed, abides with him. It was only in his wilfulness[15] that he went and told Eve to sleep with Adam. Turn to the words of the book of the Spirit God, which says: "That which is hard unto men is easy unto God," and the passage which says: "For he desireth not that one should perish." (Is this plain?) Yes.

Well, if he desireth not that anyone should perish, and all things are easy to him, wherefore was not flattery bound fast once for all in the time of Adam, that men might be pure who were to be born from his stock? I think it is easy for the God of Spirit to bind the Flatterer (Devil), but one difficulty is that he has already made a pact with the Vu of the World, namely that he should be sovereign of the life in the flesh. It lies with Jehovah to decide a thing; the objection is that the will of the God of Spirit might fall into contempt if his decision were reversed in order after all to settle a matter which concerns the body; and since he has confined himself to matters of the spirit, it is hard for his will to extend as far as the body, since there exists a sovereign of the flesh whom he has already appointed.[16]

---

14 *Mana.*

15 *Vakasausauya:* it applies to a chief who orders people about without respect for their comfort. I do not know what supposed incident he here alludes to.

16 It is here that the civil service betrays itself as the original.

The proof of it is that he was enabled thereby to give a human body to its contents in order that he[17] might die, that thereby the souls of all men should be justified[18] to the Spirit God (Jehovah) at the time when the life of the flesh ceases. I suppose, sir, this is plain.

Let me proceed.

The Devil or Enemy of Religion

How many great devils are there? I think only two. One began even with Adam's disobedience; the second those who had lately been expelled from Heaven. It is these then in truth that are the enemies of Religion; distinct from the God who is leader of men, he has dignity and might;[19] he is a god whose word has virtue[20] and is fulfilled in the life according to the flesh. We hear our fathers say that his words were fulfilled and came true in the days when he was worshipped. But when the missionaries came who brought Christianity, they proceeded to call everything devil work,[21] and thence the names of "devil" and of "Vu God" have in a way been bound together, to wit the god of us Fijians. Jehovah has given us this group of islands as our possession, and the several branches of the race, or groups of families, are severally gathered together under their several Vu Gods, the leaders of the various families in things of the flesh. As for the Christian Religion, it has come to Fiji, that is the worship addressed to the great leader of spirits, God of Spirits, Jehovah, that we may pray to him to keep our souls when the life in the flesh is at an end.

It seems to me as though the introducers of Christianity were slightly wrong in so far as they have turned into devils the Vu Gods of the various parts of Fiji; and since the Vu Gods have

---

[17] *I.e.* man.
[18] *Ndondonu:* straight back.
[19] *Sa turanga ka nggangga.*
[20] *Mana.*
[21] How the early missionaries translated *kalou* god instead of ghost, and branded spirits and ghosts as devils (*tevoro*), and some evil consequences thereof, are set forth in a paper "On the Meaning of the Word *kalou,* and the Origin of Fijian Temples," to be published shortly in the *Journal of the Royal Anthropological Institute.*

suddenly been abandoned in Fiji, it is as though we changed the
decision of the Great God, Jehovah, since that very Vu God is a
great leader of the Fijians. That is why it seems to me a possible
cause of the *Decline of Population* lies in the rule of the Church
henceforth to treat altogether as devil work the ghosts,[22] and
the manner of worshipping the Vu Gods of the Fijians, who are
their leaders in the life in the flesh, whom the Great God gave,
and chose, and sent hither to be man's leader. But now that the
Vu Gods whom Jehovah gave us have been to a certain extent
rudely set aside,[23] and we go to pray directly to the God of
Spirit for things concerning the flesh (life in the flesh), it appears as if the leader of men resents it and he sets himself to
crush our little children and women with child. Consider this:

If you have a daughter, and she loves a youth and is loved of
him, and you dislike this match, but in the end they none the less
follow their mutual love and elope forthwith and go to be married,
how is it generally with the first and the second child of such a
union, does it live or does it die? The children of Fijians so
married are as a rule already smitten[24] from their mother's womb.
Wherefore? Does the woman's father make witchcraft? No. Why
then does the child die thus?

Simply that your Vu sees your anger and carries out his crushing even in its mother's womb; that is the only reason of the child's
death.[25] Or what do you think in the matter? Is it by the
power of the devil that such wonders are wrought?[26] No, that is

---

[22] *Tevoro ndina. Tevoro,* the Tahitian form of our word "devil," was intended by the early missionaries to mean devil, but it has come to be commonly used of ghosts; in fact, *tevoro ndina* (true devils) means ghosts
proper, souls of the dead. I take this to be its present meaning, as "true
devils" would hardly make sense.
[23] It is hard to render *mbiu koto,* lit. set aside lying. *Koto* softens or de-
preciates a word, making it "low lying": *vinaka* is "good"; *vinaka koto* is
"more or less good." In this case my linguistic authority explained that it was
used "in order that the gods might appear respected, that they might not
appear despised." It makes the setting aside less downright.
[24] *Mbuta*: lit. cooked.
[25] Fijian religion is therefore not amoral, but on the contrary is closely
interwoven with the moral code. Native religions should be removed with far
more caution and science than has hitherto been usual.
[26] *Mana.*

only the power that originates from the God of Spirit, who has granted to the Prince of men, Vu God, that his will and his power should come to pass in the earthly life. The word of the Spirit God in the Bible says: "Whosoever rejecteth the Lord, rejecteth the elect of God." From this passage I conclude that Fiji erred when he who is our Vu God was set aside,[27] to whom Jehovah granted to be our head; now in so far as the worship of the Vu (Gods of the Flesh) is set aside, the will of Jehovah is opposed.

The Creation of the World

This matter Jehovah has decided once for all, and he has not given the same things to the various countries to be their fabrics, or their food, and the same skin has not been given to all men; the skin is different, the customs are different, the fabrics are different which are found in every country. Is it so, sir, or not? Yes, it is so (it is most true).

Since it is evident that the portions which Jehovah, the Spirit God, has severally assigned to the various parts of the world are different, it is right then that the various races of mankind severally follow the several customs assigned to them by Jehovah. If a man or country sets aside the custom born with him from his mother's womb to be his custom inasmuch as it is the custom given him by Jehovah, that man appears absurd and stupid in our sight. Why? For what reason but that he has set aside the custom born with him in order to get himself foreign ways, ways which the Great God did not give him to be his custom.

Well, how is Fiji? Do we abide by our customs which Jehovah gave us? Do we still follow our Vu Gods whom Jehovah gave to be our leaders or not? No, we have come to follow imported maxims, maxims let fall by the various destitute lands that keep entering into Fiji, to wit those lands that surely have no Vu Gods, or have plants to their Vu Gods, and are not like Fiji, a land beloved of Jehovah, who gave them their land and its

---

[27] *Ko koya* shows that it is singular. The author is vague on the point of numbers; sometimes as if there were only one *kalou vu,* sometimes as if there were many.

Vu Gods to return oracles and tell his vessel[28] what must be done to burn down a village, or what must be done to save the country. Now, the words of power[29] or the words of truth of the Vu God are due to Jehovah having given him the sovereignty of the body; I think it were hard for the Vu God's words to have power, if Jehovah had not previously approved of him as Vu God of the Fijians.

It is not clear to me, sir, whether there are at all Vu Gods in all countries or not? If any has not, then it is a weak and destitute land, and not like Fiji; from this fact it is plain that Fiji is indeed a land in favour at the Great House; a leader has forthwith been sent us to return oracles through his vessel, and to set forth what must be done, and what must not be done, that the country may prosper.

But now that Fiji has by the introducers of Christianity been placed on the same level as various foreign lands,[30] that our Vu Gods have come to be lightly set aside as a thing of nought, or have received the name of devil, that is the only cause that has brought about the increase of disease. If you look at the quarterly report, you will see that there are few deaths of old and middle-aged men, and that there are many and numerous deaths from children up to young men, that is even we who have just deserted quite the way of our people and are led astray by the words of foreigners to this effect: "Other times have come, chiefs are no use; money alone is chief."[31] Because this our generation is straying from our right path, therefore the deaths that come from the sins of the country become many, (1) because the Vu Gods are set aside, (2) because the temporal chiefs are set aside or despised, that is the transmitters of power from the Vu God who shows it forth in the light of the flesh, because, I say, we of this generation are thus gone wrong in these two points; for that

---

[28] *I.e.* the priest who is the vessel (*wangga*) of the spirit.
[29] *Mana.*
[30] The sequel shows that we are included in these foreign lands, though the home [English] reader might find it hard to believe that savages pity us and despise us.
[31] Is the native so very stupid when he is slow to accept our ways? In justice to ourselves, he sees most of our faults and few of our virtues; but is the reproach he here casts at us altogether unfounded?

reason alone do men flow like water to the grave with hairs that
are not grey. Alas! Fiji! Alas! Fiji is gone astray, and the road to
the salvation of its people is obstructed by the laws of the Church
and the State.[32] Alas! you, our countrymen, if perchance you
know, or have found the path which my thoughts have explored
and join exertions to attain it, then will Fiji increase.

A word of the Spirit God in his Holy Bible runs thus: "The
earnest prayer of the faithful bringeth things to pass." How is it?
Is it true? Yes, it is true. Why then does not Fiji increase?

Christianity has now been many years in Fiji, and many scores
of Fijians have passed away in their faith, and they have often
made this petition in our prayer meetings: "Lord, here is Fiji
lying before the glory of Thy face; we the inhabitants (the natives) are declining; oh! cause us to increase that we may become
many."

Well, how is it? Does God hear that prayer? Yes, he hears it.
Why then does he not bring it to pass?

I think it is hard for the Spirit God (Jehovah) to fulfil this
prayer because it belongs to another class. He is God of Spirit;
the petition is to increase the life of the flesh. It is impossible
that Jehovah should handle the body directly since he abides as
God of Spirit, and impossible that his will should apply immediately to the body, since there already is a kind[33] of sovereign of
the flesh, to wit the Vu God, Vu of men. If only the Vu God who
has been granted to us[34] Fijians had been placed at our head and
we then paid homage to the God of Spirit together, we men who
live in the flesh and the might of the God of men who live in the
flesh, then would the answer to our prayer on behalf of earthly

---

[32] Christianity is not obligatory, but natives have an idea it is, because
heathen revivals, being connected with nationalism, have had to be put
down. It is a question, however, whether this connection is not itself due to an
idea that heathendom is illegal. There seems to be a belief that the white
man is suppressing heathendom because he knows it would be the salvation of Fiji. Hence suppression keeps it alive, while publicity might discredit
it by proving its failure to arrest the decline, and would give confidence in
the Government.

[33] *Sa ndua toka: toka* is a softening word like *koto*.

[34] *Soli toka:* my informant explains that *toka* shows that it is given as a
present (*ka ni iloloma*), not once for all.

life in the flesh come from the Great House from the God of
Spirit in Heaven in less than the twinkling of an eye.

(I am Jehovah, I am a God of Spirit.) The proof of my sup-
position stands thus:

I observe that there appear to be two kinds of answers to
prayers coming from Heaven to us men who abide in the life of
the flesh. I think and believe that there are really two kinds of
answers to prayers.

I have already said above that Jehovah hears all prayers. As
for the answer in matters pertaining to the spirit, most rapid is the
answer to matters pertaining to the spirit, the proof thereof goes
on every Sunday, the conversions of the people when the Holy
Ghost of the Spirit God is hot in their souls. But petitions addressed to the Spirit God concerning the flesh, that we may increase to be many, are delayed and not fulfilled. What is the
reason? Because it is not possible for Jehovah to go past him who
is already appointed leader of the life in the flesh, and that is
precisely why it is hard for him to assist in the increase of the
life of the flesh since he is Spirit God, and moreover his decision as Spirit God has passed, inasmuch as there is a sovereign
of men already appointed by him, to wit the Vu of the Fijians or
Vu God:[35] if the Vu God had been worshipped first, and then
we went together to Jehovah (Spirit God), the answer to our
prayer would come from Heaven in less than . . .[36]

Is this plain, sir? Consider this also: Jehovah, he is Spirit God
and remains hidden and does not deliver oracles to us: that is
why men are emboldened to do evil. But if we worshipped him
first whom he has sent hither as leader of men, to wit the Vu
God, who returns oracles through his vessel, then would our
present evildoers and thieves be continually revealed to us, and
our evil deeds be a disgrace and a fearful thing in the sight of us
men in the earthly life, and the wages thereof would be revealed
to us, which would come to pass even in the earthly life. I believe that this is verily the purpose of the Spirit God, being twofold: to have a deputy in things to be done in the bodily life to be
his interpreter to us earthly men, to wit the existing Vu God, who

---

[35] *I.e.* He has exercised His will once for all in appointing His deputy.
[36] My text has *rui,* which no one can explain.

will tell us what must be done for the land to prosper, and what
not. As for his deputy in matters pertaining to the soul of man,
the Holy Ghost is established,[37] the same gives instruction in
matters pertaining to the soul. In the boldness with which men
handle evil because they think that the Spirit God does not give
oracles, lies one part of the decline. But if the Vu God, who
reveals in oracles the wages of evil works, were worshipped first,
our hands would fear to lay hold of evil. Or what, sir, do you
think?

Consider this:

There stood Mbau, and there stood Namata or Nakelo, and in
both those villages there was a born chief who was known[38] at
the Great House to Ratu Dhakombau. Well, what about the
inhabitants of both these villages, Namata and Nakelo: could
they disregard their true Chiefs who are well known personally
to Ratu Dhakombau[39] and go direct to the Great House?[40]
Would those Namata or Nakelo men be acceptable, if they set
aside their chiefs? Do you imagine[41] that Ratu Dhakombau
would attend to them in a joyful spirit, if he, who was their
sovereign, was absent? No. Why? For what reason but that their
official visit from their town to Mbau was incorrect?

Is this true, reverend sirs? Yes, it is most true. Well, if it is so,
how can Jehovah (Spirit God) hear, or how fulfil the prayer on
behalf of Fiji that it may increase, if we set him aside, who is our
sovereign in the life of the flesh and whom God created with the
World, to wit the Vu God? He will indeed hear the prayer, but it
is hard for him to accomplish what is necessary that the life in
the flesh may increase and become plentiful so long as the gods of
the flesh, Lords of men, to wit the existing Vu Gods of Fiji, are

---

37 *Voli:* "It is not weak, it goes about." *Toka voli* is applied to coconuts:
"if one is planted in the place of another and flourishes like its predecessor,
it is said: *sa toka voli.*"

38 *Kilai tiko:* related? To know each other and to be related are one and the
same to Fijians.

39 *Kilai tu vei R. Dh.:* "whatever the place he may be in." *E. kilai tu mai
vei R. Dh.:* he remains in one place, and R. Dh. knows where he is. The
second is clearer: R. Dh. knows he is a chief and knows his rank.

40 Namata and Nakelo were vassal to Mbau.

41 *Mbeka.*

set aside, and petitions are addressed direct to the God of Spirit
that the life in the flesh may increase and be plentiful. Impossible. From this fact, which demonstrates the various points I
have set forth above, I know by this my reasoning that if Fiji
returned to its proper constitutions according to the customs with
which we were endowed, then would Fiji be justified, and it would
be impossible that it should decline or infant deaths be many.
But if the various countries of the world do not follow this path
and yet are justified, no wonder since they have no Vu Gods.
But for Fiji, it is a small land which Jehovah loves exceedingly; the proof of this is that when our respective districts in
Fiji were created, they were created each with its own Vu. And if
the Vu were placed at our head and we then went up together to
our goal, to the Great God, to wit the Spirit God (Jehovah),
there would be no still births and Fiji would then be indeed a
people increasing rapidly, since our conforming to our native
customs would combine with progress in cleanly living at the
present time.[42] Now, in the past, when the ancients only worshipped Vu Gods and there was no commandment about cleanly
living, yet they kept increasing. Then if the Vu Gods were worshipped in Fiji (the deputy of the Spirit God in matters pertaining to the life in the flesh), and this were also combined with the
precept of cleanly living, I think the villages would then be full of
men. Or what, sir, is your conclusion?

I have mentioned in the above discussion that some parts of
the World are weak countries; the reason is that perhaps they
have not a single Vu God; blessed and strong is a land when there
is a deputy of the Spirit God who gave him to be his deputy, to
speak oracles through his medium. (How was it, sir, of old? Did
they prophesy, and tell the things to do?)

If this is right, then it is plain how far removed we are from
certain big countries. How wretched they are and weak, whose
medicines are constantly being imported and brought here in
bottles![43] Not so Fiji. If a disease begins to pain, you simply go

---

[42] The endeavours of the Government to introduce more sanitary conditions
of life have borne good fruit. Cleanly living seems to be the aspect of civilisation which the naturally clean Fijian appreciates most.
[43] Whites pity Fijians, but they find reasons to pity us. That is what white

and pull up a kava plant for some medium of the Vu God; then he arises and prophesies and says: "So and so, go out, stretch out thy hand to the right; the first leaf thou touchest, go and strain it: the patient will thereby recover." When this is carried out, it is wont to be most effective.[44] And what makes it effective? The power of the devil? No, that it is merely the power of the Spirit God who conferred it upon him; had not such been the intention of Jehovah, it were impossible for that medicine to be effective, or his words would have no power.

Or what is your opinion, reverend sirs, of this my argument? I do believe if the Vu Gods are properly worshipped, they will be able to go on prophesying to us what must be done to save the country, or what must be done to make Fijians wealthy, thus: "Do this, you will attain your end if it is done thus; you will go about the world and do it by power to achieve money." (Even as is commonly done in circuses.)[45] Or thus: "You go and wait for me at such and such a place. I will convey thither a ship for you to tour to America." A mere shoot of a banana tree may become our vessel to America if he so pleases.

I think, sir, my demonstration will suffice concerning our fathers who introduced Christianity; and they must not be angry with me on that account, or imagine that I am one ignorant of the Spirit God (Jehovah).

If any one of them is of this mind, he must be wrong; as for me, I simply do my duty in saying what appears in my mind when I think of my country and my friends who are its inhabitants; for since it wants only a few years to the extinction of the people, it is right that I reveal what has appeared in my soul, for it may be God's will to reveal in my soul this matter. Now it is not expedient for me to suppress what has been revealed to me,

---

men generally fail to realise; they put down to laziness or stupidity their reluctance to assimilate our civilisation, whereas it arises from a different point of view; and that point of view is not always wrong or devoid of common sense. Is Fijian medicine more absurd than our patent medicines, or as expensive?

[44] *Mana.*

[45] Fijians believe there is spiritualism (*luve ni wai*) in circuses; it is no use denying it, they won't believe you. They seem to suspect the white man forbids *luve ni wai* so as to reserve the monopoly to himself.

and if I do not declare what has appeared from forth my soul, I have sinned thereby in the eyes of the Spirit God: I shall be questioned regarding it on the day of judgment of souls: nor is it fitting that one of the missionaries should be angry with me by reason of my words; it is right that they should consider everything that I have here said, and judge accordingly. It is no use being ashamed to change the rules of the Church, if the country and its inhabitants will thereby be saved.

Part III | THE "HIGH PERIOD" OF THE STUDY
OF CULTURE CHANGE—FROM THE
MID-THIRTIES TO THE LATE FIFTIES

11 MEMORANDUM FOR THE STUDY OF ACCULTURATION

Robert Redfield, Ralph Linton,
and Melville J. Herskovits

RECOGNIZING THE IMPORTANCE of the study of acculturation, and the varying points of view from which the problem has been approached, the Social Science Research Council, early last year, appointed the undersigned as a Committee to analyze the work on the problem already done, to study the implications of the term "acculturation," and to explore new leads for further investigation. After a number of meetings, the following outline was drawn up as a first step toward clarifying the problem and to serve as an aid in the classification of studies already made.

The work of the Committee will be facilitated, and its final report the more complete, if its members have knowledge of as many of the studies of acculturation now being carried on as is possible. To this end, the tentative outline which has been drawn up to help organize its work is presented with the suggestion that information concerning acculturation studies now in progress be sent to the Chairman, or any member of the Committee, at the addresses indicated below. It will be particularly helpful if, in sending such material, the extent to which the data do or do not fall in with the categories set up in this outline might be indicated. It is expected that the results of the Committee's work will be made available to persons who communicate with it. The file of their names, and of the problems on which they are engaged, will also be available for the exchange of information and methods.

Originally published in *American Anthropologist*, Volume 38 (1936), 149–52. Reprinted with permission of the editor of *American Anthropologist*, and of Mrs. Robert Redfield, Mrs. Ralph Linton, and Mrs. M. J. Herskovits.

OUTLINE FOR THE STUDY OF ACCULTURATION

I Definition

"Acculturation comprehends those phenomena which result when groups of individuals having different cultures come into continuous first-hand contact, with subsequent changes in the original cultural patterns of either or both groups."

(NOTE: Under this definition, acculturation is to be distinguished from *culture-change,* of which it is but one aspect, and *assimilation,* which is at times a phase of acculturation. It is also to be differentiated from *diffusion,* which, while occurring in all instances of acculturation, is not only a phenomenon which frequently takes place without the occurrence of the type of contact between peoples specified in the definition given above, but also constitutes only one aspect of the process of acculturation.)

II Approach to the problem

A Listing of materials available for study

1 Published materials—of prehistoric contacts (to indicate how acculturation has characterized human contacts from early times), as well as of contacts between primitive groups, between primitive and literate groups (both mechanized and non-mechanized), and between literate groups of either or both categories.

2 Unpublished materials of studies in acculturation which are completed or in progress.

B Classification of the above materials

1 Do these studies treat of entire cultures or specific phases of culture?

2 If the studies are restricted ones, what phases of the culture are treated?

3 What are the motivations of the studies (insofar as this affects the type of material treated), e.g., are they scientific, or are they designed to aid in the formulation of administrative, educational, or missionary policy?

C Techniques employed in the studies analyzed

1 Direct observation of acculturation in process.

2 Recent acculturation studied through interviews with members of acculturated groups.

3 Use of documentary evidence which gives historic testimony concerning early contacts which have resulted in acculturation.

4 Deductions from historical analyses and reconstructions.

III Analysis of acculturation

(NOTE: The significance of physical type in determining attitudes operative in acculturation, as well as the importance of the concomitant occurrence of race-mixture or its prohibition, must not be overlooked as a factor which may pervade any situation, process, or result envisaged in this section.)

A *Types of contacts*

1 Where contacts are between entire groups; or are between an entire population and selected groups from another population, e.g., missionaries, traders, administrators, special craftsmen, pioneers and their families, and immigrant males (all these considered with special reference to the elements of culture likely to be made available by the members of such special groups to the population among whom they live).

2 Where contacts are friendly, or are hostile.

3 Where contacts are between groups of approximately equal size, or between groups of markedly different size.

4 Where contacts are between groups marked by unequal degrees of complexity in material or non-material aspects of culture, or both, or in some phases of either.

5 Where contacts result from the culture-carriers coming into the habitat of the receiving group, or from the receiving group being brought into contact with the new culture in a new region.

B *Situations* in which acculturation may occur

1 Where elements of culture are forced upon a people, or are received voluntarily by them.

2 Where there is no social or political inequality between groups.

3 Where inequality exists between groups, in which case any of the following may result:

a   political dominance by one group, without recognition of its social dominance by the subject group;

b   political and social dominance by one group;

c   recognition of social superiority of one group by the other without the exercise of political dominance by the former.

C   The *processes* of acculturation

1   *Selection* of traits under acculturation:

a   the order in which traits are selected (in specific cases);

b   the possible relationships to be discerned between the selection of traits under the various types of contacts leading to acculturation, and the situations in which acculturation may occur (as set down under III A and B above);

c   partial presentation of traits under forced acculturation;

a′   types of traits permitted and forbidden to receiving group;

b′   techniques employed by donor group for imposing traits;

c′   types of traits whose acceptance can be forced;

d′   limitations of forced acceptance;

d   resistance of receiving group to traits presented to them;

a′   reasons for this resistance;

b′   significance of understanding resistance to traits as well as acceptance of them.

2   *Determination of* traits presented and selected in acculturation situations:

a   traits presented by the donor group because of

a′   practical advantages, such as economic profit or political dominance;

b′   desirability of bringing about conformity to values of the donor group, such as humanitarian ideals, modesty, etc.;

c′   ethical and religious considerations;

b   traits selected by the receiving group because of

a′   economic advantages;

b′   social advantages (prestige);

c′   congruity of existing culture-patterns;

d′   immediacy and extensiveness of changes necessitated in certain aspects of the culture by the adoption of functionally related traits;

c   traits rejected by receiving group.

3 *Integration* of traits into the patterns of the accepting culture:

a the factor of *time* that has elapsed since the acceptance of a trait;

b the element of *conflict* produced within a culture by the acceptance of new traits at variance with pre-existing ones, and the degree of conflict which ensues;

c the process of *adjustment* in acculturation;

  a′ modification and reinterpretation of traits taken over;

  b′ modification of pre-existing patterns resulting from the taking over of new traits;

  c′ displacement of older traits in a pattern by new ones;

  d′ "survivals";

  e′ transfer of sanctions;

  f′ shifts in cultural focus caused by acculturation.

IV *Psychological mechanisms* of selection and integration of traits under acculturation

A The rôle of the individual

1 As member of the selecting group; personality of the first individuals to accept foreign traits and their position in society as influencing selection and acceptance of new traits.

2 As member of the donor group: personality of the individuals who are in contact with the receiving group, their attitudes and points of view, and the way in which the group to which they belong is regarded by members of the receiving group, as making for favorable and unfavorable reception of traits.

3 The individual as member of a special group in his society (priestly class, sib, secret society, etc.) and his position in this group, as accelerating or retarding acceptance of new traits.

B Possible consistencies in personality types of those who accept or reject new traits.

C Differential selection and acceptance of traits in accordance with sex lines, differing social strata, differing types of belief, and occupation.

D Initial hostility and subsequent reconciliation of individuals to the new culture as a factor in integrating new culture-traits, and caused by

1 intensity of contact;

2   duration of contact and resulting habituation to new cultural elements;

3   social, economic or political advantages resultant upon acceptance;

E   Psychic conflict resulting from attempts to reconcile differing traditions of social behavior and different sets of social sanctions.

V   The *results of acculturation*

A   *Acceptance:* where the process of acculturation eventuates in the taking over of the greater portion of another culture and the loss of most of the older cultural heritage; with acquiescence on the part of the members of the accepting group, and, as a result, assimilation by them not only to the behavior patterns but to the inner values of the culture with which they have come into contact.

B   *Adaptation:* where both original and foreign traits are combined so as to produce a smoothly functioning cultural whole which is actually an historic mosaic; with either a reworking of the patterns of the two cultures into a harmonious meaningful whole to the individuals concerned, or the retention of a series of more or less conflicting attitudes and points of view which are reconciled in everyday life as specific occasions arise.

C   *Reaction:* where because of oppression, or because of the unforeseen results of the acceptance of foreign traits, contra-acculturative movements arise; these maintaining their psychological force (a) as compensations for an imposed or assumed inferiority, or (b) through the prestige which a return to older pre-acculturative conditions may bring to those participating in such a movement.

12 CULTURE CONTACT
AND SCHISMOGENESIS

Gregory Bateson

THE MEMORANDUM written by a Committee of the Social Sciences Research Council has stimulated me to put forward a point of view which differs considerably from theirs; and, though the beginning of this article may appear to be critical of their Memorandum, I wish to make it clear from the outset that I regard as a real contribution any serious attempt to devise categories for the study of culture contact. Moreover, since there are several passages in the Memorandum (among them the Definition) which I do not perfectly understand, my criticisms are offered with some hesitation, and are directed not so much against the Committee as against certain errors prevalent among anthropologists.

1 THE USES OF SUCH SYSTEMS OF CATEGORIES In general it is unwise to construct systems of this sort until the problems which they are designed to elucidate have been clearly formulated; and so far as I can see, the categories drawn up by the Committee have been constructed not in reference to any specifically defined problems, but to throw a general light on "the problem" of acculturation, while the problem itself remains vague.

2 From this it follows that our immediate need is not so much the construction of a set of categories which will throw a light on all the problems, but rather the schematic formulation of the problems in such a way that they may be separately investigable.

3 Although the Committee leave their problems undefined, we may from a careful reading of the categories gather roughly what questions they are asking of the material. It seems that the Com-

Originally printed in *Man,* Volume 35 (1935), 178–83. Reprinted with permission of the author and of the Hon. Editor of *Man.*

mittee have, as a matter of fact, been influenced by the sort of questions which administrators ask of anthropologists—"Is it a good thing to use force in culture contacts?" "How can we make a given people accept a certain sort of trait?" and so on. In response to this type of question we find in the definition of acculturation an emphasis upon difference in culture between the groups in contact and upon the resulting changes; and such dichotomies as that between "elements forced upon a people or received voluntarily by them"[1] may likewise be regarded as symptomatic of this thinking in terms of administrative problems. The same may be said of the categories V., A, B, and C, 'acceptance,' 'adaptation' and 'reaction.'

4   We may agree that answers are badly needed to these questions of administration and, further, that a study of culture contacts is likely to give these answers. But it is almost certain that the scientific formulation of the problems of contact will not follow these lines. It is as if in the construction of categories for the study of criminology we started with a dichotomy of individuals into criminal and non-criminal—and, indeed, that curious science was hampered for a long while by this very attempt to define a 'criminal type.'

5   The Memorandum is based upon a fallacy: that we can classify the traits of a culture under such headings as economic, religious, etc. We are asked, for example, to classify traits into three classes, presented respectively because of: (*a*) economic profit or political dominance; (*b*) desirability of bringing about conformity to values of donor group; and (*c*) ethical and religious considerations. This idea, that each trait has either a single function or at least some one function which overtops the rest, leads by extension to the idea that a culture can be subdivided into 'institutions' where the bundle of traits which make up one institution are alike in their major functions. The weakness of this method of subdividing a culture has been conclusively demonstrated by Malinowski and his pupils, who have shown that almost the *whole* of a culture may be seen variously as a mechanism for modifying and satisfying the sexual needs of the individuals, or for the en-

---

[1] In any case it is clear that in a scientific study of processes and natural laws this invocation of free will can have no place.

forcement of the norms of behaviour, or for supplying the individuals with food.[2] From this exhaustive demonstration we must expect that any single trait of a culture will prove on examination to be not simply economic or religious or structural, but to partake of all these qualities according to the point of view from which we look at it. If this be true of a culture seen in synchronic section, then it must also apply to the diachronic processes of culture contact and change; and we must expect that for the offering, acceptance or refusal of every trait there are simultaneous causes of an economic, structural, sexual and religious nature.

6   From this it follows that our categories 'religious,' 'economic,' etc., are not *real* subdivisions which are present in the cultures which we study, but are merely *abstractions* which we make for our own convenience when we set out to describe cultures in words. They are not phenomena present in culture, but are labels for various points of view which we adopt in our studies. In han-

---

[2] *Cf.* Malinowski, *Sexual Life* and *Crime and Custom;* A. I. Richards, *Hunger and Work.* This question of the subdivision of a culture into 'institutions' is not quite as simple as I have indicated; and, in spite of their own works, I believe that the London School still adheres to a theory that some such division is practicable. It is likely that confusion arises from the fact that certain native peoples—perhaps all, but in any case those of Western Europe—actually think that their culture is so subdivided. Various cultural phenomena also contribute something towards such a subdivision, *e.g.,* (*a*) the division of labour and differentiation of norms of behaviour between different groups of individuals in the same community, and (*b*) an emphasis, present in certain cultures, upon the subdivisions of place and time upon which behaviour is ordered. These phenomena lead to the possibility, in such cultures, of dubbing all behaviour which, for example, takes place in church between 11.30 and 12.30 on Sundays as 'religious.' But even in the study of such cultures the anthropologist must look with some suspicion upon his classification of traits into institutions and must expect to find a great deal of overlapping between various institutions.

An analogous fallacy occurs in psychology, and consists in regarding behaviour as classifiable according to the impulses which inspire it, *e.g.,* into such categories as self-protective, assertive, sexual, acquisitive, etc. Here, too, confusion results from the fact that not only the psychologist, but also the individual studied, is prone to think in terms of these categories. The psychologists would do well to accept the probability that every bit of behaviour is—at least in a well integrated individual—simultaneously relevant to all these abstractions.

dling such abstractions we must be careful to avoid Whitehead's "fallacy of misplaced concreteness," a fallacy into which, for example, the Marxian historians fall when they maintain that economic 'phenomena' are 'primary.'

With this preamble, we may now consider an alternative scheme for the study of contact phenomena.

7   SCOPE OF THE INQUIRY   I suggest that we should consider under the head of 'culture contact' not only those cases in which the contact occurs between two communities with different cultures and results in profound disturbance of the culture of one or both groups; but also cases of contact within a single community. In these cases the contact is between differentiated groups of individuals, *e.g.,* between the sexes, between old and young, between aristocracy and plebs, between clans, etc., groups which live together in approximate equilibrium. I would even extend the idea of 'contact' so widely as to include those processes whereby a child is moulded and trained to fit the culture into which he was born,[3] but for the present we may confine ourselves to contacts between groups of individuals, with different cultural norms of behaviour in each group.

8   If we consider the possible end of the drastic disturbances which follow contacts between profoundly different communities, we see that the changes must theoretically result in one or other of the following patterns:—

  a   the complete fusion of the originally different groups,

  b   the elimination of one or both groups,

  c   the persistence of both groups in dynamic equilibrium within one major community.

9   My purpose in extending the idea of contact to cover the conditions of differentiation inside a single culture is to use our knowledge of these quiescent states to throw light upon the factors which are at work in states of disequilibrium. It may be easy

---

[3] The present scheme is oriented towards the study of social rather than psychological processes, but a closely analogous scheme might be constructed for the study of psychopathology. Here the idea of 'contact' would be studied, especially in the contexts of the moulding of the individual, and the processes of schismogenesis would be seen to play an important part not only in accentuating the maladjustments of the deviant, but also in assimilating the normal individual to his group.

to obtain a knowledge of the factors from their quiet working, but impossible to isolate them when they are violent. The laws of gravity cannot conveniently be studied by observation of houses collapsing in an earthquake.

10 COMPLETE FUSION Since this is one of the possible ends of the process we must know what factors are present in a group of individuals with consistent homogeneous patterns of behaviour in all members of the group. An approach to such conditions may be found in any community which is in a state of approximate equilibrium but, unfortunately, our own communities in Europe are in a state of such flux that these conditions scarcely occur. Moreover, even in primitive communities the conditions are usually complicated by differentiation, so that we must be content with studies of such homogeneous groups as can be observed within the major differentiated communities.

Our first task will be to ascertain what sorts of unity obtain within such groups, or rather—bearing in mind that we are concerned with *aspects* and not classes of phenomena—what aspects of the unity of the body of traits we must describe in order to get a whole view of the situation. I submit that the material, to be fully understood, *must* be examined in, at least, the following five separable aspects:

a A STRUCTURAL ASPECT OF UNITY The behaviour of any one individual in any one context is, in some sense, cognitively consistent with the behaviour of all the other individuals in all other contexts. Here we must be prepared to find that the inherent logic of one culture differs profoundly from that of others. From this point of view we shall see, for example, that when individual A gives a drink to individual B, that behaviour is consistent with other norms of behaviour obtaining within the group which contains A and B.

This aspect of the unity of the body of behaviour patterns may be re-stated in terms of a standardization of the cognitive aspects of the personalities of the individuals. We may say that the patterns of thought of the individuals are so standardized that their behaviour appears to them *logical*.

b AFFECTIVE ASPECTS OF UNITY In studying the culture from this point of view, we are concerned to show the emotional setting of all the details of behaviour. We shall see the whole body of behaviour as a concerted mechanism oriented towards affective satisfaction and dissatisfaction of the individuals.

This aspect of a culture may also be described in terms of a standardization of affective aspects of the personalities of the individuals, which are so modified by their culture that their behaviour is to them emotionally consistent.

c ECONOMIC UNITY   Here we shall see the whole body of behaviour as a mechanism oriented towards the production and distribution of material objects.

d CHRONOLOGICAL AND SPATIAL UNITY   Here we shall see the behaviour patterns as schematically ordered according to time and place. We shall see A as giving the drink to B 'because it is Saturday evening in the Blue Boar.'

e SOCIOLOGICAL UNITY   Here we shall see the behaviour of the individuals as oriented towards the integration and disintegration of the major unit, the Group as a whole. We shall see the giving of drinks as a factor which promotes the solidarity of the group.

11   In addition to studying the behaviour of members of the homogeneous group from all these points of view, we must examine a number of such groups to discover the effects of standardization of these various points of view in the people we are studying. We have stated above that every bit of behaviour must be regarded as probably relevant to all these viewpoints, but the fact remains that some peoples are more inclined than others to see and phrase their own behaviour as 'logical' or 'for the good of the State.'

12   With this knowledge of the conditions which obtain in homogeneous groups, we shall be in a position to examine the processes of fusion of two diverse groups into one. We may even be able to prescribe measures which will either promote or retard such fusion, and predict that a trait which fits the five aspects of unity can be added to a culture without other changes. If it does not fit, then we can search for appropriate modifications either of the culture or of the trait.

13   THE ELIMINATION OF ONE OR BOTH GROUPS   This end result is perhaps scarcely worth studying, but we should at least examine any material that is available, to determine what sort of effects such hostile activity has upon the culture of the survivors. It is

possible, for example, that the patterns of behaviour associated with elimination of other groups may be assimilated into their culture so that they are impelled to eliminate more and more.

14 PERSISTENCE OF BOTH GROUPS IN DYNAMIC EQUILIBRIUM
This is probably the most instructive of the possible end results of contact, since the factors active in the dynamic equilibrium are likely to be identical or analogous with those which, in disequilibrium, are active in cultural change. Our first task is to study the relationships obtaining between groups of individuals with differentiated behaviour patterns, and later to consider what light these relationships throw upon what are more usually called 'contacts.' Every anthropologist who has been in the field has had opportunity of studying such differentiated groups.

15 The possibilities of differentiation of groups are by no means infinite, but fall clearly into two categories (*a*) cases in which the relationship is chiefly symmetrical, *e.g.*, in the differentiation of moieties, clans, villages and the nations of Europe; and (*b*) cases in which the relationship is *complementary, e.g.,* in the differentiation of social strata, classes, castes, age grades, and, in some cases, the cultural differentiation between the sexes.[4] Both these types of differentiation contain dynamic elements, such that when certain restraining factors are removed the differentiation or split between the groups increases progressively towards either breakdown or a new equilibrium.

16 SYMMETRICAL DIFFERENTIATION To this category may be referred all those cases in which the individuals in two groups A and B have the same aspirations and the same behaviour patterns, but are differentiated in the orientation of these patterns. Thus members of group A exhibit behaviour patterns A,B,C, in their dealings with each other, but adopt the patterns X,Y,Z, in their dealings with members of group B. Similarly, group B adopt the

---

[4] *Cf.* Margaret Mead, *Sex and Temperament,* 1935. Of the communities described in this book, the Arapesh and the Mundugumor have a preponderantly symmetrical relationship between the sexes, while the Tchambuli have a complementary relationship. Among the Iatmul, a tribe in the same area, which I have studied, the relationship between the sexes is complementary, but on rather different lines from that of the Chambuli. I hope shortly to publish a book on the Iatmul with sketches of their culture from the points of view *a, b* and *e* outlined in paragraph 10.

patterns A,B,C, among themselves, but exhibit X,Y,Z, in dealing with group A. Thus a position is set up in which the behaviour X,Y,Z, is the standard reply to X,Y,Z. This position contains elements which may lead to progressive differentiation or *schismogenesis* along the same lines. If, for example, the patterns X,Y,Z include boasting, we shall see that there is a likelihood, if boasting is the reply to boasting, that each group will drive the other into excessive emphasis of the pattern, a process which if not restrained can only lead to more and more extreme rivalry and ultimately to hostility and the breakdown of the whole system.

17 COMPLEMENTARY DIFFERENTIATION To this category we may refer all those cases in which the behaviour and aspirations of the members of the two groups are fundamentally different. Thus members of group A treat each other with patterns L,M,N, and exhibit the patterns O,P,Q, in dealings with group B. In reply to O,P,Q, the members of group B exhibit the patterns U,V,W, but among themselves they adopt patterns R,S,T. Thus it comes about that O,P,Q is the reply to U,V,W, and *vice versa*. This differentiation may become progressive. If, for example, the series, O,P,Q includes patterns culturally regarded as assertive, while U,V,W includes cultural submissiveness, it is likely that submissiveness will promote further assertiveness which in turn will promote further submissiveness. This *schismogenesis,* unless it is restrained, leads to a progressive unilateral distortion of the personalities of the members of both groups, which results in mutual hostility between them and must end in the breakdown of the system.

18 RECIPROCITY Though relationships between groups can broadly be classified into two categories, symmetrical and complementary, this subdivision is to some extent blurred by another type of differentiation which we may describe as *reciprocal*. In this type the behaviour patterns X and Y are adopted by members of each group in their dealings with the other group, but instead of the symmetrical system whereby X is the reply to X and Y is the reply to Y, we find here that X is the reply to Y. Thus in every single instance the behaviour is asymmetrical, but symmetry is regained over a large number of instances since sometimes group A exhibit X to which group B reply with Y, and sometimes group A exhibit Y and group B reply with X. Cases, in

which group A sometimes sell sago to group B and the latter sometimes sell the same commodity to A, may be regarded as reciprocal; but if group A habitually sell sago to B while the latter habitually sell fish to A, we must, I think, regard the pattern as complementary. The reciprocal pattern, it may be noted, is compensated and balanced within itself and therefore does not tend towards schismogenesis.

19 POINTS FOR INVESTIGATION *a* We need a proper survey of the types of behaviour which can lead to schismogeneses of the symmetrical type. At present it is only possible to point to boasting and commercial rivalry, but no doubt there are many other patterns which will be found to be accompanied by the same type of effect.

b We need a survey of the types of behaviour which are mutually complementary and lead to schismogeneses of the second type. Here we can at present only cite assertiveness *versus* submissiveness, exhibitionism *versus* admiration, fostering *versus* expressions of feebleness and, in addition, the various possible combinations of these pairs.

c We need verification of the general law assumed above, that when two groups exhibit complementary behaviour to each other, the internal behaviour between members of group A must necessarily differ from the internal behaviour between members of group B.

d We need a systematic examination of schismogeneses of both types from the various points of view outlined in paragraph 10. At present I have only looked at the matter from the ethological and structural points of view (para. 10, aspects *a* and *b*). In addition to this, the Marxian historians have given us a picture of the economic aspect of complementary schismogenesis in Western Europe. It is likely, however, that they themselves have been influenced unduly by the schismogenesis which they studied and have been thereby prompted into exaggeration.

e We need to know something about the occurrence of reciprocal behaviour in relationships which are preponderantly either symmetrical or complementary.

20 RESTRAINING FACTORS But, more important than any of the problems in the previous paragraph [1935], we need a study of the factors which restrain both types of schismogenesis. At the

present moment, the nations of Europe are far advanced in symmetrical schismogenesis and are ready to fly at each other's throats; while within each nation are to be observed growing hostilities between the various social strata, symptoms of complementary schismogenesis. Equally, in the countries ruled by new dictatorships we may observe early stages of complementary schismogenesis, the behaviour of his associates pushing the dictator into ever greater pride and assertiveness.

The purpose of the present article is to suggest problems and lines of investigation rather than to state the answers, but, tentatively, suggestions may be offered as to the factors controlling schismogenesis:

a It is possible that, actually, no healthy equilibrated relationship between groups is either purely symmetrical or purely complementary, but that every such relationship contains elements of the other type. It is true that it is easy to classify relationships into one or the other category according to their predominant emphases, but it is possible that a very small admixture of complementary behaviour in a symmetrical relationship, or a very small admixture of symmetrical behaviour in a complementary relationship, may go a long way towards stabilizing the position. Examples of this type of stabilization are perhaps common. The squire is in a predominantly complementary and not always comfortable relationship with his villagers, but if he participate in village cricket (a symmetrical rivalry) but once a year, this may have a curiously disproportionate effect upon his relationship with them.

b It is certain that, as in the case quoted above in which group A sell sago to B while the latter sell fish to A, complementary patterns may sometimes have a real stabilizing effect by promoting a mutual dependance between the groups.

c It is possible that the presence of a number of truly reciprocal elements in a relationship may tend to stablize it, preventing the schismogenesis which otherwise might result either from symmetrical or complementary elements. But this would seem to be at best a very weak defence: on the one hand, if we consider the effects of symmetrical schismogenesis upon the reciprocal behaviour patterns we see that the latter tend to be less and less exhibited. Thus, as the individuals composing the nations of

Europe become more and more involved in their symmetrical international rivalries, they gradually leave off behaving in a reciprocal manner, deliberately reducing to a minimum their former reciprocal commercial behaviour.[5] On the other hand, if we consider the effects of complementary schismogenesis upon the reciprocal behaviour patterns, we see that one-half of the reciprocal pattern is liable to lapse. Where formerly both groups exhibited both X and Y, a system gradually evolves in which one of the groups exhibits only X, while the other exhibits only Y. In fact, behaviour which was formerly reciprocal is reduced to a typical complementary pattern and is likely after that to contribute to the complementary schismogenesis.

d   It is certain that either type of schismogenesis between two groups can be checked by factors which unite the two groups either in loyalty or opposition to some outside element. Such an outside element may be either a symbolic individual, an enemy people or some quite impersonal circumstance—the lion will lie down with the lamb if only it rain hard enough. But it must be noted that where the outside element is a person or group of persons, the relationship of the combined groups A and B to the outside group will always be itself a potentially schismogenic relationship of one or the other type. Examination of multiple systems of this kind is badly needed and especially we need to know more about the systems (*e.g.,* military hierarchies) in which the distortion of personality is modified in the middle groups of the hierarchy by permitting the individuals to exhibit respect and submission in dealings with higher groups while they exhibit assertiveness and pride in dealing with the lower.

e   In the case of the European situation, there is one other possibility—a special case of control by diversion of attention to outside circumstances. It is possible that those responsible for the policy of classes and nations might become conscious of the processes with which they are playing and co-operate in an at-

---

[5] In this, as in the other examples given, no attempt is made to consider the schismogenesis from all the points of view outlined in paragraph 10. Thus, inasmuch as the economic aspect of the matter is not here being considered, the effects of the slump upon the schismogenesis are ignored. A complete study would be subdivided into separate sections, each treating one of the aspects of the phenomena.

198 *Beyond the Frontier*

tempt to solve the difficulties. This, however, is not very likely
to occur since anthropology and social psychology lack the prestige necessary to advise; and, without such advice, governments
will continue to react to each other's reactions rather than pay
attention to circumstances.

21 In conclusion, we may turn to the problems of the administrator faced with a black-white culture contact. His first task
is to decide which of the end results outlined in paragraph 8 is
desirable and possible of attainment. This decision he must make
without hypocrisy. If he chooses fusion, then he must endeavour
to contrive every step so as to promote the conditions of consistency which are outlined (as problems for investigation) in
paragraph 10. If he chooses that both groups shall persist in
some form of dynamic equilibrium, then he must contrive to establish a system in which the possibilities of schismogenesis are
properly compensated or balanced against each other. But at
every step in the scheme which I have outlined there are problems
which must be studied by trained students and which when
solved will contribute, not only to applied sociology, but to the
very basis of our understanding of human beings in society.

13 CULTURE CHANGE
AMONG THE NILGIRI TRIBES

David G. Mandelbaum[1]

FOUR TRIBES, isolated together, mutually interdependent, yet culturally distinct, are simultaneously exposed to alien custom. The culture of each takes a different course of adaptation to the new circumstance. Our purpose is to indicate some reasons for these differences and, if possible, to discern certain general trends underlying the variant processes of acculturation.

For many centuries the tribes of the Nilgiri Hills in South India were isolated from the people of the plains below. The steepness of the hills and the climate of the plateau discouraged any extensive contacts with the Hindus of the lowlands. So the tribes formed a social enclave which was geographically close to Hindu life but culturally remote from it. The Nilgiri folk lived in economic and social symbiosis, the Todas being pastoral people, the Badagas agriculturalists, the Kotas artisans, the Kurumbas food gatherers and sorcerers.

It was about a hundred years ago that the English discovered the plateau and there found a godsend as a haven from the summer heat of the plains. They soon pushed a road through to the summit and before long moved the seat of the provincial government up to the hills for six months every year. With the British administrators and vacationists came an influx of lowland Hindus

Originally published in *American Anthropologist,* Volume 43 (1941), 19–26. Reprinted with permission of the author and of the editor of *American Anthropologist.*

[1] Read before the Central Section of the American Anthropological Association, Indianapolis, April 26, 1940. Field work sponsored by National Research Council and Institute of Human Relations, Yale University.

and Mohammedans, servants, merchants, wanderers looking for a living—men from many castes and areas.

The natives of the Nilgiris were thus subject to the impact of two levels of invading culture, Hindu and European. From both sources each tribe took over certain things, rejected others—each group according to its own tastes and inclinations. Before attempting to assess these borrowings, it is well to consider the nature of cultural interchange before Europeans appeared in the area.

There was some cultural give and take among the tribes; the great wonder is that it amounted to so little. The four peoples lived in constant and close contact with each other, yet were culturally and linguistically segregate. Any village of one tribe was, and still is, within a short walk of villages of each of the other tribes. But the four cultures have relatively little in common. The complex Toda ritual and social organization had only vague parallels in Kota life. While Kota dress and housing are similar to that of the Badaga, other phases of the two cultures bear but little resemblance. Both Kota and Badaga admired and respected the Todas, yet in spite of the high prestige rating of the Toda, the others took over very few Toda traits and those unimportant.

There are several reasons why so little trait diffusion went on among these four groups who lived almost literally cheek by jowl. For one thing, each of the cultures operated on a totally different economic base. All of Toda life had to do with the buffalo herds. Kota religion and interest centered about the smithy, Badaga life was engrossed with the welfare of the crop. Each group had a different focus of interest to which the other societies could contribute little.

Perhaps more important is the nature of social intercourse. Kurumbas are often called from their jungle homes to minister to Kotas and Badagas. Their magical services are indispensable. In the practice of their profession, Kurumbas may have occasion to call on their Kota clients several times a week. Yet whenever a Kurumba comes into view, the word flashes through the village, women and children run for the safety of home, cower inside until the Kurumbas have gone. All transactions between Kota and Kurumba take place outside the village limits, rarely is a Kurumba allowed within the home confines of another tribe.

In like manner, Kota musicians have to be present at all major Toda ceremonials; yet if the band comes too close to a dairy, the place is polluted and can only be resanctified by elaborate purificatory rituals. So it goes for the relations among all the tribes. Although contact was frequent, social intercourse was confined to a fixed number of narrowly defined activities. Any intimate contact, of a kind which would allow members of one group to mingle freely with another, was stringently tabooed.

A third bar to intertribal diffusion is the matter of prestige symbolism. A unique tribal trait tends to be interpreted as a symbol of group status. Any attempt to imitate it by another group is violently resisted. For example, Badagas wear turbans, Kotas do not. When a few Kotas once took to wearing turbans, the Badagas felt that the Kotas were getting above themselves. Some of the Badagas ambushed and beat up the Kota offenders, tore off their headgear, and effectively blocked the borrowing of this trait.

This situation is typical of conditions which prevail throughout India. Each caste and tribe has its own unique configuration of custom, represents a distinct cultural compartment. Diffusion is impeded by barriers against intimate connections and symbolic considerations of group status.

All the factors which made for frequent contact without acculturation in the Nilgiris are still valid. But there have been certain important modifications. In aboriginal times the ultimate sanction in tribal or intertribal disputes lay with a council composed of the headmen of the tribes. Now the British administrator, not the council, is the court of last appeal. Economic changes have been quick to appear. The former subsistence crop of the Badagas, millet, is being replaced by a cash crop, potatoes. The cash so acquired can be used to buy imported tools, and so the economic base of the Kotas is endangered. For fifty years past, the tribesmen have been coming into the weekly market where they see strange goods and customs, even movies.

The effect of these changes on the Kurumbas cannot be gauged at present. They still live in their jungles, still come forth to purvey magical protection, still slink quickly back. No field work was conducted among these people and my acquaintance with them is slight.

The Badagas, however, have been deeply affected by the opening of the area. They, of all the Nilgiri people, were closest akin culturally to caste Hindus. Renewed contact with Hinduism has engendered a drive to align their ways with those of the caste structure. This requires the eliminating of old traits as well as the adopting of new practices. For example, musicians rank very low in the caste system and do not merit as important a place as Kota musicians held among the Badagas. Hence many Badagas want to eliminate Kota music from ritual performances. The more conservative Badagas see a threat to the whole tenor of tribal life in this change and stubbornly retain their old relations with the Kota. This conflict has crystallized factional differences, and a fight between the pro-music and the anti-music party recently led to several Badaga deaths. Here as in other acculturative situations, we find the growth of factions, one striving to effect the change, the other bitterly resisting it.

The Badagas have borrowed little directly from the English, but the very establishment of an authority superior to any native sanction has undermined the old way of life. When disputes of a serious nature are decided by the British official instead of by the tribal headmen, then all of the old societal structure loses some of its grip. Whites have had a great effect on the Badagas, not so much because of positive contributions to Badaga life, nor because of the suppression of previous custom, but rather because of the general debilitating effect they have had on the compulsive value of aboriginal sanctions.

The Todas have been exposed to the ways of the whites more, perhaps, than any of the other groups. Two of their villages are within the limits of the largest English settlement. They constitute one of the famed sights of the town and every newcomer to the Nilgiris is dutybound to inspect and photograph the Toda soon after arrival. A mission for the tribe was established just fifty years ago and intensive missionary efforts have gone on ever since. A few Todas have been employed as herders by Europeans and some serve as ornamental guards for the palace of one of the Maharajas.

Dr Murray B. Emeneau, who conducted linguistic studies

among the Toda over a period of three years, has written a paper
called *Toda Culture Thirty-Five Years After: An Acculturation
Study* (Emeneau 1938). This paper traces the changes in Toda
culture during the thirty-five years which intervened between Rivers' studies and Emeneau's stay with the tribe.

In 1901 Rivers found the Todas but little affected by invading
peoples. True, they sold their ghee in the market and occasionally
paid vows to Hindu or Mohammedan shrines, but all the rest
of their way of life remained inviolate. A few had become converts, but they lived apart from the tribe and had no effect on the
tribal career. Emeneau diligently searched for further changes and
found but one that could be noted for most of the tribe. The
young men have taken to wearing gaily colored neckerchiefs. Only
a single sib exhibits more than this trifling change through three
decades.

Just as Toda life has furnished some standard textbook examples in other matters anthropological, so does it offer a classic
case of contact without acculturation. Toda culture is so highly
integrated, so tightly knit around the care and cult of the buffalo,
that unless the buffalo cult breaks down, other influences can
hardly penetrate. And the buffalo herds of the tribe, save for the
one sib above mentioned, are larger and more flourishing than
ever. The English have seen to it that Toda pastures are not
encroached upon, that Todas cannot sell pasture land. British
motives for this consideration have been twofold; they cherish
the Todas as they do ancient monuments and game preserves;
secondly, the Toda pastures make excellent cover for the hunt
(with jackals as quarry) which the English and the native Rajas
maintain in the Nilgiris. Since the basis of Toda economics remains unimpaired, all of the complex structure erected on this
basis is unfractured.

All, save in the sib-village *wṇkitj.* Only this solitary settlement
has taken to raising potatoes, only they keep cattle as well as
buffalo. The reason for their deviance is not far to seek. The
heart of the Toda cult is in the sacred dairies, and the sacred
dairies of this sib lie beneath the parade ground of the canton-
ment of Wellington. The site chosen for the military station covered the pastures of these Todas and they were moved to a neighboring hillside. But there they muddied the water supply of the

soldiers and they were shifted again to a more distant ridge. In this new location, they can keep buffalo easily enough but cannot carry on the buffalo ritual since they have no sacred places. For the sacred dairy sites of a sib are one, inalienable, and irreplaceable. Deprived of the hub of their ritual, this group has lost its zest for buffalo care and has taken over certain non-buffalo traits.[2]

The history of this single deviant sib illustrates the potentialities of Toda acculturation. The amputation of dairy ritual, unintentional though it was, affected the economic life of this group, weakened the cohesiveness of the whole culture, made possible the infiltration of new elements. While other alien influences have little marred the surface of Toda society, this blow struck at the vitals of the culture. Every culture is especially vulnerable to profound change in certain of its spheres. One such strategic area in Toda life is the sphere of ritual. The other Toda sibs continue to maintain their ritual, retain the old economic pattern, remain impervious to foreign ways.

The Kotas have been more susceptible to change than have the Todas but have not yielded as greatly as have the Badagas. Not so immured within a single pursuit as to be insensible to all else, they still have not been as sensitive to Hindu manners as have their agricultural neighbors. A great cultural and social distance separates the Kotas from lowland Hindus. As blacksmiths, musicians, carrion eaters, their presence cannot be tolerated by caste men and so they have less opportunity than have the Badagas to associate with plains folk. Since the gap between Kota and lowlander is bridged by a few tenuous contacts only, the tribesmen have greater reluctance to cross over into strange cultural territory, have less longing to identify with Hinduism than have the Badagas. They have had to make certain adjustments because of the partial breakdown of the old system of intertribal relationships, but these changes have not yet involved any great departure from aboriginal custom. The diminishing return from their handicraft has been supplemented by an enlargement of their old cultivations. They still carry on the traditional exchange of goods and services with Toda, Kurumba, and some Badaga.

The direct impress of European influence on Kota life meets

---

[2] I am indebted to Dr Murray Emeneau for this information.

even the casual eye. Chevrolet axles have replaced native ore as raw material for spades. Tea and potatoes are ousting millet and barley from the tribal fields. Tiled roofs and tailored jackets are supplanting ancient thatch and tribal toga. But these in themselves are mere surface substitutions. Whatever the source of the metal, the tribesmen still are smiths, and the smithy plays much the same part in social and religious life as before. The new crops have not altered ideas of land ownership or familial usufruct. Beneath the tile and store clothing reside ancient concepts of manly demeanor, of sib solidarity, of supernatural sanctions. These innovations have not really affected the core of Kota life.

More significant have been certain less conspicuous happenings, whose repercussions have created series of disturbances through the whole of the society. A single seemingly innocuous order by a British official may profoundly disturb the tribal equilibrium. Such a train of events was set going when the villagers of Kotagiri were ordered to use latrines.

The village happened to be located in a place of great scenic and climatic attraction. In the words of the interpreter and informant,

> Then the English came and bought land from the Kotas of Kotagiri and built bungalows around the village. Police station, bazaar, English hotels, all come. These civilization people have latrines but the jungle people, the Kotas, go out of the village and in the night they just sit where they wish. The government built two latrines, one for males, one for females, and the government ordered that the Kotas use them. The priests and headmen and diviners had a council about it, but they wanted to ask the *pembačol,* the woman who becomes possessed to the music of the flute.

The woman who was consulted forbade the use of latrines, and when a council of the whole tribe was called, the decision was taken to move the entire village. The proponents of this move tellingly argued that the smell of the new institution would offend the sensibilities of the village gods. To avoid offending either British or divine powers, the whole community was shifted to a new locale.

This resistance, however, raised fresh problems. For the two priests of the village could not agree on a site. The followers of one settled in his chosen spot and there built a temple, while the adherents of the other built their houses and temple in another place, about a mile away. Never before in tribal memory had the village deities been separated or a village so sundered. Since protracted argument, threats of force, and tribal pressure failed to bring either side to yield, the quarrel eventually reached the British court. True to the diplomacy of colonial administration, the court ordered a compromise; the united village was to be located on a third site, midway between the two previously selected.

Thus the resistance to one minor regulation of British authority led to submission in a matter of much greater import. Since the government official had the last word to say in matters pertaining to the gods, he had unknowingly usurped some of the sanctions formerly accorded to the gods and their retainers. The weakened prestige of the priests led to this further incident.

A few of the villagers had kept title to their lands in Kotagiri and in time received considerable revenue from rents. In the course of some years, one of these wealthy men was chosen to be priest. He chafed under the ritual taboos incumbent upon priests since they prevented him from enjoying the tastes his wealth had enabled him to acquire. Moreover, as I understand the case, the lowered prestige of the priesthood caused him to take the duties of his office less seriously than he might otherwise have done. On a grand spree one fine day he violated many of the rules of priestly conduct in a single fell swoop. He got drunk, had a barber cut his sacerdotal beard, donned footgear.

But the group had not so far relinquished its old values as to tolerate this breach. The priest was promptly subjected to the direst punishment—he was made an outcaste. The society was still sure enough of its scale of values and well enough integrated to make this punishment stick and rankle. Only by dint of great expenditure and abasement did this wayward priest secure readmittance to the tribe.

The chain of events started by the latrine edict is one index of the degree of acculturation—in matters of basic importance—among the people of Kotagiri. At least one individual, the priest, was ready to throw over an important sector of the integrating framework of the society. His unique position and experiences as a man of wealth brought him to that juncture. But his fellow villagers had not shared those experiences, for them the aboriginal patterns were still satisfactory, and in the end they forced the vagrant to reaffirm publicly the continuing validity of the traditional way. Had the group been subject to deeper frustrations, some men would very probably have supported the dereliction. Or if the priest had been a more forceful personality, if he had so manipulated the prestige set-up of the society as to accrue to himself greater power over his relatives and neighbors, then too he might have been able to flout tradition without recanting.

In another Kota village there lives a man who has done that very thing. He is a vigorous personality who has been able to bring about significant changes in several villages. This individual, Sulli, is the one Kota who can speak English. He alone of all the tribesmen has lived among Hindus, as he had to do in the course of receiving enough education to become a school teacher. Whole complexes of behavior which are significant in present day Kota life, behavior toward Europeans, literacy in Tamil and English, are carried only by him.

A life history of this individual shows that he has sought to deviate from the established patterns of his culture since childhood. The very fact that he went through a long and painful process of education is one reflection of his desire to deviate. Sulli's perpetual drive to seek new ways and to induce others to follow him finds expression in his present efforts to get his tribesmen to cut their hair, to abandon music as a tribal vocation, to give over the eating of carrion, to abolish the menstrual seclusion hut. This last reform probably stems from lessons in hygiene, but the other traits are stigmas of group inferiority according to Hindu concepts.

Sulli himself has gone beyond the reforms he advocates. The prestige value imparted by contact with an ethnographer and a linguist lent him enough courage not only to cut his hair but also to tog himself out in shorts, topee, and stockings in the style of an Englishman. Although his reforms are savagely opposed by many, some of the younger men have followed his example in cutting their hair and in abandoning other tribal practices. Had Sulli been a weaker personality, he could not have held his followers or himself to his schedule of acculturation. Much of Kota culture change is channelled through and directed by a single individual, the leitmotif of whose personality is deviation from established tradition.

A study of recent history in the Nilgiri area reveals differences in degree of change and in the nature of the acculturation process among the tribes. The old structure of Badaga society was generally weakened by the advent of the English so that many Badagas were ready to take over new traits. Since these Badagas felt more closely identified with Hinduism than with other cultures, they took over new behavior patterns mainly from the plains folk. Toda life, narrowly concentrated on the buffalo, has little time for or interest in extra-buffalo behavior. The conditions under which the integrity of Toda culture can be shattered are illustrated by the career of one aberrant sib. The sketch of Kota change reveals the varying force of different acculturative impacts and demonstrates the role which personality may play in mutations of the social mass.

14 ASSIMILATION OF AN
AMERICAN INDIAN GROUP

Elizabeth Colson

THE PHRASE 'Melting Pot' has been applied to the United States
because of its success in turning immigrant peoples into more
or less standardized American citizens within a generation or so.
The native peoples of America have also been subjected to the
'Melting Pot', but of this less is heard. In 1941 and 1942 I studied one of the American Indian tribes and attempted to assess
how they had been incorporated into American society. What
happened to the Fishers,[1] the Indians whom I studied, did not
happen to all Indian tribes. Each tribe had its own particular
difficulties of adjustment, and the results are equally varied. This
paper does not attempt to generalize for all tribes, though much
said here would apply to other groups as well.

One constant factor to which all Indian groups had to adjust
was the common policies enunciated by the American Government for dealing with such groups. One government office has
charge of all Indian tribes in the States. This is the Office of Indian Affairs in the Department of Interior. During the westward
expansion of the United States, when new tribes were encountered the Government attempted to make treaties with them. If

Originally published in *Human Problems in British Central Africa,* No. 8
(1949), 1–13. Republished with permission of the author and of the publications director of the Rhodes-Livingstone Institute.

[1] The name of the tribe has been disguised to protect informants. The field
work on which this paper is based was financed by fellowships from the
American Association of University Women and from Radcliffe College. The
material is incorporated in an unpublished doctoral dissertation on file at
Radcliffe College and Peabody Museum, Cambridge, Massachusetts, U.S.A.

this failed, they were conquered in war. In either case the final result was the same. The tribal lands were alienated, and the tribe was given a reserve, sometimes a portion of its old range, and sometimes in an entirely different part of the country. Its people were declared wards of the United States Government. This meant that they were declared incapable of administering their own affairs. As a tribe and as individuals, they were placed under the Office of Indian Affairs. Agents, who in the early years were always Europeans, were sent to the reserves to take charge of the tribes.

For many years the declared policy of the Indian Office was the extinction of tribal cultures and tribal organizations. It was assumed that eventually the Indians would become civilized and that they would be incorporated into the general American society just as were the immigrants who came flooding into the country from Europe. There was thus no need to attempt to develop tribal organization. Instead efforts were made to wean individual Indians away from their old customs and to enable them to establish themselves as independent American citizens. There were men in the Indian Service who regarded any measures which would lead to this end as thoroughly justified. Since the Indians were wards they had no legal redress even against rulings which now seem to us incredibly harsh. About 1932 this policy was changed and an attempt was made to form the tribes into political bodies with the right to handle internal affairs. The Indian Department now declared that Indian customs were valuable, perhaps because there was no longer current the same acceptance of the belief that western civilization was the ultimate goal in human development. These doubts, however, came after most of the tribes had spent at least half a century under a repressive system aimed at destroying their identity and refusing to recognize native customs as an acceptable standard. The results of such a system, of course, depend on many variables—the number of people with whom it deals, the accessibility of their areas, and the available personnel for carrying out the programme. One would expect rather different results according to whether the tribe consisted of six hundred individuals or 20,-000, whether it was set down close to developing European centres or in the midst of a howling desert where only the Indian agent could be induced to go and only he by the thought of the possibilities for embezzling the money granted for tribal improvements. To-day there are tribes such as the Navaho, who number some 50,000 or so and who still retain a distinctive culture, though it bears plentiful marks of long years of contact with European settlers. There are tribes in the east which have completely disappeared, or will soon do so. And there are tiny tribes which by some miracle still persist although there is little to differentiate them now from neighbouring Americans of European descent. The Fishers are such a people.

From time immemorial they inhabited a stretch of the coast in what is now the state of Washington. Probably they have never numbered more than two or three thousand people. Culturally they were akin to the North-West Coast peoples. The old culture of the region was marked by a dependence on hunting sea mammals and on fishing; the use of large plank houses and much wood carving; the existence of ceremonial secret societies which had great winter performances; the quest for individual guardian spirits through vigil and self-torture; the class system of nobles, commoners and slaves, with the nobles engrossed in a form of competition known as the Potlatch. In this the wealthy man gave away a vast accumulation of goods, in an attempt to humiliate his rivals. These lost face and standing if they failed to engineer a return feast in which they either gave away or destroyed more goods than did the first man. The Fishers were participants in this general culture, though they lay far south of what ethnographers regard as the most typical representatives, and they had many individual variations on the old themes. They had a modification of the potlatch system, with much less stress laid on the destruction of property than among the northern people. In their secret societies, they seem to have lacked the cannibal motives which were strong among the Kwakiutl and some of the northern Nootka. The social system seems to have been rather more fluid, perhaps because they were a whale hunting group and tended to lay more stress upon the accomplishments of the successful whale hunter than upon hereditary position in their prestige system. Their social and political organization was based on extended family groups integrated into villages rather than on clan and lineage structure as was true further north.

There are indications that Fisher culture was always in a state of flux, and borrowed freely from neighbours on all sides. With their large canoes they carried on a coastal traffic far up the Vancouver Coast, along the water ways leading into Puget Sound and the Inside Passage, and far down the Pacific Coast to the mouth of the Columbia River. They were quite accustomed to incorporating new customs they learned through such trips or through intermarriages with distant groups. Many of the individual rites which made up the winter ceremonies of the two secret societies had been acquired in this way. Foreign women whose families had the prerogative to perform certain rites in their home villages would bring these rites with them when they married Fisher men and their descendants would now maintain the privilege in the local societies. I rather think that the ceremonial life of the tribe had been radically changed in this way between about 1750 and 1850. But while the Fishers seem never to have been intensely conservative, they adapted foreign customs to fit into their own culture. They borrowed, adapted, or rejected, in line with their own interests. When they passed under the Indian Service they were faced with a different problem—a demand that they swallow wholesale an entirely different system, along with its attendant values, no matter how foreign these were.

The Fishers first came into contact with Europeans at the close of the eighteenth century when the first assault on the North-West Coast began. Captain Cook sailed past their shores on the trip when he discovered Nootka Sound. The reports that the Cook Expedition brought back about the riches of the region spurred on the traders and soon every inlet along the coast was filled with British, Spanish and American ships busy trafficking for seal and otter furs. There was even an unsuccessful attempt before the end of the century to found a trading station at Big Bay, in Fisher territory. After it was abandoned no European traders settled in the area again until 1853. This did not mean that the Fishers were left completely isolated during this period. In the early 19th century a Japanese junk was shipwrecked on their coast, and the survivors were enslaved for a few years. The same fate overtook a Russian boat. American and British trading vessels continued to call in along the coast for whale oil and furs. By 1850 many Fishers were half-breeds. It was a rough period and neither Fishers nor Europeans seem to have had much regard for the others' rights. The Fishers on their hand were not averse to looting any ship which got into difficulties in their waters. At one time they were notorious as pirates and looters and were called menaces to coastal navigation. The first American who attempted to found a trading post in their country lived a harrowing existence with daily delegations coming to order him out of Fisher country. More than one plot was made to murder him and take over his store of goods. Not that the Fishers seem to have been averse to all contacts with Europeans—they made trading expeditions up the Strait to the town of Victoria where Hudson Bay Company had established a post, and to trading centres on the American side of the border. But they were suspicious of European settlement and wanted no truck with Europeans within their own area.

About 1850 American colonization was already reaching the Pacific Coast. The Government decided that it would make treaties with the Indian tribes in the area before any land disputes could start. One day the Governor of the Territory arrived with an interpreter and some troops. The matter was explained to the assembled Fishers, probably by now shrunk to a mere 600 after several disastrous small-pox epidemics. The important men of the group put their marks to some papers. Under instruction everybody shouted 'Hurray'. And the Fishers had ceased to be an independent people and were now wards of the Government.

By the terms of their treaty they ceded all of the land they occupied, with the exception of a portion six miles square, and agreed to accept the authority of the United States Government. In return they were to be given an agent to look after their affairs. They were also to be paid a sum of money, which apparently was held for them by the Government and used to supply them with certain services. They were to be sent a farmer to teach them farming—something completely foreign to their culture and for which incidentally their country was not suitable—a blacksmith, and a teacher to start a school to educate their children. At certain periods they were also supplied with a doctor. These were standard arrangements included in most treaties with Indian tribes made at this period. When the treaty money ran out the Fishers were regarded as still far from civilized, as still in need of their instructors, and the Government assumed the direct financial burdens.

And with this the struggle began to turn the rambunctious Fishers into the Sunday-school variety of American citizen. The zest with which the struggle went on depended a good deal upon the agents. At one time the Indian Service decided that what it needed in general was army discipline so it turned the reserves over to the War Department and the agents were seconded officers of the regular army. At other times, the Indian Services decided the religious zeal would be most effective and it allowed the different mission boards to appoint missionaries as agents and school-masters. Later still it developed its own body of employees. But since Indian Service Appointments were for many years under the 'spoils system', the agents and other employees on the reserve were likely to change with every presidential election. Despite these changes in personnel, there are remarkable uniformities running through the reports of the Agents from 1860 to about 1900, when reports were no longer published. If they did half the things they said they did, being an Indian on the reservation must have been rather like being a student in a very strict boarding school, only that there was no prospect of leaving. Probably by this time there was about one European employee for every hundred Fishers, which made things even more difficult.

One of the agents wrote for instance: 'I have made it a part of my duties to visit each separate lodge once a week and examine their daily mode of living, correct irregularities, reprimand any cases of misdemeanours, and impress on their minds the importance of a higher standard of morality, which, added to their expanding ideas of civilization, is having the desired effect on the Indian mind'. This may have been the man whom the Fishers still remember for his housewifely instincts. If he found that a woman's housekeeping was below his standards he would give her a week in the agency jail to meditate upon the great virtues of cleanliness.

They worried constantly about the morals of their charges and each agent boasted about how his energetic attacks had solved the problem or were on the way to do so. Polygamy was no longer tolerated. Divorce according to Indian custom was looked on askance. Some agents went even further. One declared that he prosecuted all couples living together without a proper marriage, that he recognized no re-marriages unless the couple had previously been properly divorced and that he refused to grant divorces.

These were but a few of the places where the agents were at loggerheads with the Fishers. Any customs which differed obviously from the American customs of the periods were likely to fall under the agent's interdict, and the Fishers were put to considerable ingenuity in adapting their customs to suit the agent's whims. The rites of the secret societies were first ordered purged of all traits which offended the agents and then were banned altogether. At one time, it was illegal to have any gathering at which Indian songs and games were used and the sound of the drum was enough to bring the agency police with orders from the agent to disperse the gathering and to jail or fine the offenders. Most agents could see nothing good in potlatch, apparently on the grounds that the people merely gave away their property with nothing to show for it. The potlatch was prohibited. One of the brighter members of the tribe who had some acquaintance with European custom found a way out of this difficulty. He waited until Christmas time, put up a spruce tree, hung his goods on this and gave them away as Christmas presents, with the blessings of the agent and the missionary. For some years after this the Fishers spent much of the profits of their poaching expeditions to the arctic seal rookeries in seeing who could give the biggest Christmas parties. Later they adapted birthday parties with equal enthusiasm. During the most repressive periods, they also evaded their agents by going off in their canoes or boats and landing just beyond the reservation boundaries. There they proceeded to have their parties with full enjoyment of their agent's helplessness in the territory beyond his jurisdiction. They still snicker reminiscently about the agent sitting glowering on his porch as they came paddling home from a glorious day spent in defiance of his orders. Some of them even think that one of the reasons why their parties and Indian games have fallen away in the period since 1930 when the ban on Indian custom was lifted, is that they no longer have the fun of defying the agent and therefore the parties have lost their point.

The social structure of the people was also attacked. Partly, indirectly through the attack on the potlatch through which the prestige system operated. Partly by more direct measures. Slavery was forbidden almost immediately, and the agents refused to recognize the old class system of slaves, commoners and nobles. They also tended to ignore the established leaders of the tribe, for these embodied the Indian customs which the agents were intent on extirpating. Instead they chose young men who had grown up in the reservation school and who were more pliable. They did not understand the land-holding system of the tribe, in which each extended family had certain rights to stretches of the coast and to fishing spots. These were assumed to be common property of the tribe. Later an attempt was made to turn to a system of individual land-holding. The reservation was surveyed and each member of the tribe was allotted a certain portion of the reserve. This was now his private property, but for a period it was held in trust for him by the Indian Service. When the trust period expired, the land was to pass into his control, and he would be free to rent or sell or to use it as he pleased. The trust period for the Fisher Reserve, however, had not expired by the time the Indian Reorganization Act came along, and the land was reconverted into a tribal trust. Members of the tribe say that one of their reasons for accepting the Reorganization Act was their fear that the trust period would expire, and that individual people in the tribe would sell their holdings to the Europeans who were hovering on their borders ready for the chance to acquire the valuable timber holdings and fishing sites.

While these attacks on the old culture of the Fishers were going on, there were simultaneous attempts to convert them as individuals into ordinary Americans. The most important measure for this was the school, which was established about 1862 as a day school. Soon it was seen that a day school was inadequate, because it left the children with their older relatives through much of the day. So a boarding school was built about a mile or so away from the nearest Indian village. And here for almost twenty years every Fisher child who could be rounded up was incarcerated for much of the year. The ideal of the school was enunciated by an early agent who declared that it should 'result in such a change in the child's tastes and habits that he will never return to Indian life, but will seek new social alliances and a better form of life'.

At some periods children were kept in school throughout the year and allowed to visit their homes for only a few hours once a week; at other times they were less strictly regulated and much time was spent in the village and with older relatives. In general the policy of the school was to prevent contact with Indian life and to inculcate 'civilized' behaviour. Girls were trained in housework and sewing; boys in farming and other crafts, though usually they lacked a teacher sufficiently skilled himself to take them very far. The children were forced to speak English, and were punished for using the Fisher language. They seem not to have been entirely repressed, however. Probably even a missionary school-teacher was inadequate for this. Children used to take needles and soot with them, and while the teacher knelt with his eyes shut to recite a long incomprehensible morning prayer, they passed the time tattooing their arms and legs and thinking out new devilments for the time when they were released from classes. Later on the boarding school was abandoned, and a day school again instituted. Now, however, older children were encouraged to go right away from the reservation to the big Indian boarding schools which served the children of many tribes. And many did go away, sometimes for several years.

Meantime, many things were happening to the Fishers which were not bound up directly with the agency. During the years of the big sealing industry in the latter half of the 19th century, boats would stop at Big Bay to recruit Fisher hunters to follow the seal herds up into Alaska waters. Later the Fishers themselves began to enter this trade. A number of men used the profits from such expeditions to buy their own boats, and then having recruited a Fisher crew and hired a European navigator, they were off to Alaska and a poacher's existence. They lost interest in hunting other sea mammals—perhaps because sealing was much more profitable and they now needed European goods for the potlatch system. It is still one of their grievances against the Government that it has banned sealing, and even more pertinently that it has set up a policing of the seal herds which makes poaching risky and unprofitable. With sealing closed, they began to wander afield to the fish canneries and the berry fields and clam diggings on Puget Sound. Some of them took jobs in lumber camps. Then with the development of new methods of preserving

fish for shipment, they rushed into commercial fishing. Their
home lies just a few miles from rich fishing grounds and here
they were soon competing with European fishing boats which also
began to frequent the waters. Over-enthusiastic fishing began to
deplete even these vast fisheries, but by that time the Indian
Service had sold the lumber on the reserve to a lumber company
and there were jobs for the men in the lumber camp now situated on the reserve. A road was built connecting the Fisher area
with the neighbouring settlements of Europeans. Soon nearly
every Fisher family had some sort of car, and they were busy
racing back and forth to neighbouring towns or recovering. Some
Europeans settled in the reserve, either at the lumber camp or
within the Indian village itself. While they could not own land on
the reserve, they could rent this from the Fishers for their homes
and businesses and this they proceeded to do. The local school
was then converted into a regular government school, to which
all children of the area, both European and Indian, went.

This was the state of affairs when I went to the reservation in
1941, approximately eighty years after the Fishers had come
under the Indian Office. Only one member of the tribe had been
born in the days when the Fishers were independent. All the rest
were born and reared as reservation people. It seemed to me that
it might be rather a good place to see how effective a policy for
the re-education of a group of people can be. The Indian Service
had had eighty years to carry it out, though for the ten years
before I went to the area it had relaxed the old repressive measures and no longer favoured the extermination of Indian culture
—it had dealt with only a tiny group, never more than six hundred
since the Indian Service took over, and it had not had to pay even
lip service to some creed of human and cultural rights which might
affect its policy.

In 1941, the Fishers numbered only about four hundred people, most of whom lived on the reserve in the village of Big Bay.
In 1940 there had probably been about 100 Europeans in the
village, but within a year it must have increased to three or four
times this figure due to wartime developments. There was thus
an excellent chance to see how the Fishers fitted in among other
Americans. At first glance it was impossible to segregate the Fishers
as a group of individuals from these Europeans who lived among

them. There were people who were obviously Indian from their features, though not all of these were Fishers. There were others who were as obviously European from their features, though many of these turned out to be members in good standing of the Fisher tribe. The president of the tribal council showed almost no sign of his Indian background—his European father and his half-breed grandfather had determined his physical type. He was married to a European woman, whose parents had immigrated to the United States from Sweden, and their baby daughter though still a Fisher will probably grow up in every way an American child. Even her father, though raised by his Indian grandmother, lived part of his time in Seattle where his grandmother went to live to give him better schools; he attended a University for about a year, and finally started to learn something about Fisher customs when this University's teachers suggested that they might be something worthwhile. He had begun to learn the Fisher language only after he was chosen a member of the tribal council, where he sometimes had to deal with old men and women who felt more at home in it than in English. And the Indian Service regarded his administration with approval because he looked on matters in the same way as did the officials, liked to get things decided and was impatient of long delays and much discussion.

But the case of one individual is no real evidence of the degree to which the Fishers as a group and as individuals had managed to assimilate themselves to American society. Physically, there is considerable variation as we have seen. Slightly over 40 per cent to-day acknowledge that they have European ancestors, and probably there is not a member of the tribe who is wholly Indian. In many cases, the European ancestry was purely physical and not social. That is the man involved never lived as father to his children or made any attempt to acknowledge them or to look after them. But other Europeans had married into the tribe and had lived in close contact with their children and made an effort to give them something of their own background. At the present time there are six or seven Europeans married to Fishers and living in the village with their families; others have married Fisher women and taken them away with them—although there is still visiting back and forth.

The village in which the people live looks much like any other coast village, though it may be slightly more dilapidated. In the stores the range of goods is much what it would be any place in the region. The only exotic articles are those carried to sell to tourists who want some souvenir of their visit to an Indian reservation. The clothing of the people is pretty much the same that you would find anywhere in the general region and does not distinguish European from Indian in the village. In the restaurants, the food is bad, but not Indian. And the restaurants are equipped with the standard juke box, soda fountain and pop cooler which seem to be common American culture traits from coast to coast. The Fishers like the juke box, patronize the local motion picture showings and spend their earnings on radios to which they listen interminably. In working with them, part of the anthropologist's job may include listening to them retail with full details the latest installment of the radio soap opera.

In language the picture is not quite so clear, but there can be no doubt that the Fisher language is dying. I should imagine that in another ten years it will have ceased to exist as a common medium of speech. Already in 1941 there were only five people in the tribe who maintained they could not speak English and two of these could but wouldn't. They were old people who had managed to escape the reservation schools by hiding when European officials were around and by bribing the Indian employees. In only two families were any of the small children learning to speak Fisher. In a few other households small children understood a little but never had been known to speak it. And even most of those in their twenties never used Fisher if they could help it. In general tribal meetings where both old and young came together, English was the medium of speech.

Economically the Fishers had managed to integrate themselves into general American system. Most of them were commercial fishermen. All the moneys spent on paying a farmer to teach them to farm was wasted—a few of them had a garden or raised a few cattle, but all of them were fishermen, competing with Europeans, and making quite an adequate living in a good year. Those who fished industriously and were lucky, in a year with fair prices, probably made from a hundred to five hundred pounds in the fishing season. After that they either rested for the winter, or they went off to the lumber camp where they were paid the same wages as the European workers. Some of them owned their own enterprises in the village—restaurants, tourist cabins and garages. In the past they had also owned stores, but these failed under the kinship obligation to provide credit. Restaurants, tourist cabins, and garages which depended primarily on the tourist were much safer investments for the Fishers.

Socially they were also integrated to some extent with their European neighbours. There was some informal social exchange among them. It was not uncommon for Indian and White women to exchange visits; Indians and Whites might go on parties together, and if they drank on the reserve, they might even get thrown into jail together. Children played together on the streets, were taught in the same classes at the school, and took part in the same school activities. At the Presbyterian Church Indians and Whites attended the same service, and children took part in the same Sunday school. When the church gave a Christmas programme all the children took part together in the same entertainment.

Despite this, the Fishers still remain a distinctive group. Partly this is due to recent shifts in Indian Service policy, which has encouraged the incorporation of tribal groups. But the Fisher tribe is not a purely artificial affair backed by nothing but the approval of the Service. Their unity as a group is admittedly partially centred in the joint ownership of the reserve. Of this they are extremely jealous. According to their belief, all foreign Indians and all Whites are there only on their sufferance. They resent any infringement on what they regard as their prerogatives. But my data indicate that the attitude toward their reserve is due not only to its intrinsic value and to the prerogatives which centre in it but because it does symbolize the tribal group itself. When plans were afoot during the war to transfer them to another part of the area to remove them from an exposed portion of the coast, the people refused to consider the possibility. They felt that they must hold this particular piece of land on which all their traditions centred or they would cease to exist as a group. It was evident that they still felt themselves a people distinct and apart from the Europeans in the area.

They clung not only to their reservation but also to their status as wards of the Government, which they still held over eighty

years after they had first come under government supervision.
While they resented the status in many ways, none would have
shouted louder if any attempt had been made to change it. For
it gave them many special privileges which they now regarded as
their right. They did not have to pay state taxes; they were entitled
to free medical care and hospitalization; their children were
given free school lunches. In these respects they were better off
than their European neighbours who had to meet such bills themselves. Moreover their property in the reserve could not be seized
for debts, even if these were contracted elsewhere. Europeans
who ran up big bills at the trading post would find their pay
cheques attached. Fishers might lose their credit, but their pay
cheques were immune from seizure. If they bought cars and failed
to meet the payments, the dealers had no recourse, for they could
not seize the car while it was on the reserve nor could they force
an Indian to pay up. The Fishers were well aware of this privileged position, and exploited it. While they complained bitterly
about any theory that they were incapable of looking after themselves—and it is just this theory on which the status is based—
they hugged the privileges to them and regarded any attempts to
reduce them as an encroachment on their just rights. But they
tried to change the basis of the privileges. They maintained that
the Europeans had robbed them of their lands and possessions
and had destroyed their old culture. Therefore any special privilege which the Fishers received were but part payment on a debt
so large that it could never be paid in full. Even those who had
more European than Indian in their ancestry, and who had become most acculturated took this view. In a sense then, the
Fishers were kept a distinctive people who must nurse a grievance
by this peculiar status, though the status had originally been
thought to give the Government a free hand in forcing them to
adopt American culture and to assimilate to the rest of American
society. There were no indications that this would break down.
It held them to the reserve, where they could best exploit the
status, and encouraged even those who could easily have stood
by themselves to maintain their contact with the group.

In other respects the Fishers showed themselves a group of
people with a distinctive outlook which differentiated them from
their neighbours. Although seal hunting had vanished, the pot-

latch was a thing of the past, and the guardian spirit quest and the winter ceremonials were gone, many of the old values may have persisted. At least such values are reflected in their tales of their old culture as they are throughout present day behaviours. There is space here to deal with only one such value or motive. The Fishers interpret life in terms of rivalry and a fight for prestige. Where formerly this was somewhat channelized through the potlatch system, it is now diffused through every activity of the group.

This fight for prestige has two aspects—one the positive striving after prestige for oneself, and the other an intense jealousy of the efforts of all other members of the group which leads to attempts to cut the ground from under their feet. They do this by murmuring that the man has slave ancestors, that he has failed to accomplish anything noteworthy, that he does not know how to behave in the way that a person of high status should. These are standards of judgement based on the old class system. It is assumed that every person will try to direct the activities of the entire group to reflect and add to his own prestige. Therefore the moment he begins to accomplish something, the group withdraws its support and sits back to enjoy his failure. So long as they succeed in preventing an individual from improving his status or from demonstrating that his status has always been higher than theirs, they are content to let the group welfare pass by. Each person claims to be a chief. The others refuse to acknowledge his claims while they advance their own pretensions to status.

Thus you have the situation outlined by one of the Fishers who said:

> I know some places they had one chief until he died and the next generation took over. We didn't have it here. I think that's why we can't get along at all. We had too many chiefs and we had too many minds to think about. Here, if I talk to one of the boys they don't care what I say. I think it's what is troubling us. My grandfather told me when I was a little boy: 'When you become a man, you'll see all your life that these people have a jealous feeling against each other. I've been living a long time and I know it. Anything these Indians want to do, they always mix it up. It's because of the jealousy.' Well, I found out my grandfather was right. Now if I work

and make lots of wood and catch lots of fish, all the people will get jealous. That's how they feel now. They don't like to have a man do anything because they can't do it too. That's why we couldn't get this co-operative fish business going: They thought I was going to get rich on it, and so they found a way to stop it. It was just the jealous feeling. We paid higher prices for the fish. But Jake and Frank told the boys we were stealing money from them. So the boys went back to where they had to sell their fish cheap.

This is but one instance. There are many more. If anyone obtains undue prominence through some political or communal office, the Fishers turn on him and his family and throw him out for fear he will use the status as a marker in the tribal system of prestige. A few years ago when the road opened, the president of the tribal council took part in the ceremonies along with prominent European citizens of the area. Immediately other Fishers were moaning that he had slave ancestry and was therefore quite unfit to represent the tribe on such an important occasion. Once a year the tribe has a day on which it attempts to produce such fragments of the old ceremonial dances as are still remembered. The management of the day has been a bone of contention from the very beginning, if the following quotation is any evidence:

> My father was the first one to ask for this Fisher Day celebration. He thought they should have it so they wouldn't forget all their old dances and ceremonies, and so the younger people growing up would learn about it. He told one of Dave Trapper's boys that he should be president of the first celebration. But people started to talk about Dave's son and to say that he didn't know how things should be done and that he had common blood in him. So he came to my father and said he didn't want to be president because the people talked too much about him. My father said he shouldn't listen to them but just to do his best. Next day he came back and said he just couldn't stand the way people were talking about his people and about him to his face. So he said that my father should be president and he would help him—only my father would be head of it. My father agreed. He started deciding what should be done. Some of the people were talking just as mean as they could to him too. They didn't like the way things were going.

By 1941 no one person could be found who was willing to put up with the insults, and the festivities were in the hands of a

committee or club chosen for this purpose. Immediately insults
and complaints were directed against its chairman, who was finally even accused of embezzling the funds, with the implication
that he was poor and needed the money and also that he did not
know how to behave properly in a position of responsibility. A
woman from another tribe who had lived for some years on the
reserve commented at the time: 'I never lived among people until
we moved here, but gradually I've been learning how they are
here on the reserve. If somebody does something, then the rest
find out about it and aren't interested in helping. They don't seem
to care to be mixed up with it at all, but just sit off and laugh at
them for doing it. I think they're jealous of each other. It shows
up in Fisher Day too. That used to be wonderful I thought, but
this last time I nearly cried when I saw it. Instead of getting in
and helping with it, the people who used to help just sat back and
laughed about what people were doing'.

No member of the tribe has ever held slaves or lived as a slave
—that status vanished so long ago. But accusations of descent
from slaves are still hurled right and left in the struggle to subdue
one's rivals and keep them from competing with one's own position. The Fishers at present have a society in which every individual claims to be of chiefly descent; for heredity has always
been one of the determining factors in prestige. Other members
of the tribe refuse to recognize such hereditary claims and attempt
to prove that the person making the claim has really come out
from among the slaves. They will do this even where it rebounds
against their material advantage as a group. In 1941, the tribe
was fighting in the courts to preserve their rights to certain fishing
sites which lay outside the reserve. Yet important as this fishing
was for everyone, they were quite prepared to ruin their case by
denying that the man who held the site at the time of the treaty
was a man of any standing in the community or that he even
belonged to the tribe. Instead they swore that he was a runaway
slave from some Canadian tribe and thus successfully attacked
the prestige claims of his descendants while they lost themselves
the case.

This peculiar form of rivalry which gives spice to the dealings
of Fisher with Fisher is lacking in relations with Europeans. It
permeates the present day culture of the group to such an extent

that while superficially the culture seems comparable to that of other Americans it is geared to a different value system. Even the younger people are at times preoccupied with questions of status which can find expression only within the confines of their own small society. This may explain partially why despite the ideal held up to generation after generation that they should leave the area and merge themselves into the general population, few Fishers have done so. They have gone for short periods and apparently made successful adjustments. But the overwhelming majority of them have returned.

It appears then that eighty years passed as wards of the Government failed to obliterate completely the cultural differences which distinguish Fishers from other Americans. Instead differences of culture remain. Meantime the ward status and the reservation system have developed new barriers to complete assimilation which may well live on after the complete disappearance of Fisher culture as such.

15 OJIBWA PERSONALITY
AND ACCULTURATION

A. Irving Hallowell

IN RECENT YEARS anthropologists have devoted increasing attention to problems of acculturation, or contact between peoples
with different modes of life. The cultural consequences of such
contacts have been found to be highly variable and often unpre-
dictable. Cultural changes may range all the way from the adoption, by one people, of a few borrowed traits which they easily
fit into their own pattern of life, through cases where whole areas
of a traditional culture pattern have been affected, to those instances in which a sweeping transformation in the life of one
people has resulted from their intimate contact with another.

So far, much more attention has been paid to *what* has happened than to the acculturation process itself. The latter, of
course, is exceedingly complex, since it involves all the various
readjustments in the habits, attitudes, goals, and motivations of
the individuals through whom the novel cultural patterns that
emerge are mediated. For if there were no personal readjustments
in the lives of the people concerned, there would be no subsequent changes observable in the culture pattern of any group.
Consequently, one of the crucial questions is the nature, character, and psychological depth of such readjustments. A comprehensive understanding of the acculturation process, therefore,
demands an approach that is psychologically, as well as culturally,

Originally published in *Acculturation in the Americas,* Proceedings and
Selected Papers of the XXIXth International Congress of Americanists,
edited by Sol Tax, pp. 105–12. Reprinted with permission of the author and
the University of Chicago Press.

oriented. Yet so far even the most obvious psychological aspects of acculturation have received but scanty attention.

If we pursue our inquiries into the psychology of acculturation still further, however, we are faced with another type of problem. This further problem naturally arises out of the recent studies whose major focus has been the relations between culture and personality structure. If contact between peoples with different modes of life may sometimes be the source of basic cultural changes, it seems reasonable to inquire whether, as a result of the same set of readjustments, a parallel reconstellation occurs in the typical psychological characteristics of the people so affected. In other words, are changes in the modal or typical personality organization of the individuals of a society a necessary and intrinsic part of the readjustments that acculturation implies, or can acculturation take place under certain conditions without radical changes in personality structure?

In the first place, it is obvious that we cannot initiate an inquiry of this sort by asking: What are the incentives to personality change? We cannot go out and investigate this question in the same way that we might study the conditions that led to the borrowing of new types of tools or motivated people to acquire a new language or attend the local mission.

Indeed, we may better ask ourselves why the structural basis of the personality should undergo a change at all, so long as individuals can manage to get along without any such change. Furthermore, if the set of personality structure in man is acquired and stabilized early in life and is not under conscious control, we can hardly adopt the hypothesis that changes in personality organization throughout a society would be among the earliest effects of acculturation. In fact, it is hard to imagine how a psychological change of this order could be brought about in less than three generations. Therefore, it seems reasonable to conclude that personality structure, once established, is highly resistant to change. If this is so, then one of our fundamental hypotheses might be that the modal personality structure of a society would be expected to persist until conditions arose that *enforced* some change.

Thus, while all acculturation may be said to involve some psychological readjustment in the sense that, among other things, new habits must be learned or new attitudes or values acquired, there is no reason to assume that such readjustments *in them-selves* involve the psychological core of the personality. Surely iron tools may be substituted for those made of stone, or guns replace bows and arrows, or pidgin English be learned, without any effect upon the personality organization. Let us say, then, that the culture of one group of people may be influenced by that of another in *some* respects without the people of the borrowing group undergoing any necessary change in personality organization.

The crucial question is how far can one language displace an-other, a new world-view or new religion be acquired, moral values be reconstituted, and sweeping changes in technological and ma-terial culture take place without deep and penetrating psychologi-cal effects? Certainly the polar case would be one in which people A in intimate contact with people B had been so transformed in their mode of life that they were culturally indistinguishable from B. In such an instance we might well infer that in modal personality structure they were likewise the equivalent of B.

But in any actual study of acculturated groups this is hardly the situation. What we are usually faced with concretely are differ-ential effects of acculturation processes. This is what complicates the psychological problem and even makes it difficult to compare one acculturated group with another. Especially where there have been continuous contacts over a long period of time, as in the case of the North American Indians and Euro-Americans, varying levels of acculturation are discernible not only in different tribal groups with different cultural backgrounds but among peoples belonging to the same ethnic unit who once shared the same aboriginal culture. Although we have not developed precise meas-ures of acculturation to compare one group with another, never-theless, it is possible to distinguish roughly between different levels of acculturation. This is particularly the case in those in-stances where we know what the native culture was like and where it is apparent that the source of acculturation was Western civilization in its most recent and familiar phases.

The Ojibwa Indians, a food-gathering people originally and now living in communities scattered over a considerable geo-graphical area, represent an ethnic group with a common cultural background but now exhibit varying levels of acculturation. None, of course, live in a purely aboriginal state and few if any have been completely assimilated to Western culture, although some of the Ojibwa in the Province of Ontario closely approximate this situation. In between these extremes four levels of acculturation can be distinguished, on a more or less impressionistic basis, for the purpose of further discussion.

LEVEL 1   The Ojibwa of certain parts of Western Ontario (Canada), e.g., Deer Lake, Sandy Lake, etc. They represent the *least* acculturated groups about which I have any knowledge. No one has studied them, but even the Berens River Indians thought them "primitive."

LEVEL 2   The Inland Ojibwa (Saulteaux) of the Berens River (Canada), whom I first visited in 1932. Some of these Indians are not Christianized and speak no English.

LEVEL 3   The Lakeside Indians of the Berens River. These people are Christianized; they use no aboriginal dwellings, and no former rites or ceremonies persist. As contrasted with the Inland group, no drum is ever heard in this community. Some speak English. About 20 per cent are mixed white and Indian.

LEVEL 4   The Lac du Flambeau Ojibwa (Northern Wisconsin). About 80 per cent are mixed white and Indian. Practically all of them speak English; the children attend an excellent government school; some have radios, etc. This group was in close contact with whites during the lumbering period in Wisconsin and today their reservation is in the midst of a summer tourist area. Nevertheless, a small group still cling to the Midewiwin.

What have been the psychological effects of acculturation upon the Ojibwa? In what respects are they similar to or different from their aboriginal ancestors? Has there been a complete psychological break with the past at one of these levels of acculturation, or is there a demonstrable psychological continuity in personality structure? Is it possible that the psychological readjustments that the acculturation process, or certain stages of it, imply can take place without any radical change in the personality organization of the people involved? If there are modifications, what is their nature? How is the actual behavior of these people affected?

One of the intrinsic difficulties in answering such questions has been the necessity of obtaining the kind of personality data that furnishes a reliable collective picture of a group of individuals, or segments of such a group (men, women, children), as well as data on intra-group variability. In my studies I have found such projective techniques as the Rorschach and TAT to be highly useful instruments. They provide independent psychological data with which other types of observation may be correlated.

Another methodological difficulty has been the necessity of establishing some kind of psychological base line from which changes in personality organization can be measured. Suppose we do manage to obtain reliable information on the modal personality structure of a group of acculturated Indians. How can we tell whether this psychological picture is a function of some stage in the acculturation process or whether it represents the persistence of the same personality organization that was characteristic of people of this ethnic group before acculturation took place? In short, how can we infer change, or continuity, or modification in personality structure without a psychological base line that represents either the pre-contact period or its nearest equivalent?

In my studies of the Ojibwa during the past few years, I have attacked the problems mentioned by taking the following steps:

a In order to obtain some kind of psychological base line from which subsequent changes could be measured, the accounts of observers who had intimate contacts with the Indians of the Eastern Woodlands in the seventeenth and eighteenth centuries were examined. A generalized characterological picture was pieced together which seemed to make psychological sense. Briefly stated, the psychological picture that emerged was that of a people among whom emotional restraint, stoicism, fortitude under torture, the inhibition of all expression of aggression in interpersonal relations, a culturally demanded amiability and mildness in the face of provocation to anger, and suppression of all open criticism of one's fellows are typical characteristics. The whole psychological picture is one that suggests a suffusion in anxiety—anxiety lest one fail to maintain the standard of fortitude required no matter what the hardship one must endure, anxiety lest one provoke resentment or anger in others. This pattern of inhibition was coexistent with an absence of superordinate authority, and, despite the minimal power of chiefs, open conflicts were rare. But *covert* slander was a constant expression of the inhibited aggressive impulses. There was also an institutionalized means of covert aggression—sorcery.

Since there were no highly institutionalized agencies of reward and punishment, individuals functioned in terms of a highly internalized conscience. It is an introverted picture, with individuals highly sensitive to others and friendly only in a reserved way, for they are always wary of the powers of others that may menace them through witchcraft. Any fancied rebuff could be taken as a slight. With so little real give and take on an open, confident, and genuinely friendly basis, there was a high degree of projection in interpersonal relations.

b Field work over a period of years among the Ojibwa of the Berens River, buttressed by the collection and interpretation of a sample of 151 Rorschach records (102 adults, 49 children) was made the basis of a personality characterization of these Indians. The results were similar to those derived from a study of the records of the earlier observers mentioned. There was no evidence to suggest that the levels of acculturation (2 and 3) reached by these Indians had affected the most typical aspects of their personality organization. As already pointed out, however, a cultural gradient was observed among these groups. The Indians who lived close to Lake Winnipeg (the Lakeside group) and who were more closely and continuously in contact with whites were *more* acculturated than the Indians one hundred to two hundred miles up the river (Inland group).

c Because of these observable cultural differences, the next step was to inquire whether there were any concomitant psychological differences between these two groups (Levels 2 and 3). For this purpose a detailed analysis and comparison of the Rorschach protocols of the adults of the two groups was made. Certain differences were clearly discernible. The Lakeside Indians made their responses much faster than the Inland Indians, thus approaching closer to white norms. Some of the Lakeside Indians also showed signs of developing a much more extroverted adjustment, as contrasted with the quite generalized introverted picture presented by their Inland kinsmen. In an article reporting the results of this study these differences were emphasized because one of the purposes of the study was to discover the potentialities of the Rorschach technique. But if you examine the original article, and particularly the graph which gives the means of the Rorschach determinants in the two groups, it will be evident that the personality core in both groups is the same. No radical psychological shift has occurred. There is an essential continuity in personality organization, with some modifications. What is particularly significant, however, is that the nature of some of these modifications indicated that some serious, if not actually neurotic, strains were developing within the personality structure.

On the basis of the steps taken up to this point it seems reasonable to infer (1) that the personality structure of the Berens River Indians, considered as a whole, approximates, if it is not fully identical with, an aboriginal type of modal personality structure which was characteristic not only of the Ojibwa but of other Indians of the Eastern Woodlands; (2) that a considerable degree of acculturation could occur (i.e., up through Level 3) without any radical change in this personality structure; (3) that in the most highly acculturated group thus far examined the readjustment demanded in the acculturation process did produce stresses and strains that were leading to certain modifications in the modal personality structure; and (4) that, while some individuals, especially women, were making an excellent social and psychological adjustment, there were other individuals, men in particular, who were much less successful.

d The last step of interest here is an investigation that was undertaken in the summer of 1946 among the Ojibwa of Lac du Flambeau in northern Wisconsin. On a brief visit to this reservation during the previous summer I was much impressed with the extent to which their mode of life had been affected by acculturation. The Berens River Indians seemed positively aboriginal by comparison, and, in talking with some of the older men at Flambeau, I found that I had seen some of the things that they knew about only by hearsay. As a consequence of these impressions the investigation referred to was initiated. It must be confessed that I anticipated results quite contrary to those being expounded here. At that time I expected that the Flambeau Indians would exhibit a radically different personality picture from that of the northern Ojibwa, somehow skewed in the direction of white Americans.

I took five students from Northwestern University and one student from the University of Chicago into the field to collect pertinent data. Among other things, a good Rorschach sample of the community was obtained. The 238 subjects from whom protocols were obtained represented 29 per cent of the population. Adults and children of both sexes were included. The age span ran from six to seventy years. In addition to this, a good TAT sample of children was collected and other data that need not be mentioned here.

Mr. William Caudill of the University of Chicago, who collected the TAT material on children, recently published a summary of his results. His major conclusion is that these Flambeau children exhibit the same *basic* type of characterological structure as the less acculturated Ojibwa just described. Caudill's conclusion is of special interest because the data pertain to children six to sixteen years of age, rather than adults. One might have thought that these children, many of whom do not speak and scarcely understand Ojibwa, would *not* exhibit a typically Indian pattern.

Although not yet published, parallel Rorschach data on the Flambeau children collected by Mrs. Blanche Watrous of Northwestern University support the conclusions of Mr. Caudill. The conclusions of Mrs. Watrous, moreover, are based on a precise comparison with the series of protocols of Berens River children which I had previously collected. She established the significance of the similarities and differences that appeared at the successive age levels studied in terms of approved mathematical devices.

These two studies of the Flambeau children, along with the other data already cited, furnish a considerable body of evidence that all points in the same direction—a persistent core of psychological characteristics sufficient to identify an Ojibwa personality constellation, aboriginal in origin, that is clearly discernible through all levels of acculturation yet studied. For this reason all the Ojibwa referred to are still Indians in a psychological sense, whatever clothes they wear, whatever their occupation, whether they speak English or not, and regardless of race mixture. While, culturally speaking, they appear more and more like whites at "higher" levels of acculturation, there is no evidence at all for a basic psychological shift in a parallel direction. Thus terms like "borrowing" and "diffusion" which are entirely appropriate to describe the acculturation process in a cultural frame of reference are misleading and inappropriate if the acculturation process is viewed from the standpoint of a psychological frame of reference. At least in the situation described, no identifiable constellation of psychological "traits" has been "borrowed" by the Ojibwa or "diffused" to them as a result of their contacts with whites.

All the evidence points to far more complicated psychological processes than those which have led to the acquisition of the culture traits which I have used as empirical guides to different levels of acculturation. Consequently, descriptive facts of this order are no direct index to facts pertaining to personality adjustment and personality organization.

Perhaps I can best indicate the nature of this more complex psychological problem by clarifying another fundamental point in the data. While these show, as I have said, the persistence of an aboriginal character structure among the Ojibwa, this must not be interpreted to mean that no psychological modifications have been produced in the acculturation process. Actually, quite the contrary is true. Personality structure is a dynamic construct, not a substantive one. When the data at hand are viewed in terms of the actual life-adjustments which individuals have been making, the nature and dynamics of these modifications are fairly clear, although all the evidence is not yet assembled. But it is a striking fact that all through the Rorschach data there are common trends. These are evident whether we compare the Lakeside Indians with the Inland Indians of the Berens River, or the Flambeau children as a whole with the northern children, or the Flambeau adults with the Berens River adults. The impression one receives is of a personality structure which, under the varying pressures of acculturation in the two localities, is being pushed to the limits of its functional adequacy. If, for example, we compare the Indians of Level 2 (Inland group in the Berens River) with those of Level 4 (Flambeau), we obtain a psychological picture in which the latter represent a *regressive* version of the northern group. Many psychological characteristics which in the north bear a positive relation to the adjustment of the individual have been exaggerated to a point where they assume a negative role at Flambeau. The general introverted balance in the north, for instance, is fully integrated with the belief system and other aspects of the old culture. An even greater withdrawal may appear in individuals at Flambeau under conditions where such an adjustment has a negative effect.

What seems to have happened is that the acculturation process at Flambeau has generated a situation in which the personality structure is breaking down, rather than undergoing re-integration on any new or positive level. The individual has been thrown back on his psychological heels, so to speak. He lacks the cultural fulcrum which is necessary for full psychological maturity in any society. The situation might be characterized as one in which there is a frustration of maturity. From the northern Rorschach data we can see what the steps in this process of psychological maturity are. At Flambeau it is a striking fact that the protocols of adults are so much like those of the children. This means that regressive trends in their personality structure make an optimum adjustment impossible under the conditions that now confront them. In this respect they are the antithesis of the Inland group on the Berens River, who are quite well adjusted on the whole. The over-all picture at Flambeau is one that indicates a paucity of internally integrated psychological resources. In the old culture this was largely achieved through the psychological support offered by an aboriginal type of religious belief, which laid a prime emphasis on self-reliance through direct supernatural aid. There has been no real substitute for this in a superficially acquired Christianity. Perhaps this explains why even now a few Indians at Flambeau cling to the Midewiwin, which epitomizes this aboriginal outlook.

The old Ojibwa character was also built on a psychological foundation which required a maximum of *inner* control, since, from the standpoint of their social organization, highly institutionalized outer controls and sanctions were practically absent. This psychological feature of the Ojibwa is also at the basis of the so-called "social atomism" of their aboriginal society. While this inner control is still present, it has been modified in a regressive direction so that it easily breaks down. In actual behavior evidence of this is to be seen in the tremendous incidence of drunkenness and juvenile delinquency on the Flambeau Reservation.

Such behavior may also be interpreted as a sign of the terrific psychological struggle which many individuals are experiencing in reacting to the apathy which the paucity of inner resources, brought about by the regression I have spoken of, produces. They are attempting to survive in a situation which, as yet, offers them no culturally defined values and goals that they have really made their own and which have become psychologically significant for them. Their advanced stage of acculturation as externally viewed is thus deceptive. From a psychological point of view they are not yet *acculturated enough,* in the sense that, while contact with the version of Western civilization available has enabled them to acquire innumerable culture traits, so far at least it has not provided the psychological means that might implement a satisfactory basis for personal adjustment.

Godfrey and Monica Wilson

THE DIFFERENCE between the traditional societies of Central Africa and modern Central African society is, in one respect, a difference of size. Comparatively few people were in close relations in the old societies, and their characteristics were correlates of their smallness of scale; many people are in close relations in the modern society, and its characteristics are correlates of its largeness of scale. That difference of scale is a fundamental difference between primitive and civilized society has long been recognized, but the concept has lacked precision. We seek to refine it.

THE BOUNDARIES OF SOCIETY

Society is always universal in the sense that living people everywhere are always involved, however indirectly, with all other living people and with all past generations since the emergence of man. Until recently, however, it has never been universal in the sense that all these relations have been in any degree directly realized, that is, have been sufficiently intense for men to be aware of their positive content. The extent of conscious relations, contemporary and historical, is the extent of a particular society. Only quite recently has any particular society approached universality. We to-day are conscious of relations between past groups of which they themselves knew nothing.

Originally published as Chapter II of *The Analysis of Social Change* by Godfrey and Monica Wilson, Cambridge University Press, 1945. Reprinted with permission of Monica Wilson and the Cambridge University Press.

Societies overlap and shade into one another. The men of primitive Ngonde had direct contacts with the Bemba, but not with the more distant Lala; the Bemba had direct contacts both with Ngonde and with the Lala. Thus Bemba society included both the Lala and Ngonde, while Ngonde society included the Bemba only. Every society must be given a point of reference before it can be defined. When we speak of 'Nyakyusa society' or 'Central African society' we include all the relations directly realized by the Nyakyusa, and by the inhabitants of Central Africa, respectively.

CRITERIA OF SCALE

By the scale of a society we mean the number of people in relation and the intensity of those relations. Modern Central African society is larger in scale than those which preceded it, not only because more people are in conscious relations with one another, but also because the relations between Africa and the outside world, and between contemporary Africans and long past generations, are more intense than they were. In comparing the scale of societies therefore, we compare the relative size of groups with relations of similar intensity.

The members of all societies are equally dependent upon one another, but the range of their interdependence varies geographically and historically. A Bushman, we maintain, is as dependent upon his fellows as an Englishman, but the Englishman depends upon many more people than does the Bushman. The Englishman gets his food from the four quarters of the globe, and is directly affected by the ideas of twenty-five centuries. The Bushman depends for food only upon his immediate neighbours, and is affected by the ideas of past generations only in so far as they are communicated to him by those elders whose life overlaps with his. The total degree of interdependence, or intensity of relations, is the same, but in the case of the Englishman it is more spread out. The intensity of particular relations varies in different societies, but the total intensity of all the relations of society does not. It follows, therefore, that as the range of relations increases, the degree of dependence upon neighbours and contemporaries diminishes (Durkheim 1949).

The intensity of relations in a given group is to be measured by the intensity of co-operation,[1] and of intellectual and emotional communication, both contemporary and historical. That is:

i   By the proportion of economic co-operation within that group to the total economic co-operation of the society, whether that co-operation is with contemporaries in the form of joint production, or exchange through trade and reciprocal gifts; or with past generations through the use of capital inherited from them. The area of close economic co-operation in primitive societies is much smaller than in civilized society, and the capital inherited from past generations is also smaller.

ii   By the proportion of communication of fact in speech and writing, within that group, to the total intellectual communication of the society. The area of communication is necessarily smaller in an illiterate society than in a literate one. Primitives often have little knowledge of what is going on a hundred miles away, and oral traditions beyond the memory of the oldest inhabitants are meagre.

iii   By the proportion of emotional expression communicated within that group to the total expression of the society. In primitive societies communication of feeling barely extends beyond personal contacts, for there is no literary art, and each small group being largely self-sufficient, the manufactured articles which circulate are few. Historically, it is also limited by the absence of written records and of lasting mediums. In civilized society, on the other hand, books and musical scores, tools, utensils and pictures travel far and wide, and are inherited from generations long past.

iv   By the relative value set on contemporary co-operation and continuity within and without the group. In primitive societies co-operation within small local groups was valued; co-operation with distant groups was not. In civilized society, on the other hand, loyalty to large political groups is a value constantly pursued. Religious inclusiveness is limited by race, nation and class, but a universal society is valued by some. Christians praise neighbourly

---

[1] War is included in co-operation.

behaviour even between Jews and Samaritans; Communists appeal for the unity of the workers of the world.

All societies value continuity, but the period over which it is valued varies. In primitive society the period is limited by the absence of traditions going back more than ten or twelve generations (Evans-Pritchard 1940). Civilized societies, on the other hand, boast of the continuity between their institutions, topics of discussion and modes of expression and those of the ancient world. By *continuity* we mean both the volume of material co-operation and communication with the past, and the non-material unity that exists when people act, speak and feel as if it were a reality. This non-material continuity is differently defined in different societies. Primitives tend to define it as cultural similarity, and stress observance of the *same* customs as were practised by their fathers. In modern society it is development which is stressed—there is held to be a certain continuity between feudalism and modern constitutional government, not because both are alike, but because one grew out of the other (Trevelyan 1926).

v   By the relative degree of unity and continuity dogmatically asserted within and without the group. Small groups often emphasize their common descent, larger groups their common race, others their common humanity, thus expressing both present unity and continuity with the past. Or the common bond emphasized may be cultural homogeneity. Literate groups, having greater historical knowledge, trace their common descent or common culture through more generations than illiterate groups.

vi   By the degree in which a sense of unity and continuity is expressed within the group, compared to that expressed with outsiders. Unity and continuity are expressed in a common name, a common style of dress, a common flag, or, as Professor Radcliffe-Brown has shown in his classical exposition (1922) through common myths and ceremonies. The way in which the area of application of a common symbol increases as intensity of relations increases is illustrated by the traditional and modern use of the name *Nyakyusa*. Traditionally it applied to a few chiefdoms on the north shore of Lake Nyasa. Neighbouring groups of similar culture, with whom relations were tenuous, called themselves the people of Selya, of Kukwe, and of Mwamba. Now all three groups are in close relations and commonly refer to themselves as Nyakyusa.[2] In civilized society the group using a common symbol, such as a name, extends much further historically, as well as geographically, than in primitive society.

vii By the degree of social pressure exerted within the group compared with that exerted on and by outsiders. The more intense the relations between individuals or groups the greater the mutual pressure they exert on each other. In primitive societies power is exercised only within a comparatively small group. The area in which any ruler can exert pressure by force of arms, and in which law is effective, is limited. The range of power in time is as limited as it is in space. Legal decisions are made in accordance with precedents, but since there are no written records the cases cited are necessarily comparatively recent. Ancestors are believed to have power over men, but it is the immediate ancestors who are feared. Similarly, logical and conventional pressure are exerted only within a small group. A man is not influenced by the arguments of those living at a distance or those long dead. He fears the scorn and enjoys the admiration only of neighbours and contemporaries.

In civilized societies the range of social pressure is much greater. The military power of large groups extends over the world, and law is effective over wide areas. Through written codes and records of case law, generations long dead directly affect contemporary law. The values of Christ, of Buddha and of Mohammed directly affect behaviour to-day—it is not only his immediate predecessors who have moral power over a civilized man. Similarly, his thoughts and feelings are shaped by those far from him in space and time.

We measure the intensity of relations within a group, then, by observing the proportion of economic co-operation, of communication of ideas and of feelings within and without the group; together with the relative inclusiveness of value, of dogma and of symbolism within and without the group, and the degree of social pressure exerted within and without the group.

Groups and individuals within the same society differ in the range and intensity of their relations. In Central Africa, for ex-

---

[2] We use 'Nyakyusa' in its modern sense, and 'Nyakyusa proper' for the smaller group.

ample, the Europeans are in more intense relations with the outside world than the Africans, and an educated Swahili is similarly
wider in scale in his relations than a conservative Nyakyusa. The
proportion of the population that is wide scale in their relations
is another measure of intensity in the wider relations. It *is* the
relative intensity of the wider relations compared with the narrower.

These criteria of intensity cannot of course be measured with
mathematical precision: we seek only a means of comparing relative intensity. The reasons for our choice of these criteria are
explained in the next chapter.

The intensity of relations, be it noted, is distinguished from
cultural similarity; for there may, at any moment, be considerable cultural similarity due to close co-operation and communication with a common parent society, but little present co-operation
and communication, as when sections of tribes (such as the
Makololo and Ngoni) left their traditional homes and settled at
a far distance from their relatives, but retained much of their
traditional culture.

THE BOUNDARIES OF COMMUNITY

Within society are *communities,* which, like society, we define
historically as well as geographically (Evans-Pritchard 1940).
Communities are areas and periods of common life of more or
less intensity. To facilitate the comparison of scale we distinguish
between the largest community and extra-communal relations.
The boundaries of community are the boundaries of many-sided
relationship; extra-communal relations are one-sided and tenuous.
The boundaries of community, like those of society, vary with
the point of reference, and the exact line of demarcation is not
always clear, but in cases in which the relevant facts are known it
can be defined as falling within certain narrow limits.

Historically, circles of community are always interlocking; geographically they may be interlocking or discrete. That is to say, if
we take a point of reference *A,* and *B* is a point on the boundary
of community *A,* the boundaries of community *B* may or may
not coincide with those of community *A.* Community *B* may in-

clude only part of the area of community *A*, and also part of a third area, community *C*.

Among the Nyakyusa, for example, community did not extend from any particular point of reference beyond the neighbouring chiefdoms and the lifetime of the oldest inhabitants. Historically, these circles were interlocking; geographically, they were at least partially discrete. At some points communities were separated by physical barriers, such as the wall of the Livingstone Mountains between the Nyakyusa and Kinga, and the uninhabited forest belt between Selya and the Nyakyusa proper, and therefore did not interlock; but we do not think that all the boundaries of groups of neighbouring chiefdoms were as difficult to cross as these. On this point we lack evidence.

The main productive unit of the Nyakyusa (G. Wilson 1936) was the individual family. Circulation of wealth was chiefly in the form of marriage gifts; and marriage, though most frequent within the chiefdom, occurred fairly often between neighbouring chiefdoms, but not between distant ones. Beyond the neighbouring chiefdoms there was trade in iron, salt, a red dye, and cloth, which were exchanged for cattle, food and ivory; but the volume of this trade was very small indeed, and it was usually mediated by neighbours. Only the people of chiefdoms next to the Kinga, the producers of the red dye, bought straight from them, and they in turn sold it only to neighbouring chiefdoms. There was no coming and going of traders between distant chiefdoms. Cattle raids also were made only against neighbouring chiefdoms.

Capital was inherited in the form of cattle, seed, a few tools, certain knowledge and skills, and rights over land. This involved a degree of co-operation with distant ancestors—the domesticators of cattle, the first agriculturalists and inventors, the original occupants of the land—but relations with these creators of their cultural heritage were not directly realized. Such legends as there are of the beginnings of Nyakyusa culture are put but ten generations back. Fire, for example, is said to have been brought by the chiefs who, ten generations ago, descended from the Livingstone Mountains and conquered the previous inhabitants of the Nyakyusa valley. Until then the men of the valley had eaten their food raw.

Not only were the Nyakyusa unaware of relations extending

more than ten generations back, but the volume of capital inherited was small compared with that in a civilized society, and men were wholly dependent for it on the immediately preceding generation. They did not inherit buildings and roads and irrigation schemes, made by distant ancestors about whom they knew, as do civilized men.

There was no writing, and so intellectual communication was largely confined to personal contacts which rarely extended beyond the neighbouring chiefdoms. As we have seen traditions going back ten generations existed—old men recited genealogies and told of battles lost and won—but the facts known about generations beyond living memory were few. For example, of the numbers and culture of the conquerors who came down from the Livingstones ten generations ago, and of the previous occupants of the valley, the Nyakyusa know nothing. It is difficult even to discover details of everyday life before the coming of the Europeans in 1891.

Communication of feeling was also mainly through personal contacts and confined to neighbouring chiefdoms and overlapping generations. Dancing was among the chief mediums of expression and people did not attend dances beyond the circle within which they married. Each tiny group was, as we have seen, largely self-sufficient; the only manufactured goods traded beyond neighbouring chiefdoms were iron tools and weapons and cloth, and the quantity of these was very small. Elton (1879) (the first European to travel through the country) speaks of rarely seeing cloth in 1877, and even in 1936 in remote districts the use of iron hoes was still confined to men, women using digging sticks, though near the Government station women too used iron hoes.

There were no lasting mediums except iron, baked clay, and hard wood; and since iron was scarce, clay pots shattered, and hard wood was little used, the works of art passing down the generations were as few as those circulated beyond neighbouring chiefdoms. Where the circles of community interlocked geographically, tales and dances and songs may have travelled far in space as they did in time—the great similarity of folk tales over Bantu Africa proves that they travelled at least one way—but without writing and choreography and musical scores the volume of art thus circulated was necessarily limited. What was forgotten by one generation was lost for good.

The Nyakyusa valued co-operation within the group of neighbouring chiefdoms, but not beyond it. They held that it was best to marry within the chiefdom, allowable to marry in a neighbouring chiefdom, but not good to marry at a distance. So too it was continuity with the customs of their fathers, rather than with those of distant ancestors, that was insisted upon. Since tradition did not go back further than ten generations the range of continuity valued at all was short. Whether the heroes whose names and adventures are remembered actually lived only ten generations ago is here irrelevant; beyond that, continuity was neither conceived nor valued.

The unity of groups of neighbouring chiefdoms and their distinction from others, was further asserted in a dogma of common descent—the chiefs of Selya were closely related, as were those of the Kukwe, and of the Nyakyusa proper—and expressed in a common ritual, the chief of the senior line in each group sacrificing on its behalf. This dogmatic and ritual unity applied to the groups of neighbouring chiefdoms in Selya, among the Kukwe, and the Nyakyusa proper, respectively. Thus, in so far as Nyakyusa communities were discrete, the unity of each was expressed in dogma and ritual; in so far as they were geographically interlocking, the unity of border communities was not so expressed.

These same dogmas and rituals asserted and symbolized unity with near, rather than with more distant ancestors. One of us attended a ritual in Selya to which the junior chief of the group, who traditionally should have sent a cow to be killed by the senior, refused to do so, on the ground that 'the relationship was now distant'.

Relationship was also asserted beyond the boundaries of community. Between the chiefs of Selya and the Nyakyusa proper it was actually traced, but it was much more distant than within each group. Between the chiefs of the Kukwe and other Nyakyusa, and between the Nyakyusa, the people of Ngonde, the Ndali, the Kinga, the Bena and the Hehe, it was believed to exist, but no one could trace it. The people of Selya, the Nyakyusa proper, and the Kinga were further linked by a common ritual sacrificing to a reputed common ancestor, Lwembe, but these bonds were not in themselves sufficient to create community between groups who scarcely traded or intermarried, and who knew little about one another.

The range of social pressure was likewise limited. Law was effective within each tiny chiefdom of 100 to 3,000 men, and was sometimes applied to cases between members of neighbouring chiefdoms. It did not apply to strangers from a distance unless they were under the special protection of the chief, or of a member of the chiefdom. Men of Selya feared to travel even to Tukuyu twenty-five miles away, for strangers were liable to be assaulted and robbed, and had no redress.

It was only within and between neighbouring chiefdoms, also, that there was war. Funeral dances were a common occasion of dispute. When a man went to the funeral of his kinsmen in a neighbouring chiefdom, the young men of his own chiefdom often accompanied him armed, and joined in the dancing. They danced as a group showing off before the girls of the other chiefdom, and doing everything they could to appear fiercer and braver than their rivals. In this electric situation, charged with the memory of past fights and rivalries, insults were often hurled, and then another fight would occur (G. Wilson 1939a). Attendance at funerals, however, did not extend beyond the circle within which men married, and therefore this occasion for war only occurred between members of neighbouring chiefdoms. One or two Ngoni and Sango raids are remembered, but neither Ngoni nor Sango entered Nyakyusa country in force, and their raids were few.

Supernatural sanctions were believed to be effective only against kinsmen, neighbours, and those with whom a man was in personal contact. No one feared witchcraft from outside the chiefdom (G. Wilson 1936). Historically, also, it was those who were near who were feared. A commoner only made offerings to immediately past generations; and even chiefs, whose genealogies were better remembered, and who sacrificed to more remote ancestors, sacrificed more frequently to their fathers and grandfathers. In the prayers of chiefs and commoners alike the names of the ancestors were invoked in ascending order.

With relations so tenuous, neither the arguments of those beyond neighbouring chiefdoms, nor their conventions, could influence men, any more than could their laws.

There was then considerable intensity of relations within the area of neighbouring Nyakyusa chiefdoms, and between overlapping generations, but beyond this relations were tenuous and one-sided. With some distant chiefdoms there was a tradition of common descent, and occasionally a common ritual; with others there was a small volume of trade; with the Ngoni and Sango there was occasional war; but with no distant group was there many-sided relationship. With generations beyond living memory there was a degree of religious unity appearing in morality, dogma and ritual, but little economic co-operation with them, and little knowledge of them. But few works of art were inherited from them. Nyakyusa community, therefore, did not extend beyond living memory and neighbouring chiefdoms, though Nyakyusa society went back ten generations and included the people[3] within an area of perhaps 5,000 square miles, Ngoni raiders, and Arab traders.

The boundaries of community were somewhat wider geographically in Ngonde than among the Nyakyusa: not only was the circle of extra-communal relations wider, but relations with the Arabs, though still one-sided, were much more intense than they were between Nyakyusa and Arab. Ngonde trade in ivory was considerable. In the historical moment also the scale was correspondingly greater (G. Wilson 1939b). Bemba society was likewise larger in scale than Nyakyusa society (Richards 1940).

Although the traditional societies of Central Africa differed thus in scale, the differences between them were, however, slight compared with the difference between the largest of them and modern Central African society. Taking England as the point of reference, community now extends geographically over practically the whole world—only a few remote tribes, such as those in Central New Guinea and on the Amazon, are excluded from it—and historically for well over 2,000 years. Central Africa, though not yet in as close relations with the outside world or with past gen-

---

[3] Taking Selya as the point of reference these were: the Kinga, the Kesi, the Bena, the Hehe, the Safwa, the Poroto, the Nyika, the Penja, the Lambia, the Ndali, the Sango, and the men of Ngonde; as well as the Kukwe, the Mwamba and the Nyakyusa proper.

erations as is England, is already within the circle of universal community.

As we have seen, Central Africa trades with the world and is seriously affected by fluctuations in the world market; capital accumulated by past generations, including the vast body of knowledge and skill handed down through many literate generations, is invested there. It is in communication with the world, and, through its literate inhabitants who read the Bible and the Koran and who are beginning to study history, with distant generations. Manufactured goods and works of art from the five continents circulate—cloth from Japan, books from Europe, films from America, tennis racquets from Australia—and so do the music and books and pictures of long past generations. It is common to hear the psalms of David, or a Bach choral, or to see a copy of a Renaissance Madonna in a remote African church.

With the spread of universal religions the range of morality has extended. Christians praise co-operation with all men, Mohammedans with their fellow-believers, and both seek inspiration from prophets and saints long dead. Communists, too, value co-operation on a universal scale, and though their great prophets are within living memory yet they value the continuity between their struggles and those of revolutionaries throughout the ages. So, too, in dogma and symbol the unity of universal groups are expressed. The Christian celebrates All Saints' Day, the Mohammedan the fast of Ramadan, the Communist his May Day, all remembering both the living and the dead of their faith.

Nevertheless, religious inclusiveness is still limited by nationality, race and class. Interracial marriage, for example, is as much discouraged in Central Africa to-day as was marriage with distant chiefdoms by the Nyakyusa.

Law is effective, during peace time, over most of the world. Were it not that the person and property of foreigners were protected there could be no international trade and travel, 'Violations of . . . (international) law are extremely rare. . . . The common impression to the contrary arises from the unfortunate concentration of popular interest on the laws of war, and a consequent failure to observe that the less sensational but far more important part of the system, the laws of peace, is constantly and unobtrusively observed in the daily intercourse of states' (Brierly

1928). War, like law, is on a world scale, and thought and feeling are shaped by those distant in space and time.

COMPARABLE GROUPS

We have argued that in comparing the scale of societies it is necessary to compare the range of groups with relations of similar intensity, and to facilitate comparison we have distinguished communities, groups with more intense relations, from extra-communal relations, the less intense relations of society. The relative scale of a society from any given point of reference may then be judged by (*a*) the relative number of people living and dead in conscious relation, and (*b*) the relative number of people living and dead in community. Modern Central African society includes the population of the world and all the past generations of which we are aware. Nyakyusa society included perhaps 250,-000 souls and ten past generations. The modern Central African community includes very nearly the whole population of the world and perhaps 7,000 generations; a Nyakyusa community included perhaps 30,000 of the living and those who had died within their memory.

This is, of course, only a very rough measure of relative scale, for the degree of community between distant groups may be greater or less, and the degree of intensity of extra-communal relations greater or less. Of two societies with equal numbers in conscious relation and in community, that in which the wider relations are more intense is larger in scale.

INCREASE IN SCALE

Increase in the scale of a society may be by an increase in the numbers in relation through increase in population, exploration, or historical and archaeological discovery; or by an increase in the intensity of the more tenuous relations. In the modern world geographical expansion has practically reached its limit, but there may be an increase in scale not only through increase in population and the discovery by archaeologists of previously unknown societies, but also through an increase in the intensity of the relations between races and classes, and between the present and the past. It is also possible that, if wars continue, the scale of modern society may diminish.

Our hypothesis is that the total degree of dependence upon others, i.e. the intensity of relations, is the same in all societies, but that it may be more or less spread out. Intensity in the narrower circles of relation necessarily diminishes as intensity in the wider circles increases.

Our examples so far have been framed to show increasing intensity in the wider relations, but the same facts may illustrate decreasing intensity in the narrower relations. In a small-scale society a man is wholly dependent upon his immediate circle of contemporaries for food; there may be plenty in one district and famine across the mountains; plenty in one season and famine in the next. In a civilized society men are not so dependent upon neighbours, for food comes from the ends of the earth, and in times of famine they may draw upon capital accumulated by their ancestors to buy from a distance.

Similarly, a civilized man is less dependent upon his neighbours and contemporaries intellectually and emotionally than a primitive. He reads books written by those living at a distance and those long dead; he enjoys the music of Bach or Beethoven on wireless and gramophone, and the films of America and Europe; while the primitive has no choice but the conversation and songs of his fellow-villagers. In an illiterate society without lasting mediums men are wholly dependent upon overlapping generations for the knowledge and techniques they inherit. What is not passed on during the lifetime of the wise and skilled is lost, for there can be no rediscovery of ancient manuscripts and works of art.

The corollary of this is that local patriotism declines as wider loyalties develop, and emphasis on the worship of immediate ancestors diminishes with increase in historical range. The civic sense is not as strong in a modern borough as in a city state; nor is the unity of the kinship group as great in England as in a primitive society. A civilized man who put his town or his family before his state would be judged wrong by his fellows, though one who puts his state before some wider group is still usually judged to be right. A pagan Nyakyusa believes himself to be dependent upon his deceased father for health and fertility; he acts as if he were, and expresses his sense of dependence in rituals.

A civilized man does not believe himself to be so dependent upon his immediate ancestors, but claims to follow the teaching of Christ or Confucius; Buddha, Mohammed or Marx. That Marx lived last century is from this point of view accidental—he may well be honoured many generations hence. Greater autonomy in the narrower relations as well as greater subordination in the wider, is thus an aspect of the increase in scale.

17 ACCULTURATION:
AN EXPLORATORY FORMULATION

The Social Science Research Council
Summer Seminar on Acculturation, 1953.

Leonard Broom, Bernard J. Siegel,
Evon Z. Vogt and James B. Watson

T HE PHENOMENA of acculturation continue to command wide
interest among anthropologists and, to some extent, among
sociologists and psychologists. Published literature on acculturation is accumulating rapidly (Keesing 1953); each year new research and applied programs are being formulated for further
study of the phenomena and for possible application of the knowledge to practical affairs; additional courses on the subject are
being added to academic curricula. There appears to be agreement that careful analysis of acculturation situations and sequences offers some of our best opportunities for understanding
cultural dynamics. Yet it is evident that the collection of empirical materials on acculturation proceeds faster than theoretical
attempts to order and codify the central concepts which will make
the studies yield maximum results. This theoretical lag is undoubtedly related to (*a*) the unusually rapid expansion and proliferation of empirical studies of acculturation; (*b*) the shift in
emphasis from diachronic, cultural history studies to synchronic
functional studies, with a corresponding emphasis upon the general concept of *structure* and a relative neglect of the concept of
process; and (*c*) the fact that interest in acculturation—in the
United States at least—grew out of the earlier concern with sal-
vaging "memory" cultures. This last tendency has fostered a
predominant concern with the postcontact ethnography of "recep-

Originally published in *American Anthropologist,* Volume 56 (1954), 973–
1000. Reprinted with permission of the authors and of the editor of *American
Anthropologist.*

tor" cultures, while the "donor" tacitly receives the status of an independent variable.

With this estimate as a background, a few actively interested anthropologists proposed to the Social Science Research Council that one of its interuniversity summer research seminars be devoted to acculturation problems. The seminar was held during July and August of 1953 at Stanford University, and four of the participants—three anthropologists (Siegel, Vogt, and Watson) and one sociologist (Broom)—are the authors of this article. We are especially indebted to the fifth member of the seminar, Homer Barnett, who contributed importantly to the discussions and to this paper, although he has not joined us in its final preparation. The discussions during the eight-week period ranged widely and informally over the field of culture change. The efforts in this paper follow other attempts to synthesize and codify research and theory in the field of acculturation (Thurnwald 1932; Bateson 1935; Redfield, Linton, and Herskovits 1936; Herskovits 1938; Mair 1938; Linton 1940; Malinowski 1945; Hallowell 1945; Ramos 1947; Moore 1951; Beals 1953; Wax Ms.). It should be emphasized that the paper is intended to be exploratory and suggestive, rather than conclusive and definitive. It takes previous work into account but it does not purport to be a review of our state of knowledge with respect to acculturation. Instead, it represents the authors' conception of an orderly approach to the study of cultural change as it is generated by culture contact. During the course of the seminar the authors benefited from consultations with J. B. Casagrande, A. L. Kroeber, G. Bateson, G. D. Spindler, and from the efficient service of Rose Wax, the rapporteur. We also wish to express our gratitude to the Social Science Research Council for the opportunity to engage in the seminar.

DELINEATION OF THE PROBLEM

For the purposes of the formulation under consideration, acculturation may be defined as culture change that is initiated by the conjunction of two or more autonomous cultural systems. Acculturative change may be the consequence of direct cultural transmission; it may be derived from noncultural causes, such as ecological or demographic modifications induced by an impinging culture; it may be delayed, as with internal adjustments following upon the acceptance of alien traits or patterns; or it may be a reactive adaptation of traditional modes of life. Its dynamics can be seen as the selective adaptation of value systems, the processes of integration and differentiation, the generation of developmental sequences, and the operation of role determinants and personality factors.

An autonomous cultural system is one which is self-sustaining —that is, it does not need to be maintained by a complementary, reciprocal, subordinate, or other indispensable connection with a second system. Such units are systems because they have their own mutually adjusted and interdependent parts, and they are autonomous because they do not require another system for their continued functioning. An autonomous cultural system is what is usually called "a culture" in the anthropological literature, but the more explicit denotation at once makes the concept more definitive and delimits the incidence of acculturation as defined. Thus, cultural changes induced by contacts between ethnic enclaves and their encompassing societies would be definable as acculturative, whereas those resulting from the interactions of factions, classes, occupational groups, or other specialized categories within a single society would not be so considered. Hence, socialization, urbanization, industrialization, and secularization are not acculturation processes unless they are cross-culturally introduced rather than intraculturally developed phenomena.

This delimitation of the field is dictated by strategic considerations. For unless the culture concept is construed at some broadly inclusive level (viz., a tribe) the analyst is ultimately reduced to dealing with particularized "cultures" such as those of families or even individuals. Indeed, the equating of acculturation with the socialization of the individual seems to us to make explicit this methodological error. If attention is not centered on the conjunction of markedly different cultural traditions, the analyst is confronted with effects too microscopic to yield to existing techniques of analysis. For the present it would seem to be more fruitful to concentrate upon the conjunction of cultural differences that are wide and deep.

The unit of analysis in acculturation studies is thus taken to be any given culture as it is carried by its particular society. It is recognized that individuals are empirically the culture bearers and that they are the mediators of any cultural process. Students of culture are, however, concerned with individuals as functioning members of a society and with the shared patterns of behavior constituting a body of customs. Consequently, while it is individuals who change their habits of doing and believing under the influence of alien forms, it is the body of custom of the society to which they belong that is said to be acculturated.

Our formulation envisages four principal facets of the phenomenon of acculturation: (1) the characterization of the properties of the two or more autonomous *cultural systems* which come into contact; (2) the study of the nature of the *contact situation;* (3) the analysis of the *conjunctive relations* established between the cultural systems upon contact; and (4) the study of the *cultural processes* which flow from the conjunction of the systems. Each of these facets is treated under a separate heading in this paper and embodies distinctive theoretical problems which bear upon developments following the meeting of diverse ways of life. What is said in each section has relevance to other sections as well.

CULTURAL SYSTEMS

Acculturation theory would be greatly advanced if it were possible to characterize the properties of autonomous systems in a way that would be meaningful in respect to their behavior under contact conditions. Ideally it should be possible to specify the effects that one kind of system will have on another. If such a typological approach is feasible, it must deal with those features of a system which are directly relevant to problems of change when contact occurs. There are numerous ways in which cultures can be classified, such as simple-complex, folk-urban, Apollonian-Dionysian, and so on. While these dichotomies may be important for a study of cultural change, their relevance for acculturation remains to be demonstrated.

In this section we shall explore three variable properties of cultural systems that appear to affect the course of acculturation: (*a*) boundary-maintaining mechanisms which are found in "closed" as opposed to "open" systems; (*b*) the relative "rigidity" or "flexibility" of the internal structure of a cultural system; and (*c*) the nature and functioning of self-correcting mechanisms in cultural systems. We do not wish to imply that these are the *only* variable properties of cultural systems which affect acculturation. Rather, they are properties which occurred to us as being relevant, important, and insufficiently analyzed in the acculturation literature to date.

Boundary-Maintaining Mechanisms

One order of difference among cultural systems which may be objectively verifiable, common, and therefore significant is variation in their boundary-maintaining mechanisms. These comprise the techniques and ideologies by means of which a system limits participation in the culture to a well-recognized in-group. Here the relatively "open" society of the United States, which has admitted diverse immigrants for many years, may be contrasted with the "closed" systems of the Southwestern Pueblos which admit few aliens and censure their own members who do not conform to the key values of the culture. Boundary-maintaining mechanisms appear to include the relative presence or absence of devices by which the knowledge of customs and values is restricted to in-group members and thus shielded from alien influence. In some systems the whole range of culture is open to inspection by members of other societies while in others key customs are carefully guarded from outside observers.

Some examples of specific boundary-maintaining mechanisms which may operate in a closed system are: ritual initiations into the in-group; cleansing ceremonies to reintroduce an in-group member to his society after an absence; secret activities for in-group members only; localizing ceremonies in the homeland; the cultivation of self-defining concepts, such as ethnocentrism, or racism; the posting of territory or the lowering of isolationist "curtains"; the designation of contact agents or alien "handlers"; high evaluation of the group's language or dialect; the erection of legal barriers.

All of these devices are widely practiced, but not to the same extent nor for the same purpose. However, their concentration or lack of it may be the mark of a closed or resistant system as opposed to an open or susceptible one under contact conditions. A type case which manifests most of the above mechanisms is modern Zuni (Adair and Vogt 1949); an example of an open system would be the contemporary Palauans (Barnett 1949). Before validating an "open-closed" typology based upon boundary-maintaining mechanisms it would be necessary to examine more closely the data we have on precontact conditions. It is possible that some of the proliferation of boundary-maintaining mechanisms is a postcontact phenomenon and that closed systems are really a manifestation of reactive adaptations.

"Flexible" vs. "Rigid" Systems

Another important typological distinction might be based upon the relative "rigidity" or "flexibility" of the internal structure of a cultural system. A tight or rigid interrelatedness—or its opposite —may prevail either with respect to the total value structure of a society or with respect primarily or solely to its social structure. Inclusiveness, precision, articulation, and range of variation might be utilized as yardsticks of integration in social or in over-all value configurations: multiple or single avenues to prestige or other goals, ambiguous vs. clearly defined interpersonal relations, authoritarian vs. equalitarian social controls, ascribed vs. achieved statuses, prescribed vs. situationally defined activities, specified vs. alternative patterns of conduct, and so forth. The acme of tight integration, on the social side at least, is probably achieved in systems which sanction autocratic powers in one or a few elite roles, such as absolute monarchies, theocracies, and gerontocracies. The Zulu (Gluckman 1940b), the Pueblos (Eggan 1950), the Australians (Warner 1937), and sects such as the Hutterites (Eaton 1952), and the Amish (Kollmorgen 1942) provide examples. The Ghetto Jews of Eastern Europe (Bienenstok 1950) are a related case. Loosely integrated systems may be illustrated by the Chukchi (Bogoras 1904–09), the Siriono (Holmberg 1950), and the Shoshone (Steward 1938).

In itself, degree of integration affords no basis for predicting contact reactions. If, however, the outlines of a social structure or an underlying value system are unequivocal and inflexible previous to contact, they are more likely to be so under challenge from outsiders. Furthermore, if they are of a positive and invariant nature they will probably be supported by strong rationalizations and emotional commitments. If, in addition, there are relatively few key or command values in its hierarchy, a system is likely to be rigid and self-consciously resistant to alteration on contact, since it is already organized defensively probably as a result of external or internal challenges in the past. But here again, as with boundary-maintaining mechanisms, it is important to ascertain whether we are in fact dealing with precontact phenomena.

Self-Correcting Mechanisms

While boundary-maintaining mechanisms refer to the surface tension attributes of the cultural "organism," self-correcting mechanisms refer to the ability of the cultural "organism" to shift function and to adapt internally, irrespective of its outer protective devices. The analysis of the forces of equilibrium within social structures, focusing attention upon their dynamic qualities and potentialities for variation, is also useful for the study of acculturation. This conceptual dimension recognizes the overt and covert struggles for power and position, the divisive tendencies of factionalism, and the centrifugal tensions produced by individual rejection of group expectations. It is assumed that in most, if not all, systems there is some degree of real or latent conflict, contradiction, or opposition of interests between certain segments of a society; even in groups where there are no major conflicts there is never full assent or conformance with respect to ascribed and achieved status and role. All this is another way of saying that no way of life is completely satisfying to all members of a society; and that the existing reward system will be sufficiently frustrating to some who, by their challenging attitudes, may threaten the values of the society.

Set off against this assumption of disruptive tendencies is the complementary one which asserts that there must be counterforces at work sufficient at least to maintain the pattern of a particular social order. These adjustive devices are highly variable depending on the value definitions of the culture. They include measures of social control ranging from the arbitrary use of force to techniques for insuring the personalization of a social ethic. Some operate to provide an area of permissiveness in individual role performance. Others set aside, with varying degrees of approval, occasions and contexts for the relaxation of restrictive rules of personal conduct, as in tacitly sanctioned acts of aggression or periods of license. Double standards of performance or contradictory estimates of the same behavior are often resolved by the device of compartmentalization, that is, by segregating them and giving them situational validation. Almost always potential areas of conflict are reduced by a differential allocation of rewards that is supported by some rationalization and by a recognized means of recruiting and sustaining leadership. Whatever the adjustment devices might be, they too must be meshed in some systematic way and be as mutually adjustable as the social system that they regulate.

The concept of equilibrium posits neither perfect balance of forces nor an immobilized social structure. The balance that it envisages is a labile one with the prospect of stresses developing which will call counterstresses into play (MacIver 1937; Myrdal 1944; Parsons 1951). Moreover, this type of balance entertains the possibility that such a reactive system, unlike its mechanical analogue, alters its social base as it attempts to stabilize it. For in the seesaw process of adjusting conflicts and differences, compromises must be made and new mechanisms devised; and each successive adjustment must take into account not only an initial adjustment but all those following in cumulative fashion. Change is therefore implicit in the notion of equilibrium, but as it occurs, it is internally governed change.

It would appear that there are differences among cultural systems on an equilibrium scale, but if this conceptual dimension is to be a useful one, there must be some criteria for ascertaining such differences. The rate of rule-breaking or of obligation-rejection should afford some measure of disequilibrium, as should the frequency of unsettled disputes and factional struggles. The incidence of withdrawal from social situations or of migration elsewhere where this is possible, as it once seems to have been in Polynesia, would be other indicators of disequilibrium. Under some conditions the frequency with which rules of conduct are changed would serve the same purpose, but this criterion might also be an evidence of flexibility in the adjustment machinery.

It is suggested that if equilibrium is a fruitful dimension for the analysis of a cultural system it might also be useful in ascertaining the contact reactions of the system. It is supposed that a system off balance is more vulnerable to outside influences than one under better control of its own internal forces (Gluckman 1940a).

The importance of our three typological distinctions may be pointed up by suggesting that "hard-shelled, vertebrate" cultural systems—that is, cultures with many boundary-maintaining mechanisms and with "rigid" internal structures—whose self-correcting mechanisms are functioning smoothly may be found to be least susceptible to change in acculturation. On the other hand, "soft-shelled, invertebrate" cultural systems—that is, cultures with few or no boundary-maintaining mechanisms and with "flexible" internal structures—which are off balance, or in a state of disequilibrium, are likely to be most susceptible to change in acculturation. These biological analogies are obviously meant only to be suggestive. Furthermore, it is clear that such an "outrageous hypothesis" would require modification in two directions: (1) under certain conditions of extreme acculturation pressure the "hard-shelled vertebrates" may suddenly crack up completely; and (2) under other conditions it seems possible for the "soft-shelled, invertebrate" cultures to "ingest" great quantities of alien cultural material and still preserve many of their basic patterns and values. But perhaps we have said enough to indicate the kinds of hypotheses that can be derived from this facet of our formulation.

THE CONTACT SITUATION

A comprehensive study of acculturation must include an assessment of those noncultural and nonsocial phenomena that provide the contact setting and establish certain limits of cultural adaptation. The most important of these are the ecological context and the demographic characteristics of the respective peoples.

Ecology

Ecology is significant to the extent to which the respective cultures are hinged to a specific environment and the extent to which that environment affects the acculturational setting. For example, the Australian Aborigine's accommodation to desert

Australia was not improved by European culture. Western influence was very largely that of dislocation, and Western success in mastering the desert until now has not materially exceeded the Aborigine's. This is one of the relatively rare instances where an environment which comprised a situation of "closed resources" for the aboriginal population was also closed for the emissaries of Western culture. Additional examples may be found in other extreme environments such as the tropical rain forest and the circumpolar zone (Forde 1934; Kroeber 1939; Price 1939; Mills 1942; Bates 1952). The far more common type of situation finds Western agents impinging on an area in which the indigenous peoples have "closed resources" but in which the environment affords "open resources" for Western technology (Neibohr 1900). This circumstance sets the stage for the relatively rapid modification of aboriginal technology, and the fact that this has happened repeatedly may have a bearing on the generalization that material culture forms are more amenable to change than are more purely symbolic forms.

Full assessment of the significance of ecological factors requires analysis of the main types of possible relationships to resources at each pertinent technological level. Close study of the relationship between ecology and acculturation would no doubt reveal that rather small and particular phenomena from the ecological standpoint are sometimes of major concern for acculturation research. A heavy dependence on some single resource which looms large in the mythology and ceremony of a people immediately comes to mind. On the other hand, the changes induced by acculturation may have decisive effects on the character of the environment and may thus set new limits on the possible relationships between man and nature. That is, the environment may be so modified as to foreclose certain kinds of cultural retrenchment even if the earlier modes of adaptation are still well remembered. The impact of domestic animals on the seed resources of the Basin-Plateau (Steward 1938) and the destruction of the buffalo on the Great Plains are cases in point.

Demography

A variety of demographic phenomena appear to be relevant to the study of acculturation. The relative sizes of contacting populations and the demographic characteristics of their agents clearly affect the pattern and degree of the influence they exert. If the representatives of the societies are not adequate in numbers or lack other demographic attributes necessary to maintain or reproduce an operating social order, the acculturation situation will thereby be modified in manifold ways. For example, in the impingement of Western civilization on aboriginal peoples, the bearers of Western civilization in early stages are mature males. This provides an arbitrary delimitation and a very high degree of structuring of the role network. Or, to take a more specific instance, the impingement of masculine frontier culture on an aboriginal population with matrilineal exogamous clans will have a smaller theoretical effect on the native kinship system than if the system were patrilineal (Spoehr 1947). The demographic fact is the sex imbalance of the frontier; the cultural fact, limiting the possibilities of adjustment, is the kinship system. The fact that masculine agents are the ones who employ the instruments of their culture may also explain to some extent why material culture changes first.

Another way in which population factors bear on acculturation or vice versa may be noted in the specialized demographic relations between peoples whereby personnel from one system are incorporated in the other. Adoption, or the recruitment or enslavement of a people for labor, military, or sexual purposes have two significant effects (Siegel 1945). First, the character of intercultural contact is sharply structured. Second, the integrity of the role network within each culture is seriously affected by the selective removal or addition of personnel in certain age-sex categories.

CONJUNCTIVE RELATIONS

After the properties of the two or more cultural systems which come into contact have been studied and the ecological and demographic aspects of the contact situation have been analyzed, our formulation calls for an examination of the nature of the conjunctive relations that are established between the systems. The patterns of these conjunctive relations may be conceptualized as intercultural role networks that not only establish the framework of contact but also provide the channels through which the content of one cultural system must be communicated and transmitted to the other (e.g., Fortes 1936; Ekvall 1939; Gluckman 1940a; Mandelbaum 1941; Honigmann 1952).

Intercultural Roles

The significance of this contact design is evident when the observable facts of acculturation are taken into account. Cultures do not meet, but people who are their carriers do. As carriers of traditions such contacting individuals never know their entire cultures and never convey all they know of them to one another. That part of their cultural inventory which they do transmit is conditioned primarily by their reasons for making the contact, that is, by the cultural concomitants of the role that they assume in dealing with an alien group. They may adopt a complex but limited number of roles, so that unless there is full representation on both sides there can be opportunity for only a partial intercultural transfer.

Like their internal counterparts, intercultural roles may be conceptualized as constellations of behaviors that are appropriate to particular situations. Since roles presuppose a social context, each one calls for its complement if either is to be sustained. In an intercultural system, such reciprocal behaviors are paired cross-culturally with the performance of an act by a member of one autonomous system evoking a supporting response from some member of the other. Behind each act in a paired set lies a complex of beliefs and attitudes, and together the pair constitutes a cross-cultural unit of mutually understood expectations founded upon a definition of reciprocal rights and obligations. As with role playing within the two contacting cultures, that which develops interculturally requires not only the alignment of participants in it but also an agreement, in this instance arrived at across cultural boundaries, upon its meaning and importance. Stated otherwise, the intercultural role network is made up of shared and valued behaviors as well as a structuring of relationships between contacting agents of the two systems.

Intercultural role playing reflects the interest areas that are shared by the two groups in contact, whether attention to these areas is cultivated or enforced by unilateral demands or whether the areas represent a convergence of aspirations or needs. Usually role playing mirrors one group's image of itself in relation to the other. Consequently, among other generalized components, it contains an assertion of intergroup status and a definition of intergroup power relationships. In addition to such generalized elements, particular roles demand specific purposes and entail specific expectations. In the expansion of western European culture, the roles of the administrator, the entrepreneur, and the missionary have established a stereotype in accordance with the principal incentives activating the expansion. Important subsidiary roles in this movement have been those of the educator and the physician. At the same time, going along with this master plan for contact, there have been innumerable subordinate or incidental projections of occidental culture as its representatives have individually varied in background, capacity, and purpose.

Non-Western contacts naturally have other role characteristics, as is evidenced by Kula trading partnerships (Malinowski 1922), Tungus-Cossack family visits (Lindgren 1938), and Zuni-Navaho "guest-friend" relationships (Vogt 1951). To provide a concrete illustration of the social structural characteristics and of the culturally patterned ways in which contact within the intercultural role network takes place, let us examine this Zuni-Navaho relationship. Although Navahos and Zunis have been in contact for at least 100 years, the total sociocultural systems have never been brought into conjunction. Rather the contact appears to have occurred in terms of a specifiable set of intercultural role relationships, one of the most important being the "guest-friend" relationship. Each Navaho family which visits Zuni (during large ceremonials such as the Shalako, and at other times) has one or more Zuni families whom they regard as "friends." When the Navahos enter the pueblo, they invariably go to the house of their "friends" where they are expected to leave gifts of mutton, rugs, or jewelry. The Zuni family is expected to house and feed the Navaho family during its stay and to return gifts of bread, corn, melons, or hay when the Navahos leave. The customary modes of interaction are highly patterned: there is handshaking, inquiries about the state of health of families on both sides, the communication usually takes place in Navaho rather than in Zuni, etc. At some other time during the year, the Zuni family may return the visit by going to the hogans of its Navaho friends. The Zunis bring gifts, and it is expected that they will be housed and fed and be given gifts in return when they leave. These relationships are often enduring ones—sometimes persisting through two or more generations. There are also mechanisms for severing the relationship in the event that one of the parties fails to reciprocate with the expected gifts. Nothing is said at the time, but the following season the family which came out on the short end of the deal will simply look for other friends, or retaliate by failing to bring gifts. The relationship depends upon a basic cross-cultural pattern of mutual hospitality and reciprocity, and no bargaining is involved in the gift exchanges.

Intercultural Communication

The architecture of the intercultural role network also provides communication and transmission lines between the two contacting cultures, and it organizes the acculturative flow between the two. It is at once a profile of contacting cultures and a communication system contributing to their modification.

Intercultural communication may be specifically or diffusely channeled. Specificity in this sense has to do with whether a cross-cultural message appropriately applies to any member or just to certain members of a receiving group. Extremely diffuse are forms of dominance, discrimination, fear, respect, or approbation which uniformly engage most members of one group vis-à-vis the other. Or an alien administrator may rule for all or for a great many individuals in the group under his jurisdiction. More specific directives are those restricted to a particular set of roles, as with those pertaining to the employer-employee relationship. In another sense, a dominant role, such as that of an administrator, may be the central channel for the controlling cultural directives focused by one society upon another. Such influences, furthermore, may be funneled through a single counterpart, such as a headman, in the recipient group. To the extent that cultural representations of either side are thus channeled through a few contact specialists, the communication for most of the group's members is restricted in advance. Such contact specialists are comparable to consuls in foreign service, and the very concept of "external relations" suggests the existence of a high degree of bicultural autonomy and the limited capacity of the system of communication.

An intercultural communication system is a product of purpose and cross-purpose, and there are also levels of flow in the process of cultural interchange. The result is a highly selective patterning of contacts. Two components figure in this complex design, namely, the range of presented fact and the cross-cultural interpretation of it. That is, no culture presents its full face to the other, and to the façade that is presented cross-culturally meanings are attached which may have little or no relation to their intracultural significance. The intercultural role structure fixes the framework of communication, but within this framework the perceptual orientations of the recipients are important determinants of acculturation. Concretely, representatives of one contacting system may or may not present a model of its family life, but if they do, the family configuration is certain to be refracted by the more or less distorting lens of intercommunication. A filter of traditional and idiosyncratic perception always intervenes between the fact and its alien interpretation.

As in analyzing autonomous systems, one must deal with dysfunction in an intercultural system. In communication terms this means a discrepancy between the intentions of a sender and the meaning of the message to a receiver. The fact of internal misinterpretation of intentions suggests the hypothesis that the chances for discrepant communication rise with the degree of intercultural difference. The apperceptive mass, to mention only an obvious factor, is very differently constituted for communicators reared in diverse traditions.

There remains the ever present possibility of qualification or reservation in the presentation of a cultural fact; the giver of an intercultural message may intend that it should have its face-value meaning, or he may conceal its real significance. The labor recruiter may not reveal all the implications of his offer, and the administrator may have covert reasons for reserving a knowledge of the consequences of his dictates.

The recognition that acculturation is very much a matter of range of presentation and of perceptual reality raises the issue of compatibility between contacting cultures. The number and character of compatible facets which one system presents to the other may be taken as one measure of its acculturative potential. When so considered, compatibility must be understood to have reference to selected parts of the systems and not to their whole properties. It is a relationship which obtains directly between particular ideological or behavioral sets; only derivatively and descriptively can it be said to pertain to the boundary characteristics, the modes, the structures or the tendencies of the two systems or to characterize the relationship between a specific element in one and such holistic properties of the other. Analysis of the compatibility of systemic patterns yields useful generalizations on the typological level and provides a basis for predicting acculturative influence. At the same time, systemic compatibilities are not the data of group or individual experience in culture contacts, and operationally agreement and disagreement must be treated on the level of perception.

Closely related is the factor of cultural relativism and the fact that compatibility is an intercultural variable emerging under intracultural controls. New experiences are organized by each group under the influence of its existing ideological and motivational set, and as the set varies so do the possibilities of each group for assessing sameness and difference between past and present events. In short, perceptive reality is the effective mediator in the determination of compatibility, and in the context of acculturation it is the perceptual organization of the receptor rather than the evaluation of the donor or some third party which determines the areas and degrees of intercultural agreement and disparity.

PROCESSES OF ACCULTURATION

All the evidence leads to the conclusion that any autonomous cultural system is in a continuous process of change. The change that is induced by contact therefore does not represent a shift from a static to an active state but rather a shift from one sort of change to another. Contact often stimulates change more adventitiously, more generally, and more rapidly than do internal forces. The particular effects of a conjunction of two cultures will depend upon antecedent modes of internal change together with the nature of the intercultural contact profile and the influences that are communicated through its network.

The indicated distinction between internally generated and contact-stimulated change invites comparative analysis. It is assumed that change is an inherent property of cultural systems; it cannot be assumed that the analytic properties of internal and acculturative change are identical. Detailed comparisons of the characteristics of the two situations should soon disclose orderly distinctions if, in fact, they do occur.

The processes which flow from the conjunction of two or more cultural systems are obviously numerous, varied, and complex, and it is evident that we need additional concepts to deal with these dynamic phenomena. We shall first deal with fairly specific recurring sequences of events in acculturation: (*a*) intercultural transmission (diffusion), (*b*) cultural creativity, (*c*) cultural disintegration, and (*d*) reactive adaptations. Then we shall take up the problem of more pervasive and lasting outcomes of acculturation, including progressive adjustment of two types, fusion and assimilation, and the development of a stabilized pluralism. Finally we shall explore the possibilities of discovering processual regularities in (*a*) the differential rates of change found in different aspects of culture, and (*b*) the sequential developments in acculturation over long time-spans.

Intercultural Transmission

One of the obvious invariant processes of acculturation that takes place through the intercultural networks outlined above is the transmission of cultural materials (objects, traits, or ideas) between the two systems. It may be as little as the transmission of a steel ax in exchange for furs, or it may be as much as the transmission of a whole new religious theology, but it always takes place. The classic concept of "diffusion" applies directly to this transmission process. In the most general terms we can make two statements about intercultural transmission: (1) that the patterns and values of the receiving culture seem to function as selective screens in a manner that results in the enthusiastic acceptance of some elements, the firm rejection of other elements; and (2) that the elements which are transmitted undergo transformations in the receiving cultural systems, and may also undergo transformations within the intercultural network while in the process of being transmitted. At any rate, these transformations are also probably intimately related to the value systems of receptor cultures. These value systems may be conceptualized as operating with gyroscope-like qualities; that is, the cultural elaborations of the system are kept going in certain "directions" and the cultural materials ingested appear to fall into place within the pre-existing framework. A classic example is the diffusion of masked dances from the Pueblos (where they are rain ceremonials) to the Navaho (where they have become curing ceremonials) or to the Western Apache (where they are used to celebrate puberty for girls) (Underhill 1948). Another example is the case of the diffusion of the Sun Dance among the Plains Indians (Spier 1921).

Cultural Creativity

Acculturation is, however, neither a passive nor a colorless absorption. It is a culture-producing as well as a culture-receiving process. Acculturation, particularly when not forced, is essentially creative. It is a productive process even though in consequence there may be a decrease in the number and variety of pre-existent elements. Abandonment or voluntary loss is compensated for in the same or some other area of culture; and to the extent that an introduced element may serve as an alternative to an indigenous one, there is an actual gain in number and variety. But irrespective of numerical changes, there are other creative processes which inevitably occur with the incorporation of alien elements into an autonomous system. The most notable ones have been variously described as "reorganizations" (Kroeber 1948), and "reinterpretations" and "syncretisms" (Herskovits 1948: 553–60). "Syncretism" has been recognized in the identification of African deities with Catholic saints among certain New World Negroes (Herskovits 1948: 553). As other evidence of the creativity of acculturation, it may be recalled that the very act of copying alien traits entails some modification of them since no copy is a perfect reproduction.

These considerations suggest that the conjunction of differences in culture contact provides a kind of catalyst for cultural creativity (Barnett 1953: 46–56; Beals 1953: 636). Much has been made of the melancholy process of cultural disintegration, often with the implicit value assumption on the part of the anthropologist that the older aboriginal patterns are good and what emerges in the contact situation is bad. Comparative study which is also sensitive to the generation of new and qualitatively different patterns may add significantly to our knowledge of cultural transformation and growth. The design for such research enterprises requires more than the cataloguing of the provenience of the cultural elements which form the new patterns. It should also involve a close study of the steps which lead to the creation of new patterns and the enrichment of old.

Cultural Disintegration

Although the incorporation of new traits is essentially a creative process it may have destructive consequences for the borrowing culture as an autonomous system. This result is clearly a possibility if the incorporation is forced by the donor group. Under coercion the receptor group not only loses its political independence; more important from the standpoint of its cultural autonomy, it loses its freedom to modify creatively what it is forced to accept as given. This strait-jacketing of acceptance forbids the flexibility of reinterpretation and reassociation that is essential to the independent functioning of a cultural system. When it is accompanied, as it usually is with captive cultures, by the mandatory elimination of certain customs, it is easy to understand why systems so enthralled proceed to "disintegrate." They do so because they have lost the prerogative of integrating what they want and rejecting the rest. Their creative mechanisms have been blocked.

Even when force is absent the conjunction of two systems usually creates tendencies that are at least potentially disintegrative. These tendencies develop in a system to the extent that its borrowed traits set up differentiating alternatives which demand partisan commitments by the society's members. In this way factional struggles, such as those between what are usually called "progressives" and "conservatives," develop. Contests for status and prerogatives are also common when cross-cultural influences are pronounced enough to unsettle traditional controls. Cleavages may take place along age, sex, or other social borders.

Intergenerational conflicts are commonplace features of acculturation wherever cultures meet; they undermine immigrant family life in the United States, as they do in contact situations elsewhere in the world. In addition to divisions along pre-existing group or class lines there are many others which gerrymander an exposed population in accordance with individual preferences for or against introduced objects, procedures, and ideas.

Presumably, any autonomous system is capable of indefinite growth as long as it can maintain its internal controls. Since this is evident as far as internally stimulated change is concerned, there is no reason to suppose that a radically distinct situation is precipitated by the injection of an alien trait. There are probably variable tolerances for growth, assuming that other factors, such as rate and force of presentation of new ideas, can be held constant. Some culture types may be not only more rigid in adhering to their value orientations but also for the same reason less able to assimilate new elements under contact without creating intolerable tensions among their carriers. This may be the case with a closely integrated system; extensive undermining of a command value may dispose the entire system to collapse, although the door is open for subsequent reintegration. Also it is likely that at some periods in its history a system is more vulnerable than it is at others, as, for example, when it is in a crucial phase of adjusting its conflicts or of striving to restore its equilibrium. Still, provided the shock of contact is not too unsettling, it may be assumed that a system operating under its own controls is able to absorb alien materials just as it adjusts to internal changes under the force of its own adaptive mechanisms.

When its autonomy is threatened a system may respond belligerently; that is, it may resort to force to maintain its independence. This has happened repeatedly as expanding systems have sought to dominate others in the path of their exploitations. Failure to maintain cultural and political independence often results in a reaction of defeatism which may be manifested in the neglect of ceremonial observances, the establishment of a dependency relationship with the dominant group, and population decline.

Reactive Adaptation

Another response to threat when the pressure is less nearly overwhelming is to withdraw and to encyst native values. In this instance there is, so to speak, a reactive adaptation to threat: native forms are reaffirmed and re-enforced by a renewed commitment to them. Thus when the Japanese attempted to induce Palauan men to undertake rice farming, the Palauan man's aversion to any activity resembling taro cultivation—a female occupation—was strengthened and the Japanese program rejected. More familiar and more spectacular expressions of the same phenomenon have repeatedly occurred as nativistic reactions of one sort or another, including revivalistic cults, nationalistic movements, and isolationist programs.

Progressive Adjustment

If we assume that neither withdrawal from alien contact nor the complete annihilation of a group occurs, conjunctive relations at any time must fall under one of two headings: progressive adjustment or stabilized pluralism. Progressive adjustment can lead predominantly in the direction of fusion or that of assimilation. In fusion the approximation of the two autonomous systems is roughly mutual, though probably never perfectly so. "Bilateral" could be used in describing the ideal typical pole of fusion on the continuum, with "unilateral" characterizing the opposite theoretical absolute of assimilation. Obviously, the trend of adjustment in most contact situations is toward some point between the poles of a balanced blending and the total submersion of one culture by the other. It is nevertheless useful to gauge and attempt to account for differences of trend.

CULTURAL FUSION An intercultural network can develop into a genuine third sociocultural system through a process of fusion. If it does, it must exhibit the attributes of uniqueness and autonomy possessed by parent systems. It is probable that in almost every instance some modification of unilaterally extended roles will be necessary to adjust to the peculiarities of the system with which they must articulate. Some distinctiveness is also to be expected from the emergence of *ad hoc* roles, such as those of designated go-betweens, proxies, and buffering agents, which did not previously exist in either system. It is possible, too, for a cluster of intercultural roles to give rise to a new institution, such as a plantation system or an arbitration council, which is relatively autonomous. However, isolated complexes of this character do not necessarily constitute an intercultural role network that is either an integrated system or a distinctive sociocultural body. A real third system probably emerges only with the disappearance of the original two through fusion in a given territory, as has happened to invading and resident cultures in Mexico and to some extent in China. It may be possible for a third system to emerge without the disappearance of the original two from its territory, but theoretically this seems dubious. Fusion-producing forces which are strong enough to eventuate in a new and integral third system would appear to be sufficient to eliminate completely the autonomy of the parent systems. Or if the fusion is not sufficient to insure the elimination of some and the adoption and reconfiguration of the remaining elements of the original systems, then it is unlikely that such fusion could result in a third system with full cultural qualifications. Put another way, the fusion either erases the essential outlines of both the merging cultures, or it produces no third culture with outlines clear enough to be maintained autonomously. Bearers of either or both parent traditions may theoretically continue to exist, however, if there is a territorial separation, without fundamentally inhibiting the emergence of a third system.

ASSIMILATION The second type of progressive adjustment is the assimilation of one group by another. In some ways it is the dichotomous opposite of fusion. American sociologists have given much attention to this phenomenon as manifested on both the individual level (passing, marginality, and the like) and the group level (the changing modes of ethnic self-definition and valuation, etc.). Acculturation is a necessary but not sufficient condition of assimilation (Broom and Shevky 1952). The latter requires that the erstwhile ethnics should have not only the internalized cultural skills to move freely in the large social order but also full and free access to those parts of the order for which they have the cultural prerequisites. This is not to say that assimilation is measured by some random distribution in the status and power hierarchy, except in the extreme long-run, for clearly this would assume the eradication of historical differences in the introduction of groups into the society. Although it is never fully realized, assimilation implies an essentially unilateral approximation of one culture in the direction of the other, albeit a changing or ongoing other. Complete assimilation, like complete fusion, is much less frequent in fact than is indicated by the frequency with which the term is used in the literature.

It is interesting to consider how much the difference in emphasis between anthropology and sociology in the study of culture contact may be the product of ethnographic specialization more than of basic theoretical or methodological differences. As is well known, American sociological students of acculturation have given much of their attention to United States immigrant groups, while anthropologists have concentrated on nonmigrant and non-Western peoples, albeit peoples usually under Western contact. The immigrant groups of the United States in the numerically preponderant cases were nearly all originally Western peoples, motivated toward assimilation, and were peoples who came to a milieu which may be among the most notable in history for its rapidity of ethnic absorption. Assimilation, on the whole, is taken as a positive value by both donor and receptor in these cases, and the sociological student has not been unaffected by the valuation. The anthropologist's subjects, on the other hand, besides being non-Western, have not voluntarily moved to any part of the Western world. Rather, the West has come to impinge upon or engulf them. They usually lack any initial inclination to assimilate, they have deep historical roots in the localities where they are found, and they seldom have such a relatively undisruptive solution of their difficulties as to let the "progressives" emigrate and the "conservatives" remain. Assimilation is rarely valued at any one time by all the natives or by all segments of the Western group (e.g., *apartheid*). In a sense of fairness and moral indignation the anthropologist has frequently rejected assimilation and all that it stands for and has been delighted to find evidence of the "savage" holding his own, or even striking back (Lips 1937). He has tended to emphasize evidence of fusion wherever possible, such as minor influences upon the dominant group or concessions they are obliged to make, in contrast to many sociologists' espousal of assimilation. The

American Negro is an exception to much of the above, and it is noteworthy that a controversy over the interpretation of Negro data exists between certain anthropologists and sociologists which reflects precisely the difference of emphasis described here between the two fields. These contrasting tendencies of sociologists and anthropologists, in working on problems often closely related, may account for an important part of the failure to make more of a joint and co-ordinate contribution to acculturation research.

Whether exploration of the differences between fusion and assimilation has actually been retarded by the contrasting orientation of sociology and anthropology in this matter, there can be no questioning its importance. The differences sketched above concerning the traditional locations of anthropological vs. sociological research suggest several historical and ethnographic contrasts which may be crucial themselves to the question of fusion or assimilation. Such factors as voluntary migration or deep local attachments, assimilation as a positive or a negative value, small or large degree of cultural match, differential prestige, and balanced or unbalanced numbers only indicate the crude headings under which to pursue the problem of why adjustment between some systems progresses toward fusion and adjustment of others toward assimilation.

Of late, however, evidence has been accumulating that even the "savage," for whom many an anthropologist held only timid hopes, is not in all cases so readily to be written off the rolls as had been reluctantly believed. Of other peoples in contact this indeed has long been known to be true. The fact is of direct importance for acculturation theory. It is certainly not implied in every case that a progressive trend toward fusion or toward assimilation must run its full course, at least in any given span of time. Moreover, short-run fusion or short-run assimilation may well be special phenomena, and if so they demand investigation. Each probably implies a special combination of properties of the two cultures in contact, and of the contact situation. In acculturation the reasons for differences of rate must be understood, as well as the actual occurrence of fusion or assimilation.

Stabilized Pluralism

In order to understand progressive adjustment, it is also necessary to explore cases of arrested fusion or incomplete assimilation. By this is meant stabilized pluralism, namely, the failure of two cultures in contact completely to lose their autonomy (Linton 1940: 510–11; Tax 1941; Gillin 1945; Bruner 1953; Coughlin Ms.). Theoretically, at least, stabilized pluralism implies only an extreme slackening of the rate of progressive adjustment. In any event, a common pattern of adjustment appears in the many cases of a relatively stabilized relationship between two contacting cultures, as happens in some caste systems, in the adaptations of enclaves and their dominant hosts, and in the symbiotic connection between some sedentary and nomadic groups in the Old World. In these instances an intercultural system has reached a point of institutionalized adjustment to serve the interests of both groups. Often parallel ethnic institutions develop in the two societies in continuous and stabilized contact. These institutions are significant in acculturative adaptation in at least three respects. They ameliorate the stresses of interethnic situations and provide contexts for validating acculturation under relatively permissive conditions. They also provide criteria of acculturation for members of the ethnic group and as such they may express selective emphases of dominant cultural forms, symbols, and valuations due to the socially differentiated position of the two groups. Further, they legitimatize the status system of the ethnic community in which one may expect to find transplanted important aspects of the stratification criteria of the dominant society (Broom and Kitsuse Ms.).

Differential Rates of Change

Change under contact conditions, like change under internal stimulation, seems to proceed at uneven rates in different areas of culture regardless of the nature of the intercultural system. It has often been remarked that in the conjunction between Western and non-Western cultures technology appears to alter more readily than do other aspects of a system. This may be due in part to the emphasis placed upon technology in the Western world as well as to its evident superiority over most local forms.

Since material accomplishment represents values held by the invaders in such cases, the same considerations may help to explain why Westerners, when they are affected by contact, also adopt objects rather than behaviors and ideas.

In point of fact, the conventional categories of cultural description—technology, social organization, religion, etc.—do not readily lend themselves to an analysis of differential change. *All* cultural segments have their concrete aspects, and these more explicit behaviors and apparatus are as a rule more readily mastered than symbolic and valuational aspects. In religion, for example, objects and rituals may be assimilated as rapidly as new tools. They may be integrated as long as they enhance prevailing security and orientational functions. In the absence of coercion even more clearly efficient implements have been rejected or ignored when perceived to interfere with basic cultural understandings (Hall and Trager 1953). Furthermore, adoption of a foreign object can in most cases be an individual matter; at any rate it does not necessarily raise the social complications and the need for common consent that are inescapable with the transfer of an alien kinship system or marriage custom.

Intangibles also appear to show levels of differential change. Specific and isolated ideas and behaviors are thought to be more vulnerable than those integrated with a more inclusive set of values. The more generalized values are, the more persistent they seem to be. What might be called the basic premises of a people regarding the nature of man and the universe can go unchanged despite considerable modification in technology and other aspects of culture. These inferred values of a culture appear to have a greater continuity in many, if not in all cases, and for this reason have themselves been conceptualized as selectors, molders, and integrators. If they have a controlling position they may be said to screen the incoming material and to order its placement in the existing system.

It has been suggested that the greatest resistance to change and reorganization will occur in certain universal categories of cultural adaptation: maintenance systems, communication systems, and security systems (Keesing Ms.). By contrast, there are elements which are only weakly supported by moral judgments of right and wrong, propriety and impropriety, desirability and undesirability, and hence more susceptible to change. In most cases these less resistant aspects would include what are rated as luxury products, such as ornamentation, art, and leisure activities, in so far as they are not symbolic of deeply held values. But it is evident that much additional research is needed on this problem.

Long-Range Regularities

In the search for uniformities in acculturation processes, the possibility of regularities in sequential developments over long time-spans should not be neglected. Are there in fact processual regularities in acculturation comparable to those suggested for the development of early civilizations (Steward 1949b) and for the transformations of the primitive world (Redfield 1953)? The implication is that the processes in certain phases may be determined more by earlier forms of intercultural interaction than by further changes in contact conditions. There may be a limited number of sequential types in acculturation in which later phases follow predictably from earlier phases.

The acculturation literature contains a number of attempts to identify the sequential "stage" or "phase" developments in particular cases (Thurnwald 1935; Firth 1929; LaFarge 1940; Keesing 1941; Mekeel 1943; Albrecht 1946; Gillin 1946: 165–66; Elkin 1951; Goubaud 1952; Beals 1952; Watson 1953). Some of these formulations deal with large ethnographic areas, others with single tribes. Some treat total cultural systems in process of change, others restrict themselves to statements about acculturating groups or individuals. A few take into account the intercultural nature of the process; others treat only one side of the equation, typically the "native" culture. As matters now stand, comparative study of the phenomenon is difficult, if not impossible, because the approach to the problem is so uneven. It is significant that only a few students have attempted comparative statements (Mekeel 1943; Beals 1952).

Fruitful possibilities exist in this problem area, as, for instance, in the onset of nativistic movements as acculturational phases. It has been suggested (Linton 1940: chap. 10; 1943) that nativistic movements do not typically appear during the early period of contact but tend to develop later. However, more research is needed on the problem of the conditions which trigger and sustain these reactions both in dominant and in dominated groups.

It is evident that research into the problem of identifiable and regular developmental sequences in acculturation will require the best control of the historical and archeological data that can be mustered, detailed and coordinate comparisons of various acculturative situations over long time spans, and explicit recognition of the reciprocal intercultural nature of the processes. A suggestive formulation has been provided for Australia (Elkin 1951). Similar formulations are required for other areas as well as systematic comparative treatment both of cases involving European contacts and of those in which non-Western cultures have been in conjunction.

A Methodological Note

We have provided some suggestions for a way of looking at acculturation phenomena and have suggested some of the types of hypotheses which might be derived from this theoretical framework. The next step is obviously one of continuing research enterprises which will enable us to say what combinations of conditions and patterns will produce what kinds of processes. If anthropologists were omnipotent katchinas, our task would be easy. We could take two cultural systems with specified properties and bring them into conjunction in a particular type of environmental situation, and then wait to see what happens—what kind of intercultural network develops and what kinds of processes result. After a sufficient number of such experiments using different combinations of variables, our katchina observer could predict with considerable precision.

But since anthropologists are not katchinas, we are reduced to utilizing comparative methods of analysis of cultural systems in conjunction as we find them in their natural states in the world. Typically, by the time we look at an acculturation situation first-hand, the two cultural systems are already in contact and have been in contact for a long period of time. We begin by studying the total situation as it exists at the present time; when we may move backward in time by taking earlier "readings" based upon the testimony of old informants, the data found in historical documents, or, in some cases, the data provided by archeology.

We may move forward in time and take later "readings" by observing acculturation processes in long-range field projects. These "readings" on an acculturation situation and sequence can then be compared with other situations and sequences where the variables, as found in the natural state, are different in specifiable ways. Eventually, by the use of careful comparative designs and the use of comparable categories for analysis we can hope to arrive by this long and tortuous process of study at the state of knowledge which could be readily reached by experimentation if anthropologists *were* katchinas.

APPENDIX

During the course of the seminar a number of other topics were discussed which could not be incorporated smoothly into the main body of this paper. The substance of our conclusions on the most important of these problems is briefly presented below.

Personality and Acculturation

In recent years attempts to treat responsiveness to change as an expression of personality characteristics has been given two formulations, the interrelationships of which are not yet clear. In one approach the concept of a basic or modal personality structure provides insight into what might be accepted by a given group and what types and rates of adjustment may be expected of the group in acculturative situations (Linton, in Kardiner 1945; Barnouw 1950; Wallace 1951; Caudill 1952). In the other approach the concept of deviant individuals has posed related issues concerning individual receptivity to change: whether personal conflicts predispose individuals to embrace alien patterns (Barnett 1941), the extent to which conflicts may lead to an intensified return to native patterns as well as to departures from them (Vogt 1951), whether elite rating is a variable factor in defining acceptors in different acculturative situations (Adams 1951), and the function of certain need-dispositions as determinants in acceptance (Rapoport 1954).

As far as acculturation is concerned, the psychological problem is to determine the depth of commitment to certain shared patterns and values and consequently to assess the difficulties of accepting changes. For what is important in this connection is not the structure or the orientation of personality itself but the extent to which certain basic values are internalized or rejected and the extent to which they function as selective mechanisms in acculturation.

This problem can be explored with the aid of life histories (Aberle 1951), by situational choice tests, and perhaps by projective tests such as the Rorschach and T.A.T. if the methodological difficulties of employing these devices cross-culturally can be resolved. The use of such psychological instruments may also define a spectrum of social and psychological types of more or less acculturated individuals (Hallowell 1952). Such a spectrum of co-existing types might conceivably provide insights into acculturative effects in time. It might also contribute to an ordering of the relationships between psychological variants and intercultural role playing: are contact agents always deviants in their own cultures; or does the filling of such a role tend to produce psychological variants?

There is the additional question of what happens to individual personality systems under acculturative stress. Some researches lead to the conclusion that at deep psychological levels they are persistent (Hallowell 1952). Others indicate that at least in certain cultures the conflicts induced by alien pressures tend to have disintegrative effects (Kluckhohn and Leighton 1946; Thompson 1950). Still others suggest that an integration takes place on a new level after some disintegration during a transitional stage (Spindler 1952; Spindler and Goldschmidt 1952).

Language and Acculturation

Language communication is a principal medium for the flow of cultural elements and provides an important clue for assessing the dynamics of this transfer. As long as the members of autonomous groups perceive mutual advantages and are also motivated to preserve their cultural differences, communication between them will involve either bi- or multilingualism on the part of one or both; the development of a marginal language (e.g., a jargon, pidgin or creolized language); the adoption of a lingua franca (Swahili; Chinook jargon); or, in extreme cases of intermittent and specific contacts, gestural patterns of communication (Mead 1931; Reinicke Ms.; Hall 1953). The alternative selected in a given situation is of special interest to linguists and students of acculturation alike.

The social functions of language vary in multilingual situations. Specifically, it is important to investigate the categories of individuals who become multilingual, the social contexts in which they use each language, and attraction to or withdrawal from a dominant culture in relation to skill in using the language (Barker 1947; Weinreich 1953).

Linguistic change goes on *pari passu* with changes in other spheres of culture under conditions of contact. As long as the respective language speakers retain a degree of cultural autonomy changes may be expected to occur in any or all aspects of the language systems, whether lexical, phonological, or syntactic. Internal tendencies, such as extensions or losses of prevailing constructions and sound shifts, may be reinforced or they may compete with alternative phonological and structural features. Or lexical innovations, based on the analogy of alien forms but using indigenous elements, may be introduced (Johnson 1943; Casagrande 1951).

Finally, lexical change, which is the most obvious, suggests several problems. Some groups will consistently take over words with alien objects or practices, whereas others will almost invariably coin new words from their own language resources. This may be a function of similarity or difference of formative processes, of cultural interest, or of some other factor. The proposition that a shift in the manner of linguistic adaptation is a function of a critical change in the orientation of the receptor culture merits consideration.

Use of Archeological Data in Acculturation Study

Archeological materials do not lend themselves to the extensive analysis that is envisaged in this paper for observed or historically documented contacts. The data of archeology, like those of contemporary ethnography, do offer additional instances of the consequences of acculturation, but the evidence for the meeting of autonomous systems and their conjunctive relations must be inferred. Despite these limitations, the same theoretical framework might be applicable both to ethnology and to archeology, and what is revealed by contact phenomena in the former should illuminate some kinds of problems presented by the latter. Acculturative changes can, for example, sometimes be inferred from shifts in pottery traditions, art styles, or house types (Willey 1953a). It may also be productive to treat some instances of an intensified return to earlier material culture patterns as manifestations of nativistic reactions. Archeological research alerted to the multidimensional concepts of acculturation will probably require both the careful formulation of research problems and hypotheses (Willey 1953b; Rouse 1953) and a close contextual analysis of archeological remains (Taylor 1948). Students interested in long-range acculturation processes can also profitably utilize certain bodies of archeological material to obtain readings on culture-contact situations which began in prehistoric periods. For example, a long-range analysis of Navaho acculturation processes would profit by the use of archeological data on Navaho-Pueblo contacts (Keur 1941).

18 PERSISTENCE AND CHANGE
PATTERNS IN AMISH SOCIETY

John A. Hostetler

THE STUDENT OF human society finds explicitly developed moral postulates in human institutions which Malinowski (1944: 52) calls the "charter." The charter is "the system of values for the pursuit of which human beings organize." It is "an organized system of purposeful activities." In Amish society behavior is oriented to absolute values, involving a conscious belief in religious and ethical ends entirely for their own sake and independent of any external rewards. This orientation to *Wert-rational,* or absolute values, as Max Weber (1947: 305–6) states it, requires of the individual unconditional demands. Regardless of personal considerations the members are required to put into practice what is required by duty, honor, personal loyalty, and sacrifice. Behavior is tradition-directed by unwritten norms. In Amish society there is an almost automatic reaction to habitual stimuli which guides behavior in a course which has been hallowed by the habit of long experience.

The consistency of "charter" in Amish society has been noted by a number of social scientists. Gillin (1948: 209–20), for example, has termed the Amish culture "remarkably compatible with the various components of its situation." Kollmorgen (1942: 105) observed that the integrative aspects of the culture "must have qualities that make for survival." Huntington (1956: introduction) states that in Amish society "Each community is integrated, but not self contained." Freed (1957: 55) has noted the absence of

---

Originally published in *Ethnology,* Volume 3 (1964), 185–98. Reprinted with permission of the author and of the editor of *Ethnology.*

class differences in Amish society as a factor in the acceleration of change.

The generalization that the Amish are a stable people, consistent in their moral values, has led to several misconceptions and over-statements about Amish social organization. One recent source (Schreiber 1962: 58), for example, states that "juvenile delinquency is unknown among the Amish." Consistency of major points in the charter does not mean that Amish life is relatively free from stress, sustained personal conflicts, or rebellious behavior.

It will be the purpose of this paper to develop five elements in the Amish charter which demonstrate a high degree of consistency. They are formulated from careful observation in a number of contemporary communities, from the original documents (Gascho 1937), and from personal experience as a participating member of the culture. Second, evidence for sustained personal conflicts in this seemingly "remarkably compatible" culture will be presented. The evidence is based upon depth interviews with Amish and former Amish persons and reveals stress patterns of the following character: thwarted motivations for higher education, the practice of marginal occupations, the presence of suicidal behavior, and rowdyism. Third, it will be shown how persons with unresolved personal conflicts make meaningful contacts with outgroups by means of acculturation agents.

THE CHARTER

Separation from the World

The doctrine of separation is an expression of the Amish view of reality, which is one of "nonconformity to the world." The conception of reality is conditioned by a dualistic view of human nature. Although the natural, "created" world is amoral, the world of man is categorically divided into the pure and impure, light and darkness, and the powers of good and of evil. Separation from the world is based upon this dualistic conception of reality, and it is expressed in life situations, in ecology, and social organization. Separation is furthermore based upon explicit scriptural passages which validate the practice: "Be not conformed to this world . . ." and "Be ye not unequally yoked together with unbelievers." The ark of safety for the member is within the community, and not outside of its beliefs and customs. This doctrine forbids marriage with outsiders, it prohibits members from establishing business partnerships or sustained associations with outsiders, and it keeps intimate human associations within the ceremonial community.

Biblical Tradition

The whole of the Old and New Testaments, in the German language, and to some extent the Apocrypha as well, constitute the sacred writings for the Amish. The codifications and moral principles have their basis in the teachings of Christ and his proclamation of a kingdom. The Amish have perpetuated the teachings of the sixteenth century Anabaptists from whom they are direct descendants, having been an offshoot of the Swiss Brethren in the late eighteenth century. Some of their teachings and practices are taken literally from scriptural texts, e.g., the refusal to retaliate or bear arms, to swear oaths, or to hold public office, the observance of adult baptism, the foot-washing ceremony, and mutual concern for the aged and poor. They refuse to accept or to pay social security on the grounds that it is insurance; they pay taxes without qualms of conscience, but compulsory insurance is another matter. The vow of baptism involves not only confession of faith in the Trinity but the promise to remain in the narrow path of "obedience" to the rules of the believing community.

The Ordnung *or Rules of Order*

The rules of order of the church are clearly understood by all baptized members, and the individual is committed not only to obedience but to active maintenance of the rules. Marriage, always occurring after baptism and not before, admits the individual to even greater responsibility for promoting and "building the church." The body of rules and traditions which govern behavior are rarely specified in writing; they are essentially a body of sentiments and taboos intimately shared among the members. The rules are taken for granted, and it is usually only the questionable or borderline issues which are specified in the "examination" service preceding the semi-annual communion service. A change in the rules, either toward relaxation or formalization, requires a members' meeting where each person is asked to give assent to the unanimous recommendations of the ordained functionaries. The bishop is, of course, the spokesman. The rules are not strictly the same in all communities. Those which are most nearly universal in the twenty states where the Old Order Amish live are the following: no electricity, telephones, automobiles, central heating systems, or tractors with pneumatic tires; beards but no moustaches for all married men; long hair (which must be parted in the center if parted at all); hooks-and-eyes on dress coats; and the use of horses for farming and for travel within the community. No formal education beyond grade eight is also a rule of life.

Meidung *or Shunning*

Shunning is a technique of keeping the fellowship "clean" or purged from habitual transgressors. Although a means to an end, it is so important in the total life of the society that it becomes prominent in the charter. Shunning is applied after the offender has been formally excommunicated from the fellowship by vote of the assembly. In such a state the transgressor cannot enjoy normal relations with other members of the church. He may not eat at the same table in the home. Married couples may not sleep in the same bed, and church members may not receive gifts or favors from one who is under "the ban." The offender can be restored if he so desires after a period of shunning by confessing violation of the taboos and by expressing repentance. A member can be excommunicated not only for lying or for adultery but also for buying an automobile, for possessing a driver's license, or for cutting the hair too short. Persons who voluntarily leave the church to join more relaxed groups, such as factions who drive automobiles or Mennonite groups, are excommunicated and shunned for life. They are regarded as "vow-breakers" and apostates. Members are in duty bound to regard them in this way, and any member who sides with the offender is also excommunicated. Shunning is regarded by the "strict" Amish as absolutely essential as a disciplinary measure. That it should continue to be rigidly practiced was one of the main issues on which the Amish separated from the Swiss Brethren.

Agrarianism

The Amish world view is conditioned by first-hand experience with nature. The ordered seasons, celestial objects such as the moon and stars, and the world of growing plants and animals provide the Amish with a sense of order and destiny. Hard work with the soil, where muscles and limbs ache from daily toil, provides human satisfaction. All family heads are required to limit their occupation to farming or to closely related activities such as operating a sawmill, carpentering, or masonry. Hard work, thrift, and social concern for the believing community find sanction in the Bible. The city by contrast is held to be the center of worldly progress, of laziness, of nonproductive spending, and often of wickedness. Man occupies his right place in the universe when he is caring for the things in "the garden," that is, the plants and animals created by God. The Amish agrarian experience for several centuries has been conducive to isolation characteristic of the ideal-typical folk society (Redfield 1947: 293–308), which greatly strengthens their religious outlook on life.

The above five elements of the Amish charter demonstrate a high degree of consistency and integration. Contradictions of belief appear to be at a minimum. Agrarianism, for example, is compatible with the doctrine of separation from the world. Conformity to absolute values is expressed by adherence to the Biblical formulations as interpreted by the functionaries. Powerful social controls are exercised through institutionalized rules (*Ordnung*) and shunning (*Meidung*) of offenders.

HIGHER EDUCATION: THE FORBIDDEN FRUIT

Despite the internal consistency of the charter, an increasing number of Amish persons find meaningful and satisfying experiences outside of the Amish society. As the American rural community becomes more urban the Amish, with their small familistic type of society, are less and less able to satisfy the psychological and social needs of their individual members. When individuals find personal fulfillment outside of the Amish community the relationship to the traditional community is altered. As marginal persons they frequently experience great personal stress; the individual is no longer sure of himself or of the values which he has traditionally held. Problem areas then arise within the society which threaten elements within the charter. Families who live on the fringe of the larger settlements of Amish appear to be exposed to greater stress than those living in "solid" communities.

One of the areas of internal conflict is the desire of young people to obtain education beyond the elementary grades. Attendance at high school is prohibited by the Old Order Amish, and such ambitions are blocked. The increased emphasis on education in American society as a prerequisite for adult living makes learning very attractive to the Amish boy or girl. The following life-history documents reflect the rewarding experiences of outside learning and show how such satisfying behaviors are legitimized to other members of the Amish society.

Our first case is that of an ex-Amish person whom we shall call Sam. Sam recalls his early interest in schooling, leading to his decision to enter college:

> I always loved school from the day I started. My parents didn't start me until I was seven so I wouldn't have to go to high school. They thought I couldn't learn very well, and I wanted to show them I could. When my mother was young she taught school. She wanted to go on to school but never had a chance. I sort of caught this desire from my mother. It made me mad when my father kept me home for a day's work. Sometimes, when I was to stay at home, I would switch into my school clothes at the last minute and get on the bus.

Sam was adept in making friends at school and during his last grades in school, he said, "I hated that I came from such a backward family." His animosity over his backwardness grew as he learned to know his classmates and especially a certain non-Amish girl.

> We were always the top two in the class. I could beat her in arithmetic, but she always beat me in reading. It was always tit for tat between us. We were always together in those early years. I always hated that I was an Amishman. My older brother was a "good boy" and listened to daddy but was always getting into trouble. Sunday after Sunday I would go to church, and all we would do after church was sit out in the buggies and tell filthy stories. I was the cockiest guy, I guess, as I was more or less the leader of our group of boys. My, how I used to get whippings from my father. I hear other people brag how they thank the Lord for their whippings, but mine just did not make sense.

With the completion of grade school Sam wanted to go to high school but could not. "I felt there was nothing to do but stay home and work for Dad till I was twenty-one. My life was terribly lean during those years." Sam was baptized in the Amish church. After he reached legal age he was exposed to a wider association of friends, most of them Mennonites. Following his release from service he entered a Mennonite college. Although for some years he attempted to retain his Amish affiliation, eventually he became a member of the Mennonite Church.

Another case is that of Rebecca, who turned from her Amish background at the age of eighteen without having been baptized.

I read a great many books and anything I could get my hands on. I tried to persuade my father to let me go to high school. But he would not. After grade school I was Amish for another six years, and this was a very difficult time in my life. My dissatisfaction began to show in physical ways. I had no energy. I was anaemic. Nothing interested me. I didn't fit in with the Amish young people, and I sort of despised them for their lack of learning. I made attempts to be popular among the Amish and dated a few times, but I didn't like it very much. I was pretty lonely, and it was a very miserable time for me. I was the oldest of eight, and mother kept on having children. This tied me down, and I was constantly resenting this. I was always running away to read, and I hid books. When mother was not watching I would read everything I could.

When I was eighteen, I thought mother had reached the age when she could have no more children. Finally, I thought I could begin to see daylight, have a little more time to myself, and keep the house neat without working so hard. Then I learned that mother was pregnant again, and this was the last straw. I simply could not face this. I went to the basement and just cried. I told father that I had had enough, I was leaving. While I was packing my suitcase, mother became upset. Father knew that mother needed my help. So we worked out a compromise. Father said if I would stay until the baby was born, the next year I could go to Bible school. This was enough for me; then I could get away and go where there was a library and read.

A third case is that of a lad whom I shall designate as Chris.

I wanted to go to high school so badly that I remember crying about it, trying to persuade my parents. They gave us county-wide achievement tests after grade eight, and I found out I was the highest in the county. I competed from grade one through grade eight very closely with a girl who went on and became valedictorian. In the accumulative tests which included all eight grades I had all A plusses except two. My principal talked to my father several times and told him I had possibilities. I was only fourteen, so my father made me repeat the eighth grade the next year. After getting all A plusses in grade eight I barely got As the second time. I was very athletic, though, and even though I was not going on to high school the principal let me go all out for athletics. All the time the kids and neighbors (non-Amish) wanted me to go on to high school. In my second year in the eighth grade I quit when April came because it was time to start plowing. I went home, and I remember how terrible I felt.

With all his chums now in high school, the lad returned to the principal and explained his painful experience. The principal gave him ninth grade books, and Chris promised that he would study them and appear for the semester tests.

I hardly touched the books, but I took the first semester test and got all As and Bs. But I finally gave up and returned the books. But I knew I would never stay Amish because the principal convinced me the Amish should not keep their children home from school. He told me I had brains. He told me I could be more than a farmer.

Such experiences frequently result in a reconsideration of the basic provision of the Amish charter which unilaterally forbids any formal training beyond the elementary grades. The Amish leaders know that they must consider the problem of finding teachers for their own private schools in areas where school consolidation has been put into effect. So long as the one-room public school served the Amish, they did not need to face the problem of securing teachers. Presently there are about 150 privately operated schools whose teachers are Amish, most of them offering no more than an elementary education. The realization that education is needed to prepare teachers for their own schools has helped to legitimize the teacher role. A few members have entered college for preparation without bringing upon themselves the sanctions of *Meidung*. The role of these persons as agents of change within the Amish society may have the effect of modifying the charter in the future.

MARGINAL OCCUPATIONS

The Amish charter requires that persons aspire to be laborers on farms and eventually farm owners. Investigation of current occupations reveals exceptions to this rule. Old Order Amish girls who have taken training as nurses have not remained Amish: There are no Amish physicians, and this role appears not to be a likely one. One unusual occupation is that of an Amish girl who is employed as a registered technician. She completed high school by correspondence, and by borrowing books from a local high school she qualified for a high school certificate. She had always anticipated the vocation of nursing. Upon counseling with a Director of Nursing, she learned that a professional uniform would be required for a trained nurse and that no exception could be made. She knew that she could not remain loyal to the Amish church if she followed this vocation, so she began training for work as a technician. She commuted to a college and completed the required courses. As a registered technician she is not required to wear white shoes or white stockings, and she may wear a white coat over her Amish uniform while on duty. The hospital officials have been very co-operative in helping the girl find security in her new vocation. Safeguards were taken not to give publicity which would jeopardize her relationship to the Amish church. When photographs of her graduating class appeared in the papers, for example, hers was omitted. Her Amish friends believe that, if she keeps the *Ordnung* otherwise, she may be able to continue her profession.

Sickness, incapacity, or chronic illness of a family head may lead to marginal occupations of a nontraditional type. Daniel, a man in his fifties, always loved farming. According to a neighbor, "He has been in many things." As a result of an accident in his youth, "he had surgery done on his head and has suffered many headaches since. He has taken many pills from different doctors, which now affects his heart." Besides being a sales agent for seeds, which allows him to travel in many Amish settlements, he also has been engaged in dynamite blasting as custom work. In this business he served as a supplier of dynamite for hardware stores in his region of the state. He ordered the dynamite by carload lots and stored it in a stone quarry on his farm. This occupation was perhaps more compatible with farming than many.

The question may be raised why Amish persons who are really marginal remain within the Amish community. One young Amishman, after many years of trying to remain loyal to the Amish faith, gave up, saying, "I would rather be a conservative Mennonite than a liberal Amishman." But many who are allowed to exercise a small degree of marginality prefer to remain with their kin and community. A marginal occupation may be tolerated by the community so long as it does not constitute a direct threat. However, when a person takes his marginal occupation seriously and wishes to excel, as in nursing, teaching, or business, the stresses created tend to exceed the limits of toleration.

Marginal persons who persist in their deviation, as in the cases above, frequently become effective agents of change. They create favorable attitudes toward behaviors usually forbidden. An Amish father who invokes no sanction against his son for buying an automobile becomes an innovator. Family heads who merely refrain from taking negative sanctions against violators are in a favorable position for introducing change, especially if they are from families of high status. Agents of change may accept the goals of their society but use other than institutional means for achieving the goals.

SUICIDE

The frequency of suicides, even in the face of strong Biblical injunctions against taking life, suggests the presence of unresolved personal conflicts. While most common among single unmarried Amish males, suicide also occurs among adults who occupy key positions (Hostetler 1963: 283). Two well-informed persons in one community could recall fifteen suicides, fourteen of whom were males and most of them under the age of 22. This period in life appears to be the most crucial for acceptance or rejection of the basic values of the culture. Persons "without values" (Durkheim 1951) to direct a course of action revert to apathy and despair. Anomic suicides reflect one aspect of personal disorganization. Religious functionaries who are charged with maintaining the *Ordnung* are subjected to extraordinary role stress. The threat of strong negative sanctions for suggesting alternative courses of action contributes to anxiety and conflict in persons charged with maintaining the norms.

One of the most dramatic instances of suicide was that of a very prominent leader who hanged himself to the surprise of the entire Amish community. The reason for his sudden "disgraceful act" remained a mystery to his kin and his close friends. Upon close examination of the case it is clear that the ordained man was caught between contradictory expectations.

The rate of suicide among the Amish may be higher than that of the rural United States population in general—possibly even as high as that for rural Michigan (Schroeder and Beegle 1953), which exceeds that of the urban population. This impression derives from a survey based on the memory of informants in one large community, but we shall not know conclusively until a complete investigation has been made. The Amish would need to have but four suicides per year to approximate the rate for the United States at large (10.3 per 100,000).

ROWDYISM

"Running wild" is tolerated in the normal life of the young unmarried adult male. The number of young persons who defect permanently varies considerably with each community. After marriage the individual generally conforms to the rules of the community and accepts seriously the norms of its culture. Before marriage, however, there is a great deal of rowdyism and other forms of antisocial behavior in reaction against the traditional norms. This has become especially manifest in the largest Amish settlements, where it is associated with the relaxation of traditional controls.

The geographic boundaries of the community have expanded beyond the limits encompassed by a horse and buggy. This poses no problem for the adult ceremonial community, which has explicit recognized boundaries. But for the young people of courting age there are no geographic boundaries. One result has been the development and differentiation of informal special-interest groups, especially in connection with the institution of Sunday evening "singings." Sharp differentiations are expressed in the names and modal behavior of the various "singings." According to one young man:

> The Groffies are the most liberal, then the Ammies, and then the Trailers. Each has a number of subgroupings and interests, and under the Groffies, for instance, there are the Hillbillies, Jamborees, and Goodie-goodies. The Hillbillies occupy the hill country, the Jamborees are the most unruly, and the Goodie-goodies are so called because they are the Christians.

These groups maintain social distance and display various forms of antagonism. "There are times when one gang has cut the harness of another to pieces, or they have unhooked the horses of the others and let them run off." Differentiation is also expressed in patterns of smoking, entertainment, dating, and the use of automobiles.

Indulgence in antisocial acts, within the religious community as well as outside of it, occurs with greater frequency as individuals experience problems of stress. Stealing chickens or grain and selling these products, or trading them for a dance floor for a night, is not unknown. One juvenile said: "We used to see who could do the best job of swearing and being the biggest blow gut. If there was anything daring to be done, I had to show the boys I had the nerve to do it." Problems associated with drinking alcoholic beverages have come to the attention of the wider community. There have been a number of arrests of Amish for violation of the liquor laws. After complaints from neighbors, the police conducted several raids on Sunday night singings. On one occasion, officers reported more than a dozen cases of empty beer bottles, and several youths were arrested for drunkenness. Although parents are concerned about the mischief of the boys, they appear helpless. After one arrest at a singing, an Amish father said: "What can I do? I know it's wrong for minors to drink beer, but the boys would get down on me if I didn't allow it."

Outsiders are not welcome at Amish singings and are chased off the grounds if not invited. One outsider, who was a farm hand but had worked for an Amish family, decided to attend a nearby singing. He was surrounded by a score or more of Amish boys and was accused of wanting their women and of spying. He did not escape without a beating. Just as the staunch Amish are wary of the outsider who wants to write a book about them, so the young too are suspicious of the stranger as a possible intruder.

ACCULTURATION AGENTS

After a period of permissive "wildness" the typical Amish young man returns to a state of conformity, for baptism and marriage, and to serious observance of the moral postulates of the society. Those who cannot or will not be induced to accept the basic elements in the charter usually make successful linkages with outsiders who bridge the gap between the Amish and the surrounding alien culture.

Acculturation agents are those non-Amish persons outside the Amish society but adjacent to it who are in unique positions to assist the marginal Amish person, e.g., members of nearby churches, physicians, business men, officers of the law, and neighboring farmers. They are the middlemen who mediate between the small and the great society.

To obtain a valid driver's license (forbidden by the *Ordnung*) an Amish youth must have some kind of assistance before he applies for a permit at the police headquarters. Usually he will have learned how to drive an automobile from a friend or relative in the Amish Mennonite religious group, or in some cases from an employer if, for instance, he has been employed by a non-Amish construction firm. Amish youth who wish to qualify for college entrance frequently fulfill their high school requirements by taking special examinations administered by the state. Assistance in applying for the proper forms and in acquiring the knowledge and tutorial instruction necessary to pass the examinations is often obtained from a school principal or a non-Amish friend.

Owing to their ignorance of the ways of the outside world, the Amish are sometimes exploited by outsiders, e.g., by charging an exorbitant price for an automobile. Automobile salesmen, salesmen of musical instruments, insurance salesmen, and issuers of driver's licenses do business secretly with young Amish people so that their parents and the public do not discover such activities and the special procedures involved. When Amish youth are arrested or convicted, their names are often withheld from the newspapers if they request it. Frequently a postman or mail carrier will hold certain mail until he sees the recipient personally, so that parents will not be aware that a family member has received a forbidden item such as an insurance policy or a driver's license.

Young Amish men who have been stopped for speeding, or for legal charges having to do with the condition of an automobile, e.g., a faulty muffler, are known to have been released because a police officer "favored" or was in sympathy with them. Many have passed driver's examinations with a little bribery. Some examining officers have the reputation among Amish youth for passing them easily on driver examinations. Even persons under the legal age have been issued licenses, as well as trustworthy youths who have not had adequate driver training. In return for pies, rolls of bologna, and home-cured hams these "agents" provide licenses under conditions which Amish youth can meet.

There are gasoline service stations which permit Amish boys to park their automobiles with them. One used-car salesman allows boys to keep their autos on his lot when they are not driving them on the understanding that they will buy the automobiles from and service them with his firm. A number of service stations receive much Amish patronage on weekends.

Increasing numbers of Amish youth, minors included, patronize bars and liquor stores because they are trusted and favored by many outsiders and rarely cause trouble. In general, the Amish young people enjoy an excellent reputation among outsiders because they are usually honest and industrious. There appear, however, to be a few outsiders who co-operate with the elders and parents to keep the young people "in line."

For those who leave the group, making the initial break with the culture takes place in a number of ways and is usually an adjustment to stress. Some run away from home without making a successful contact with outside reference groups. A boy aged sixteen suddenly disappeared one Saturday afternoon. The first sign of his leaving was the discovery of his Amish hat a mile away from home. The father was alarmed but could do nothing but wait hopefully. The next day a neighbor received a phone call from a large city stating the exact place where the runaway boy could be picked up. The boy had discarded his Amish clothing, had his hair cut in a barber shop, and traveled to the city, then became despondent and gave up. Unknown to any of the family members the boy had entertained the notion of running away for many months as a result of an unhappy encounter with his father.

Four Pennsylvania boys, two of whom were members, made their departure after midnight by walking and thumbing their way to Ohio. The first sign of their leaving was the discovery of their long shorn hair in an upstairs bedroom. Within two weeks all were back to their native community, though not all returned to their homes. Two of them joined the army, and the other two soon married girls outside the Amish faith. A former Amish father, when asked why boys sometimes run away, said:

> Who wouldn't? All the teaching they get is *Attnung* [*Ordnung*] and the command from their parents *"Du bliebst Deitsch"* [You must stay Dutch]. Parents are too rigid in their demands and punishment. My brother ran away from home last year, and I can tell you why. Dad was awful rough with him. He gave us boys one licking after another. Even when I was eighteen he tried to lick me, but that's when I said, "It's enough." I didn't let him.

Slipping outside the Amish community with intent to return appears to be more common now than in former years. As outside pressures exert themselves on small neighborhoods, and as young members have more and more knowledge about outside affairs, "having a fling" with the world and returning has become institutionalized. Thirty or forty years ago it was not uncommon for two or more Amish persons to go west and work their way with the harvest from Texas to North Dakota. They usually returned and after marriage settled down as members in the Amish community.

Two brothers purchased an automobile "to see the world." One of them said:

> We traveled all over the United States and visited practically all the states. We just cut a huge figure eight all over the United States. We were interested in traveling, and we told our parents, and then bought a car. We each had a half share and after returning I sold my share.

The boys left in the spring and returned in the fall.

Another type of exodus is typified by a boy who left as usual on Monday morning for work on a nearby non-Amish farm.

> I did not want to leave this way, but I decided I would write my parents a letter after I was away so they wouldn't need to worry about me. I stayed away several weeks. Then, because I was not of legal age, I got a warning from the courthouse. I told my boss I did not think the warning meant anything because I was sure my father would not go to law. Then in a few days I got a phone call from my dad, and he asked if I am coming home. I told him I would come home to visit but I didn't feel too welcome. I said I could not stay home. So he said he would have to go to the court-

house. Then I knew he was not kidding. My boss went to the court-house to find out what would happen. He found out they could only take me home, but they could make it bad for him as my employer. So I left his place and on the advice of a friend went to Florida. While down there I also got a warning from the courthouse, so I went to see them about it. They said Florida authorities could do nothing, but the Pennsylvania authorities could come and get me, but it would cost them a lot of money and they probably would not. After they heard my story, they told me not to worry.

Another young man gave the following account:

I did not run away at night. After my father accused me of some-thing I had not done, I just put on my old straw hat and walked down the road. I wanted to join the army but was too young. I worked for an English farmer not far away who hated the Amish. My father saw me in town one day and asked me why I don't come home. I said, "I'm not coming home now nor will I ever come home."

The young man then joined a traveling medicine show which visited his home town.

They needed a boy to help. Of course I was interested. I had read a lot about circuses, so I joined the show. We traveled all over the state. I ran the popcorn machine, took the tent down, and cleaned up the papers and mess afterwards. The show did not get into any of the Amish communities. I would sell tickets at the door, and if the ropes needed tightening I did that. On my birthday the recruit-ing officer got in touch with me. I left and joined the service.

CONCLUSION

The Amish charter embodies elements which tend to be con-sistent with each other. But consistency does not assure con-formity. Amish life is not free from personal stress and sustained conflict. The experiences related in the above case materials reveal problems of thwarted motivation and problems of sociali-zation common to marginal persons. The role of "agents of change" within Amish society and of "acculturation agents" out-side the society gives rise in multiple ways to meaningful personal contacts in the larger American society. Alterations of behavior patterns occur, forcing a re-evaluation of the charter. Unless the charter is reinterpreted, inconsistencies develop between doctrine and practice, and these may lead to anomie, fragmentation, and demoralization. The central doctrines remain essentially the same, but the applications change. Separation from the world, for example, remains a central doctrine, but slight modifications in dress, in mechanization, and in other living habits occur in the process of solving the existential problem and of coping success-fully with the environment.

The Amish response to change, especially when it threatens the charter, characteristically takes the form of fragmentation and division over what appear to the outsider as hair-splitting issues. Divisions are rarely peaceful or the result of deliberations. In-stead, the relations between different ceremonial groups are commonly characterized by *Meidung* and animosity. Some settle-ments have as many as five different kinds of Amish, with different symbolic behavior systems, who practice ritual avoid-ance in relation to all others. These subsystems function so as to prevent further change. Each group expels its marginal persons and controls marriage and intergroup associations. The large number of small and extinct communities of Amish is evidence of such fragmentation (Mook 1955; Umble 1933).

But extinct settlements do not mean failure of the community —only failure of its spatial dimension. The Amish take their social institutions with them to other areas where group fulfillment can be successfully resolved. Complete disintegration is rare, for staunch families generally migrate if they dislike their community or the conditions in it. Migration is frequently the only alternative for those Amish who wish to shun all progress. Amish who can-not put up with change frequently sell their farms and move to other settlements, often across state lines. Those who moved from Pennsylvania to Ontario in recent years said: "We want to go back fifty years; things are going too fast there." Thus a father faced with the possible threat of the automobile or the tractor may write to an uncle or a distant relative in another state and ask, "How are things there?" In prospecting for a new loca-tion, the strictness of *Ordnung* there is as important to him as the price of land.

Migration, for the Amish, is one of the most important factors in resisting acculturation. Freed (1957: 55) has observed that specialists and class differences are essential to the maintenance of the Jewish *shtetl* of Eastern Europe. By contrast, the Old Order Amish, who have no occupational class differences and no specialists, are able to survive by migration. Had they not migrated from Europe to America they would have become extinct long ago. Indeed, those who remained in Europe have coalesced with other Protestant sects or with Catholics (Hostetler 1955). Migrations are normally directed to new localities rather than old ones, but there is also constant family mobility between communities.

All cultures exert pressures on the individual, and in Amish culture, as in that of French Canada (Hughes 1943: 216), such pressures generate feelings of resentment. Like the French Canadians, the Amish have not had to absorb their own "misfit people," their own "toxic by-products." Their misfits and marginal persons, following their excommunication by the Amish, are absorbed by neighbors of other religions. Discontent finds expression in a variety of complaints, and rowdyism has exceeded institutionalized boundaries and become a serious problem. Marginal personalities have emerged among individuals who have identified themselves with the dominant outgroup but have encountered relatively "impermeable barriers" (Kerchoff and McCormick 1955: 54).

Amish communities, like other separatist communities, find themselves in a problematic situation. Amish society is faced with the problem of community self-realization and personal fulfillment for each new generation of members born into it. The problem must be solved within the range of its limited potentialities and by means of its available natural and human resources and its own unique local heritage. The constant striving to achieve the goals of the charter has given rise to distinctive patterns of deviancy and stress.

19 THE RESEARCH AND DEVELOPMENT
APPROACH TO THE STUDY OF CHANGE

Allan R. Holmberg

I

W HAT I HAVE to say[1] on the question of values in action
stems largely from a rather deep and personal involvement
with this question for the past five years. In 1952, quite by design, although unexpectedly and suddenly, I found myself in the
delicate position of having assumed the role of *patrón* (in the
name of Cornell University) of a Peruvian *hacienda,* called Vicos,
for a period of five years, for the purpose of conducting a research
and development program on the modernization process.

As you can readily imagine, such action on my part clearly
shook (or perhaps I should say shocked) the Board of Trustees
—to say nothing of the some 2,000 residents of the *hacienda* and
no few of my anthropological colleagues—to the extent, I might
add, that had events subsequently taken other turns than they
eventually did, I would probably not be writing this and would be
much more in disgrace as an anthropologist and human being than
I presently am. Moreover, had I known then what I now know, I
am not so sure that I would be willing to repeat the experience,
even though it has been one of the most rewarding ones of my
whole professional career. My doubts lie not so much with the

Originally published in *Human Organization,* Volume 17, No. 1 (1958),
12–16. Reprinted with permission of the publisher, the Laura Holmberg and
the Society for Applied Anthropology.

[1] The paper printed here was first given at the symposium on "Values in
Action" at the annual meeting of the American Anthropological Association,
Chicago, December 1957.

fruitfulness or legitimacy of the research and development, as contrasted with the strictly research, approach to the study of the social process but more with the wear and tear that it might cause to the inadequately financed or inadequately staffed anthropologist or other behavioral scientist who is brash enough to attempt to apply it, especially in a foreign area. On this point I shall have more to say later. For the moment, suffice it to say that having recently retired—again quite by design—from playing the dual role of God and anthropologist (the status of Vicos has recently changed from a dependent to an independent community) and having again assumed the role of a plain anthropologist, I find the change in status a highly comforting one. Nevertheless, on the basis of the past five years of experience at Vicos, I remain convinced that the interventionist or action approach to the dynamics of culture, applied with proper restraint, may in the long run provide considerable payoff in terms both of more rational policy and better science. My concern here, therefore, will be with some of the reasons why I believe this to be the case. What, then, are some of the implications—the advantages and disadvantages, the gains and losses—of the application of the research *and* development approach to the study of change, both from a value and scientific point of view?

II

On the question of values—in the ethical sense—I really have little to say, more than to state my stand. No one—professional or layman—can scientifically justify intervention into the lives of other people, whether they be of his own kind or of a different breed. However, by its very nature, the social process is an influencing process among individuals and social groups, one upon which the very existence of society depends. It is no less a necessary condition for the study of social life. Even the most "pure" anthropologist imaginable, conducting his research with "complete" detachment and objectivity, cannot avoid influencing his subjects of study or in turn of being influenced by them. In some instances, I believe, this has led to very salutory effects, both on anthropologists and their informants. Certainly the science of anthropology has been greatly enriched by those informants who were influenced by anthropologists to become anthropologists, even though it may be more questionable, perhaps, that native cultures have been correspondingly enriched by those anthropologists who were influenced by their informants to go native. While this may seem beside the point, I simply want to emphasize the fact that influence and consequently the values which motivate that influence are always part of the process of human interaction and while they can be studied by science, their validation must rest on other grounds.

This does not mean that any anthropologist—pure or applied —can manipulate his subjects without restraint. Some code of ethics must govern his behavior, as the Society for Applied Anthropology long ago recognized. In the case of Vicos, however, where power was held by us, this became an especially delicate issue because having assumed the role of *patrones* we expected and were expected to intervene in the lives of the people. It was at this point that the question of values entered and it was at this point that it was very necessary to take a value stand. What then was this stand?

I long ago made the decision for myself, which is shared by a great many people and communities of the world, that the best kind of a community in which to live is one that is, to quote Aldous Huxley, "just, peaceable, morally and intellectually progressive" and made up of "responsible men and women." To my way of thinking, and I am by no means unique in this view, the best way of approaching this Utopian state of affairs is to pursue as a goal the realization of basic human dignity to which every individual is entitled. And by basic human dignity I mean a very simple thing: a wide rather than a narrow sharing of what I regard as positive human values, some expression of which, as Professor Harold Lasswell (n.d.) has so clearly shown, is found in every society and towards a wider sharing of which, if I interpret Professor Robert Redfield (1953) correctly, the broader course of civilization itself has been moving for a considerable period of time.

For lack of better terms of my own to express the meaning I wish to convey, let me again refer to Lasswell who speaks of the following categories of value: power, wealth, enlightenment, respect, well being, skill, affection, and rectitude. The wide sharing of such values among members of the Vicos community was essentially the overall basic value position and policy goal to which we subscribed. In other words, everyone, if he so desired, should at least have the right and the opportunity, if not the responsibility, to participate in the decision-making process in the community, to enjoy a fair share of its wealth, to pursue a desire for knowledge, to be esteemed by his fellowmen, to develop talents to the best of his ability, to be relatively free from physical and mental disease, to enjoy the affection of others, and to command respect for his private life. While no such value stand, of course, can ever be validated by science we and a surprising number of Vicosinos, as I have said elsewhere, and, as revealed by a baseline study, believed them "to be good and desirable ends" (Holmberg 1955).

Movement towards such goals, of course, rests on a couple of fundamental assumptions (or better, expectations) in which I happen to have a very strong faith: 1) that human traits are such that progress can be made towards the realization of human dignity, and 2) that the natural order (physical nature) is such that with greater knowledge and skill, human beings can turn it progressively to the service of social goals.

In stating this overall value position, I have not meant to suggest that movement towards these goals can occur only through a single set of institutional practices. Like most anthropologists I subscribe to the doctrine of the relativity of culture and I firmly believe that people have the right of self-determination, as long as they respect that right in others. From the very beginning at Vicos we recognized this principle. In short, we used our power to share power to a point where we no longer hold power, which is just as matters should be.

Before leaving these value and policy matters let me simply cite a few of the developmental changes that have come about as a result of the application of the research *and* development approach to change at Vicos:

1   *Organization*

1952   Vicos had an *hacienda*-type organization. Outside renters not only had free use of *hacienda peones* for labor and personal services, but also of their animals and tools. Power was concentrated in the hands of a *patrón*.

1957   *Hacienda* system and free services have been abolished;

new system of community organization now in march is based on shared interests and local control.

2   *Land Ownership*

1952   No title to land, although Vicosinos had tried on numerous occasions to purchase the land on which they had been living as *peones* for 400 years.

1957   Based on reports of development by the Cornell-Peru Project, the Institute of Indigenous Affairs asked the Peruvian Government to expropriate Vicos in favor of its indigenous population. This expropriation has now taken place.

3   *Local Authority*

1952   Under the *hacienda*-type organization there were no responsible secular authorities within the community.

1957   The Vicosinos have organized a board of their own delegates elected from each of 6 zones of the *hacienda*. They have the legal responsibility for the direction of community affairs.

4   *Income*

1952   The indigenous community of Vicos had no source of income of its own.

1957   Former *hacienda* lands are now farmed for the public good, providing a steady income for the payment of lands and the development of public service.

5   *Education*

1952   In the aspect of education Vicos had a very small school, with one teacher, 10–15 students.

1957   Vicos now possesses the most modern school in the whole region, recently made a *nucleo escolar,* with a capacity of 400 students. There are now 9 teachers and about 200 students, many of whom have had five years of continuity in school.

6   *Production*

1952   Low economic production—each *hectare* of potato land produced a value of only $100.

1957   Each *hectare* of potato land is now producing a value of $400–$600.

7   *Health Facilities*

1952   There were no modern health facilities.
1957   A modern health center has been built by the Vicosinos and a neighboring community; a clinic is held twice a week and a public health program is underway.

Most of the cost of these developments have been borne by members of the community themselves.

As a final development outcome I should perhaps mention that the Cornell-Peru Project has had considerable impact outside of the area of Vicos. When originally undertaken there was not a single project of its kind in Peru. At the present time, the Institute of Indigenous Affairs is directing five programs of a similar nature in other areas of the country. And attached to all are Peruvian anthropologists, many of them trained in part at Vicos.

But more important have been the effects on the outside produced by the Vicosinos themselves. Word of their freedom has got around. Let me cite but one example. Recently an *hacienda* community, in conditions similar to those obtaining at Vicos in 1952, sent a commission to Vicos for advice. Their *hacienda,* a public one as Vicos has been, was about to be rented at public auction for a period of ten years and they were desirous of freeing themselves from service to a *patrón*. One of the ways in which this can be done is for the residents of an *hacienda* to rent it directly from the government themselves. But in the case of this community sufficient funds were not immediately available.

The Vicosinos sent a return commission to *Huascarán,* a fictitious name for the community under discussion. On the recommendation of this commission the community of Vicos, which had funds in the bank, lent the community of Huascarán sufficient money to rent their *hacienda* directly from the government, thus freeing them from service to a *patrón*. More than that when the commission from Vicos first went to Huascarán they noticed that the Huascarinos planted their fields by somewhat antiquated methods and suggested more modern methods of agriculture which were originally introduced into Vicos by the Cornell-Peru Project. These are the kind of developmental effects that give the applied anthropologist an occasion for joy.

III

Now what of the scientific implications of the research and development approach to the study of change? (Lasswell, Lindblom, Kennedy and Holmberg n.d.). Here again I take a positive view, particularly in a situation like Vicos, where it was possible to work in a complete cultural context, where it was possible to specify social goals for almost all aspects of culture, and where it was possible for the anthropologist to maintain some control over the interventions and variables involved. In such an environment, hypotheses can be tested by comparing actual goal achievement with predicted goal achievement.

Actually in the natural sciences, research and development are inseparable. It is even common to join them in one formal project as is the case in many technologically advanced industries, in government, and in private institutions. But whether formally joined or not, scientific discovery is sooner or later inevitably put to the test of success or failure through the application of research results in engineering and technology. In other words, a great strength of, if not a necessary condition for, natural science is feedback through development.

Anthropology, like other behavioral sciences, profits little from such corrective feedback. In part, this is because it is not systematically employed in social decision-making, as let us say, physics is employed in missile or building construction. But even if it is employed the results are either not fed back to the anthropologist or they are fed back too slowly to facilitate rapid scientific advance. Moreover, research and development work in behavioral science are seldom joined, even though they were to some extent in Vicos, for the systematic exploitation of their reciprocal benefits, as they are in the research and development laboratories of the natural sciences. To get the feedback necessary for rapid advance in a behavioral science like anthropology, policy is needed, even if policy does not need science.

The connection between research and development in anthropology and other behavioral sciences is probably even closer than it is in the natural sciences. In science, as everyone knows, every generalization is both an insight and a prediction, even though its explicit statement is usually cast in one form or another. Now when a generalization on behavior is communicated to people who are also its subjects, it may alter the knowledge and preferences of these people and also their behavior. Thus a scientific generalization on behavior, by altering behavior, appears to falsify or obsolesce itself. This is called "pliancy factor" by my philosophical colleague at Cornell, Max Black.

In general this complication has been viewed as a cross that the behavioral scientist must bear. Actually, a generalization about behavior is not falsified when predictions based upon it are made obsolete when the subject to whom it is made known prefers to modify himself rather than to conform to an earlier prediction. It is simply that the possibility of modification of behavior must be taken into account and turned to scientific advantage. In the continuous interplay between scientific generalization and goal-seeking behavior, the insight-feedback of a scientific generalization can be employed both for goal revision and as empirical data for research. This is one of the great advantages of the research and development approach. Perhaps an example will illustrate what I mean.

One of the developmental goals of the Vicos program was to bring decision-making bodies of the community up to a level of competence at which we, the *patrones,* could be dispensed with but without the community's falling victim to its most predatory members as has sometimes been the case. Thus, arrangements had to be made for group survival and stability and, through controlling the complexity of the problems dealt with and by other devices, the groups gradually brought to their highest level of competence. This required that hypotheses be formulated and acted upon—hypotheses concerning the requirements of viability and competence of groups. Once acted upon the hypotheses were tested by their results. Hence each successive developmental step was a step in the isolation of another variable for research.

Concretely, both development and research interests merge in following the consequences of such successive steps as the following, at least some of which were taken for one group of potential decision-makers at Vicos: 1) the group was asked for advice in the settlement of land disputes; 2) it was invested with prestige by calling public attention to its role; 3) the group was given the opportunity to settle land disputes; 4) the group was provided, through skilled observers, the feedback of an understandable analysis of its performance; 5) the *patrón* was withdrawn from the group meeting, reserving only the right to veto under certain conditions; 6) the jurisdiction of the group was enlarged with gradually decreasing veto.

While this detail is much abbreviated, it suggests how research on the developmental steps provides an opportunity for the dogged pursuit of whatever variables one wishes to isolate. Every insight into the variables can be put to a test; and, where predictions are disappointed, a reformulation of the hypothesis can be followed by a further test until predictions are no longer disappointed. By no means will all the unknowns of human behavior become unveiled, but development requires correct insights, hypotheses, and analytic models. It compels their never-ending revision until they pass the test of application.

The essence of the connection between research and development in this illustration is that each developmental intervention —say, introducing legal principles by which land disputes might be resolved—is both a necessary step towards reaching community goals and in the research sense a method of varying the group situation to isolate another variable in group dynamics—in this instance isolating the effect of introducing formal principles against which individual cases are to be judged. It is precisely because of feedback to the researcher from the development application that research needs development just as much as development needs research.

Whatever the particular example, the story is much the same. The researcher is compelled to follow through, to keep on trying for the refinement of an hypothesis or model that will stand the test of application. If, for example, he wants to know what is necessary to break down prejudice between Indians and Mestizos, his research is not terminated when he has tested one popular hypothesis and found it invalid, because his developmental objectives require that he try a whole series of interventions until prejudice begins to decline.

In the case of Vicos, attempts were made in collaboration with several colleagues (Lasswell, Lindblom, Kennedy, and Holmberg n.d.) to lay out about 130 specific possible lines of research and development, each matched to a specific developmental goal such as the diversification of agriculture, the development of community leadership, the reduction of social distance between Indians and Mestizos, the increase of educational opportunities for both children and adults, etc. Wherever possible an attempt was made to make fairly precise statements about the goals in question. To lay out the various possibilities in order subsequently to develop a strategy of research and development, each line of possible intervention was represented in a semi-diagrammatic way by a column on a very large bulletin or map board taking up the walls of a room. The diagram below represents how 3″ x 5″ cards were used to lay out visually the

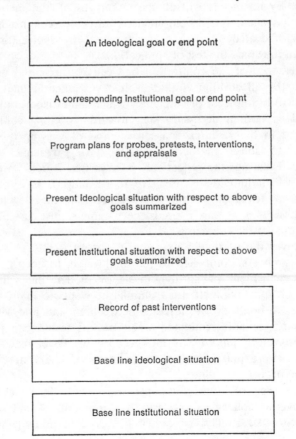

research and development sequences, subject to constant revision as research and development continues:

At the top of the column is posted for some end-point date the particular goal in question to be reached. At the bottom of the column are posted the counterpart institutional and ideological situations found at the base line period before interventions. Above them are summarized any interventions so far made, and above them the present institutional and ideological situation with respect to this one line of development. The remainder of the column is given over to a proposed schedule of probes, pretests, interventions, and appraisals.

By utilizing such a method, interventions are not likely to be hit or miss and their developmental and research gains can be fully appreciated. Scheduling them requires the careful appraisal of the facts describing the existing situation and trends, probes of readiness of the community to take the proposed step, pretests of interventions on a small scale, then the intervention itself and subsequent appraisal, which in turn becomes the first step in a still further intervention. Hence in diagrammatic terms, the upper part of the column, including the goals themselves, is constantly undergoing revision on the basis of the growing lower part of the column representing past experience.

To illustrate the distinctiveness of research, where the whole life of the community is available for study, as it was to a considerable extent in Vicos, it may be helpful to visualize a great many columns such as have just been described, set side by side. The interrelationships among these columns can hardly go unnoticed, and it becomes both possible and necessary to consider these interrelationships in devising a research and development strategy.

One more thing should be said about this contextual mapping in a research and development approach to change. It makes possible, for *development,* an economy of intervention. For example, one way in which to reduce social inequality between Mestizos and Indians is to schedule public functions in Vicos attractive enough to draw neighboring Mestizos in and then conduct these functions in such a way as to break down the traditional acceptance of segregation. One can conceive of an experiment along this line that might test the hypothesis that prejudice between Indians and Mestizos will be reduced by contact under conditions of social equality.

Now with reference to quite a different goal of reducing communal binges, movies are an effective competitor with alcohol because the Vicosinos prefer to be sober when watching a movie. Movies are also an obvious method for adult education, including literacy. Finally, the importation and showing of films may become the nucleus of a small-scale experiment in Indian entrepreneurship. Hence a variety of lines of desirable research and development converge on a movie program for Vicos. Actually such an experiment is now underway at Vicos and a skillful plan for introducing movies into the community may turn out to be a strategically sound intervention because many birds may be killed with one small stone.

I have now said enough to indicate what I believe some of the value and scientific implications of the research and development approach to the study of change to be. Most of what I have said is positive and I have not suggested that this approach be applied to the exclusion of others. My greatest doubts about it, on the basis of my experience at Vicos, stem from the unlikelihood of mobilizing sufficient funds and personnel to do a research and development job well. It is a man's job that a boy cannot be sent to do. I hope that the powers supporting research will soon take cognizance of this fact.

20 THE BACKWASH OF THE FRONTIER:
THE IMPACT OF THE INDIAN
ON AMERICAN CULTURE

A. Irving Hallowell

A LTHOUGH Frederick Jackson Turner and his disciples have made little point of the influence of the American Indian upon our civilization, it is the Indian's continuing presence throughout our whole colonial and national history that has given many aspects of our culture a special coloring. In this respect, our national experience differs from that of any western European nation, though our culture is continuous with that of Europe. Recently, Bernard De Voto has stressed the manifold nature of this unique historical situation and its neglect by historians (Howard 1952):

> Most American history has been written as if history were a function solely of white culture—in spite of the fact that till well into the nineteenth century the Indians were one of the principal determinants of historical events. Those of us who work in frontier history—which begins at the tidal beaches and when the sixteenth century begins— are repeatedly nonplused to discover how little has been done for us in regard to the one force bearing on our field that was active everywhere. Disregarding Parkman's great example, American historians have made shockingly little effort to understand the life, the societies, the cultures, the thinking, and the feeling of the Indians, and disastrously little effort to understand how all these affected white men and their societies.

It is discernible Indian influences of this sort that have formed

---

Originally published in *The Frontier in Perspective* edited by Walker D. Wyman and Clifton B. Kroeber, Madison, University of Wisconsin Press, 1957, pp. 229–58. Reprinted with permission of the author and of the University of Wisconsin Press.

what I have called "the backwash of the frontier," fertile silt carried on the currents and eddies left by the turmoil on the borderlands. Many other factors beside frontier conditions were involved in the further development of these influences—factors too complex to analyze here. And the problem is complicated by the extreme diversity of America's reactions to the Indian and his cultures; by the manner in which Indian influences have been mediated, the varying forms they have assumed at different periods of our national existence, and their depth. Most often they have been manifested at the vernacular level of American culture, one expression of our cultural provincialism, which is perhaps the reason so little systematic attention has been paid to them. Our contacts with the Indians have affected our speech, our economic life, our clothing, our sports and recreations, certain indigenous religious cults, many of our curative practices, folk and concert music, the novel, poetry, drama, even some of our basic psychological attitudes, and one of the social sciences, anthropology.

To the outside world there is a closer association of the Indian with the image of America than perhaps we are aware of. For example, Cooper's *The Last of the Mohicans* is not only read by every American schoolchild, it has been said to be the best known American novel in the world. So too, *Hiawatha,* Longfellow's poetic image of the Indian, is widely read and translated in other countries. Ivan Bunin, the Russian poet and novelist, "is probably as well recognized for his translation of *Hiawatha* as for any of his original works" (Golides 1950).

Americans have created a whole succession of images of the Indian, some literary and interpretative, some growing out of direct contact of particular types of white men with him and changing with historical circumstances. Although the Pope declared as far back as 1512 that the natives of America were descended from Adam and Eve, in colonial New England, Cotton Mather thought that "probably the *Devil* decoy'd . . . [them] . . . hither, in hopes that the gospel of the Lord Jesus Christ would never come here to destroy or disturb his absolute empire over them." As God's elected agents and under his "wonder-working Providence," the colonists must convert these "tawney serpents" or annihilate them. However, the Indian was never simply The Enemy. On the earliest frontiers, the colonists were befriended by the natives. Who has not heard of Squanto? White men from the beginning profited in many practical ways from the Indians' knowledge of their own country and through intimate contacts learned about their customs, manner of thought, and character, and were influenced by them.

During the eighteenth century, when in England and on the Continent a literary image of the Noble Savage, partly derived from ideas about the Indian, was being created, the colonists greatly deepened their firsthand knowledge of the American natives. Trading activities brought tribal groups over a wider range into contact with the colonists. The Indians were not always fought against; on occasion they were comrades-in-arms, and aboriginal methods of fighting influenced the colonists. The speeches made by Indians in treaty negotiations aroused so much interest in native oratory that a novel literary form, with no prototype in Europe, emerged. Verbatim reports of these conferences were widely circulated and read in printed form. It has even been said that information about the organization and operation of the League of the Iroquois, which Franklin picked up at various Indian councils, suggested to him the pattern for a United States of America. In any case it was Franklin whose appreciation of the attitude of the Indians toward their own culture led him to express the anthropological principle of the relativity of culture norms when, in 1784, he wrote: "Savages we call them, because their manners differ from ours, which we think the Perfection of Civility: they think the same of theirs" (Aldridge 1950).

As the eastern frontier receded westward and for most Americans the contemporary Indians could be viewed at a comfortable distance, it was their decline that became a romantic literary theme. As expressed in poetry, drama, and the novel, it was an early backwash of the frontier. But it was by no means always the Noble Savage that was depicted; a double image was created —the savage as ignoble as well as noble. During this period, the first half of the nineteenth century, when the Indian was such a popular figure in American literature, it is particularly significant that most of the authors who dealt with Indian themes derived their information from written sources rather than from direct observation. Cooper depended on Heckewelder's writings, and Longfellow on Schoolcraft's *Algic Researches* (1839). It has been said that "Cooper poured the prejudices of John Heckewelder into the Leather-Stocking mold, and produced the Indian of nineteenth century convention" (Wallace 1952). The authors who were busy writing about the Indians were far removed from the men who faced them on the new frontiers.

Two and a half centuries after Englishmen on the eastern frontier faced the Indian, American frontiersmen in the Mississippi Valley and the Far West found themselves in a parallel situation and regarded him in much the same hostile light—the Indian blocked the path of America's "manifest destiny." In 1867, the Topeka *Weekly Leader* spoke for the West when it characterized the Indians as "a set of miserable, dirty, lousy, blanketed, thieving, lying, sneaking, murdering, graceless, faithless, gut-eating skunks as the Lord ever permitted to infect the earth, and whose immediate and final extermination all men, except Indian agents and traders, should pray for" (Taft 1953). Cotton Mather's terser characterization of the "tawney serpents" seems almost mild and dignified beside this scathing blast.

Wrestling with his own day-to-day problems, with the Long Hairs not far off, the trans-Mississippi frontiersman was in no position to appreciate the extent to which the Indians *already* had affected American culture. And it would be interesting to know how many Americans on this frontier had read *Hiawatha*. Certainly, few of them could have imagined that, when the West was won and the Indians were safely settled on reservations, native arts and crafts would be appreciated for their aesthetic values and widely exhibited, musicians and poets would visit these remaining enclaves of Indian culture to study their music and songs at first hand, and a museum devoted exclusively to the preservation and exhibition of Indian objects would be established in the largest city of the nation. What would have surprised them more, perhaps, if they could have looked at a Boy Scout Handbook of the twentieth century, is the statement that it "is a pity that most boys think of head-dresses, war whoops, tomahawks, and scalps the instant Indians are mentioned. . . . There are so many thousands of beautiful and desirable things in their lives that it is safe to say that they can offer boys a mighty good code of sport and happiness." And among the other things that would strike the frontiersman forcibly would be the requirement that, in order to win a merit badge in Indian lore, the Boy Scout must learn the Omaha Tribal Prayer. Yes, the Omaha, one of those dastardly Siouan tribes—the gut-eating skunks!

But if the Midwestern frontiersman had been interested enough, he would have discovered that the word *skunk,* which he could so glibly hurl at the Long Hairs as a derogatory epithet, was derived from an Indian language and had entered American speech in the seventeenth century. The borrowing of words as well as traits of Indian culture, like the use of corn, had been going on for a long time. Referred to by anthropologists as cultural diffusion, this kind of cultural borrowing is a process that has been occurring throughout the entire history of man. It has been one of the main stimuli of cultural change. When people of different cultures meet and social interaction takes place, this situation inevitably eventuates in some cultural borrowing on the part of either or both peoples.

In the past two decades, cultural anthropologists in this country have devoted increasing attention to detailed studies of the effects of Euro-American culture upon the Indians, that is, acculturation, rather than confining themselves, as was once the case, primarily to the collection of data that would make it possible to reconstruct an ethnographic picture of aboriginal life in its undisturbed form. On the other hand, although recognizing that in principle acculturation is seldom if ever a one-way process, anthropologists have paid scarcely any attention to the total effects upon American culture of our continuing contacts with Indians.

One of the things that anthropologists have discovered is that while Indians may "clothe" themselves, so to speak, with many of the accouterments of white man's culture, this is often no more than skin-deep. Even when the Indian is brought into close contact with the white man for more than a generation, and despite missionary efforts and educational opportunities, there is a psychological lag to be taken into account which indicates a dimension of the acculturation process about which we know too little.

In contrast to this side of the acculturalization picture in the

United States, it is interesting to recall, when white adults, and especially children, were captured in the seventeenth, eighteenth, and early nineteenth centuries by many different groups of Indians and lived among them in daily intimacy, the apparent ease with which these individuals adjusted themselves to Indian culture. Turner speaks of the "occasional instances of Puritans returning from captivity to visit the frontier towns, Catholic in religion, painted and garbed as Indians and speaking the Indian tongue, and the half-breed children of captive Puritan mothers." While there were many hundreds of white captives taken, we have detailed and reliable information on only a few cases, including individuals who were abducted as children. These "white Indians" often refused to return to the mode of life into which they had been born, even when given an opportunity (Ackerknecht 1944). In the eighteenth century Crèvecoeur asked: "By what power does it come to pass, that children who have been adopted when young among these people, can never be prevailed on to readopt European manners?" Such individuals sometimes forgot their native speech, like Cynthia Ann Parker, captured by the Comanches in 1836 at the age of nine. When recaptured by the whites as a grown woman, all she could remember was her name. Other captives praised Indian character and morals and some of them adopted an Indian world view and religious beliefs. It was said of Mary Jemison, abducted in 1758 at the age of fifteen, that "she was as strong a pagan in her feelings as any Indian," that all her religious ideas conformed to those of the Senecas, and that "the doctrine taught in the Christian religion she is a stranger to." Of William Failey, abducted in 1837, his brother-in-law and biographer wrote: "In fact, his long residence among the Indians has made him an Indian." Don Ryan in *The Warriors' Path* (1937) and Conrad Richter in *The Light in the Forest* (1953) have given this theme modern novelistic treatment. The latter book was soon republished in paper-back form (1954), and Walt Disney is planning a movie version of it.

Benjamin Franklin must have been highly impressed by the attitude which the Six Nations assumed towards the values of their own culture as compared with that of the whites. An anecdote, in several forms, appears in his writings which presumably was derived from the considered response these Indians made when, during the Lancaster conference in 1744, it was suggested that if they so desired some of their boys might be sent to Williamsburg for a white education. The Iroquois countered with the proposition that "if the English Gentlemen would send a Dozen or two of their children to Onondago, the great council would take care of their Education, bring them up in really what was the best Manner and make men of them" (Aldridge 1950).

These Indians not only felt secure in their own values; they felt free to appraise those of the white man. And the captives who became "white Indians" discovered that the actual manner of life of the natives was something other than the literary images of the Noble Savage or the fiendish red man. The Indian cultures contained values which the white child could assimilate, live by, and in adulthood refuse to relinquish. Old White Boy and all his sons became Seneca chiefs. Even aside from captives, there were white men on the frontier who became semiacculturated to Indian ways. Sam Houston, in his early days, lived with the Cherokees. It has not been sufficiently stressed that *Leatherstocking,* the most famous internationally of all characters in American fiction, falls into this category. Although a white man by "nature," he had Indian "gifts." He is said to have "acquired some knowledge of most of the Indian dialects." During his early life, he lived among the Delawares and long before they called him Deerslayer, he had successively borne three other Indian nicknames. On occasion, he identified himself with the Delawares and their aboriginal values. When contemplating torture by the Hurons, he says he will strive "not to disgrace the people among whom I got my training." And the Huron chiefs, uncertain about his return from the brief furlough granted him, entertained "the hope of disgracing the Delawares by casting into their teeth the delinquency of one held in their villages." While they would have preferred to torture his Indian comrade Chingachgook, they thought the "pale face scion of the hated stock was no bad substitute for their purposes." Quite aside from his characterization as the honest, resourceful, intrepid frontiersman and scout, the uniqueness of Leatherstocking as the first white man in fiction represented as acculturated in his youth to Indian languages, customs, and values, should not be overlooked.

From a contemporary vantage point, I believe that our relations with the Indians involve one distinct peculiarity which might have been difficult to predict at an earlier period of our history. Despite our achievement of political dominance, considerable race mixture, and the effects of acculturation on the native peoples, neither the Indian nor his culture has completely vanished from our midst. The question arises, have the Indian cultures of the post-frontier period completely ceased to influence us? The answer is no. One effect of the reservation system has been the conservation of those aspects of the native cultures that had survived all the vicissitudes of previous contacts with the white race. A new potential source of influence on our twentieth-century culture was created. Before we can turn to the nature of this influence, however, it is necessary to obtain the wider historic perspective that a more systematic consideration of the older lines of influence will provide us.

In the first place, it could have been predicted that, as a result of the colonization of the New World, loan words would appear in various Indo-European languages that could be traced to aboriginal American languages. Besides the nouns borrowed to designate objects unknown in England, there are many expressions in American English that reflect Indian influence—*burying the hatchet, Indian summer, Indian giver, happy hunting ground,* and *warpaint,* used by the American woman. *Buck* as a slang expression for *dollar* harks back to the Indian fur trade when prices had reference to beavers or buckskins. Place names of Indian origin are, of course, legion—the names of twenty-six states, eighteen of our largest cities, thousands of small towns, most of the long rivers and large lakes, and a few of the highest mountains are of Indian derivation.

Having come to a country new to them, it was inevitable that the colonists, whose traditional culture had not prepared them to live as they had to live here, should be influenced by those aspects of Indian culture that had immediate practical advantages in daily life. In any case, the determinative importance of the fact that this was not in any sense a virgin land must not be forgotten. The countless generations of Indians had left their imprints upon the landscape. Without the plow, the soil had been cultivated, and the raising of native crops was as typical over wide areas as was hunting and fishing. It is still debatable how far the actual virgin terrain had been radically modified by burning, girdling, and tilling.

There were narrow forest trails, trodden by moccasined feet, that were already old, and the whites made use of them in their own system of overland communication, developing some of them into highways eventually connecting great centers of American civilization. Then there were the earthworks of an older Indian population in the Old Northwest Territory which influenced the patterning of some early white settlements. The "pilgrims" who founded Marietta, Ohio, found it convenient to moor their flatboats "at the foot of a raised terrace the Mound Builders had once used as an avenue between their temple and the river." Circleville takes its name from the fact that in the laying out of the original town, concentric circles of aboriginal earthworks were closely followed by the outlying streets. An octagonal courthouse, surrounded by a circular green, became the hub of the town. And it is said that "in the Wabash River bottoms, in the early spring, many farm houses stand high and dry on a wooded burial mound while all the fields are under water" (Havighurst 1946).

Among the early settlers, communication by water was everywhere the most important. While they were familiar with certain types of watercraft in their own culture, they and their descendants have been influenced by at least two types used by the Indians, the Chesapeake Bay log canoe and the bark canoe of the north.

From a European point of view, the Indians wearing moccasins, leggings, and breechclouts were considered to be relatively naked compared to themselves. However, considered in a very broad culture-historical perspective, their own style and that of the aborigines shared a generic train in common: throughout the boreal regions of the Northern Hemisphere, clothing of the fitted or tailored type prevails, standing in marked contrast to the untailored style once found in the ancient Mediterranean region, Africa, and Central and South America. In all these latter regions, for example, nothing like the fitted footgear represented by the boot, shoe, or moccasin is found. While the practice never spread beyond the frontier itself, nevertheless there were white men who adopted the wearing of not only Indian moccasins, but leggings and a breechclout as well. The moccasin, of course, is the most noted item of Indian clothing that was used by white men very early. It was a fitted type of footgear, and if the colonists had been Romans, this item of clothing might not have been borrowed so quickly, or its use continued. Turner has noted that the General Court of Massachusetts once ordered five hundred pairs each of snowshoes and moccasins for use in the frontier counties. Much later, footgear of this type was used by lumbermen. In the backwoods of Manitoba in the 1930's, a clergyman of my acquaintance always wore a pair of his best beaded moccasins in the pulpit on Sundays. It would be interesting to know more about the commercialization of the moccasin type of shoe which we see increasingly on the feet of Americans today.

It was, however, the discovery of the plants cultivated by the New World aborigines that from the very first produced the most profound impact on both European and American culture, revolutionizing the food economy and diet of Old World peoples and at the same time laying one of the foundations on which was to rise the distinctive structure of American agriculture. Of the several plants—maize, beans, pumpkins, squash, and others—maize in particular was important from the start, taking precedence over the grain which the settlers had brought from Europe. It became a primary factor in the acculturation of the Englishmen to an American way of life. We need think only of corn on the cob, corn bread, Indian pudding, hominy, mush, grits, succotash, and corn syrup; of breakfast cereals, cornstarch, and popcorn; or of corncob pipes and bourbon, to understand the extent of this Indian contribution to our civilization today.

Tobacco is an equally significant "gift" of the American Indians, symbolized by the once-familiar figure of the "wooden Indian" inextricably linked with the tobacco shop in the nineteenth century. The history and use of it in our culture present a number of features in cultural borrowing at large. Readaptation to the values of the borrowing people is well illustrated. The consumption of tobacco was completely divorced from the ceremonial context in which it appeared among the Indians and became purely secular.

Peruvian bark, now known as quinine, proved highly sensational since it was a specific for malaria. It reached Spain before the middle of the seventeenth century and was soon introduced into the English colonies. In Virginia, Governor Berkeley said in 1671 that whereas formerly one person in five had died of fever in his first year, now almost no one succumbed. When one considers that in this same century Governor Winthrop's famous remedy for ulcers consisted of "one ounce of crabbe's eyes and four ounces of strong wine vinegar," the general state of colonial medicine can be well appreciated, and the reason why Peruvian bark, an Indian herbal, achieved such high fame can be easily understood. Indian medicine was likewise given a boost when, in 1738, Dr. John Tennent was awarded one hundred pounds by the Virginia House of Burgesses for curing pleurisy with Seneca rattlesnake root. As William Fenton well says, when Western medicine met Indian herbalism, the former "was still carrying a heavy burden of medieval practices so that the first few physicians in the colonies were but several centuries advanced from the Indian shaman who selected his herbs thinking of the effect that their appearance might contribute to the disease and guaranteed their efficiency with incantations and feats of magic. Moreover, the average settler had brought from the Old World a knowledge of herbs that in kind was not unlike that of the Indian, but as newcomers they were unfamiliar with New World plants, and although the level of their own popular medicine did not set them above adopting Indian remedies, the Indian herbalist whose knowledge was power was not always a ready teacher" (Fenton 1941). In *The Pioneers,* Cooper pictures for us how "Doctor" Elnathan Todd managed to steal one of John Mohegan's remedies.

Popular confidence in Indian medicine remained strong during the early nineteenth century, when the population was flowing over the Appalachians. The "yarb and root" doctor, red or white, played a prominent role in many communities. In 1813 in Cincinnati there was published *The Indian Doctor's Dispensatory.* Other books followed, including Selman's *The Indian Guide to Health* (1836) and Foster's *The North American Indian Doctor, or Nature's Method of Curing and Preventing Disease According to the Indians* (1838). In a lecture given at the New York Academy of Medicine in 1936, Dr. Harlow Brooks (emeritus professor of clinical medicine, New York University) said:

> The Universal testimony of those qualified to judge has been that even within the memory of my generation we have incorporated into our pharmacopoeia and practice a good many practices and drugs of our Indian predecessors. . . . The leading doctor in my boyhood

memory, in the district in which my parents settled, was an old Sioux medicine man, whose services were considered by the territorial government so valuable that when his tribe was removed to a reservation he was asked to remain with his white patients, among whom were my own parents. I am sure that much of the medicine I received as an infant and child was derived directly from the lore of this fine, learned, and much respected old man. In those days it was on the service of these men that our pioneers relied for medical help; otherwise, little or none at all was available to the early settler (Brooks 1936).

What is particularly interesting is not merely the incorporation in our pharmacopoeia of some aboriginal drugs, but the positive attitude towards Indian medicine and charms that has persisted into the twentieth century. For instance, old Seneca families still sell wild flowers and sassafras on certain street corners in Buffalo, and the Pamunkey Indians of Virginia until a decade ago went to Washington every spring to sell sassafras and other herbs. In *Triple Western* (Fall, 1954) there is a short item on "Medicine Man's Wisdom."

The potencies attributed to Indian herbal remedies have had still other manifestations in our culture, an important one being the medicine show. While not all these shows made use of the Indian, most of them did. It has been said that "as a symbol" the native "was as important to the med-show platform as the wooden Indian was to the tobacco shop." It exploited the image that had already been created of him as a "healer." When Chief Chauncey Kills-in-the-Bush Yellow Robe died, eulogies appeared in the theatrical press. Rolling Thunder, the owner of the Kiowa Indian Medicine and Vaudeville Company, commented on these as follows:

> It is fine to see this intelligent recognition of the life work of an Indian. Too many people have always thought of the American Indian as next to a beast. There are some who are now learning the truth: that the Indian's drugstore was always the field and the forest, where the herbs he uses in his medicines are gathered as God placed them for him to use, and God gave the Indian the knowledge to gather and compound them. That is why the Indian as a healer has been a success (Johnston 1936).

The authors of *Show Biz* say that "when the Kickapoo Indian Medicine Company went on the block in 1911, after thirty years roaming the American plains and hamlets, it still brought $250,-000. At one time, there were 150 medicine shows on the road, all of them featuring one or more Kickapoo Indians" (A. Green and Joe Laurie, Jr. 1953). It may be pointed out in passing that at the same time that the image of the Indian as a healer was being exploited in the medicine show, the old image of him as a bloodthirsty enemy was being dramatized by the wild West show that William F. Cody took on the road in 1883 and which in various incarnations and imitations continued until 1931, when the 101 Ranch closed down.

The red man also became involved in another characteristic area of American cultural development in the years before the Civil War—religion. In Spiritualism, the United Society of Believers (Shakers), and the Church of Latter-day Saints (Mormons), the American Indians had special significance for the founders or adherents. According to Shaker tradition, "it was a native of the forest who first recognized the saintliness of Mother Ann. One poor Indian saw a bright light around her, and prophesied that the Great Spirit had sent her to do much good. In another story it is related that when Ann was returning from her eastern mission, she was met at the Albany ferry by a number of Indians, who joyfully cried: 'The good woman is come! The good woman is come!'" (Andrews 1953). What other religious sect in the world has turned to an aboriginal people for validation of the saintliness of the founder? Besides this, some of the Shaker "gift songs" received in trance came from Indian spirits. Once the spirits of a whole tribe of Indians, who had died before Columbus discovered America and had been wandering homeless ever since, turned up at a Shaker meetinghouse, where they were made welcome. As described by an eyewitness, more than a dozen of the Shakers present became possessed by these Indian guests. A powwow ensued. There were yells, whoops, and strange antics. The Indian spirits asked for succotash, which they ate, and after some instruction were sent off under guidance "to the Shakers' heavenly world."

Although "speaking in tongues" had a long history in Europe as well as in America, one of the striking facts in the early develop-

mental phases of American Spiritualism is the frequency of references to mediums speaking Indian languages and to those who had
an Indian "control" or "guide." The names of more than a dozen
mediums, men and women and their Indian controls, appear in
the *Encyclopaedia of Psychic Science*. Such historic figures as Red
Jacket, Black Hawk, and Tecumseh are on the list, as well as spirits
with such names as White Feather, Bright Eyes, and Moonstone.
What is particularly significant is that these Indian spirits were
thought to be beneficent in their influence, especially because of
their healing powers, although they often manifested themselves
at seances in a somewhat rambunctious manner. As time went on
and spirit photography was introduced, some of these spirits appeared in native costume in the photographs.

It would seem that no other American religious sect, with the
possible exception of the Shakers, felt such a genuine affinity with
the aborigines. While there was no question of borrowing Indian
beliefs as such, nevertheless the Spiritualists saw analogies to their
own views and practices. One of these was the "shaking tent" rite
of the Algonkians of the eastern woodlands (which has been described elsewhere) (Hallowell 1942). Into a framework of poles
covered with birchbark or canvas a conjurer goes; the tent sways
and voices are heard which, however, are usually believed to be
nonhuman. An early historian of American Spiritualism, writing
in 1870, after referring to some of these rites, says:

> Such are some of the phases in which communication exhibits itself
> amongst a people whom we call 'savage' and whom, in comparison
> to our more advanced civilization, we may justly call so; and yet,
> does our knowledge of the occult and invisible forces in nature fur-
> nish us with any clue to the mystery of these astounding manifesta-
> tions or the power by which the unlettered 'savage' can avail himself
> of a knowledge which all our control over the elements fails to com-
> pete with? In a word, the red Indian can do what we can neither
> explain nor imitate (Hardinge 1944).

This interest of the Spiritualists in the Indian and his ways has continued down to the present. At Lily Dale, New York, the summer
mecca of Spiritualists, which commemorated its fiftieth anniver-
sary in 1929, it has been customary to celebrate Indian Day with
parades and dances given by natives from near-by reservations.

To turn now to the Church of Jesus Christ of Latter-day Saints, the attitude of the adherents of this indigenous American sect towards the Indians is in sharp contrast with that of the Spiritualists. According to *The Book of Mormon,* the red men are essentially the degenerate posterity of a rebellious segment of a small group of Jews who, migrating to the New World before the beginning of the Christian era, brought with them an advanced culture. Consequently, it is said that *The Book of Mormon* supplements the Bible, since it is a history of God's dealings with remnants of Israel and the Saviour's ministrations among them in the Western Hemisphere (Hanson 1945). For in America, the great Nephrite prophecy has been fulfilled—the second coming of Christ. After the Resurrection He appeared to a multitude of nearly 3,000 people in Mexico, before a greater assembly the next day, and after this "he did show himself unto them oft." The occurrence of the legendary figure of a so-called "white god" with certain associated attributes among the Incas, Mayas, Aztecs, and Toltecs, the Mormons interpret as supporting evidence for the historic appearance of Christ in America.

In the Mormon view, the aborigines of the United States were the descendants of the Lamanites, the "bad" people of the Mormon epic. Unlike the Spiritualists, the Mormons had nothing they could look to them for; still, a strange affinity connected them with the Indians. In Mormon hymnals there are songs about the red man. In the days before the rise of archaeology or anthropology in the contemporary sense, *The Book of Mormon* was representative of the speculations that had been going on in Europe for several centuries about the peopling of the New World. These earlier theories had to be reconciled first of all with the account given in the Bible of man's creation and dispersal. What is peculiar in the Mormon case, however, is the fact that a particular theory of the peopling of the New World was incorporated as a dogma of a religious sect. This could hardly have occurred anywhere but in early nineteenth-century America. The early Mormons easily reconciled their theory with the Bible, but since the sect has survived into a period of American culture when an enormous increase in our knowledge of New World prehistory from archaeological investigations has taken place, a further reconciliation of the inspired history found in *The Book of Mormon* with this new knowledge is now being sought.

Outside the Mormon church, the consensus is that in its nondoctrinal aspects *The Book of Mormon* is derived from a romance written but not published by Solomon Spaulding, a clergyman who left the church and was in business in Ohio by 1812. There he dug into some mounds and became interested in the origin of the extinct people who had erected them. The theory that they were of Jewish origin was not original with him, since it was maintained by many prominent men in this country. If Spaulding's manuscript had been printed in its original form as fiction, he would have anticipated those writers in America who were soon to exploit the Indian in the historical novel. Even when *The Book of Mormon* was published in 1830, it fell precisely in the period when the Indian was assuming great prominence in American literature. Three of Cooper's *Leatherstocking Tales* had met with acclaim by this date, and at least thirty-nine novels published between 1824 and 1834 included Indian episodes.

There was a parallel development in the drama. Barker's *Indian Princess* (Pocahontas), staged in 1808, had a long line of successors. There were at least thirty so-called Indian plays staged between 1820 and 1840 and twenty or more between the latter date and the Civil War. Some of these were dramatizations of the novels of Cooper, Bird, and Simms. The peak in the popularity of these Indian dramas also falls within the period (1830–70) that has been called "the golden days of the American actor." Perhaps the most outstanding example is *Metamora, or The Last of the Wampanoags,* which was in the repertoire of Edwin Forrest for almost forty years. It was played in Philadelphia every year— except two—for a quarter of a century. Forrest had specifically advertised in 1828 for a play in which "the hero, or principal character, shall be an aboriginal of this country." William Cullen Bryant was the chairman of the committee which selected *Metamora* from the fourteen plays submitted. It proved to be one of the most popular plays of the nineteenth-century American theater. *Metamora* was played even after Forrest's death, and a radio version was broadcast in 1939. During its theatrical lifetime, more Americans are said to have seen *Metamora* than *Abie's Irish Rose* or *Tobacco Road* in the twentieth century.

In poetry, the Indian had appeared as a subject ever since the time of Freneau, but there was nothing that could compare with the initial impact and continuing popularity of *Hiawatha*. It became *the* poem of the American Indian. Before publication in 1855, there was an advance sale of four thousand copies; in five months the sale had risen to fifty thousand copies. It has been said that what was unique about Longfellow's poem was the fact that "*Hiawatha* was the first poem of its kind in America based on Indian legend rather than on Indian history" (Schramm 1932). While true enough, it is clarifying to note that until 1839, when Schoolcraft published his *Algic Researches,* there were no reliable collections of Indian myths or tales on which a poet could draw. It was, therefore, a historical accident that Longfellow came to exploit Ojibwa material; he had no other choice. Paradoxically, Schoolcraft himself published a poem dealing with the Creek Indian wars twelve years before *Hiawatha* appeared. He did not know the Creeks at first hand, while he knew the Ojibwas intimately, his wife being of that tribe. Evidently it never occurred to him to use his Ojibwa myths as the basis of a narrative poem. Thus Schoolcraft epitomizes the force of the traditional literary approach to the use of Indian themes.

Longfellow bore the same sort of relation to Schoolcraft as Cooper did to Heckewelder. Generally speaking, there was no inclination on the part of eastern novelists, dramatists, or poets who selected Indian themes to become acquainted with living Indians of the contemporary frontiers as a background for their productions. Indeed, a volume of short stories, *Tales of the Northwest,* about Indians in the Upper Mississippi region, written by one who knew them intimately, was ignored after its publication in 1839. William Joseph Snelling, the author, had insisted that "a man must live, emphatically, live with Indians; share with them their lodges, their food, and their blankets, for years, before he can comprehend their ideas, or enter their feelings." American writers were not yet ready for this early call to realism. But for American readers, a novel entitled *Altowan; or Incidents of Life and Adventure in the Rocky Mountains,* by Sir William Drummond Stewart, an eccentric Scot, who during the 1830's had spent six years in the West, was published in New York in 1846. Although the novel was undistinguished in writing and had some romantic trappings, in this case the author *had* seen a great deal of Indian life. What makes the book unique is that one of the leading characters, as pointed out by De Voto, is an Indian transvestite—a berdache— and this individual is depicted in highly realistic terms. The author pictures his behavior and dress in detail, and no doubt is left about what he was. "I know of no English or American novel of that time or for many years later that is half so frank about homosexuality," writes De Voto (1947).

In painting and popular music there was a parallel romantic tradition. Gleanings from historical documents or tradition were tinctured by an extremely free use of imagination. It is obvious, for instance, that the artist who provided the frontispiece for Mrs. Morton's *Ouabi, or The Virtue of Nature* (1790) knew as little about Indians at first hand as did the author of this poem in the Noble Savage tradition. And Benjamin West's painting of one of Penn's treaties with the Indians, dating from about 1771, offers a direct parallel to the literary artist who drew on historical documents for his source material.

Part of Mrs. Morton's poem was set to music by Hans Gram the year after its publication. This composition, the first orchestral score published in the United States, was entitled *The Death Song of an Indian Chief,* although there is no evidence that the composer knew anything about aboriginal music. In 1799, a musical arrangement of *Alkamoonok, the Death Song of the Cherokee Indians,* reputedly based on a genuine Indian melody, was published and soon became very popular. It had been sung in *Tammany* (1794), the first American opera. An eccentric musician, Anton Philip Heinrich, who died in 1861, was the composer of the *Pocahontas Waltz* for piano and is said to have been the first to use Indian themes in larger orchestral works. The heroine of the big song hit of 1844, *The Blue Juniata,* was an Indian girl, "Bright Alforata."

Actually, it is at this vernacular level that the backwash of the frontier is most clearly discernible in American music of the nineteenth century. This was due to the role the Indian played in the subject matter of folk songs. In one group of songs, the Indian appears "merely as an incidental personality" and the attitudes towards him are vague. In a second group, however, negative attitudes are sharply defined since many songs in this class are long narrative ballads which depict actual frontier conflicts. Folk songs about historic events, "including songs about dramatic episodes in the relationships of Indians and White, have been sung regularly since the earliest days of colonization and have faithfully reflected changing relationships between the two culture groups at least down to the present century when modern techniques for the commercialization of popular songs may have beclouded the issue." A third category of songs reflects a positive attitude towards the Indian varying "from vague references to good Indians or Indians with heroic qualities, to songs and ballads exclusively about romanticized Indians, who are admired for their stamina and other heroic qualities" (A. E. Fife, and F. Redden 1954). An anonymous, undated example of America's folk painting, depicting the rescue of John Smith, belongs to this earlier period (American Folk Art 1932). The same motif was subsequently as popular in prints as it was in fiction, drama, poetry, and music.

However, in the midst of all this romanticizing of the Indian, a trend toward greater realism developed, particularly in painting. Here and there in colonial times there had been some realistic paintings of the Indians, for example, the masterly portraits of Lenape chiefs painted in 1735 by Gustavus Hesselius (1682–1755). But about 1821, many of the western chiefs who came to Washington on business with the government sat for their portraits. A collection of these became the nucleus of the famous "Indian Gallery." The magnificent reproduction of 120 of these portraits in a folio edition of three volumes (McKenny and Hall, *History of the Indian Tribes of North America, 1836–44*) gave the eastern public an opportunity to see what contemporary Indians looked like. On the other hand, artists themselves began to go west (Seymour, Rindisbacher, Lewis, Catlin, Miller, Eastman, Stanley, Kane, Bodmer, Kurz), so that greatly enriched images of the natives, the kind of life they led, and the grandeur of the country they inhabited soon became more widely known to those living far removed from the contemporary frontier. It was the author of *Altowan* who induced Alfred Jacob Miller—now one of the most famous of these artists, whose true accomplishments have only become known to the public in recent years—to accompany him west in 1837. Catlin is particularly important, however, not only because he was a pioneer, but because he was a showman. He toured eastern cities in the late 1830's exhibiting his "Indian Gallery," which has been called the first wild West show. It included Indian "curios," featuring pipes, and in exhibition halls he erected a real Crow tepee. Catlin appeared in person and, taking selected pictures as a point of departure, lectured to his audiences about Indian life. He would dress lay figures in Indian clothing and frequently had some Indians on hand to pantomime native activities. Although Catlin was not an anthropologist, his Indian Gallery did mediate to Americans a more realistic type of knowledge about the Plains tribes than had been available. After touring American cities, he took his show to England and the Continent. In 1954, an exhibition of Catlin's work, sponsored by the United States Information Agency, was again on tour in Europe, while in this country Bodmer's water colors were being exhibited.

Even though Catlin "had been there," he had detractors, like Audubon, who challenged the accuracy of his paintings. The same thing had happened to Cooper and Longfellow. The romantic tradition in America was strong, and the application of a purely realistic standard of judgment was, in effect, an attack upon the tradition. Cooper may have idealized the Indian in some respects and erred in many details, but he idealized the pioneer and backwoodsman too. The Indian was enveloped in the romantic tradition and what is interesting is how long he has remained a part of it.

When the dime novel sprang into popularity in the sixties, the Indians of the Cooper tradition became an integral part of this literature. In one way or another, Indians play a role in at least 45 per cent of the 321 stories in the original dime-novel series. *Maleska, the Indian Wife of the White Hunter* (1860), the first one published by Beadle and Adams, actually was a reprinting of a story that had been serialized in 1839. "The death of the dime novel, if it ever really occurred, was accompanied by the birth of the nickelodeon, the motion picture, and the radio, which simply transferred the old stories of cowboys, desperadoes, and Indians to more dynamic forms" (Hart 1950). In fact, as soon as the silent cinema began to flicker, the Indian of the old romantic tradition was in. There was a screen version of *Hiawatha* as early as 1909, the *Deerslayer* was shown in 1911, *The Last of the Mohicans* in 1920. And, until very recently, what Stanley Vestal called the "Hollywooden Indian" has persisted in that typically American movie genre—the western.

On the other hand, there was an increasing awareness that authentic knowledge of the aboriginal cultures was relevant and desirable in the arts. Perhaps this attitude developed along with the emergence of a more realistic tradition in American writing. However this may be, I think that the publication of Edna Dean Proctor's *Song of the Ancient People* in 1893 represents a transitional case. While it is in the high romantic tradition, there is an appended commentary to this poem by F. H. Cushing (1857–1900), a pioneer anthropologist who went to the Southwest in 1879 and lived among the Zuñi for five years. He says he can bear witness to the poet's "strict fidelity of statement, and attempt to show, as one of the Ancient People themselves would be glad to show, how well she has divined their spirit." The volume was illustrated with realistic aquatints made by Julian Scott in the Hopi country. No other Indian poem had ever been offered to the public with such an aura of authenticity about it—it was bound in buckskin with a design taken from Southwestern pottery on the cover.

The inauguration of genuine Indian themes in American concert music is ordinarily attributed to Edward MacDowell, whose *Indian Suite* was first performed in 1896. But where did he find such themes? He was not a frontier boy. He entered the Paris Conservatory at the age of fourteen and did not take up residence here until he was twenty-seven. The fact is that MacDowell exemplifies a repetition of the same kind of relationship to the source of his thematic material as was noted in the case of Cooper and Longfellow. He got them from Theodore Baker, the first trained musician to go into the field and study Indian music at first hand. Baker, a German, visited the Seneca Reservation and the Carlisle Indian School in the summer of 1880, offering the results of his analysis to Leipzig University as a doctoral dissertation. But he was not a composer, nor was Alice C. Fletcher, whose monograph on Omaha songs (1893) initiated the study of Indian music in American anthropology. However, two of the songs she collected, *Shupida* and the *Omaha Tribal Prayer,* undoubtedly have been among the most widely circulated examples of authentic Indian music in American culture. Together with three other Indian songs, they appear in *Indian Lore,* a pamphlet in the Merit Badge Series of the Boy Scouts of America. In the past six years, approximately forty-seven thousand copies of this booklet have been printed. Scouts who aspire to the merit badge in Indian lore must be able to "sing three Indian songs including the Omaha Tribal Prayer and tell something of their meaning." Since 1911, there have been 18,719 American boys who have won this distinction.

Following the lead of MacDowell, other composers began to make increasing use of Indian themes, though only a few made direct contact with the reservation Indians. Among them were Burton, Cadman, Farwell, Jacobi, Lieurance, Arthur Nevin, Skilton, and Troyer, who found native music interesting to them, because as Skilton has said, "many devices of the ultra modern composers of the present day have long been employed by Indians —unusual intervals, arbitrary scales, changing tune, conflicting rhythm, polychoral effects, hypnotic monotony" (Skilton 1939). Indian songs were harmonized and arranged for performance by white musicians; Indian themes were handled freely in the composition of original works, much in the same way that Longfellow handled Ojibwa myths.

In the field of operatic composition, despite the popularity of other compositions of Herbert and Cadman, neither the former's *Natoma* (1911) nor the latter's *Shanewis* (1918) became established in operatic repertoire. Some compositions based on Indian themes have received high acclaim in the repertoire of orchestral music, others as popular songs. Skilton's *Indian Dances,* along with MacDowell's *Indian Suite,* were among the twenty-seven compositions of twelve American composers which had the greatest number of performances in the United States during the seven years following World War I. Jacobi's *String Quartet on Indian Themes* was selected to represent American music at the International Festival of Contemporary Music at Zurich in 1926. Elliott Carter's ballet *Pocahontas,* presented in New York in 1939 (and later developed into a suite for orchestra), received the Juilliard Publication Award the following year. Cadman, who went to the Omaha Reservation in 1909 with Francis LaFlesche, an Indian anthropologist, wrote one of his most famous songs that year, *From the Land of the Sky Blue Water.* It vied with *The Rosary* in popularity. He likewise wrote two operas on Indian themes. *By the Waters of Minnetonka* (1921), composed by Thurlow Lieurance, who had visited the western reservations as early as 1905, has had a phenomenal success. At mid-century, it appears in the Victor Album *Twelve Beloved American Songs* along with *The Rosary* and *A Perfect Day.* Nor should commercialized popular songs of a lower order—some Indian in name only —be forgotten. Among those composed early in this century were *Navajo* (1903), *Tammany* (1905), *Red Wing* (1907), and *Hiawatha's Melody of Love* (1920), to say nothing of *The Indian Love Call* (1924), and *Ramona,* a hit of 1927.

In the early years of this century, some American poets, like the musicians, sought out the Indians, and those of the Southwest became a focal point of interest. These were the same people that Edna Proctor had written about. They had been the subject, too, of a novel, *The Delight Makers* (1890) by A. F. Bandelier, said by Alfred L. Kroeber to be "a more comprehensive and coherent view of native Pueblo life than any scientific volume on the southwest."

A few American painters (Sharp, Phillips, Blumenschein) had also discovered the Southwest before the opening of the twentieth century. Blumenschein's graphic commentary on the acculturation process, which shows two Indians mounted on merry-go-round horses, had appeared in *Harper's Weekly* in 1899.

Among the poets who became interested, Mary Austin soon took the lead. She became the key figure in the use of Indian material for literary purposes, and her extremely positive attitude toward the cultures of the Indians influenced many others to seek inspiration in their art. She characterized her *Amerindian Songs* as being "Re-expressed from the Originals." Some of these first appeared in *Poetry* (1917), along with comparable interpretations by Frank S. Gordon, Alice Corbin Henderson, and Constance Lindsay Skinner. Mary Austin wrote plays and stories, too. She seems to have moved from a romantic primitivism to a more and more realistic handling of Indian themes, as exemplified by her play *The Arrow Maker,* produced on Broadway in 1911, and her *One-Smoke Stories* (1934), one of her last books. Nor should the fact be overlooked that four anthologies containing translations of American Indian songs and poetry have appeared in this century (George W. Cronyn, *The Path of the Rainbow,* 1918 and 1934; Nellie Barnes, *American Indian Love Lyrics and Other Verse,* 1925; Margot Astrov, *The Winged Serpent,* 1946; and A. Grove Day, *The Sky Clears,* 1951).

In the twentieth century, the Indian has also reappeared in American plays, particularly in the work of the regional dramatists. While the setting is frequently the historic past, the problems the native faces in the acculturation process are sometimes dramatized. Both *Strongheart* (1905) and *Cherokee Night* (1936) are examples of this theme. In prose fiction, we also find that anthropologists, inspired by Bandelier and the stories collected in Elsie Clews Parsons' *American Indian Life* (1922), entered the field. *Laughing Boy,* a Literary Guild book of 1929, by Oliver La Farge and *Hawk Over Whirlpools* by Ruth Underhill (1940) are outstanding illustrations. In *America in Fiction,* the authors call attention to the fact that "now that he is on reservations, not a military foe, and generally not an economic competitor, the Indian is a subject of great interest, so much so that more fiction has been written about him in recent years than about any other ethnic group except the Negro. In many works of fiction, he has been given central prominence, his cultural complex has been detailed, and much attention has been paid to his problems of adjusting himself to the dominating civilization that surrounds him" (O. W. Coan and R. G. Lillard 1949). Their bibliography lists thirty-seven novels or collections of stories published between 1902 and 1947. "Where once we had melodrama about the Indian with his bloody tomahawk," they say, "now we have clear-cut realism." Whatever the art form may be, what is striking is the more intimate acquaintance with contemporary Indians that informs the work of the painter, musician, poet, dramatist, or novelist who has drawn upon aboriginal cultural forms or used the problems of the Indian for his thematic material.

Finally, it seems to me that among these more recent influences, the impact of the Indian on modern anthropology should not be omitted. The social sciences as they have developed in the United States during the past half-century have attained an unusual prominence in American culture. Among these, anthropology in its modern form was just getting under way about the time the frontier closed. It was in the 1890's that Franz Boas began to teach at Columbia University and to train students in field work. Boas was a specialist in studies of the American Indian and a majority of his early students followed in his footsteps. Indeed, practically all the chief authorities on North American Indian ethnology, archaeology, and linguistics have been American. A historical accident? Of course. But that is the point. It is only recently among the younger generation that more attention is being devoted to peoples in the South Seas, Africa, and Asia. But it was the study of the Indians, and the problems that emerged from the investigation of the Indian as a subject, that gave American anthropology a distinctive coloring as compared with British, French, and German anthropology. Recently an American psychologist has remarked that "if the word 'anthropology' were presented to a sample of psychologists in a word-association test, I would venture 'culture' would probably be the most popular response, with 'Indians' a runner-up" (Smith 1954). The presumption, no doubt, is that these hypothetical responses would be those of *American* psychologists.

The more detailed and reliable accounts of native Indian cultures that have emerged from the field work of American anthropologists have made possible a more objective appraisal of the values inherent in the aboriginal modes of life. To those who look at the record, the Indian no longer appears as either a noble or ignoble savage. He has moved into a clearer focus as a human being. Like our own, his traditional cultural background and historical situation have determined the nature of his experience and made him what he is.

Viewing the panorama of our colonial and national history as a whole, I have referred to many diverse aspects of our culture—speech, economic life, food habits, clothing, transportation, medicine, religion, the arts, and even a social science—which have been influenced by our relations with the Indians at different times and in differing ways. Some of these influences have been mediated directly, others indirectly. Contacts with the Indian on the frontier have by no means been the source of all of them.

In summing up, we may ask: how deeply have such influences

penetrated our culture? To what extent are our relations with the Indians one key to our differentiation as Americans, not only culturally but psychologically? Constance Rourke once wrote, "The Backwoodsman conquered the Indian, but the Indian also conquered him. He ravaged the land and was ravaged in turn." Phillips D. Carleton, concluding his comments on the captivity literature, writes: "it emphasizes the fact that it was the line of fluid frontiers receding into the West that changed the colonists into a new people; they conquered the Indian but he was the hammer that beat out a new race on the anvil of the continent" (Carleton 1943). Carl Jung, who has probably analyzed more persons of various nationalities than anyone else, thought he could discern an Indian component in the character structure of his American patients, and D. H. Lawrence asked whether a dead Indian is nought. "Not that the Red Indian will ever possess the broadlands of America," he said and then added, "But his ghost will."

In America we faced the Indian on receding frontiers for a long period; but outside the frontier there was the shadow of the Indian. This shadow is still upon us. We still mouth words and idioms that reflect intimate contacts with the aborigines of our land. We still make use of plants originally cultivated by them. We wear derivative forms of the footgear they wore. We have collected objects made by them in our homes and in our museums. Our artists have found inspiration in their artistic modes of expression. We constantly see the Indian sweep past our eyes on the movie screen. He persists in our historical novels and westerns. In 1954, *The Leatherstocking Saga* reappeared, compressed into one handsome volume. We Americans have seen the Indian come and go on the commonest national coins we have fingered. The first Bible to be printed in colonial America was in the Indian language, John Eliot's translation of the Old and New Testament into an Algonkian tongue. Over the generations thousands of American men have belonged to the more-than-a-century-old *Improved Order of Red Men*. American anthropologists have labored most industriously to provide more and more authentic information about aboriginal modes of life and the influence of American culture on the Indian. The Indian has never been rejected from the American consciousness. Perhaps his shadow upon us is even disappearing—he has become a part of us: in the *Dictionary of American Biography* will be found side by side with other famous Americans, Pontiac and Tecumseh, Blackhawk and Osceola. In 1931 a brief popular biography of Osceola—only a few pages in length—was printed at Palm Beach; it was entitled *Osceola the Seminole. Florida's Most Distinguished Historical Character!* And it is said that more statues have been erected of Sacajawea than of any other American woman.

Now that the frontier has passed, our children discover the Indian in the comic books, as well as in the library. They are familiar with Cooper's tales in *Classics Illustrated.* Indeed, there appears to have been a marked increase in number, variety, and quality of children's books about Indians published in the last two or more decades. There are biographies of Indians famous in our history as well as historical romances. The stories of famous white captives have been retold; there are excellent books on Indian crafts and simplified but accurate accounts of tribal life, besides well-written stories which center around Indian children as major characters. Nevertheless, the average American is by no means aware of all the ramifications of Indian influence upon our culture. Perhaps the Red Indian ghost D. H. Lawrence saw here and what Jung discerned in the character of his patients provide clues to an aspect of the American ethos that invites deeper scrutiny in the future.

21 THE ROLE OF TRADITIONALISM IN THE POLITICAL MODERNIZATION OF GHANA AND UGANDA

David E. Apter

SOCIAL ANALYSTS have long been preoccupied with those features of traditional culture and belief which affect the direction of change and the receptivity of a society to innovation. In spite of the very considerable literature concerned with acculturation, there have been few efforts to examine different types of traditional systems with respect to the problems they pose for political modernization. We attempt this form of analysis here.[1] The plan is to examine two countries, Ghana and Uganda, which are engaged in the effort to build a national society. Each is experimenting with constitutional forms and each has had to deal with the problem of traditionalism. Indeed, the central problem of those concerned with building national, as distinct from local, political institutions has been to create overarching political parties, voluntary associations, and governmental forms that bridge older parochialisms. Moreover, just as tradition is a source of parochial strengths and social pride, so its characteristics vary

Originally published in *World Politics,* Volume XIII (1960), 45–68. Reprinted with permission of the author and the publisher.

[1] In an earlier form, this article was presented at the Dobbs Ferry Conference of the SSRC Sub-Committee on Comparative Government in 1959.

Research by the author in West Africa was first made possible through the generosity of the Social Science Research Council in 1952. Subsequent work was done in West Africa under the auspices of the West African Comparative Analysis Project, a Carnegie-supported research project that is still under way. Work on Uganda was undertaken in 1955–56 through a Ford Foundation Area Research Training Fellowship. None of these agencies is responsible for the opinions expressed in this article.

widely. There are some who argue that any understanding of modernity in Africa must be based on an examination of the variants of the traditional systems.

In this article, we shall compare recent political events in Ghana and Uganda, and try to show how they have been shaped by the nature of traditionalism. By this means we can illustrate the implications of two different kinds of traditionalism and the problems they pose for modern nation-builders.

I   TRADITIONALISM

The importance of traditional factors in change was not the discovery of Max Weber, as some have thought. Such antecedent greats as Marx and Coulanges sought to link to the problem of modernization those stable symbols, artifacts, and values transmitted by the people of a society through generations. Marx was particularly concerned with its economic aspects; Coulanges with its religious aspects. Since that time, the study of tradition has been either directly or indirectly brought into the most contemporary concerns. Most recently, Lerner has observed the behavioral consequences and durability of tradition by exploring degrees of participation in mass media of communication. Fallers has dealt with it in terms of bureaucracy. My own concern has focused on the functional implications of traditional political forms for modern ones (Lerner 1958; Fallers 1956; Apter 1955).

Nor is interest in tradition a peculiarity of social scientists. Politicians, no less than academics, recognize that traditional factors which under some circumstances seem to create immobilities in social structure, and abort or minimize innovation, at other times can open the door to an entirely different range of behaviors. Administrators who in Mali Federation (formerly Senegal and French Sudan) for years sought with only small success to establish effective local units of government, possessing cultural and solidary features satisfying to the population, now find the very same measures enthusiastically taken up by African leaders and interpreted as peculiar to the genius of Africans. Under the ideology of *negritude,* the meaning attached to community development, co-operation, and communalism has been transformed into a living and continuous feature of the African past. By this means, innovation has been "traditionalized" and made comfortable. Change is not strange or foreign, requiring new roles or learning. Traditionalism puts novelty on trial rather than the people that novelty is supposed to serve. The lesson of Mali is that contemporary administrators and political leaders in Africa who can learn to enlist traditionalism in the service of innovation will indeed be contributing to successful political modernization.

Traditionalism, as distinct from tradition, we can define as validations of current behavior stemming from immemorial prescriptive norms. It is not that traditionalist systems do not change, but rather that innovation—i.e., extra-systemic action—has to be mediated within the social system and charged to antecedent values. Modernism, in contrast, presupposes a much remoter relationship between antecedent values and new goals. Modern systems, with their complex and highly differentiated social structures, value change itself.

These distinctions between modernism and traditionalism, valid as they are, leave unanswered the question why some traditional systems can innovate more easily than others. Answers have been sought in the structural features of traditional societies, while traditionalism has remained a more or less undifferentiated concept.

The discussion here accordingly distinguishes between two types of traditionalism. The first can be called *instrumental;* the second, *consummatory.*[2] Each kind exhibits certain structural

---

[2] As we are using the terms, "instrumental" systems are those characterized by a large sector of intermediate ends separate from and independent of ultimate ends; "consummatory" systems are those characterized by a close relationship between intermediate and ultimate ends. The terms are derived from Parsons' categories of "cognitive-instrumental meanings" and "expressive-integrative meanings." See T. Parsons *et al., Working Papers in the Theory of Action,* Glencoe, Ill., 1953, p. 105.

In our sense, the difference between instrumental and consummatory values can be illustrated by the following example. Consider two traditional systems, one consummatory and the other instrumental in value type. Both are short-hoe cultures and an effort is made to introduce new agricultural techniques, particularly the use of tractors. In the consummatory system, changing from the short hand-hoe system will so corrupt the ritual of hoe-making, the division of men's and women's work, the religious practices associated with both, and the relationship between agricultural rituals and the

tendencies. The combination of value type and structural tendency determines the problems that confront political leaders as they seek to build modern nations. We shall examine these combinations in Ghana and Uganda.

As we are using the term, instrumental systems are those which can innovate easily by spreading the blanket of tradition upon change itself. In such systems, those who are called upon to arbitrate in matters of custom, and to interpret in some official capacity, are easily persuaded to find traditional counterparts in contemporary events. Such systems can innovate without appearing to alter their social institutions fundamentally. Rather, innovation is made to serve immemoriality. The characteristic structural expression of instrumental traditionalism is a military type of system, with hierarchical authority stemming from a single king or command figure (Southall 1956; Apter 1961). Appointive ranks in the system tend to underwrite the king as the central source of authority. A heavy reliance on performance is a characteristic of office and the chief who fails to serve his king loyally and well is subject to removal or death. Religion is decidedly secondary in such a system, whose primary value is service to the king or state. Examples of such systems are Morocco, Ethiopia, and Buganda.[3]

The traditionalism of consummatory systems is much more complex. They were first described by Fustel de Coulanges when, deploring the simplistic interpretations of Greece and Rome as prototypes for modern societies, he wrote that examining the institutions of those two systems without a knowledge of their re-

---

authority of chiefs that it would be impossible to consider a tractor only in terms of increasing agricultural productivity. In the instrumental system, by contrast, the tractor would simply be viewed in terms of its ability to expand agricultural output and would not affect the ultimate ends of the system. In the first instance, such an innovation represents a threat to the system. In the second instance, it is far likelier to strengthen the system by increasing farm income.

[3] The reader should note that the name Uganda refers to the entire country, the Uganda Protectorate, which includes many different tribes; Buganda is a tribe within Uganda; the Baganda are the people (plural) of Buganda; a Muganda is a single member of the Buganda tribe; and Kiganda is the adjective form.

ligious notions left them "obscure, whimsical, and inexplicable." He went on to say: "A comparison of beliefs and laws shows that a primitive religion constituted the Greek and Roman family, established marriage and paternal authority, fixed the order of relationship, and consecrated the right of property, and the right of inheritance. This same religion, after having enlarged and extended the family, formed a still larger association, the city, and reigned in that as it had reigned in the family. From it came all the institutions, as well as all the private laws, of the ancients. It was from this that the city received all its principles, its rules, its usages and its magistracies" (Fustel de Coulanges n.d.).

Thus society, the state, authority, and the like are all part of an elaborately sustained, high-solidarity system in which religion as a cognitive guide is pervasive. Such systems have been hostile to innovation. Change has produced fundamental social upheavals such as migration to towns. Broken are the warmth and intimacy of custom. Not only were ancient Greece and Rome examples of such systems, but so was Ashanti (Dia 1957a and 1957b).

Our general hypothesis is that the instrumental-hierarchical type of system can innovate with ease until the kingship principle is challenged, at which point the entire system joins together to resist change. In other words, such systems are highly resistant to political rather than other forms of modernization, and in particular cannot easily supplant the hierarchical principle of authority with a representative one.

Consummatory values are most significantly rooted where the structural expression of authority is pyramidal rather than hierarchical. Pyramidal structure means that patterns of subordinacy and superordinacy are limited to such activities as war or court appeals. For most purposes a chief or political leader is responsible to his social group rather than to a senior chief or official. The chiefs at each level of the pyramid thus have similar powers and are relatively autonomous of one another. Such a structural form relies heavily on semi-segmental kinship relationships. The autonomy of the chief or political leader is thus a reflection of the autonomy of the kinship unit itself.

The consummatory-pyramidal systems are highly resistant to all forms of innovation, and the consequences of change are external political groupings that form as new solidary associations cutting across the older ones. In other words, new social structures with a political focus emerge, with the object of tearing down the older ones. Let us examine these processes in Ghana and Uganda.

II TWO TRADITIONAL SYSTEMS

Buganda, one of the most important kingdom states in the lake area of Eastern Africa, was regarded very favorably by Europeans who first came upon the country in the latter half of the nineteenth century. First Arabs, and then British and French missionaries, were welcomed by the king, or *Kabaka,* of Buganda. Kabaka Mutesa I encouraged competitive performances by the three religious groups—Muslim, Catholic, and Protestant. Although he died a pagan, he was intensely interested in Christianity.

To the Baganda, adoption of Christianity came to denote a superior technological and educational status. The older religious system, associated with the institution of clanship which was itself giving way to a hierarchical chieftaincy system, disappeared without producing much internal strain. Christianity easily passed muster as an aid to the Baganda in maintaining their society. The only point of concern was the fact that missionaries, in gaining adherents, tended to usurp the functions of chiefs. Since the latter remained responsible to the Kabaka, while the missionaries were not, a disturbing element was introduced into the political system.

Competition among religions, however, resulted in religious wars. These were eventually resolved by allocating fixed numbers of chieftaincies to Catholics, Protestants, and Muslims. The religious factions became tantamount to political parties within Buganda.

The missionaries themselves commented on how quickly the Baganda took to education and became ardent religionists as well (Ashe 1894; Tucker 1908). After British intervention and the establishment of the Protectorate over Uganda, regular Catholic and Protestant school systems were established. The chiefs were the best-educated group in the population. Catholic chiefs were products of Kisubi, the Catholic school, and Protestant chiefs were products of King's College, Budo. Both were modeled after British public schools.

Moreover, freehold land tenure was introduced and 8,000 square miles were distributed among 1,000 chiefs and notables, who thereby became a kind of squirearchy. The recipients of the land were mainly Catholics and Protestants.

Whatever the innovated structure, whether civil-service chieftaincy, a parliament and council of ministers, modern education, or freehold tenure, it strengthened the system. The instrumental quality of hierarchical kingship was never defeated. The innovations that were most easily accepted were those that strengthened the Buganda government and also facilitated the individual's efficiency within it.

As a result, the organization of political life, which had been the crucial social structure in Buganda, was regarded as continuing from the past, with each innovation simply perfecting and strengthening an established system. All novelty came to be regarded as a device for strengthening tradition. As we shall indicate below, the main form of nationalism which emerged was that of a modernizing autocracy in which the government of the Kabaka and the Kabaka himself represented effective nationalism.

In Ashanti, on the other hand, responses to innovation were relatively complicated. Chieftaincy, despite its tiers of relatively autonomous powers with respect to various units of government, was nevertheless hemmed in with restrictions. Chieftaincy faced inward to the people to whom, by lineage and totem, the chief or headman was related. Instead of the individual atomism of Buganda, which was held together by regard for the Kabaka and the external force of hierarchical authority, the Ashanti chief was linked with an elaborate system of religiously sanctioned self-restraints on behavior. When land alienation began to occur in undue measure, for example, chieftaincy was affected and the stable confines of the social system were undermined. When Christianity was introduced, it helped to weaken the traditions of chieftaincy and removed the control that the dead ancestors exercised over the living. The result was excesses by chiefs, who turned to British authorities for their support. When education was introduced, chiefs had to be ordered to send their children to school. While they could not disobey the orders of district officers, they often sent the children of their slave lineages rather than the children of royal blood. The succeeding generations of chiefs were thus by no means the best educated. The support required for the authority of the chiefs violated customary restraints on behavior. The excesses of the chiefs soon came to be regarded as perversions of traditional society, from which younger and more educated elements began to disaffiliate. Christianity helped ease the process of disaffiliation and there developed, along with an increase in urbanization and the growth of villages, the phenomenon of the urban village Christian and the rural village pagan. Most important, a series of wars between the British and the Ashanti was a token of the inability of Ashanti to absorb those innovating effects of a system of colonial rule which was basically common to both Buganda and Ashanti. In the end the *Asantehene,* or king of Ashanti, had to be exiled. Indeed, from 1901 to 1935, the Ashanti Confederacy did not exist as such (Matson 1941).

Within the context of the term "traditional," both Ashanti and Buganda were traditional systems. Both required validations of current behavior by appeal to immemoriality. Both had myths of origin involving a powerful figure associated with the formation of the society, and with whom the king had claims to ancestry. In the case of the Ashanti, the powers of origin descended to the Golden Stool rather than to a person. In Buganda, descent was reckoned through the line of kings, or Kabakas. That the preservation of power and continuity should reside in an object in the case of Ashanti—as distinct from a person, as in Buganda—is not without significance. For, in Ashanti, those in power serve the present by serving the past. It is a symbol of ancestral concern which is the visible repository of authority. In Buganda the king was, as both Roscoe and Fallers have called him, despotic (Roscoe 1911). While there was—and still is—pomp and ceremony around the king, he was not regarded as a descendant of living ancestors. He was rather the punishing, aggressive, and virile representative of a dynamic people expanding their military hegemony in the Lake Victoria region. Hence the essentially religious and theocratic nature of the Ashanti state, and the more secular and military character of Buganda.

There were other important differences between these societies. In Ashanti, the system of political organization had its prototype in the extended family, which included up to a hundred members, possessing strong solidary affiliations. Families lived together in villages and it was unusual for an Ashanti to live alone or with only his immediate family.

In addition, the Ashanti had an elaborate lineage system whereby recruitment to office and the allocation of rights and duties were organized. The core political unit was the village. The largest unit was the division, over which there was a paramount chief. Kumasi, which established a compact with the other Ashanti divisions in a historical episode veiled in mystery and magic, became the center of a Confederacy. An elaborate balance of checks and controls on authority extended from the village level to the division, including restrictions on the exercise of power by the Asantehene, or king of the Ashanti Confederacy.

The system in Buganda was much simpler in one respect, and much more complex in others. Unlike the chief in Ashanti, who was a religious figure, a lineage figure and, moreover, elected to office, the chief in Buganda was appointed by the king, or Kabaka, and was responsible to him. The chief was subject to summary dismissal at the pleasure of the Kabaka. Much closer to the Ashanti pattern was an earlier, pre-Kabaka, clan system which continued to play a part in subsequent periods. The king was both *Sabataka* (head of all the clans) and Kabaka.

Every Muganda is a member of a clan. Clans are hereditary. The elders of clans had responsibilities over the family, the social conduct of individuals, and inheritance. Chiefs, who were appointed, reflected the powers of the Kabaka. Clan elders, who were appointed, reflected the powers of the Kabaka. Clan elders, who were elected from eligible lineages, reflected religious and immemorial powers. These two principles of authority were in constant conflict. Increasingly, performance in serving the Kabaka and thereby the state became the basis of chieftaincy. Performance and service became readily identifiable since Buganda, as a military system, was in process of expanding at the expense of her neighbors.

The acceptance of hierarchical authority thus was associated with successful national aggrandizement and the pure authority of the Kabaka was not mitigated by any other countervailing principle. Tension within the system was produced by conflicts between clanship and chieftaincy. But the Kabaka represented the central authority in both systems—i.e., Sabataka or head of all the clans, and Kabaka or head of all the chiefs.

Two effects were immediately observable from the twin systems of organization in Buganda united by a system of autocratic and hierarchical kingship. Clans were scattered throughout the country. In any area an individual on the move could find a clansman and receive certain benefits from him. This not only facilitated mobility but also ensured considerable uniformity of custom and behavior throughout the system.

The chiefs, who were territorial governors for the king, were also military leaders. Their followers were loyal to the chief because the chief reflected the Kabaka's authority. This military-administrative system of organization included a massive network of military roads converging, radially, upon the center or capital. Yet the capital itself was often moved, so that there was no "center" and "hinterland."

The result was a "suburban" pattern of life in which clanship counterpoised chieftaincy in daily life, but each man's eyes centered upon the king. In time of war, which was often, the military administrative system required almost no modification. The necessary mobilizations took place under the chiefs. Food continued to be produced, and family life managed to go on quite well. In contrast, Ashanti had to shift to a quite different military formation in time of war, and then returned to their peacetime pyramidal organization when war was over.[4]

What were some of the controversial issues which the Kiganda system was unable to absorb? The most characteristic one was an inability to adjust to any permanent limitation on the power of the Kabaka. Whether a Muganda were chief or peasant, educated or not, he maintained the same unabashed veneration for

---

[4] Ashanti had a complex hierarchy of chiefs. At the pinnacle of the hierarchy was the *omanhene,* or divisional chief. Independent in his sphere of authority, he was nevertheless hedged about with restrictions. His was a religious role symbolizing lineage relationships to ancestors, and only members of a founder's or royal lineage were eligible to be elected to chieftaincy. The same held true for village chiefs and headmen. During war a division chief and others would take a position in the army and a more hierarchical system of authority would come to prevail (Meyerowitz 1951).

the office of the Kabaka. Or, to put the matter another way, the principle of national aggrandizement was never lost, and the Kabaka was its symbol. Each of the major conflicts which aroused the Baganda and posed serious problems for the Protectorate government centered around possible dangers to the autonomy of Buganda or diminutions of the authority of the Kabaka.

In contrast to Ashanti, then, the Baganda have instrumental values. Ends are relatively well defined and essentially patriotic.

Both Baganda and Ashanti developed their own forms of tribal parochialism. The former were adept in retaining considerable political autonomy, and the Uganda Agreement of 1900, which stipulated the relations between Baganda and British, became a legal bulwark of ethnic nationalism and political parochialism. In Ashanti, where no such constitutional relationship existed, internal conflict was widely manifested throughout the entire area, creating instabilities which eventually led to mass nationalism. In more contemporary terms, in Buganda nationalist politicians have so far been able to make little headway and are regarded by the Buganda government as malcontents and ne'er-do-wells. One finds there an absorbing situation, in which the British authorities are anxious to see nationalist political parties develop on an all-Uganda pattern as the solution to building a modern state (Wild 1959). In Ghana, the party nationalists have become tantamount to the state itself, regarding chiefs dimly, to say the least. Not only have they taken active steps to break the chief's power, but the Asantehene, the paramount chief of Ashanti, has been their particular target. In the last encounter between the Asantehene and the party government, it was the former who had to admit defeat. The quasi-religious character of traditional society has been replaced by the quasi-religious character of modern nationalism in Ghana. We can analyze these developments more closely.

III   CONTRASTING EFFORTS AT POLITICAL MODERNIZATION

Uganda and Ghana are in the process of modernization. Practically, this has meant establishing parliamentary institutions by means of which the whole country is governed. Ghana achieved the level of political development in 1950 which Uganda now hopes to achieve. In other respects as well, Ghana has developed more rapidly. National income per head in Ghana is double that of Uganda. More effective internal transport and trade facilities are found in Ghana and Africans participate actively in all aspects of technical and commercial life. In Uganda, Asians and Europeans still monopolize the more important sectors of the economy and are the predominant racial groups in the civil service. In contrast, Africanization of the civil service in Ghana is virtually complete, with only a few senior positions and technical services still performed by Europeans, and these mostly on contract.

Ghana is economically well off for an African country.[5] Since 1951, 80 per cent of its internal savings has been based upon a single cash crop, cocoa. Other sources of income are gold, bauxite, manganese, industrial diamonds, and timber. It has advanced economically under a series of development plans, the first of which was primarily concerned with expanding basic transportation facilities. Railways were extended, a deep-water port built at Takoradi. The principle of a reserve fund for economic contingencies was established early. The first ten-year development plan was launched at the end of World War I and, except during the period of the world depression, Ghana has been development-conscious. Both under the later stages of colonialism and under her present nationalist government, she has been a social-welfare state.

What was the effect of innovation? Traditional chieftaincy and social organization increasingly became a focus for internal resentments. Bitter conflict over land developed. The pattern of self-restraints on behavior was upset. Land alienation in the form of concessions was common. Considerable friction developed between chiefs who took their seats not only in traditional coun-

---

[5] A population of approximately 5 million in an area of over 90,000 square miles is divided into several main tribal groups. The northern peoples are chiefly grouped in Muslim kingdoms. The central group is the seat of the once-powerful Ashanti Confederacy. The southern groups—Fante, Ga, Ewe, and others—have had the longest contact with Western commerce and education. There are old families inhabiting the former "factories" of early traders who intermarried with the local people and established their own family dynasties. See J. Boyon, *Le Ghana,* Paris, 1958, pp. 7–10.

cils, but on the legislative council and other conciliar bodies set up by the government, and the urban, educated elites which emerged with the spread of modern commerce. Each emerging group thought itself destined to inherit political power. The result was cultural withdrawal which prepared the ground for mass nationalism in Ghana after the Second World War. The chiefs, failing to consider the sources of mass nationalism, regarded it as simply an event in a long and stable cultural tradition which would only help to restore chieftaincy to its proper role.

The Western-educated elites regarded the nationalists as usurpers of their roles. The British viewed them as dangerous malcontents, subversive of public peace and good order. Such rejection gave fervor to the nationalists of the Convention People's Party (CPP), who by adherence to the party gave a new coherence to Ghana as a national society. They brought about a closer integration of the different peoples making up the territory, and they made economic and political institutions African rather than foreign by using them in the interests of self-government. Politics had already become polarized between traditional and secular authorities during the colonial period. Now the fundamental issues of traditionalism and modernity became wrapped up in more complex conflicts over democracy itself.

The major achievement of the CPP in Ghana was the organization and maintenance of an effective mass political organization. This resulted in centers of communication in the towns and villages, requiring members who could co-ordinate the activities of others. By building the CPP into a social group, a fraternity of the disadvantaged was encouraged to mold society in its favor by means of national political institutions and political freedom. A widely diverse membership was provided with a feeling of confidence in the future. Self-government was the goal. New opportunities were to be achieved thereby. A vision of a new society which was as vague as it was powerful was the moral claim of the CPP.

Yet in creating a mass political organization devoted to achieving independence, the CPP incorporated elements which had no long-run natural inclinations toward one another. More particularly, traditional groupings formed centers of opposition to Dr. Nkrumah both inside and outside the party. The main source of opposition was Ashanti. The Asantehene and his council helped plan the organization of an opposition, the National Liberation Movement (NLM), which itself renewed an old alliance between intellectuals and traditional authorities.[6]

With demands for a federal system of government, the situation rapidly grew dangerous. One Cabinet minister, a leading CPP figure from Ashanti, was ambushed outside his house and his sister killed. Government leaders did not dare to go to Ashanti for almost two years. Moreover, the appearance of successful traditionalism in Ashanti encouraged other opposition groups to form. In Accra, in Nkrumah's own constituency, there was formed an Accra people's movement which was essentially parochial and anti-Nkrumah. Everywhere traditionalism and the natural organization of the ethnic and tribal group seemed the only possible alternative to party rule by the Convention People's Party.

The conflicts over traditionalism and the future of democracy were sharpest during the period just prior to independence. In the general election of 1956, the candidates of seven parties and 45 independents ran for office. In spite of the fact that the NLM was able to put only 39 candidates in the field, and the CPP was well enough organized to contest all 104 seats, the latter received only 398,141 votes and the combined opposition received 299,-116. This opposition vote was extremely high, considering the fact that a vote for the CPP was considered a vote for independence. Approximately 50 per cent of the electorate voted. In the post-independence period, the opposition was smashed. A series of acts rushed through Parliament were designed to break the power of traditional authorities. So successful were these efforts that, when elections to the Kumasi Municipal Council were held in February 1958, the CPP won 17 out of 24 seats—a remarkable achievement.

In attacking traditionalism, movements of the CPP type take on the characteristic of inviolability. They have a tendency to brand splinter groups and the opposition as playing into the

---

[6] In 1957 the NLM joined with other tribal parties like the *Ga Shiftimo Kpee* to become the United Party. The former leader of the party, Dr. K. A. Busia, is currently in Holland, Ghana's first real political exile.

hands of the "feudal" elements in society. The idea of party fealty is stressed more than any other.

The pattern which can be clearly seen in this conflict between traditionalism and modernism is thus the continuous affiliation to and disaffiliation from powerful social groupings that each make total claims on the allegiance and support of its members. The clear loser in such a situation is the opposition. In crucial respects, therefore, countries like Ghana find that in attacking tradition and supporting modernity they become one-party systems. It is not that there is no opposition, but that organized party opposition finds itself in difficult circumstances. Traditionalism, which serves the opposition as an effective rallying ground for popular support, is branded as subversive.[7] Indeed, at the Accra African Peoples' Conference in December 1958, tribalism and religious separatism were defined as evil practices by Africa's leading nationalists. It was resolved that "those African traditional institutions whether political, social, or economic which have clearly shown their reactionary character and their sordid support for colonialism be condemned" (Conference Secretariat 1958).

What, then, has political modernization meant in Ghana? Attacking tradition has resulted in the development of an "organizational weapon" type of party which, constantly on the attack, probes for weaknesses in the system. It seeks to jostle the public into functionally useful roles for the pursuit of modernization. To prevent the loss of power, and to modernize as rapidly as possible, are the basic goals of those who have inherited the mantle of British power. Modernization has come to require a host of attitudes of mind and social organizations antithetical

---

[7] At the same time, the parliamentary opposition in Ghana has been effective on occasions. There are times when the CPP backbench threatens to bolt party whips and vote with the opposition. Such a threat has been a useful means of modifying the position of the government on several issues, not the least of which was modification of the Emergency Powers Bill, while the constitutional changes of early 1957 were incorporated under pressure from the opposition. Bitterly contested decisions which often resulted in suspensions of parliamentary sessions have been those involving basic liberties. Three such measures were the Ghana Nationality and Citizenship Bill, the Emergency Powers Bill, and the Deportation Bill (Austin 1958).

to traditional ways of doing things. Political modernization therefore attacks head-on traditional ways of believing and acting.

In these respects, the Ghana government has been unable to
make use of traditionalism to support innovation. The past has
become a dead weight on the present government, which by the
use of inducements, and by occasional kicks and blows as well,
seeks to drive people toward a new way of life. Because of the
government's loss of support in the traditional sectors of society,
the burdens of modernization on Ghana have become more intense. Unlike Senegal, where the blending of traditionalism and
modernity has eased the transition to new political and economic
forms, in Ghana traditionalism has not provided a genuine source
of pride and inspiration. Unlike the French African concept of
negritude, the slogan "African personality" has remained largely
devoid of content.[8] Ghana, in assuming the heavy burdens of
modernization without the supports of traditionalism, has become a relatively autocratic system.

Uganda shows a completely different political pattern. Unlike
Ghana, which is a maritime nation, Uganda is situated inland on
the shores of Lake Victoria.[9] It is roughly the same size as
Ghana, with an area of 80,000 square miles and a population of
approximately 6 millions (*Colonial Report* 1959).

By virtue of its superior institutions and successful collaboration with the British, Buganda was made a privileged area. The
Uganda Agreement of 1900 formally recognized these privileges,
and elsewhere in the country the Kiganda pattern of territorial
organization was established—a three-tiered system of local government, each with a chief and a council (*Lukiko*) and ranging
in scope from the parish to the county. The British retained an

---

[8] It is interesting to note that while the term "African personality" is widely
attributed to Nkrumah, it is in Nigeria that an effort is being made to give it
content. Examples of such efforts are the journals *Black Orpheus* and *Odú,*
which, as cultural and literary journals, seek to give a philosophic and
cultural significance to the term.

[9] Blessed with an exceedingly good climate and well-distributed rainfall,
most of Uganda is fertile agricultural country. To supplement her two main
crops, cotton and coffee, she needs more diverse export commodities, and
copper and other raw materials are being successfully exploited on an increasing scale.

appointive chieftaincy system, but one which followed the practice of a regular civil service, with chiefs being promoted, transferred, and retired. Theirs was the task of maintaining peace and good order, collecting taxes, and otherwise taking care of the areas under their jurisdiction. Buganda, as a province, formed the model for the other ethnic groups to follow in the districts. In more recent times the parliament of Buganda, the Great Lukiko, has been the model for the district councils, which have become the object of considerable tribal parochialism in the districts outside of Buganda.

The three races, African, Asian, and European, live in uneasy proximity. Asians are involved in petty commerce, and increasingly in larger commercial enterprises in urban centers such as Kampala, while Europeans generally remain in charge of major commercial operations. Few Europeans were successful in farming in Uganda, where a situation comparable to that of the white settlers in Kenya never developed. Asians and Europeans have always tended to collaborate in representing the commercial interests of the country.[10] Asians were represented on the Legislative Council along with Europeans from the very onset, after World War I. No Africans were represented on the Legislative Council, nor was it regarded as desirable that they should be, until after the Second World War. It was widely held that Buganda's own Lukiko served as her political outlet, and the same situation was thought to prevail in the districts. It was regarded as essential to the interests of Africans that the principle of trusteeship, the mainstay of administration during the interwar period, should be maintained through the Governor and his staff (Ingham 1958).

Until the present day, nationalism in Uganda[11] was largely expressed through the Buganda government "establishment." There is now stirring the kind of "modern" nationalism which is increasingly inclined to limit the powers of the Kabaka and make of Uganda a united, self-governing nation. But modernism as an ideology is confined to a very few. Indeed, it has been

---

[10] The Indian Association and the Uganda Chamber of Commerce were instruments of that co-operation.

[11] I.e., Buganda.—W.J.H.

largely pre-empted by the Buganda government. Let us examine the process by which this occurred.

Although the Baganda did not suffer national defeats as did the Ashanti, religious wars in the latter part of the nineteenth century resulted in the deposition and restoration of the Kabaka by Europeans on two occasions. The Baganda have never gotten over that. Given the special position of the Kabaka in the structure of Kiganda society, cavalier treatment of them on the part of the Europeans deeply wounded and aggrieved the Baganda. Even during the period of their closest collaboration with the British (roughly from 1900 to 1926), such grievances were nursed. A singular touchiness has thus characterized relations between the British and the Baganda. Unlike the more typical case in the districts, changes in political organization have, if they originated with the Protectorate government, been stoutly resisted. The Kabaka as a symbol of modern nationalism has been continuously strengthened and now has more power than at any time since British control.

When the Agreement of 1900 was signed, the Lukiko, or African parliament, dominated by the chiefs, was empowered to distribute land on a freehold basis to the most important people in Buganda. The three chief ministers received the largest estates (with the exception of the Kabaka himself), while others were given land according to their chieftaincy rank, or their general status (*Laws* 1936). Few pagans received any land.

Since chieftaincies had been divided up according to religion, both Protestants and Catholics of wealth came to have a considerable stake in the modified system. By fixing the proportions of chieftaincy along religious lines, family wealth and position were distributed in the same manner. Both Protestants and Catholics had some wealthy families in possession of land, and in important positions in the community. The Muslims suffered most of all the religious groups, while paganism quickly disappeared.

Those in the clan system who had been traditionally entitled to certain burial estates or clan lands, and who lost those lands during the parceling-out of freehold, became the first political force in Buganda. The clan system thus formed the "natural" opposition to a government of chiefs. This resulted in considerable internal dissension. Gradually the *bataka,* or clan groups, came to represent the *bakopi,* or peasantry. Land holding had become almost synonymous with prestige and social position.[12] Indeed, it appeared for a time that the system would become based on dynastic land-holding families, and the principle of easy access to political office and performance would be eliminated. Yet other innovations helped to prevent this. For example, the expanded educational system, which was enthusiastically supported by the Baganda, did not limit facilities to the children of chiefs, but included peasant children as well. Education was regarded as a major basis for entry into the political hierarchy (which remained the only major social organization throughout Buganda).

The instrumental values of the Baganda, colliding with a threatening monopoly of political roles by families of the senior chiefs who had received land, or by important Protestant and Catholic leaders, prevailed over both elites without altering the autocratic principle of hierarchical kingship. This allowed progressive modification of the Lukiko and greater opportunities to the public as a whole. Unlike the consummatory system of Ashanti, where individuals had virtually to withdraw from the traditional system in order to seek new careers and opportunities in a different kind of society, the Kiganda system was modified in practice, while posing few contradictions in principle.

Although the Buganda government was often in conflict with the peasantry, such conflicts appeared in the guise of government and its loyal opposition. The British, through a Resident, built up the influence of the chiefs and the ministers of the Buganda government. They regarded them as modern because of the ease and alacrity with which they learned to collect taxes, adapted

---

12 Important in preventing such dissension from assuming proportions of "class conflict" was the fact that peasants could, and did, buy freehold land. Moreover, no landless peasantry was created. Everyone could get a leasehold property at a nominal and fixed rental. This deterred migration to towns, and no urban-rural cleavage developed. Buganda remains a rural "suburbia." See A. W. Southall and P. C. W. Gutkind, *Townsmen in the Making,* East African Studies No. 9, Kampala, East African Institute of Social Research, 1956, *passim.*

themselves to methods of bookkeeping, and were able to control the public.

Thus the autocratic principle has prevailed in Buganda until the present. Innovations, it is widely believed, have come not from an alien source, but through the Buganda government itself. With the country's leaders able to maintain social discipline, because to act irresponsibly is to act against the Kabaka, a sense of awe and formality in social relations has helped retain public support. To keep the public "on the alert" and politically conscious, skirmishes against the intervention of the Residency are constantly fought.

As a result, the Baganda have regarded themselves as exceedingly blessed in a state of political autonomy. The Buganda government has been the most successful nationalist "party" in the country. Success in the economic field as well, particularly with the cotton and coffee crops, brought the Baganda considerable wealth as compared with the rest of Uganda. To add to their complacency, they had, by such visible indicators as tin roofs on their houses, number of bicycles, number of laborers from elsewhere working for them, and number of educated people, the highest standard of living in the Protectorate. They were able to absorb new forms of income, and to accept the standards of education, knowledge, skill, and training as requirements for a job such as chieftaincy, while retaining the essential character of their political system.

The freehold system, the chieftaincy system, the method of recruitment, the standards of selection, the acceptance of cash crops, all helped to make Buganda extremely modern in many ways. *But the prerequisite to accepting any modern feature on the political level was that some real or mythical traditional counterpart had to be found for it.* Hence, if the Lukiko was now a regular council with minutes, committees, and a budget, it was nevertheless regarded as an age-old institution. If chiefs were now almost invariably large landowners or related to the original holders of freehold, in custom those responsible for the control over "heads," i.e., over families and soldiers, were found to be the equivalent.

In 1955 several important measures were passed. In the districts, the District Councils Ordinance gave the councils both executive and legislative powers, enabling them to make bylaws on a wide range of subjects (*District Councils* 1955). In Buganda, after the deportation of the Kabaka for refusing to co-operate with the Protectorate government (part of his effort to retain autonomy for Buganda), a new Agreement was signed which enhanced the powers of the Lukiko, made the Kabaka in effect a constitutional monarch, and gave the Baganda three new ministries—Health, Education, and Natural Resources—in addition to the three they already had (Prime Minister, Chief Justice, and Treasurer) (*Buganda Agreement* 1955). These reforms in effect gave to Buganda and to the district governments substantive warrants of authority and responsibility to attend to most of the economic and social schemes which are regarded as necessary to modernization. In Buganda the autocratic nature of the system has now come under attack—but the attack is still exceedingly mild. Elsewhere, in the districts, the effort to achieve local autonomy is regarded as the essence of political modernity.

What the system in Buganda cannot resolve are challenges to the principle of autocratic or hierarchical kingship. Resisting the first direct elections to be held in Buganda in 1958, the Baganda saw themselves threatened by devolution of authority to an African national government. Opposed to the nationalism of political parties, they regard representative government on an all-Uganda basis as tantamount to the destruction of their own society. In a pamphlet justifying the position of Buganda, the *Katikiro,* or Prime Minister, recently pointed out that the "peaceful growth of Western democracy in Buganda has been possible because the Baganda's customs and traditions are adaptable to new ideas which do not seek to uproot their fundamental political conceptions. . . ." Yet the pamphlet also warns that "The Baganda cannot exist as a people unless the Kabaka is the Head of the political structure in his Kingdom. Therefore, any constitution which envisages placing any other ruler or any foreign monarch in the position of the Kabaka of Buganda has no other intention but to cause the Baganda to cease to be a nation." More importantly, he concludes: "From time immemorial the Baganda have known no other ruler above their Kabaka in his Kingdom, and still they do not recognize any other person whose authority does not derive from the Kabaka and is exercised on his behalf" (Kintu 1960).

As a result of this position, it is the Protectorate government and British officials who are trying to build a modern national state in Uganda. How well they have succeeded is indicated by the fact that in the first direct elections in 1958, Buganda refused to participate, as did several other districts (Allen 1959).

Still more recently, a constitutional committee has recommended the establishment of responsible government at the center, with a legislature possessing 72 elected seats (Wild 1959). The Buganda government voiced its bitter opposition, but non-Baganda see in it the possibility of a political society not dominated by Buganda. With the Baganda anxious to secede from Uganda entirely if that is necessary to maintain the position of the Kabaka and the Buganda kingdom, there is bitter conflict between the Buganda government, on the one hand, and party politicians allied to British authorities, on the other.

There is now emerging among many Baganda an awareness that the absorptive capacity of the traditional system and its instrumental values has been reached. This is taken by the traditionalists to indicate a need for secession if the system is to be preserved. Younger groups are anxious to build a larger national society, a united Uganda. These are regarded as traitors by the traditionalists. However, the traditionalists are not antimodern. Quite the contrary, as we have seen, they have built up a modern if miniature state in Buganda and now that very modernity is used as a justification for autonomy.

The result is that political parties remain largely ineffective both in Buganda and in Uganda as a whole. Recently, in an effort to gain popular support, several parties induced anti-Asian riots aimed at reducing the economic and commercial power of Indians. But in spite of such efforts, political parties remain weak and the Buganda government continues to be the main source of parochial nationalism. Political party leaders hoped that when responsible government develops at the center and the financial resources of the country are allocated on the basis of popular government, the strength of the Buganda government will be diminished. The struggle to obtain parliamentary institutions is less concerned with Britain or the colonial administration than was the case in Ghana. Rather, it is directed against the Buganda government because of its unwillingness to subordinate hierarchical authority to the principle of representative government. Thus the ethnic nationalism of Buganda remains the most important political obstacle to self-government and has crippled political party growth, rendering the political heart of the country virtually lifeless.[13]

As has been pointed out above, however, non-Baganda groups are developing a new political party that has been launched by recently elected African representatives of the Legislative Council. They seek to make the Legislative Council the crucial political organ in Uganda, and are reluctant to be tied to the tail of Kiganda parochialism. Thus the possibility presents itself that the central conciliar institutions of Uganda will now tend to favor the rest of the country. Grants in aid, development plans, and educational schemes can now become the target of competitive nationalism, fought out in the context of competing parochialisms. In that event, neither the traditional institutions nor their insularity will long be maintained.

Moreover, direct elections to the Buganda Lukiko will bring party politics strongly into the Buganda sphere.[14] It is possible that competitive nationalism can be transformed into federal government at the center. Federal government is a compromise system brought about by conflict among the constituent states, and conflict is necessary for its vitality. What is possible in the Uganda situation is political modernization in a federal system, in which the several traditional states will be allowed to modernize their

---

[13] It must be pointed out, however, that in Uganda, unlike colonial Ghana, everyone knows that self-government is forthcoming. Lack of such certainty helped to develop an effective nationalist movement in Ghana, where to remain outside the party was tantamount to being pro-colonialist. In Uganda, all groups know that the country will eventually get self-government, and there is far more effort on the part of each of them to retain and expand their influence and power. Foreknowledge of self-government, in that sense, has helped to diminish the urgency of nationalism.

[14] Already in the new Lukiko, elected in 1959 (without direct election methods), five political parties are represented, a predominantly Catholic party supplying 80 per cent of all party representatives. The Buganda government has accepted the principle of direct elections but has steadfastly refused to implement it.

institutions on their own terms. In the demand for federalism all groups see some hope for their survival. Federalism itself has come to mean political modernism.

IV   CONCLUSION

In both Ghana and Uganda tribal or ethnic parochialism has persisted with widely varying results. Kiganda parochialism has itself been a form of modernism. Civil-service chieftaincy and bureaucratic norms have bolstered the kingdom. Indeed, the Buganda government is widely regarded as the most progressive force in the country. Hence, for the Baganda, to be modern is to be parochial.

In Ashanti, modernism clashed directly with traditionalism. The religious aspect of the traditional political and social structure was an important part of a network of suitable restraints on behavior. When these were disrupted by innovations in commercial enterprise and colonialism, traditional authority was quickly undermined. Yet because traditional authority was so much a part of daily life and custom, those who broke with tradition found themselves in drastic need of new and powerful social affiliations, for to break with tradition was to break with family, lineage, and ancestral fidelity.

In contrast to Ashanti, Buganda remains the most powerful solidary association possible. Social satisfactions are still achieved within Buganda and its government for all those who belong to the kingdom. In Ashanti the formation of a new political party was itself a process of forming new and powerful symbolic attachments. The Ashanti members of the CPP became fiercely devoted to the organization. The messianic role of the leader was based on the development of a new morality to supplant the old. Hence the deep cleavages in society which remained after self-government had been obtained posed the problem of nation-building after independence rather than before it.

We can summarize some of the more salient points of contrast between the two systems as follows:

1 *Absorption of Innovation*

Ashanti, with its consummatory-pyramidal system, was unable to control the effects of innovation. Ashanti tended to shrink from contact with the modern world. Early missionaries were imprisoned. The Ashanti wars were efforts to expel the British, as a foreign body, from the body politic. The effects of contact loosened the hold of traditionalism, although it remained a powerful force.

Buganda was able to control innovation. The European presence was absorbed and rendered useful. By careful planning and the use of modernizing agencies, the Buganda government increased its autonomy and control as time went on, rather than suffering partial decay.

2 *Internal Divisions and Discontinuities*

What had hitherto been reinforcing social institutions of the consummatory system of Ashanti rapidly broke down into competing power groups and sources of internal antagonism and weakness. Thus the development of conflicts between youth and age, royals and non-royals, slaves and non-slaves, were all examples of conflict over the continuing strength of particularistic criteria which could be reconciled only so long as older religious and institutional checks were sustained. Such social controls were highly internalized, with authority variously distributed. As soon as the continuity of past and present was disrupted, the various groupings rapidly came to compete.

In Buganda the internal conflict continued, as in the period prior to contact, between clanship and chieftaincy—all, however, under the umbrella of the king as both Sabataka, head of all the clans, and Kabaka, or king. The advantages of appointive chieftaincy had long been apparent in the military undertakings of the kingdom and a secular tendency inherent in the system was simply reinforced by contact with the British. The system was able to modify itself to restrain the old conflicts sufficiently so that the principle of hierarchic kingship did not require substantial alteration. Allegiance did not become confused.

3   *Competition for Affiliations*

Internal conflict in Ashanti produced widespread attitudes of guilt. Cleavages divided the extended and nuclear families. Social breaks which meant modifying one's religious practices and sundering ties with the past (and one's ancestors) led to migration of individuals to urban areas which supported very different patterns of social life. These created more fundamental differences in outlook between urban and rural groups who, within one generation had grown apart but were still not socially distant. The Ashanti were able to retain affiliations among those who represented orthodoxy. However, breaking such affiliations could not be resolved by the simple acceptance of heterodoxy. Rather a new orthodoxy had to be posed against the old. Thus the new affiliations of the political party assumed the proportions of a militant church movement.

In Buganda, there was relatively easy adaptation of internal cleavage to serve the larger purposes of the state. As a result, no Baganda repudiated their chiefs or the Kabaka. The Buganda government was itself a source of modernism, and no incompatibility between modernism and traditionalism resulted in the enforced disaffiliation of discontented groups. No discontented urban groups emerged, anxiety-ridden and seeking drastic change.

4   *Legitimacy Conflicts*

Just as innovation could not be controlled in Ashanti, so the secular authority of the colonial government was posed against the traditional authority of the chiefs. Immemorial prescriptive rights clashed with concepts of efficiency and performance as a basis of authority. In Buganda, the autocratic principle prevailed and two oligarchies, British and Baganda, worked alongside one another. They were in constant competition, but they did not challenge each other's legitimacy. Both were oriented to efficiency and performance.

In Ashanti almost any outside activity, by being resisted, posed an ultimate legitimacy problem. So closely interrelated were the elements of social life and belief that they conformed nicely to Durkheim's concept of a fragile and mechanical society. Ultimately all threats were threats against legitimacy. Hence not only was colonialism viewed as a threat to traditional legitimacy, but nationalism was even more so. The conflict between lineage and ancestral sanction (immemoriality) for current acts and secular forces was introduced by colonialism, and helped to produce the nationalism which then had to break the power of traditionalism and its residual hold upon the public. Thus modern nationalism in Ghana is essentially an effort to create a wider legitimacy which introduces some of the same instrumental characteristics which Buganda possessed traditionally. *The result is a growth of an autocratic principle of leadership in Ghana*—the organizational weapon serving as its own justification.

In contrast, in Buganda, the conflict over legitimacy never emerged in sharp form in the colonial-Buganda government relationship. Indeed, even when the Kabaka was exiled, early in the relationship, or more recently when the present Kabaka was deported, the principle of the Kabakaship was not questioned by the Protectorate government authorities.

However, now that the problem of building wider affiliations has been tackled effectively by the Protectorate government, political parties are challenging the principle of hierarchical authority. *They are seeking to supplant hierarchical authority with representative authority* as a means of building a modern nation. They do not, however, need to create attitudes of universalism and performance as the basis of political recruitment since these are already widespread and traditional.

Where the consummatory-pyramidal system prevailed, there developed fierce competition between traditional and secular leaders to monopolize allegiance. This was expressed by the latter in efforts to build overarching and autocratic institutions which by autocratic means fostered egalitarianism in political recruitment and the exercise of authority. The problem was to prevent social atomism while mobilizing those resources of the society which could capitalize on change itself. This put exceedingly heavy burdens on political nationalists, whose need for organizational control and support became all important.

In the instrumental-hierarchical system prevailing in Buganda, change has aided parochialism and modernism of a local sort, making political modernism of the national state more difficult to achieve. Where consummatory values prevail in the traditional sector, the political leaders lose the advantages of traditionalism. Their need is to find new ways and means of employing it to ease the burdens of political development. Where instrumental values prevail, the local and national forms of modernism need to be brought into some kind of useful identity so that instrumental traditionalism can reinforce political modernization at the national level.

Ghana shows the effects of a single-party unitary government and its difficulties in modernization. Can a modernizing nation be created through a federal system of government in which the parts will reinforce the whole? In this respect, Uganda represents a potential alternative to the Ghana pattern. Out of regard for instrumental traditionalism, Uganda may find a political compromise proximate to the needs of the public, achieving modernity with both prudence and freedom.

Modernism and traditionalism have become key political issues. Buganda has retained both her tribalism and her separatism, penalizing the political advance of the country as a whole. Ashanti, the last stronghold of tribalism in Ghana, has been defeated by modernism in the form of nationalism. Buganda and Ashanti, Uganda and Ghana, both facing similar problems in different ways, shed some light on the politics of modernization in contemporary Africa.

22 THE WRETCHED OF THE EARTH

Frantz Fanon

COME, THEN, COMRADES; it would be as well to decide at once to change our ways. We must shake off the heavy darkness in which we were plunged, and leave it behind. The new day which is already at hand must find us firm, prudent and resolute.

We must leave our dreams and abandon our old beliefs and friendships of the time before life began. Let us waste no time in sterile litanies and nauseating mimicry. Leave this Europe where they are never done talking of Man, yet murder men everywhere they find them, at the corner of every one of their own streets, in all the corners of the globe. For centuries they have stifled almost the whole of humanity in the name of a so-called spiritual experience. Look at them today swaying between atomic and spiritual disintegration.

And yet it may be said that Europe has been successful in as much as everything that she has attempted has succeeded.

Europe undertook the leadership of the world with ardour, cynicism and violence. Look at how the shadow of her palaces stretches out ever further! Every one of her movements has burst the bounds of space and thought. Europe has declined all humility and all modesty; but she has also set her face against all solicitude and all tenderness.

She has only shown herself parsimonious and niggardly where men are concerned; it is only men that she has killed and devoured.

Originally published in English as the Conclusion, pp. 252–55, of *The Wretched of the Earth* by Frantz Fanon, New York, Grove Press, 1966. Reprinted with permission of the publisher and MacGibbon & Kee, Ltd.

So, my brothers, how is it that we do not understand that we have better things to do than to follow that same Europe?

That same Europe where they were never done talking of Man, and where they never stopped proclaiming that they were only anxious for the welfare of Man: today we know with what sufferings humanity has paid for every one of their triumphs of the mind.

Come, then, comrades, the European game has finally ended; we must find something different. We today can do everything, so long as we do not imitate Europe, so long as we are not obsessed by the desire to catch up with Europe.

Europe now lives at such a mad, reckless pace that she has shaken off all guidance and all reason, and she is running headlong into the abyss; we would do well to avoid it with all possible speed.

Yet it is very true that we need a model, and that we want blueprints and examples. For many among us the European model is the most inspiring. We have therefore seen in the preceding pages to what mortifying set-backs such an imitation has led us. European achievements, European techniques and the European style ought no longer to tempt us and to throw us off our balance.

When I search for Man in the technique and the style of Europe, I see only a succession of negations of man, and an avalanche of murders.

The human condition, plans for mankind and collaboration between men in those tasks which increase the sum total of humanity are new problems, which demand true inventions.

Let us decide not to imitate Europe; let us combine our muscles and our brains in a new direction. Let us try to create the whole man, whom Europe has been incapable of bringing to triumphant birth.

Two centuries ago, a former European colony decided to catch up with Europe. It succeeded so well that the United States of America became a monster, in which the taints, the sickness and the inhumanity of Europe have grown to appalling dimensions.

Comrades, have we not other work to do than to create a third Europe? The West saw itself as a spiritual adventure. It is in the name of the spirit, in the name of the spirit of Europe, that Europe has made her encroachments, that she has justified her crimes and legitimised the slavery in which she holds the four-fifths of humanity.

Yes, the European spirit has strange roots. All European thought has unfolded in places which were increasingly more deserted and more encircled by precipices; and thus it was that the custom grew up in those places of very seldom meeting man.

A permanent dialogue with oneself and an increasingly obscene narcissism never ceased to prepare the way for a half delirious state, where intellectual work became suffering and the reality was not at all that of a living man, working and creating himself, but rather words, different combinations of words, and the tensions springing from the meanings contained in words. Yet some Europeans were found to urge the European workers to shatter this narcissism and to break with this unreality.

But in general, the workers of Europe have not replied to these calls; for the workers believe, too, that they are part of the prodigious adventure of the European spirit.

All the elements of a solution to the great problems of humanity have, at different times, existed in European thought. But the action of European men has not carried out the mission which fell to them, and which consisted of bringing their whole weight to bear violently to bear upon these elements, of modifying their arrangement and their nature, of changing them and finally of bringing the problem of mankind to an infinitely higher plane.

Today, we are present at the stasis of Europe. Comrades, let us flee from this motionless movement where gradually dialectic is changing into the logic of equilibrium. Let us reconsider the question of mankind. Let us reconsider the question of cerebral reality and of the cerebral mass of all humanity, whose connections must be increased, whose channels must be diversified and whose messages must be re-humanised.

Come, brothers, we have far too much work to do for us to play the game of rear-guard. Europe has done what she set out to do and on the whole she has done it well; let us stop blaming her, but let us say to her firmly that she should not make such a song and dance about it. We have no more to fear; so let us stop envying her.

The Third World today faces Europe like a colossal mass whose aim should be to try to resolve the problems to which Europe has not been able to find the answers.

But let us be clear: what matters is to stop talking about output, and intensification, and the rhythm of work.

No, there is no question of a return to Nature. It is simply a very concrete question of not dragging men towards mutilation, of not imposing upon the brain rhythms which very quickly obliterate it and wreck it. The pretext of catching up must not be used to push man around, to tear him away from himself or from his privacy, to break and kill him.

No, we do not want to catch up with anyone. What we want to do is to go forward all the time, night and day, in the company of Man, in the company of all men. The caravan should not be stretched out, for in that case each line will hardly see those who precede it; and men who no longer recognise each other meet less and less together, and talk to each other less and less.

It is a question of the Third World starting a new history of Man, a history which will have regard to the sometimes prodigious theses which Europe has put forward, but which will also not forget Europe's crimes, of which the most horrible was committed in the heart of man, and consisted of the pathological tearing apart of his functions and the crumbling away of his unity. And in the framework of the collectivity there were the differentiations, the stratification and the bloodthirsty tensions fed by classes; and finally, on the immense scale of humanity, there were racial hatreds, slavery, exploitation and above all the bloodless genocide which consisted in the setting aside of fifteen thousand millions of men.

So, comrades, let us not pay tribute to Europe by creating states, institutions and societies which draw their inspiration from her.

Humanity is waiting for something other from us than such an imitation, which would be almost an obscene caricature.

If we want to turn Africa into a new Europe, and America into a new Europe, then let us leave the destiny of our countries to Europeans. They will know how to do it better than the most gifted among us.

But if we want humanity to advance a step further, if we want to bring it up to a different level than that which Europe has shown it, then we must invent and we must make discoveries.

If we wish to live up to our peoples' expectations, we must seek the response elsewhere than in Europe.

Moreover, if we wish to reply to the expectations of the people of Europe, it is no good sending them back a reflection, even an ideal reflection, of their society and their thought with which from time to time they feel immeasurably sickened.

For Europe, for ourselves and for humanity, comrades, we must turn over a new leaf, we must work out new concepts, and try to set afoot a new man.

Aberle, David F.
   1951 "The psychosocial analysis of a Hopi life history." *Comparative Psychological Monographs* 21, No. 107.
Ackerknecht, Erwin H.
   1944 "White Indians." *Bulletin of the History of Medicine*, XV.
Adair, John and Evon Z. Vogt
   1949 "Navaho and Zuni veterans: a study of contrasting modes of culture change." *American Anthropologist* 51: 547–61.
Adams, Richard N.
   1951 "Personnel in culture change: a test of a hypothesis." *Social Forces* 30: 185–89.
Aiton, Arthur S.
   1940 "Latin American Frontiers." Canadian Historical Association, *Report*, 100–4.
Albrecht, A. C.
   1946 "Indian-French relations at Natchez." *American Anthropologist* 48: 321–53.
Aldridge, Alfred O.
   1950 "Franklin's Deistical Indians." *Proceedings of the American Philosophical Society*, XCIV.
Alexander, Fred
   1947 *Moving Frontiers: An American Theme and Its Application to Australian History.* Victoria: Melbourne University Press.
All-African Peoples' Conference
   1958 Resolution on Tribalism, Religious Separatism, and Traditional Institutions. *Conference Resolutions*, Vol. 1, No. 4. Accra.
Allen, C. P. S.
   1959 *A Report on the First Direct Elections to the Legislative Council of the Uganda Protectorate.* Appendix J. Entebbe, Uganda: Government Printer.
Almack, John C.
   1925 "The Shibboleth of the Frontier." *Historical Outlook*, XVI, May, 197–202.

1932 *American Folk Art. The Art of the Common Man in America, 1750–1900.* New York: Museum of Modern Art Publication No. 19.
Andrews, E. D.
1953 *The People Called Shakers* . . . New York: Oxford University Press.
Apter, David E.
1955 *The Gold Coast in Transition.* Princeton: Princeton University Press.
1961 *The Political Kingdom in Uganda: A Study of Bureaucratic Nationalism.* Princeton: Princeton University Press.
Ashe, R. P.
1894 *Chronicles of Uganda.* London: Hodder & Stoughton.
Austin, D. G.
1958 "The Ghana Parliament's First Year." *Parliamentary Affairs,* XI, No. 3, Summer, 350–60.
Barker, George
1947 "Social functions of language in a Mexican-American community." *Acta Americana* 5: 185–202.
Barnett, Homer G.
1941 "Personal conflicts and cultural change." *Social Forces* 20: 160–71.
1949 *Palauan Society.* Eugene: University of Oregon Publications.
Barnouw, Victor
1950 *Acculturation and personality among the Wisconsin Chippewa.* American Anthropological Association Memoir No. 72.
Barraclough, G.
1954 "Metropolis and Macrocosm." *Past and Present,* III, May, 77–93.
Bates, Marston
1952 *Where Winter Never Comes: A Study of Man and Nature in the Tropics.* New York: Scribner.
Bateson, Gregory
1935 "Culture Contact and Schismogenesis." *Man,* Art. 199.
Beals, Ralph
1951 "Urbanism, urbanization and acculturation." *American Anthropologist* 53: 1–10.
1952 "Notes on acculturation." In *Heritage of Conquest,* ed. Sol Tax, pp. 225–32. Glencoe, Illinois: Free Press.
1953 "Acculturation." In: *Anthropology Today,* by A. L. Kroeber and others, pp. 621–41. Chicago: University of Chicago Press.
Beard, Charles A.
1921 "The Frontier in American History." *New Republic,* XXV, February 16, 349–50.
1928 "Culture and Agriculture." *Saturday Review of Literature,* V, October, 272–73.
Beazley, Raymond
1942 "Democratic Factors in Russian History." *Contemporary Review,* CLXI, March, 139–43.
Beck, Roland H.

1955 *Die Frontiertheorie von Frederick Jackson Turner, 1861–1932.* Zurich.

Belaunde, Victor A.

1923 "The Frontier in Hispanic America." *Rice Institute Pamphlets,* X, October, 202–13.

Beyer, H. Otley

1948 "Chinese Elements in the Tagalog Language." In: *Influence of Chinese on Philippine Language and Culture.* Manila: Filipiana Publications.

Bienenstok, Theodore

1950 "Social life and authority in the East European Shtetl community." *Southwestern Journal of Anthropology* 6: 238–54.

Billington, Ray A.

1945 "The Origin of the Land Speculator as a Frontier Type." *Agricultural History,* XIX, October, 204–12.

1963 "The Frontier in American Thought and Character," in Archibald R. Lewis and Thomas F. McGann, eds., *The New World Looks At Its History.* Austin: University of Texas Press.

Binney, George

1931 *The Eskimo Book of Knowledge.* London: Hudson's Bay Company.

Bogoras, W.

1907 "The Chukchee." Part 2. *Memoirs of the American Museum of Natural History* XI: 277–733.

Bogoraz-Tan

1934 *Chukchi.* Leningrad: [Reference incomplete in original]

Bogue, Allan G.

1958 "Pioneer Farmers and Innovation." *Iowa Journal of History,* LVI (January), 1–36.

1960 "Social Theory and the Pioneer." *Agricultural History,* XXXIV (January), 21–34.

Bogue, Allan G. and Margaret B. Bogue

1957 " 'Profits' and the Frontier Land Speculator." *Journal of Economic History,* XVII, March, 1–24.

Brierly, J. L.

1928 *The Law of Nations.* Oxford: Clarendon Press.

Brooks, Harlow

1936 "The Contribution of the Primitive American to Medicine." In *Medicine and Mankind,* ed. Iago, Galdston. New York: Appleton-Century.

Broom, Leonard, and E. Shevky

1952 "Mexicans in the United States: a problem in social differentiation." *Sociology and Social Research,* 36, No. 3.

Broom, Leonard, and John I. Kitsuse

1955 "The validation of acculturation: a condition to ethnic assimilation." *American Anthropologist* 57: 44–48.

Bruner, Edward M.
  1953 "Assimilation among Fort Berthold Indians." *The American Indian* 6: 21–29.
Burkhart, J. A.
  1947 "The Turner Thesis: A Historian's Controversy." *Wisconsin Magazine of History*, XXXI, September, 70–83.
Burt, A. L.
  1940 "The Frontier in the History of New France." Canadian Historical Association, *Report*, 93–99.
Campisi, Paul J.
  1947 "A scale for the measurement of acculturation." Unpublished Ph.D. dissertation, University of Chicago.
Careless, J. M. S.
  1954 "Frontierism, Metropolitanism, and Canadian History." *Canadian Historical Review*, XXXV, March, 1–21.
Carleton, Phillips D.
  1943 "The Indian Captivity." *American Literature*, No. 15.
Casagrande, Joseph B.
  1951 "Comanche linguistic acculturation: a study in ethnolinguistics." Unpublished Ph.D. dissertation, Columbia University.
Caudill, William
  1949 "Psychological characteristics of acculturated Wisconsin Ojibwa children." *American Anthropologist* 50: 409–27.
  1952 "Japanese American personality and acculturation." *Genetic Psychology Monographs* 45: 3–102.
Cheyney, E. P.
  1907 "Some English Conditions Surrounding the Settlement of Virginia." *American Historical Review*, XII.
Child, Irvin
  1943 *Italian or American? The Second Generation in Conflict.* New Haven: Yale University Press.
Coan, Otis W., and Richard G. Lillard
  1949 *America in Fiction. An Annotated List of Novels that Interpret Aspects of Life in the United States* (3d ed.). Stanford: Stanford University Press.
Coedes, G.
  1944 *Historie ancienne des états hindouisés d'extrême orient.* Hanoi: Imprimerie d'Extrême-Orient.
1959 *Colonial Report.* Entebbe: Government Printer.
Cook, S. F.
  1945 "Demographic consequences of European contact with primitive peoples." *Annals of the American Academy of Political and Social Sciences* 237: 107–11.
Coughlin, Richard J.
  1953 "The Chinese in Bangkok: a study of cultural persistence." Unpublished Ph.D. dissertation, Yale University.

Coulanges, Fustel de
n.d. *The Ancient City*. New York: Doubleday Anchor Books.

Curti, Merle
1955 "Intellectuals and Other People." *American Historical Review*, LX, January, 259–82.

Davis, Kingsley
1951 *The Population of India and Pakistan*. Princeton: Princeton University Press.

De Villiers du Terrage, Baron Marc
1924 "Une vente de terrain ou Gregor mac Gregor, 'cacique des Poyais.'" *Journal de la Société des Américanists de Paris,* Vol. 16, 197–200.

De Voto, Bernard
1947 *Across the Wide Missouri*. Boston: Houghton.

Dia, M. Mamadou
1957a *L'économique africaine*. Paris: Presses universitaires de France.
1957b "Economie et culture devant les élites africaines." *Présence africaine,* Nos. 14–15, June–September, 58–72.

Durkheim, Emile
1893 *De la Division de Travail Social,* translated as *The Division of Labor in Society,* 1949. Glencoe: Free Press.
1951 *Suicide*. (Original edition, 1897.) Glencoe: Free Press.

Eaton, J. W.
1952 "Controlled acculturation: a survival technique of the Hutterites." *American Sociological Review* 17: 331–40.

Eggan, Fred
1950 *Social Organization of the Western Pueblos*. Chicago: University of Chicago Press.

Ekirch, Arthur A.
1944 "The Idea of Progress in America 1815–1860." Unpublished Ph.D. dissertation, Columbia University.

Ekvall, Robert B.
1939 *Cultural relations on the Kansu-Tibetan border*. Chicago: University of Chicago Press.

Elkin, A. P.
1944 *Citizenship for the Aborigines*. Sydney: Australasian Publishing Co.
1949 "Man and His Cultural Heritage." *Oceania,* XX, No. 1.
1951 "Reaction and interaction: a food gathering people and European settlement." *American Anthropologist* 53: 164–86.

Elton, J. F.
1879 *Travels and Researches among the Lakes and Mountains of Eastern and Central Africa*. London: J. Murray.

Emeneau, Murray B.
1938 "Toda Culture Thirty-Five Years After: An Acculturation Study." *Annals of the Bhandarkar Oriental Research Institute,* Vol. XIX, January.

Evans-Pritchard, E. E.
   1940 *The Nuer.* Oxford: Clarendon Press.
Fallers, Lloyd A.
   1956 *Bantu Bureaucracy.* Cambridge: Heffer.
Fenton, W. N.
   1941 "Contacts Between Iroquois Herbalism and Colonial Medicine."
   Smithsonian Institution *Report,* 505–6. Washington, D.C.
Fife, Austin E., and Francesca Redden
   1954 "The Pseudo-Indian Folksongs of the Anglo-American and the
   French-Canadian." *Journal of American Folklore,* LVII.
Fiji, Colony of
   1896 *Report of the Commission appointed to inquire into the Decrease
   of the Native Population,* Suva.
Firth, Raymond W.
   1929 *Primitive Economics of the New Zealand Maori.* New York:
   Dutton.
Fitzpatrick, Brian
   1947 "The Big Man's Frontier and Australian Farming." *Agricultural
   History,* XXI, January, 8–12.
Forbes, Jack D.
   1962 "Frontiers in American History." *Journal of the West,* I, July,
   63–73.
Ford, H. J.
   1915 *The Scotch-Irish in America.* Princeton: Princeton University Press.
Forde, C. Daryll
   1934 *Habitat, Economy and Society.* London: Methuen.
Fortes, M.
   1936 "Culture contact as a dynamic process." *Africa* 9: 24–55.
Fox, Dixon R.
   1935 *Ideas in Motion.* New York: Appleton-Century.
Freed, S. A.
   1957 "Suggested Type Societies in Acculturation Studies." *American Anthropologist* 59: 55–68.
Furnivall, J. S.
   1948 *Colonial Policy and Practice.* Cambridge: The University Press.
Gascho, M.
   1937 "The Amish Division of 1693–1697 in Switzerland and Alsace."
   Mennonite Quarterly Review 22: 235–66.
Gates, Paul W.
   1936 "The Homestead Act in an Incongruous Land System." *American
   Historical Review,* XLI, July, 652–81.
   1942 "The Role of the Land Speculator in Western Development." *Pennsylvania Magazine of History and Biography,* LXVI, July, 314–33.
   1954 *Fifty Million Acres: Conflicts over Kansas Land Policy, 1854–1890.*
   Ithaca: Cornell University Press.
   1963 "The Homestead Act: Free Land Policy in Operation, 1862–1935,"

in Howard W. Ottoson, ed., *Land Use Policy and Problems in the United States.* Lincoln, Nebraska: University of Nebraska Press.

Gillin, John

1945 "Parallel cultures and the inhibitions to acculturation in a Guatamalan community." *Social Forces* 24: 1–14.

1948 *The Ways of Men.* New York: Appleton-Century.

1949 "Mestizo America." In *Most of the World,* ed. Ralph Linton, pp. 156–211. New York: Columbia University Press.

Gluckman, Max

1940a "Analysis of a social situation in modern Zululand." *Bantu Studies* 14: 1–30, 147–74.

1940b "The kingdom of the Zulu in South Africa." In *African Political Systems,* eds. M. Fortes and E. E. Evans-Pritchard, pp. 25–55. London: Oxford University Press.

Golides, Clarence

1950 "The Reception of Some Nineteenth Century American Authors in Europe." In *The American Writer and the European Tradition,* eds. Margaret Denny and W. H. Gilman. Minneapolis: University of Minnesota Press.

Gookin, Daniel

1674 *Historical Collections of the Indians in New England.* Boston: Belknap and Hall. Massachusetts Historical Society Collections, Ser. 1, Vol. 1.

Goubaud, A. Carrera

1952 "Indian adjustments to modern national culture." In *Acculturation in the Americas,* Proceedings and Selected Papers of the XXIXth International Congress of Americanists, 1949 ed. Sol Tax, pp. 244–48. Chicago: University of Chicago Press.

Green, Abel, and Joe Laurie, Jr.

1951 *Show Biz, from Vaude to Video.* New York: Holt.

Gregory, D.

1881 *The History of the Western Highlands and the Isles.* 2d edition. London: Hamilton, Adams and Co.

Gressley, Gene M.

1958 "The Turner Thesis—a Problem in Historiography," *Agricultural History,* XXXII, October, 227–49.

Guppy, H. B.

1887 *The Solomon Islands and Their Natives.* London: S. Sonnenschein, Lowrey and Co.

Gwynn, S.

1923 *The History of Ireland.* London: Macmillan.

Hacker, Louis M.

1933 "Sections—or Classes?" *The Nation,* CXXXVII, July 26, 108–10.

1935 "Frederick Jackson Turner: Non-Economic Historian." *New Republic,* LXXXIII, June 5, 108.

Hall, Edward T., Jr., and George L. Trager
  1953 *The Analysis of Culture*. Washington, D.C.: Foreign Service Institute.
Hall, Robert A., Jr.
  1953 *Haitian Creole*. American Anthropological Association Memoir No.
  74.
Hallowell, A. Irving
  n.d. "Preliminary Report on a Field Investigation of the Psychological
  Effects of Acculturation upon a Group of Ojibwa Indians." Ms.
  1934 "Some Empirical Aspects of Northern Saulteaux Religion." *American Anthropologist* 36: 389–404.
  1941 "The Rorschach Method as an Aid in the Study of Personalities in
  Primitive Societies." *Character and Personality* 9: 235–45.
  1942a "Acculturation Processes and Personality Changes as Indicated by
  the Rorschach Technique." *Rorschach Research Exchange* 6: 42–50.
  1942b *The Role of Conjuring in Saulteaux Society*. Philadelphia: University of Pennsylvania Press.
  1945a " 'Popular' Responses and Cultural Differences: An Analysis Based
  on Frequencies in a Group of American Indian Subjects." *Rorschach
  Research Exchange* 9: 153–68.
  1945b "The Rorschach Technique in the Study of Personality and Culture." *American Anthropologist* 42: 95–210.
  1945c "Sociopsychological aspects of acculturation." In *The Science of
  Man in the World Crisis,* ed. Ralph Linton, pp. 171–200. New York:
  Columbia University Press.
  1946 "Some psychological characteristics of the Northeastern Indians."
  In *Man in Northeastern North America,* ed. Frederick Johnson, pp.
  195–225. Papers of the Robert S. Peabody Foundation for Archaeology,
  Vol. III. Andover, Massachusetts.
  1950 "Values, Acculturation and Mental Health." *American Journal of
  Orthopsychiatry* XX: 732–43.
  1951 "The Use of Projective Techniques in the Study of the Sociopsychological Aspects of Acculturation." *Journal of Projective Techniques*
  XV: 27–44.
  1952 "Ojibwa personality and acculturation." In *Acculturation in the
  Americas,* Proceedings and Selected Papers of the XXIXth International
  Congress of Americanists, 1949, ed. Sol Tax, pp. 105–12. Chicago:
  University of Chicago Press.
Hancock, W. K.
  1940 *Survey of British Commonwealth Affairs,* Vol. II, Part 1, pp. 4–5.
  London: Oxford University Press.
Hannay, D.
  1926 *The Great Chartered Companies*. London: Williams & Norgate.
Hanson, Paul M.
  1945 *Jesus Christ among the Ancient Americans*. Independence, Missouri:
  Herald Publishing House.

Hardinge, Emma (Emma Hardinge Britten)
  1945 *History of Modern American Spiritualism.* Independence, Missouri: Herald Publishing House (New York: The Author, 1870).
Hart, James D.
  1950 *The Popular Book. A History of America's Literary Taste.* New York: Oxford University Press.
Havighurst, Walter
  1946 *Land of Promise, the Story of the Northwest Territory.* New York: Macmillan.
Hayes, Carlton J. H.
  1946 "The American Frontier—Frontier of What?" *American Historical Review,* LI, January, 199–216.
Herskovits, Melville J.
  1938 *Acculturation: the Study of Culture Contact.* New York: Augustin.
  1948 *Man and His Works.* New York: Knopf.
Hofstadter, Richard
  1949 "Turner and the Frontier Myth." *American Scholar,* XVIII, Autumn, 433–43.
Holmberg, Allan R.
  1950 *Nomads of the long bow; the Siriono of Eastern Bolivia.* Smithsonian Institution: Institute of Social Anthropology Publication 10. Washington, D.C.
  1955 "Participant Observation in the Field." *Human Organization,* 14: 1, Spring, 23–26.
Holt, W. Stull
  1948 "Hegel, the Turner Hypothesis, and the Safety-Valve Theory." *Agricultural History,* XXII, July, 175–76.
Honigmann, John J.
  1952 "Intercultural relations at Great Whale River." *American Anthropologist* 54: 510–22.
Horton, Donald
  1943 "The functions of alcohol in primitive societies: a cross-cultural survey." *Quarterly Journal of Studies on Alcohol* IV: 199–320.
Hostetler, J. A.
  1955 "Old World Extinction and New World Survival of the Amish: A Study of Group Maintenance and Dissolution." *Rural Sociology* 20: 212–19.
  1963 *Amish Society.* Baltimore: Johns Hopkins Press.
Howard, Joseph K.
  1952 *Strange Empire: A Narrative of the Northwest.* New York: Morrow.
Hughes, E. C.
  1943 *French Canada in Transition.* Chicago: University of Chicago Press.
Huntington, G. E.
  1956 "Dove at the Window. A Study of an Old Order Amish Community in Ohio." Unpublished Ph.D. dissertation, Yale University.

Ingham, K.
  1958 *The Making of Modern Uganda*. London: Allen & Unwin.
1888 *Izvestiya Imperatorskago, Geograficheskago, Obshchestva*, Vol. XXIV: 180–87. St. Petersburg.
1909 *Izvestiya Imperatorskago, Russkago Geograficheskago Obshchestva*, Vol. XIV, 516. St. Petersburg.
Johnson, Jean B.
  1943 "A clear case of linguistic acculturation." *American Anthropologist* 45: 427–34.
Johnston, Winnifred
  1936 "Medicine Show." *Southwest Review* XXI.
Kardiner, Abram, and others
  1944 *The Psychological Frontiers of Society*. New York: Columbia University Press.
Keesing, Felix M.
  1941 *The South Seas in the Modern World*. New York: Day.
  1949 "Cultural dynamics and administration." Prepared for the Seventh Pacific Science Congress. Manuscript at Stanford University, Stanford.
  1953 *Culture Change: An Analysis and Bibliography of Anthropological Sources to 1952*. Stanford: Stanford University Press.
Kerchoff, A. C., and T. C. McCormick
  1955 "Marginal Status and Marginal Personality." *Social Forces* 34: 48–55.
Kershner, Frederick D., Jr.
  1953 "George Chaffey and the Irrigation Frontier." *Agricultural History*, XXVII, October, 115–22.
Keur, D. L.
  1941 *Big Bead Mesa: An Archaeological Study of Navaho Acculturation, 1745–1812*. Society for American Archaeology Memoir 1.
Kintu, M.
  1960 *Buganda's Position*. Information Department, Kabaka's Government. Kampala: Uganda Printing and Publishing Co.
Kluckhohn, Clyde
  1943 "Covert culture and administrative problems." *American Anthropologist* 45: 213–27.
Kluckhohn, Clyde, and Dorothea C. Leighton
  1946 *The Navaho*. Cambridge: Harvard University Press.
Kluckhohn, Florence
  1950 "Dominant and substitute profiles of cultural orientations." *Social Forces* 28: 376–93.
Kollmorgen, W. M.
  1942 "The Old Order Amish of Lancaster County, Pennsylvania." *United States Department of Agriculture Rural Life Studies* 4: 1–105.
Kroeber, A. L.
  1923, 1948 *Anthropology*. New York: Harcourt.

1939 *Cultural and Natural Areas of Native North America.* University of California Publications in American Archaeology and Ethnology 38.

1942 "The Societies of Primitive Men," in *Levels of Integration in Biological and Social Systems,* Biological Symposia, Vol. 8, ed. Robert Redfield, 205–17. Lancaster, Pa.: Cattell Press.

Krzywicki, Ludwik
1934 *Primitive Society and Its Vital Statistics.* London: Macmillan.

La Farge, Oliver
1940 "Maya ethnology: the sequence of cultures." In: *The Maya and their Neighbors* (dedicated to Alfred M. Tozzer), pp. 281–91. New York and London: Appleton-Century.

Landon, Fred
1941 *Western Ontario and the American Frontier.* Toronto: The Ryerson Press.

Lasswell, Harold
n.d. "Law, Science and Policy Papers." Mimeographed, Yale University, New Haven.

Lasswell, Harold, Charles Lindbloom, John Kennedy, and Allen Holmberg.
n.d. "Experimental Research in the Behavioral Sciences and Regional Development." Unpublished ms.

1936 *Laws of the Uganda Protectorate, Native Agreements and Buganda Native Laws.* London.

LeDuc, Thomas
1950 "The Disposal of the Public Domain on the Trans-Mississippi Plains: Some Opportunities for Investigation." *Agricultural History,* XXIV, October, 199–204.

Lerner, D., and others
1958 *The Passing of Traditional Society: Modernizing the Middle East.* Glencoe: Free Press.

Lindgren, Ethel J.
1938 "An example of culture contact without conflict: Reindeer Tungus and Cossacks of northwestern Manchuria." *American Anthropologist* 40: 605–21.

Linton, Ralph (ed.)
1940 *Acculturation in Seven American Indian Tribes.* New York: Appleton-Century.

Linton, Ralph
1943 "Nativistic movements." *American Anthropologist* 45: 230–39.

Lips, Julius
1937 *The Savage Hits Back.* New Haven: Yale University Press.

Lipset, Seymour M., and Reinhard Bendix
1959 *Social Mobility in Industrial Society.* Berkeley: University of California Press.

Lokken, R. L.
1941 "The Turner Thesis: Criticisms and Defense." *Social Studies,* XXXII, December, 356–65.

Lottick, Kenneth V.

    1959 "Cultural Transplantation in the Connecticut Reserve," *Historical and Philosophical Society of Ohio Bulletin,* XVII, July, 154–66.

    1961 "The Western Reserve and the Frontier Thesis," *Ohio Historical Quarterly,* LXX, January, 45–57.

Lower, A. R. M.

    1930 "The Origins of Democracy in Canada." Canadian Historical Association, *Report,* 65–70.

McDougall, John L.

    1929 "The Frontier School and Canadian History." Canadian Historical Association, *Report,* 121–25.

McGee, W. J.

    1896 "Anthropology at Buffalo." *American Anthropologist,* Vol. IX, September.

MacIver, Robert M.

    1937 *Society: A Textbook of Sociology.* New York: Farrar.

MacLean, J. P.

    1900 *An Historical Account of the Settlements of the Scottish Highlanders in America Prior to the Peace of 1783.* Cleveland: Helman-Taylor Co.

MacLeod of MacLeod, Rev. Canon R. C.

    1927 *The MacLeods of Dunvegan: From the Time of Leod to the End of the Seventeenth Century.* Edinburgh: Clan MacLeod Society.

MacManus, Seumas

    1921 *The Story of the Irish Race.* Subscriber's Edition. New York: Irish Publishing Co.

Mair, L. P. (ed.)

    1938 *Methods of Study of Culture Contact in Africa.* International Institute of African Languages and Cultures, Memorandum XV. London: Oxford University Press for the Institute.

Malinowski, B.

    1922 *Argonauts of the Western Pacific . . . Native Enterprise and Adventure in the Archipelagoes of Melanesian New Guinea.* London: Routledge.

    1944 *A Scientific Theory of Culture and Other Essays.* Chapel Hill: University of North Carolina Press.

    1945 *The Dynamics of Culture Change: An Inquiry into Race Relations in Africa.* New Haven: Yale University Press.

Mandelbaum, D. G.

    1941 "Culture change among the Nilgiri tribes." *American Anthropologist* 43: 19–26.

Mason, John

    1637 *A Brief History of the Pequot Wars.* Boston: S. Kneeland and T. Green. Reprinted in 1736.

Matson, J. N.

    1941 *Warrington's Notes on Ashanti Custom* (2d ed.). Cape Coast Gold Coast [Ghana]: Prospect Printing Press.

Mayer, A. C.
1952 *Land and Society in Malabar.* London: Oxford University Press.
Mead, Margaret
1931 "Talk boy." *Asia* 31: 144–51.
Mekeel, Scudder
1943 "A short history of the Teton-Dakota." *North Dakota Historical Quarterly* 10: 137–205.
Melchin
1909 *Amerikanskaya Interventsiya na Sovetskom Dalnom Vostoke* [American Intervention in the Soviet Far East]. Moscow [Publisher unknown].
Mendaña, Alvaro de
1901 *The Discovery of the Solomon Islands.* (Edited and translated by Baron W. A. T. A. Amherst.) London: Hakluyt Society.
Meyerowitz, E.
1951 *The Sacred State of the Akan.* London: Faber.
Mills, Clarence A.
1942 *Climate Makes the Man.* New York: Harper.
Miyakawa, T. Scott
1964 *Protestants and Pioneers.* Chicago: University of Chicago Press.
Mood, Fulmer
1945 "The Concept of the Frontier, 1871–1898: Comments on a Select List of Source Documents." *Agricultural History,* XIX, January, 24–30.
1948 "Notes on the History of the Word *Frontier.*" *Agricultural History,* XXII, April, 78–83.
1952 "Studies in the History of American Settled Areas and Frontier Lines: Settled Areas and Frontier Lines, 1625–1790," *Agricultural History,* XXVI, January, 16–34.
Mook, M. A.
1955 "A Brief History of Former, Now Extinct, Amish Communities in Pennsylvania." *Western Pennsylvania Historical Magazine* 38: 33–46.
Moore, Arthur K.
1957 *The Frontier Mind: a Cultural Analysis of the Kentucky Frontiersman.* Lexington, Kentucky: University of Kentucky Press.
Moore, Wilbert Ellis
1951 *Industrialization and Labor: Social Aspects of Economic Development.* Ithaca: Cornell University Press.
Morton, Thomas
1637 *The New English Canaan.* Boston: Prince Society. Reprinted in 1883.
Morton, William L.
1951 "The Significance of Site in the American and Canadian Wests." *Agricultural History,* XXV, July, 97–104.
Myrdal, Gunnar
1944 *An American Dilemma: the Negro Problem and Modern Democracy.* New York: Harper.

394 *Beyond the Frontier*

Neibohr, H. J.
1900 *Slavery as an Industrial System*. The Hague: Martinus Nijhoff.
Neumark, S. Daniel
1957 *Economic Influences on the South African Frontier, 1652–1836*. Stanford: Stanford University Press.
Opler, Morris E.
1945 "Themes as dynamic forces in culture." *American Journal of Sociology* 51: 198–203.
Parsons, Talcott
1951 *The Social System*. Glencoe: Free Press.
Pearce, T. M.
1962 "The 'Other' Frontiers of the American West," *Arizona and the West*, IV, Summer, 105–12.
Pierson, George A.
1940 "The Frontier and Frontiersmen of Turner's Essays." *Pennsylvania Magazine of History and Biography*, LXIV, October, 449–78.
1942 "The Frontier and American Institutions. A Criticism of the Turner Theory," *New England Quarterly*, XV, June, 224–55.
Pitcairn, Robert (ed.)
1830 *Criminal Trials . . . before the High Court of Justiciary in Scotland*. No. 42. Edinburgh: Bannatyne Club Publications.
Pitt-Rivers, George Henry Lane Fox
1927 *The Clash of Cultures and the Contact of Races*. London: Routledge.
Pomeroy, Earl
1955 "Toward a Reorientation of Western History: Continuity and Environment." *Mississippi Valley Historical Review*, XLI, March, 579–600.
Price, A. C.
1939 *White Settlers in the Tropics*. New York: American Geographical Society.
Radcliffe-Brown, A. R.
1922 *The Andaman Islanders*. Cambridge: The University Press.
Ramos, Arthur
1947 *Introdução à antropologica brasileira*. Rio de Janeiro: Coleção Estudos Brasileiros.
Rapoport, Robert N.
1954 *Changing Navaho religious values: a study of Christian missions to the Rimrock Navahos*. Papers of the Peabody Museum of Harvard University 41, No. 2.
Reavis, William A.
1957 "The Maryland Gentry and Social Mobility, 1637–1676," *William and Mary Quarterly*, 3rd. Ser., XIV, July, 418–28.
Redfield, Robert
1947 "The folk society." *American Journal of Sociology* 52: 293–308.

1953 *The Primitive World and Its Transformations.* Ithaca: Cornell University Press.

Redfield, Robert, Ralph Linton and M. J. Herskovits
1936 "Memorandum on the study of acculturation." *American Anthropologist* 38: 149–52.

Reinicke, John
1937 "Marginal languages." Unpublished Ph.D. dissertation, Yale University, New Haven.
1938 "Trade jargons and Creole dialects as marginal languages." *Social Forces* 17: 107–18.

Richards, Audrey I.
1940 "The Political System of the Bemba Tribe." In *African Political Systems,* M. Fortes and E. E. Evans-Pritchard, eds. Oxford: Clarendon Press.

Riegel, Robert F.
1952 "Current Ideas of the Significance of the United States Frontier." *Revista de Historica de America,* June 1952, 25–43.
1956 "American Frontier Theory." *Journal of World History,* III, No. 2: 356–80.

Rivers, W. H. R.
1910 "The Genealogical Method of Inquiry." *Sociological Review,* III, No. 1, January, pp. 1–12.
1914 *The History of Melanesian Society.* Cambridge: The University Press.

Rivers, W. H. R. (ed.)
1922 *Essays on the Depopulation of Melanesia.* Cambridge: The University Press.

Robbins, Roy M.
1933 "Horace Greeley: Land Reform and Unemployment, 1837–1862," *Agricultural History,* VII, January, 18–41.

Roberson, Nancy C.
1960 "Social Mobility in Ante-Bellum Alabama," *Alabama Review,* XIII, April, 135–45.

Roscoe, John
1911 *The Baganda.* London: Macmillan.

Rouse, Irving
1953 "The strategy of culture history." In *Anthropology Today,* by A. L. Kroeber and others, pp. 57–76. Chicago: University of Chicago Press.

Rundell, Walter, Jr.
1959 "Concepts of the 'Frontier' and the 'West'." *Arizona and the West,* I, Spring, 13–41.

Sage, Walter N.
1928 "Some Aspects of the Frontier in Canadian History." Canadian Historical Association, *Report,* 62–72.

Sansom, G. B.
1950 *The Western World and Japan.* New York: Knopf and London: Cresset.
Sastri, K. A. Nilakanta
1949 *South Indian Influences in the Far East.* Bombay: Luzac and Co., Ltd.
Schramm, W. L.
1932 *"Hiawatha* and Its Predecessors." *Philological Quarterly,* XI.
Schreiber, W. I.
1962 *Our Amish Neighbors.* Chicago: University of Chicago Press.
Schroeder, W. W., and J. A. Beegle
1953 "Suicide: An Instance of High Rural Rates." *Rural Sociology* 18: 45–56.
Scott, W. R.
1912 *The Constitution and Finance of English, Scottish and Irish Joint Stock Companies to 1720.* 3 vols. Cambridge: The University Press.
Semyonov, Yuri (Iurii Nikolaevish Semenov)
1944 *The Conquest of Siberia* . . . London: Routledge.
Sergeev, M. A.
1934 *Kamchatsky Kray* [The Territory of Kamchatka]. Moscow.
Shannon, Fred A.
1936 "The Homestead Act and the Labor Surplus." *American Historical Review,* XLI, July, 637–51.
1940 *An Appraisal of Walter Prescott Webb's The Great Plains: A Study in Institutions and Environment.* New York: Social Science Research Council.
Sharp, Paul F.
1955 "Three Frontiers: Some Comparative Studies of Canadian, American and Australian Settlement." *Pacific Historical Review,* XXIV, November, 369–77.
1951 *Sibirskie Ogni,* No. 3, May–June, 116–22.
Siegel, B. J.
1945 "Some methodological considerations for a comparative study of slavery." *American Anthropologist* 47: 357–92.
Silnitsky, A. P.
1897 *Poyezdka v Kamchatku i na Reku Anadyr* [Journey to Kamchatka and the Anadyr River]. Khabarovsk.
Skilton, Charles S.
1939 "American Indian Music." In *International Cyclopedia of Music and Musicians.* New York and Toronto: Dodd.
Smith, Henry Nash
1950 *Virgin Land: The American West as Symbol and Myth.* Cambridge: Harvard University Press.
1951 "The West as an Image of the American Past" *University of Kansas City Review,* XVIII, Autumn, 29–39.

Smith, John
1910 *Travels and Works of John Smith* (ed. E. Arber). 2 vols. Edinburgh: J. Grant.

Smith, M. Brewster
1954 "Anthropology and Psychology." In *For a Science of Social Man. Convergences in Anthropology, Psychology and Sociology,* ed. J. P. Gillin. New York: Macmillan.

Southall, Aidan
1956 *Alur Society.* Cambridge: Heffer.

Spier, L.
1921 *The Sun Dance of the Plains Indians: Its Development and Diffusion.* Anthropological Papers of the American Museum of Natural History, XVI, No. 7, 451–527.

Spindler, George D.
1952 "Personality and Peyotism in Menomini Indian acculturation." *Psychiatry* 15: 151–59.

Spindler, George D., and Walter Goldschmidt
1952 "Experimental design in the study of culture change." *Southwestern Journal of Anthropology* 8: 68–83.

Spoehr, A.
1947 "Changing kinship systems." *Field Museum of Natural History, Anthropological Series* 33: 159–235. Chicago.

Stanley, G. F. G.
1940 "Western Canada and the Frontier Thesis." Canadian Historical Association, *Report,* 105–17.

Steckler, Gerald G.
1961 "North Dakota versus Frederick Jackson Turner," *North Dakota History,* XXVIII, Winter, 33–43.

Steward, Julian H.
1938 "Basin-Plateau aboriginal sociopolitical groups." Smithsonian Institution, *Bureau of American Ethnology Bulletin* 120. Washington, D.C.
1949a *Handbook of South American Indians,* Vol. 5. Smithsonian Institution, *Bureau of American Ethnology Bulletin* 143. Washington, D.C.
1949b "Cultural causality and law: a trial formulation of the development of early civilizations." *American Anthropologist* 51: 1–27.
1951 "Levels of socio-cultural integration." *Southwestern Journal of Anthropology* 7: 374–90.

Still, Bayrd
1941 "Patterns of Mid-Nineteenth Century Urbanization in the Middle West." *Mississippi Valley Historical Review,* XXVIII, September, 187–206.

Strickland, Rex W.
1960 *The Turner Thesis and the Dry World.* El Paso: Texas Western Press.

Strieby, M. E.
1895 "Scotch-Highlanders and American Indians: the Process of Civiliz-

ing them Compared." Washington, D.C.: 27th *Annual Report,* Board
of Indian Commissioners, pp. 58–63.
Surtees, R.
   1816–40 *History of the County Palatine of Durham.* London: J. D.
   Nichols and Son.
Syomushkin,
   1948 *Alitet Ukhodit v Gory* [Alitet Goes to the Hills]. Moscow: [Pub-
   lisher unknown].
Taft, Robert
   1953 *Artists and Illustrators of the Old West, 1850–1900.* New York:
   Scribner.
Tax, Sol
   1941 "World view and social relations in Guatemala." *American Anthro-
   pologist* 43: 27–42.
   1958 "The Fox Project" in "Values in Action: a symposium." *Human
   Organization* 17: 17–19.
Tax, Sol, and others
   1952 *Heritage of Conquest: the Ethnology of Middle America.* Glencoe:
   Free Press.
Taylor, Walter W.
   1948 *A study of archaeology.* American Anthropological Association
   Memoir No. 69.
Thompson, James Westfall
   1913 "Profitable Fields of Investigation in Medieval History." *American
   Historical Review,* XVIII, April, 490–504.
Thompson, Laura M.
   1950 *Culture in Crisis: A Study of the Hopi Indians.* New York: Harper.
Thurnwald, Richard C.
   1932 "The psychology of acculturation." *American Anthropologist* 34:
   557–69.
   1935 *Black and White in East Africa.* London: Humanities Press.
Treadgold, Donald W.
   1952 "Russian Expansion in the Light of Turner's Study of the American
   Frontier." *Agricultural History,* XXVI, October, 147–52.
   1956 "Siberian Colonization and the Future of Asiatic Russia." *Pacific
   Historical Review,* XXV, February, 47–54.
Trevelyan, G. M.
   1926 *History of England.* London, New York: Longmans. New York:
   Doubleday Anchor, paper.
Tucker, A. R.
   1908 *Eighteen Years in Uganda and East Africa.* London: E. Arnold.
Turner, Frederick Jackson
   1906 *Rise of the New West.* New York and London: Harper and Bros.,
   68.
   1935 *The United States, 1830–1850.* New York: H. Holt and Company,
   278.

1951 *Uchitelskaya Gazeta,* October 10.

Uganda, Government of
1955a *Buganda Agreement of 1955.* Entebbe: Government Printer.
1955b *District Councils Ordinance.* Entebbe: Government Printer.

Umble, J. S.
1933 "The Amish Mennonites of Union County Pennsylvania." *Mennonite Quarterly Review* 7: 71–96, 169–90.

Underhill, Ruth
1948 *Ceremonial Patterns in the Greater Southwest.* Monographs of the American Ethnological Society 13.

Vasiliev, A. A.
1952 *History of the Byzantine Empire, 324–1453* (2d Eng. ed., rev.). Madison: University of Wisconsin Press.

Vogt, Evon Z.
1951 *Navaho veterans, a study of changing values.* Papers of the Peabody Museum of Harvard University 41, No. 1.

Wallace, A. F. C.
1951 "Some psychological determinants of culture change in an Iroquoian community." In *Symposium on Local Diversity in Iroquoian Culture.* Bureau of American Ethnology Bulletin 149: 55–76.

Wallace, Paul A. W.
1952 "John Heckewelder's Indians and the Fenimore Cooper Tradition." *Proceedings of the American Philosophical Society* XCIV.

Ward, John W.
1960 "Individualism Today," *Yale Review,* XLIX, Spring, 380–92.

Warner, W. Lloyd
1937 *A Black Civilization: a Social Study of an Australian Tribe.* New York: Harper.

Watrous, Blanche
n.d. "A personality study of Ojibwa children." Ms.

Watson, James B.
1952 *Cayuá culture change.* American Anthropological Association Memoir No. 73.
1953 *Way Station of Westernization: the Brazilian Caboclo.* Brazil: Papers, Institute for Brazilian Studies, Vanderbilt University, Nashville.

Wax, Rose
1953 "An analysis of acculturation abstracts." Manuscript at Stanford University, Stanford, California.

Webb, Walter P.
1931 *The Great Plains.* Boston: Ginn.
1952 *The Great Frontier.* Boston: Houghton.

Weber, M.
1947 *The Theory of Social and Economic Organization.* Glencoe: Free Press.

Weinreich, Uriel
1953 *Languages in Contact* . . . New York: Columbia University Press.

400 *Beyond the Frontier*

(Wild Report)
1959 *Report of the Constitutional Committee, 1959.* Entebbe: Government Printer.

Willey, Gordon R.
1953a "A pattern of diffusion—acculturation." *Southwestern Journal of Anthropology* 9: 369–84.
1953b "Archaeological theories and interpretation: New World." In *Anthropology Today,* by A. L. Kroeber and others, pp. 361–85. Chicago: University of Chicago Press.

Williams, F. E.
1935 "The blending of cultures: an essay on the aims of native education." *Territory of Papua, Anthropological Reports* 16. Port Moresby.

Williams, Roger
1634 *Key to the Language of America.* London: G. Dexter. Providence: Rhode Island Historical Society, reprinted in 1827.

Wilson, Godfrey
1936a "An Introduction to Nyakyusa Society." *Bantu Studies* X.
1936b "An African Morality." *Africa* X: 75–99.
1939a "Nyakyusa Conventions of Burial." *Bantu Studies* XIII: 1–32.
1939b *The Constitution of Ngonde.* Livingstone, Rhodesia: Rhodes-Livingstone Institute.

Wilson, Godfrey and Monica
1945 *The Analysis of Social Change: based on observations in Central Africa.* Cambridge: the University Press.

Winstedt, R. O.
1950 *Malaya and Its History.* London: Hutchinson's Universal Library.

Wright, Louis B.
1955 *Culture on the Moving Frontier.* Bloomington, Indiana: Indiana University Press.

Zaslow, Morris
1948 "The Frontier Hypothesis in Recent Historiography." *Canadian Historical Review,* XXIX, June, 153–67.